ARABIC BOYS AND GIRLS NAMES FROM ALPHABET A TO M

AHSRAH AYIR

Made with ♥ on the Notion Press Platform
www.notionpress.com

Contents

Preface

The physical identity of a man is his name, through which his intrinsic qualities and behaviour are revealed. Therefore, while naming the child, the parents emphasize that the name should be auspicious and should reflect its personality well. It is also taken care that the meaning of the child's name should not be odd.

According to the naming principles, it is concluded that the name has a special relation to our behaviour. The name in our life not only gives information about our personality but it is also an important part of our future.

Any person is named for his/her identity. We often hear "what is there in the name" and apart from this, you may have heard some other proverbs which reveal that the name does not cause symptoms. The name has been accepted in most human traditions. In Hinduism, sixteen rites have been performed in the scriptures from before the birth of the child till after his death. One of these rites is the naming ceremony. Many people in Hinduism carry out this process of naming with full legal practice, which is called a naming ceremony. A few days after the birth of the child, its naming ceremony is performed with pomp. Relatives and friends are also invited along with family members. A feast is also given to everyone as soon as possible.

The child's parents or the parents who name it at birth are often identified with age by the same name. There are very few people who change the parents' given names. Sometimes the name of the child is changed under the circumstance.

Scholars say that the name has a great influence on the life of a human being, so the name should be meaningful. By the way, the child doesn't need to behave according to the name. Also, if two persons with the same name have the same character and nature, it is not necessary, but it may be more likely that they are opposite like the two poles. Nevertheless, understanding the importance of the name, give the child a reasonable and meaningful name.

If seen, the first identity of the child is the name, which is associated with it throughout life. While naming the child, many things have to be taken care of - such as family customs, traditions, social rules and many other things.

All the aspects should be considered while choosing the name. The name should be kept which is easy to pronounce as well as being meaningful. Sometimes a person keeps the old and traditional name of the child, but they should not forget that if their child is born in modern times, then the name given by you may not cause him to become a comic character in the future. At the same time, some people also believe that if we name our child after a famous person, then he will get fame like that person. So let us tell you that a person becomes greater by his actions and moves forward only because of his efforts. That is why always keep the name afterthought.

In many places, you can guess the religion of the child by name. By the way, in present modern times, people do not give much preference to religion etc. while naming. All they need for their child is just a catchy and easy name.

Despite all these things, naming a child is difficult for any parent. Everyone wants their child's name to be the most out of place and attractive. Some people even keep their child's name separate from their religion. Sometimes you are so attracted by the name of a child that you feel that the name of your child should be the same. But keep in mind that once you name your child something, then it is known by the same name throughout life, so do not make the mistake of naming it in a hurry.

Name the child as one that is popular and soon everyone will be on the tongue. Nicknames are easy and are quickly remembered by everyone. To name the children, you can take the help of the books present in the market. All kinds of names and their meanings are present in these books.

The baby is usually named after a baby who is sweet and beautiful to listen to. The name should not be too difficult. It is the right of the person to keep the name, but at times it is very difficult for the baby to be named like the most famous people when he grows up and becomes a part of the functioning of this world. It is better than naming very famous people to make the baby worthy so that he makes his name meaningful. Even if the name is someone else.

Usually, the baby should be named so that it is sweet and beautiful to listen to. Very difficult names can sometimes cause problems for that child in the future. Often, mistakes occur in documents while writing difficult names, which have to be circulated by government offices to fix them, and a lot of problems, have to be faced. Therefore, the name should be such that while it is beautiful, it is also easy to speak and write. This will save you and your baby from many problems.

Often the original name of many infants is later confined to documents and school, and the family changes their name. Though it is the right of every family to show affection to boys and girls, it is better to give importance to its original name as well. For example, in villages, there is a practice of naming the baby as Giga, Babu etc. There is no harm in this, but when the baby gets older, it should gradually leave those names and call on his real name.

The name is not just a group of some letters. It is the identity of a person who remains alive even after his life.

Many names in the world are banned. For example, Portugal prohibits writing Tom's name on a birth certificate. In Mexico, you cannot name yourself Traffic and the name Linda in Saudi Arabia can bring trouble for you; naming Alice is also prohibited. Similarly, if you think of living in Germany, never keep the name, Hitler.

Even before the birth of the child, the whole family along with the parents starts thinking of the name of the little guest coming. Even if this is the case, after all, the name is our identity for a lifetime. Every parent wants to give their child the most beautiful and unique name. If you are also pregnant and thinking of the name of your child, then know what is the way to name the children.

If you keep in mind the things mentioned here, then you will be able to choose the best name for your child. The name should be such that the heart will be happy to hear it. Do not choose a name that pricks your ears and sounds strange when you are calling fast. At the same time, the name should also match with the surname.

Trendy Name

They are like the uplift of the rainy river. They may be in trend right now, but when your child grows up or goes to school, then the names may not be trending and then those names seem strange. So avoid having trendy names.

Meaningful Name

Always give your child a name that means something cute. Choose a simple name that has a deep message or meaning hidden. Nowadays the practice of naming such names has increased considerably. At the same time, it is believed that the meaning of the name also affects the nature of the people. Therefore, whatever name you will give, the meaning will affect your child's behaviour.

Short and Easy Name

The child may get upset due to having too long a name. At the same time, when he grows up and fills the form, he may still get annoyed to fill a long name. Give the child an easy and easily spoken name. Spelling the name should also be easy.

In the end, we can say that naming children is a very important and difficult task. Even before the child is born, the parents spend a lot of time thinking about the name of the child and sometimes even after the birth of the child, no name is finalized. In such a situation, keeping in mind the above-mentioned tips, you can give the right name to your child and this book can prove to be helpful in this. It contains alphabetically chosen and meaningful names for your child. So it can become a useful and collectable book for you, your family and friends.

—Author

ONE

Arabic Baby Names—A

Aaban—(m)—of an angel

Aabdar—(m)—bright, like glass

Aabdeen—(m)—worshipper

Aabel—(m)—breath

Aabidaat—(f)—adorer of the god

Aabidah—(f)—adorer

Aabida—(f)—adorer, devotee

Aabideen—(m)—worshippers

Aabidha—(f)—devotee, adorer

Aabidh—(m)—worshipper

Aabidoon—(m)—worshipper of god

Aabidullah—(m)—worshipper of allah

Aabid—(f)—a adorer of the god

Aabid—(m)—worshipper, devotee

Aabinus—(m)—ebony

Aabirah—(f)—fleeting, transitory, ephemeral

Aabira—(f)—colour

Aabir—(f)—fragrance, scent, aroma

Aabir—(m)—fragrance, cloud

Aabisha—(f)—a gift of god

Aabish—(m)—one with divine wisdom

Aabis—(f)—austere, stern

Aabis—(m)—austere stern

Aabraham—(m)—father of a multitude

Aabriq—(m)—one with divine wisdom
Aabroo—(f)—fame, honour, dignity
Aadab—(f)—hope and need
Aadab—(m)—good wish
Aadam—(m)—the first prophet of allah
Aadan—(m)—acceptance, holding
Aada—(m)—to bind, fasten
Aadeeba—(f)—cultured, literary woman
Aadeel—(m)—just
Aadeen—(m)—one with divine wisdom
Aadeez—(m)—beloved, dearest, treasured
Aadel—(m)—reasonable
Aaden—(m)—warmth of the home, fire, flame
Aadham—(m)—one with divine wisdom
Aadheen—(m)—obedient, submissive
Aadhila—(f)—sincerity
Aadhil—(m)—honourable judge
Aadibaa—(f)—refined, civilised
Aadiba—(f)—polite, cultured, respect giving
Aadifa—(f)—one which we can proud
Aadilah—(f)—unique, divine aura
Aadila—(f)—honest, upright, justice
Aadil—(m)—justice, upright, sincere, truth
Aadina—(f)—friday
Aadin—(m)—first, at the very beginning
Aadiqa—(f)—unique, divine aura
Aadir—(m)—origin, beginning
Aadiya—(f)—beginning, the first power
Aaedah—(f)—unique, divine aura
Aaeedah—(f)—visiting, returning, reward
Aaeefa—(f)—gift, a gift of god
Aaeeshah—(f)—living prosperous, life
Aaeesha—(f)—life, vivaciousness
Aaeeza—(f)—beautiful, obedient
Aaeisha—(f)—obedient, life, beautiful
Aaema—(f)—leader, ruler
Aaen—(f)—precious
Aaera—(f)—honourable, noble, respectful

Aaerin—(f)—enlightened
Aaesha—(f)—obedient
Aaezah—(f)—obedient
Aaeza—(f)—beautiful, pretty, obedient
Aafaaq—(f)—horizons
Aafaaq—(m)—horizons
Aafana—(f)—virtuous, chaste, the forgiver
Aafan—(m)—forgive
Aafaqia—(f)—vertex of grace, generosity
Aafaque—(m)—horizon
Aafa—(f)—forgiver, pardoner
Aafa—(m)—forgiver
Aafeen—(f)—forgiveness
Aafeen—(m)—one who forgives others
Aafera—(f)—colour of the earth, pink
Aaferin—(f)—blessing, praise
Aafesha—(f)—shining, pretty
Aaffiya—(f)—freedom from illness
Aafia—(f)—healthy, wise - beautiful, vigor
Aafida—(f)—hearts, consciences
Aafidha—(f)—consciences, hearts
Aafifa—(f)—unique, divine aura
Aafii—(m)—honesty
Aafika—(f)—knowledge, vertex of grace
Aafila—(f)—intelligent
Aafil—(m)—honest, prince
Aafina—(f)—young doe
Aafiqa—(f)—generosity, knowledge
Aafiq—(m)—pinnacle of grace, generosity
Aafir—(m)—one with divine wisdom
Aafisha—(f)—unique, divine aura
Aafiyah—(f)—healthy
Aafiyana—(f)—healthy
Aafiyan—(m)—khuda ka banda
Aafiyat—(f)—freedom from illness
Aafiya—(f)—freedom from illness, appropriate health
Aafiya—(m)—good health
Aafizah—(f)—unique, divine aura

Aafiza—(f)—unique, divine aura
Aafrah—(f)—happiness
Aafra—(f)—white, colour of earth, happiness
Aafreeda—(f)—created, produced
Aafreena—(f)—enlightenment
Aafreen—(f)—encouragement, brave, acclaim
Aafreen—(m)—encouragement, sun
Aafree—(f)—beautiful, happiness
Aafrein—(f)—brave, encouragement
Aafrim—(m)—fruitful, productive, fertile
Aafrina—(f)—light of self-confidence
Aafrin—(f)—lucky, happiness, praise
Aafrin—(m)—praise, blessing
Aafsana—(f)—storey, fiction
Aafseen—(f)—shine like a star
Aafsha—(f)—pretty, shining
Aafsheen—(f)—shine like a star
Aafshin—(f)—shine like a star, golden
Aaftab—(m)—the sun, sunlight
Aafyan—(m)—great king, leader, emperor
Aafya—(f)—health, freedom from illness
Aafzaan—(m)—one with divine wisdom
Aafzan—(m)—one with divine wisdom
Aagaz—(m)—start, beginning
Aaghaaz—(m)—awake
Aaghaa—(m)—master, owner
Aahaana—(f)—first rays of the sun
Aahaan—(m)—auspicious dawn, sword
Aahad—(m)—devotee of the only one
Aahail—(m)—thankful
Aahana—(f)—first rays of the sun
Aahana—(m)—first rays of the sun
Aahan—(m)—iron, sword, dawn, early morning
Aaheel—(m)—prince, king
Aaheer—(m)—fearless, devotee
Aahida—(f)—strong, beautiful
Aahid—(m)—sponsor, representative, promised
Aahila—(f)—pleasant

Aahil—(m)—emperor, great king, prince
Aahin—(f)—pure
Aahira—(f)—brilliant, dazzling
Aahira—(m)—one with divine wisdom
Aahir—(m)—dazzling, brilliant
Aahnaf—(m)—name of the narrator of hadith
Aahnan—(m)—one with divine wisdom
Aahna—(f)—exist, beautiful, traditional
Aahona—(f)—first ray of sun, morning
Aaiat—(f)—verses, clue, signs
Aaidah—(f)—narrator of hadith
Aaidam—(m)—one with divine wisdom
Aaida—(f)—visiting, returning, healer
Aaidha—(f)—a flame, splendour
Aaidun—(m)—those who are returning
Aaid—(m)—restore
Aaiefa—(f)—beautiful, forgiver
Aaiela—(f)—beautiful, moonlight
Aaiema—(f)—leader
Aaiera—(f)—honourable, noble, respectful
Aaifah—(f)—forgiver
Aaifa—(f)—forgiver, fearless
Aaif—(m)—fearless, friend
Aaiisha—(f)—beautiful
Aailayah—(f)—unique, divine aura
Aaila—(f)—beautiful, like moon, leader
Aaiman—(f)—righteous, door of the paradise
Aaiman—(m)—righteous
Aaima—(f)—leader, ruler
Aainaa—(f)—pure, mirror, the only one
Aainah—(f)—reflection, mirror
Aaina—(f)—mirror, reflection
Aaini—(f)—flower, spring, the eye
Aairaa—(f)—honourable, respectful
Aairah—(f)—noble, respectful
Aaira—(f)—noble, respectful, honourable
Aairha—(f)—respectable
Aairin—(f)—unique

Aaisah—(f)—woman, life, also spelt as aisha
Aaisa—(f)—obedient, lively person
Aaishaa—(f)—prosperous, lively
Aaishah—(f)—a lively person
Aaisha—(f)—beautiful, obedient
Aaishu—(f)—obedient, god blessings
Aaish—(m)—god blessings
Aaisya—(f)—unique, divine aura
Aaiysha—(f)—obedient, beautiful
Aaizaa—(f)—respected
Aaizah—(f)—radiance, the moon, dear one
Aaizan—(m)—fire, soul of the moon
Aaiza—(f)—pretty, wonderful, god's gift
Aaizulrahman—(m)—great
Aajaan—(m)—one with divine wisdom
Aajad—(m)—independence
Aajam—(m)—respectable, great
Aajira—(f)—a winner
Aajisa—(f)—strong - proud
Aajmeen—(f)—unique, divine aura
Aajmee—(f)—moon
Aakeeb—(m)—one with divine wisdom
Aakeel—(m)—world
Aakeerah—(f)—graceful strength
Aakiba—(f)—cute
Aakib—(m)—god gift
Aakifah—(f)—devoted, dedicated
Aakifa—(f)—worship allah in solitude
Aakif—(m)—given, attached, devotee
Aakila—(f)—intelligent
Aakil—(m)—intelligent, smart
Aakir—(m)—one with divine wisdom
Aaki—(m)—eye
Aakqib—(m)—one with divine wisdom
Aalaa—(f)—highest
Aaladin—(m)—prince
Aalaish—(m)—one with divine wisdom
Aalamgeer—(m)—conqueror of the world

Aalam—(f)—world
Aalam—(m)—the whole world, universe
Aalan—(f)—normal
Aalasa—(f)—protected by god, nobility
Aalaya—(f)—pure
Aalayna—(f)—princess, beautiful
Aala—(f)—bounties, she who hunts and heals
Aala—(m)—supreme, exalted, high in status
Aaleah—(f)—ornament, noble, ascent
Aaleena—(f)—unique, divine aura
Aalee—(m)—sublime, high
Aalema—(f)—loveable
Aalesha—(f)—of the noble sort
Aaleyah—(f)—exalted, highest social standing
Aaleya—(f)—superior, high born
Aale—(m)—noble
Aalfeez—(m)—one with divine wisdom
Aalfiya—(f)—unique, divine aura
Aaliah—(f)—high, to ascend, exalted one
Aalia—(f)—exalted, highest social standing
Aalifa—(f)—compassionate, friendly
Aalifsha—(f)—one in thousand
Aalif—(m)—compassionate, affectionate, kind
Aaliha—(f)—unique, divine aura
Aalijah—(f)—the lord is god, variant of elijah
Aalik—(m)—defender
Aalimah—(f)—woman scholar, authority
Aalima—(f)—authority, woman scholar
Aalimeen—(m)—knowledgeable one
Aalimoon—(m)—knowledgeable one
Aalim—(m)—religious scholar
Aalina—(f)—beautiful, nice
Aaline—(f)—unique, divine aura
Aalinna—(f)—unique, divine aura
Aalisa—(f)—great happiness, god is salvation
Aalisha—(f)—truthful, noble
Aalish—(m)—one with divine wisdom
Aaliyaa—(f)—bright, sunshine

Aaliyah—(f)—to ascend, high, lofty, sublime
Aaliyah—(m)—sunshine, bright
Aaliyana—(f)—beautiful, beauty
Aaliyan—(m)—high, tall
Aaliya—(f)—beauty, high, tall, towering
Aaliyha—(f)—noble, ornament, ascent
Aaliza—(f)—joyous, happiness, pious
Aali—(f)—beautiful
Aali—(m)—name of allah, sublime
Aalma—(f)—caring, nourishing soul
Aalmeen—(f)—knowledgeable one
Aalmin—(f)—knowledgeable one
Aalmir—(m)—prince
Aalyah—(f)—honourable, ascent, noble
Aalyan—(m)—one with divine wisdom
Aalya—(f)—smooth, soft, sublime
Aalyiah—(f)—ascent, ornament, noble
Aamaal—(f)—hopes, aspirations, wishes
Aamad—(f)—plural of amad, periods of time
Aamad—(m)—plural of amad, periods of time
Aamaira—(f)—one who is beautiful forever
Aamal—(f)—work, hope, aspiration
Aamana—(f)—unique, divine aura
Aamanee—(f)—appropriate wish
Aaman—(m)—peace, friendly disposition
Aamara—(f)—one who is beautiful forever
Aamariah—(f)—given by god, pledged by god
Aamariya—(f)—pledged, given by god
Aamash—(m)—one with divine wisdom
Aamayraa—(f)—princess
Aambar—(f)—sky
Aamber—(f)—sky
Aameena—(f)—unique, divine aura
Aameen—(f)—oh allah, accept our prayer
Aameen—(m)—trustworthy, faithful
Aameera—(f)—princess, leader
Aamela—(f)—beloved, flatterer
Aamenah—(f)—god's swear of life

Aamena—(f)—truthful, trustworthy, faithful
Aamerah—(f)—high-born girl
Aamera—(f)—leader, princess
Aamer—(m)—ordering person, leader
Aamid—(m)—one with divine wisdom
Aamiera—(f)—abundant, full of life, inhabited
Aamilah—(f)—righteous, doer of appropriate deeds
Aamil—(m)—doer, work man, worker, effective
Aaminabee—(f)—blessed
Aaminah—(f)—safe, secured
Aamineen—(m)—safe, unharmed
Aaminoon—(m)—safe
Aamin—(f)—grace of god, divine grace
Aamin—(m)—divine grace, grace of god
Aamirah—(f)—inhabiting in a place, princess
Aamirah—(m)—inhabitant
Aamira—(f)—imperial, abundant, prosperous
Aamiruddin—(m)—leader of the faith
Aamir—(m)—full, prosperous, amply settled
Aamish—(m)—successful, honest
Aamiya—(f)—night
Aami—(f)—powerful
Aamnah—(f)—peace
Aamna—(f)—peace, soft, all
Aamra—(f)—princess, leader
Aamreen—(f)—ruler of sky, height
Aanaa—(m)—moments
Aanabia—(f)—unique, divine aura
Aanaiza—(f)—beauty, mercy
Aanam—(f)—god blessing
Aanaya—(f)—blessed with god, god gifted
Aana—(f)—young, food grain, most precious
Aandaleeb—(f)—nightingale.
Aaneseh—(f)—virtuous, eloquent woman, miss
Aani-fatimah—(f)—literary poetess
Aania—(f)—mirror
Aanifah—(f)—dignified
Aanifa—(f)—dignified, bright

Aanisah—(f)—young lady, maiden
Aanisa—(f)—young lady, maiden
Aanisha—(f)—beautiful
Aaniyah—(f)—happy
Aanjum—(f)—symbol, star, angel
Aansa—(f)—portion
Aanshi—(f)—god's gift
Aansh—(m)—portion
Aan—(f)—bring, pride, respect
Aapsana—(f)—fiction
Aaqaa—(m)—master, owner
Aaqibah—(f)—result, aftermath, consequence
Aaqiba—(f)—consequence, result
Aaqib—(m)—follower
Aaqid—(m)—one who promises
Aaqifa—(f)—unique, divine aura
Aaqif—(m)—means in
Aaqilah—(f)—intelligent, wise, discerning
Aaqila—(f)—intelligent
Aaqil—(f)—wise, discerning, sensible
Aaqil—(m)—intelligent, wise, discerning
Aaqsa—(f)—intelligent, a mosque
Aaquib—(m)—follower of allah
Aaquil—(m)—one with divine wisdom
Aaraaf—(m)—heights
Aaraa—(f)—embellishing, adorning
Aarab—(m)—powerful, pray
Aaraf—(f)—heights
Aaraf—(m)—beautiful
Aaran—(m)—exalted, on high, light bringer
Aarash—(m)—a hero, a hero in persian folklore
Aarat—(m)—quiet, gentle, important, anxious
Aara—(f)—adoring, brilliant, knowledgeable
Aareef—(m)—expert, knowledgeable
Aareen—(f)—full of joy, rejoice
Aareez—(m)—first ray of sun
Aaree—(m)—water
Aarefa—(f)—female who recognises (islam)

Aarefina—(f)—unique, divine aura
Aaref—(m)—knowledgeable
Aaren—(m)—lofty, inspiration, inspired
Aarfaa—(f)—very high
Aarfah—(f)—the mighty, high, greatness
Aarfa—(f)—great, high
Aarfa—(m)—honourable
Aarfeen—(m)—one with divine wisdom
Aarhaan—(m)—ruler, winner, king
Aarhan—(m)—ruler, king, leader
Aariaz—(m)—leader, ruler of nation
Aaria—(f)—gentle music, brings rain
Aaribah—(f)—winner
Aarib—(m)—fortunate, handsome, healthy
Aaric—(m)—rule with mercy
Aaridh—(f)—clouds
Aaridh—(m)—cloud
Aarief—(m)—wise, intelligent, learned
Aarifaa—(f)—knowing
Aarifah—(f)—knowing
Aarifa—(f)—female who recognises islam, wise
Aarif—(f)—forgiven, acquainted
Aarif—(m)—acquainted, knowledgeable
Aarin—(m)—mountain of strength
Aarish—(m)—first ray of sun, smart
Aaris—(m)—brave, character
Aariyah—(f)—blossom, purity, powerful, bold
Aariyaz—(m)—ruler of nation, leader
Aariza—(f)—urge
Aariz—(f)—sacred, diving
Aariz—(m)—respectable man, intelligent
Aari—(m)—mountain
Aarjoo—(f)—wish
Aarju—(f)—wish
Aarmaan—(m)—wish, desire
Aarman—(f)—wish, desire
Aarman—(m)—desire, wish
Aarnav—(m)—ocean, sea

Aaron—(m)—mountain of strength, exalted one
Aarooshee—(f)—appropriate, peaceful
Aarshad—(m)—honest, pious
Aarshan—(m)—good
Aarshin—(f)—beautiful, above every thing
Aarshiya—(f)—above of everything
Aarshi—(f)—first ray of sun
Aarva—(f)—unique, divine aura
Aaryan—(m)—respectable, of utmost strength
Aaryf—(m)—learned, wise, knowledgeable
Aarzam—(m)—war, battle, quarrel
Aarzoo—(f)—wish, desire, hope
Aarzoo—(m)—desire, wish
Aarzu—(m)—wish, hope, love
Aasaal—(f)—evenings
Aasaal—(m)—real, pure, evening time
Aasad—(m)—lion
Aasaf—(m)—clear, lined up
Aasal—(m)—afternoons, evenings
Aasama—(f)—sky
Aasar—(m)—heavy, torrential rain
Aaseamah—(f)—appropriate
Aaseayah—(f)—unique, divine aura
Aaseemah—(f)—unique, divine aura
Aaseem—(m)—one with divine wisdom
Aaseeyah—(f)—unique, divine aura
Aasefa—(f)—guardian, protector
Aaseiyah—(f)—unique, divine aura
Aasemah—(f)—guardian angel
Aaseyah—(f)—unique, divine aura
Aasfa—(f)—protector, guardian
Aashan—(m)—name of a tree
Aashar—(m)—fire
Aashfiya—(f)—supporter
Aashia—(f)—place to live
Aashifah—(f)—unique, divine aura
Aashifa—(f)—unique, divine aura
Aashif—(m)—bold, courageous

Aashika—(f)—lovable, affection
Aashik—(m)—lover, romantic, sharp, adorer
Aashil—(m)—derived from aash
Aashima—(f)—limitless, one who is full of hope
Aashim—(m)—one with divine wisdom
Aashina—(f)—derived from aash
Aashiq-ali—(m)—adorer of ali
Aashiq-muhammad—(m)—adorer of the prophet muhammad
Aashiqah—(f)—adorer, lover, one without sorrow
Aashiqa—(f)—lovable, adorer, lover
Aashique—(m)—lover
Aashiq—(m)—adorer, suitor, lover
Aashira—(f)—blessing, wealthy
Aashir—(m)—living, wealthy, thankful to god
Aashiya—(f)—place to live, habitat
Aashi—(f)—love, full smile, queen of family
Aashlina—(f)—unique, divine aura
Aashlin—(f)—meadow of ash trees
Aashmi—(f)—from the sky
Aashna—(f)—hope, devoted to love, beloved
Aashna—(m)—familiar, friend
Aashra—(f)—shelter
Aashreen—(f)—unique, divine aura
Aashya—(f)—long live
Aasia—(f)—hopeful
Aasia—(m)—one with divine wisdom
Aasiba—(f)—unique, divine aura
Aasieyah—(f)—unique, divine aura
Aasifah—(f)—spotless, pure, organiser
Aasifa—(f)—pure, organiser, spotless
Aasif—(m)—an able minister
Aasika—(f)—goddess laxmi
Aasik—(m)—a swordsman
Aasimah—(f)—protector, defendant, central
Aasima—(f)—protector, central, defendant
Aasim—(m)—protector, guardian, central
Aasira—(f)—bond
Aasir—(m)—fascinating, captivating

Aasiyah—(f)—pharaoh's wife who embraced islam
Aasiyana—(f)—beautiful home
Aasiya—(f)—appropriateness
Aasmaa—(f)—excellent, precious
Aasma—(f)—precious, excellent, sky
Aasma—(m)—sky
Aasmeen—(f)—sweet-smelling, jasmine flower
Aasmin—(f)—jasmine
Aasmi—(f)—i am soul
Aasna—(f)—purity
Aasqeen—(m)—one with divine wisdom
Aasya—(f)—related to mouth, face
Aasymah—(f)—unique, divine aura
Aatheef—(m)—one with divine wisdom
Aathef—(m)—one with divine wisdom
Aathifa—(f)—unique, divine aura
Aathif—(m)—generous
Aathika—(f)—dignified female
Aathila—(f)—deep-rooted, firmly established
Aathiqa—(f)—dignified female
Aathiq—(m)—dignified
Aatifah—(f)—affection, emotion, feeling
Aatifa—(f)—affection, sympathy
Aatif—(m)—kind affectionate
Aatikah—(f)—kind affectionate, gorgeous
Aatika—(f)—kind affectionate
Aatikha—(f)—kind affectionate
Aatiqah—(f)—d, shoulder (support) old
Aatiqa—(f)—free
Aatiq—(f)—young woman, free, baby pigeon
Aatiq—(m)—liberated, independent, free
Aatirah—(f)—fragrant
Aatish—(m)—fireworks, explosive
Aatiya—(f)—giver, bestowed
Aati—(m)—giver, best ower
Aatoon—(f)—educator, teacheress
Aatun—(f)—educator, teacheress
Aauf—(m)—guest, fragrance, lion

Aavan—(m)—water, earth owner
Aavez—(m)—fire
Aawad—(m)—one with divine wisdom
Aawej—(m)—fire
Aawf—(m)—fuel, lion
Aayaan—(m)—lord bless
Aayaat—(f)—quran verse
Aayah—(f)—proof, sign, verse
Aayan-malik—(m)—allah ka banda
Aayana—(f)—beautiful blossom, innocent one
Aayansh—(m)—the sun, gift of god
Aayanuddin—(m)—one with divine wisdom
Aayan—(m)—speed, bright
Aayash—(m)—gold, long life
Aayath—(m)—mark, sign
Aayat—(f)—verses, signs, plural of ayah
Aayat—(m)—proof, signs, clue
Aayaza—(f)—unique, divine aura
Aayden—(m)—bright, enlightened
Aayeesha—(f)—living, life
Aayema—(f)—ruler, leader
Aayerah—(f)—noble, vision filler, respectful
Aayera—(f)—appropriateness of love
Aayesa—(f)—obedient, precious, beautiful
Aayesha—(f)—obedient
Aayet—(f)—phases of quran
Aayet—(m)—phases of quran, signature of god
Aayeza—(f)—obedient, beautiful
Aayid—(m)—trustable
Aayira—(f)—respectful, noble, honourable
Aayisha—(f)—unique, divine aura
Aayish—(m)—god's blessings
Aayizah—(f)—replacement
Aayiza—(f)—dear one, noble
Aayiz—(m)—replacement
Aayla—(f)—top of the mountain
Aayman—(m)—blessed, gift of god
Aaymon—(m)—one with divine wisdom

Aayna—(f)—mirror
Aayrah—(f)—respectful, noble, vision filler
Aayra—(f)—respectable person
Aayrin—(f)—beautiful, enlightened, unique
Aaysa—(f)—precious, obedient
Aayshah—(f)—one who lives, alive
Aaysha—(f)—obedient
Aayub—(m)—to repent
Aayun—(f)—eyes, plural of ain
Aayzah—(f)—respected, gift of god
Aayza—(f)—gift of god, respected
Aazaad—(m)—independent, free
Aazaan—(m)—prayer
Aazad—(m)—independent, free
Aazam—(f)—fearless
Aazam—(m)—supreme, powerful, greatest
Aazan—(m)—prayer
Aazar—(m)—the th month of celebration
Aazath—(m)—one with divine wisdom
Aazbad—(m)—one with divine wisdom
Aazeb—(m)—one with divine wisdom
Aazeem—(m)—greater, defender
Aazeen—(f)—shining star, beautiful
Aazia—(f)—rising sun, holy
Aazif—(m)—breeze
Aazil—(m)—protector, guardian
Aazima—(f)—resolution, defender
Aazim—(m)—determined
Aazina—(f)—jewellery
Aazin—(m)—beauty, decoration
Aazira—(f)—a rising star
Aaziya—(f)—unique, divine aura
Aazmeen—(f)—sweet-smelling
Aazmina—(f)—fortunate, beautiful
Aazmin—(f)—a star
Aazz—(m)—mightier, stronger, dearer
Abaabeel—(f)—flocks
Abaabeel—(m)—flocks

Abaal—(f)—wild rose
Abaan—(m)—old arabic name, angel of god
Abaasa—(f)—lioness
Abaas—(m)—lion
Ababeel—(m)—flocks
Ababil—(f)—flocks
Ababil—(m)—crowd, band, swallow
Abab—(m)—softness gracefulness of youth
Abadah—(m)—endurance, durability, strength
Abadard—(m)—prosperous
Abadilat—(m)—abdullah
Abadiyah—(m)—one with divine wisdom
Abadi—(m)—eternal, endless, immortal
Abadullah—(m)—one with divine wisdom
Abad—(m)—everlasting, eternal, father
Abahat—(m)—correct, accurate
Abaidullah—(m)—one with divine wisdom
Abaid—(m)—worshipper of god, god knows
Abaj—(m)—eternity
Abakhtar—(m)—planet, north
Abal—(f)—wild rose
Abam—(m)—tower, pigeon house, fortress
Abanhir—(f)—possessing the essence of aban
Abanjar—(m)—tall, stout
Abannah—(f)—tall, strong
Abannak—(m)—firm, strong
Abanna—(f)—tall, strong
Abann—(m)—tall, strong
Abanus—(m)—ebony
Aban—(f)—water, clear, eloquent
Aban—(m)—old arabic name
Abaranji—(f)—unique, divine aura
Abaravand—(m)—above all
Abarinnotavan—(m)—great rejuvenate
Abarr—(f)—most of very pious, upright
Abashsh—(f)—friendly, talkative, affable
Abasin—(m)—the indus river
Abasi—(m)—stern

Abass—(m)—lion
Abas—(m)—lion
Abay—(f)—always listening, world
Abazir—(f)—spices, sweet herbs
Abbaad—(m)—great worshipper
Abbaar—(m)—strong
Abbaasah—(f)—lioness, sister of haroon rashid
Abbaas—(m)—gloomy look, description of lion
Abbadi—(m)—one with divine wisdom
Abbad—(m)—great worshipper
Abban—(m)—abbot, white
Abbar—(m)—peace, strong
Abbasahamed—(m)—one with divine wisdom
Abbasah—(f)—lioness
Abbash—(m)—one with divine wisdom
Abbasiyah—(m)—pertaining to abbas
Abbasi—(m)—pertaining to abbas
Abbasuddin—(m)—lion
Abbas—(f)—stern
Abbas—(m)—description of a lion
Abba—(m)—leader, father
Abbes—(m)—one with divine wisdom
Abbey—(m)—my father is light, intelligent
Abbe—(m)—nobleman, father in rejoicing
Abbiah—(f)—great, joy of my father
Abbia—(f)—great, joy of my father
Abbira—(f)—strong, powerful, noble
Abbir—(f)—fragrance, aroma
Abbobaker—(m)—one with divine wisdom
Abbood—(m)—devoted worshipper of allah
Abbott—(m)—the father of the abbey
Abbubakar—(m)—one with divine wisdom
Abbudin—(m)—worshippers
Abbud—(m)—worshipper of allah, devoted
Abbuzer—(m)—name of sahabi
Abbu—(m)—father
Abd-al-ala—(m)—slave of the high
Abd-al-alim—(m)—devotee of the all knowing

Abd-al-bari—(m)—devotee of allah
Abd-al-hakim—(m)—devotee of the wise
Abd-al-jabbar—(m)—devotee of the mighty
Abd-al-matin—(m)—devotee of the strong
Abd-al-qadir—(m)—devotee of the capable
Abd-al-rashid—(m)—devotee of the guided
Abd-al-sami—(m)—devotee of the all hearing
Abd-allah—(m)—devotee of the moon god
Abd-almuhsin—(m)—one with divine wisdom
Abd-al—(m)—allah's slave of the high
Abd-er-rahman—(m)—devotee of the merciful one
Abd-khayr—(m)—goodness, happiness
Abdaal—(m)—replacements
Abdah—(f)—adorer of allah
Abdalala—(m)—slave of the high
Abdalalim—(m)—devotee of the all-knowing
Abdalati—(m)—devotee of allah
Abdalaziz—(m)—devotee of the mighty one
Abdalbari—(m)—devotee of allah
Abdalhadi—(m)—devotee of the leader
Abdalhakim—(m)—devotee of the wise one
Abdalhalim—(m)—devotee of the patient one
Abdalhamid—(m)—devotee of the praiseworthy one
Abdaljabbar—(m)—devotee of the comforter
Abdaljabir—(m)—devotee of the comforter
Abdaljawwad—(m)—devotee of the noble one
Abdalkadir—(m)—devotee of the capable
Abdalkarim—(m)—devotee of the generous one
Abdallafif—(m)—devotee of the kind one
Abdallah—(m)—devotee of allah
Abdalla—(m)—devotee of god
Abdall—(m)—devotee of god
Abdalmajid—(m)—devotee of the glorious one
Abdalmalik—(m)—devotee of the king
Abdalmatin—(m)—devotee of the strong
Abdalmufi—(m)—devotee of the donor
Abdalmuhsin—(m)—devotee of the charitable one
Abdalqadir—(m)—devotee of the capable

Abdalrahim—(m)—devotee of the compassionate
Abdalrahman—(m)—devotee of the merciful
Abdalrashid—(m)—devotee of the guided
Abdalrauf—(m)—devotee of the compassionate
Abdalraziq—(m)—devotee of the provider
Abdalrazzaq—(m)—devotee of the provider
Abdalsalam—(m)—devotee of peace
Abdalsami—(m)—devotee of the all-hearing
Abdalwahab—(m)—devotee of the giving
Abdal—(m)—substitutes
Abdan—(m)—powerful man
Abdarrahman—(m)—devotee of the merciful
Abdar—(m)—glittering with water, wealthy
Abdas—(m)—devotee of god
Abda—(f)—extraordinary, original, beautiful
Abda—(m)—strength, power
Abdeali—(m)—follower of ali
Abdeel—(m)—a vapour, a cloud of god
Abdeladir—(m)—devotee of the capable
Abdelatif—(m)—one with divine wisdom
Abdelati—(m)—devotee of allah
Abdelazim—(m)—devotee of the mighty
Abdelaziz—(m)—devotee of the mighty one
Abdelgawwad—(m)—devotee of the noble one
Abdelhadi—(m)—devotee of the leader
Abdelhakim—(m)—devotee of the wise one
Abdelhak—(m)—devotee of the truth
Abdelhalim—(m)—devotee of the patient one
Abdelhamid—(m)—devotee of the praiseworthy one
Abdelilah—(m)—devotee of god
Abdelkader—(m)—devotee of the capable
Abdelkadir—(m)—devotee of the capable
Abdelkarim—(m)—one with divine wisdom
Abdelkerim—(m)—devotee of the generous one
Abdelkrim—(m)—devotee of the generous one
Abdellafif—(m)—devotee of the kind one
Abdellah—(m)—devotee of allah
Abdellatif—(m)—one with divine wisdom

Abdella—(m)—devotee of allah
Abdell—(m)—devotee of god
Abdelmajid—(m)—one with divine wisdom
Abdelmalik—(m)—devotee of the king
Abdelmufi—(m)—devotee of the donor
Abdelouahid—(m)—one with divine wisdom
Abdelqadir—(m)—devotee of the capable
Abdelrahim—(m)—devotee of the compassionate one
Abdelrahman—(m)—devotee of god
Abdelsalam—(m)—devotee of peace
Abdel—(f)—devotee
Abdel—(m)—devotee of god
Abderrahim—(m)—devotee of the compassionate
Abderrahmane—(m)—servent of relief
Abderrahman—(m)—devotee of the merciful
Abderraouf—(m)—one with divine wisdom
Abderrazak—(m)—one with divine wisdom
Abderrazi—(m)—devotee of the provider
Abderrazza—(m)—devotee of the provider
Abdeslam—(m)—devotee of peace
Abdhullah—(m)—devotee of allah
Abdhulla—(m)—devotee of allah, god
Abdikarim—(m)—devotee of god
Abdillah—(m)—one with divine wisdom
Abdinatif—(m)—one with divine wisdom
Abdiqani—(f)—unique, divine aura
Abdirahman—(m)—devotee, slave of allah
Abdiyah—(f)—devotee of allah
Abdiya—(f)—devotee of allah
Abdi—(f)—slave to allah, ocean
Abdi—(m)—abbreviated form of abdul
Abdmanaf—(m)—devotee of manaf
Abdnan—(m)—one with divine wisdom
Abdnasha—(m)—one with divine wisdom
Abdollah—(m)—one who serves the god
Abdolrahem—(m)—devotee of god
Abdoolah—(m)—one with divine wisdom
Abdoullah—(m)—devotee of allah

Abdoul—(m)—devotee of god
Abdou—(m)—one with divine wisdom
Abdo—(m)—very sensitive and kind
Abdualla—(m)—devotee of allah
Abdual—(m)—devotee of the lord
Abdud-daar—(m)—devotee of the depriver
Abduddaar—(m)—devotee of the depraver
Abduh—(m)—one with divine wisdom
Abdukhdra—(m)—one with divine wisdom
Abdukrahman—(m)—slave of the merciful god
Abduk—(m)—lucky
Abdul-aakhir—(m)—devotee of last one
Abdul-aala—(m)—devotee of allah
Abdul-aalee—(m)—devotee of the most high
Abdul-adal—(m)—devotee of the just
Abdul-adheem—(m)—devotee of the most great
Abdul-adl—(m)—devotee of the just
Abdul-afw—(m)—the devotee of the forgiver
Abdul-ahad—(m)—devotee of the only one (allah)
Abdul-aleem—(m)—devotee of the all-knowing (allah)
Abdul-alim—(m)—devotee of the omniscient
Abdul-aliyy—(m)—devotee of the most high
Abdul-ali—(m)—devotee of the most high
Abdul-asad—(m)—lion
Abdul-atheeq—(m)—fresh air
Abdul-awwal—(m)—slave of the first one
Abdul-azeem—(m)—the devotee of the mighty
Abdul-azeez—(m)—devotee of most powerful, mighty
Abdul-azim—(m)—devotee of the mighty (allah)
Abdul-aziz—(m)—devotee of the mighty
Abdul-azzam—(m)—great
Abdul-baaqi—(m)—devotee of the everlasting
Abdul-baari—(m)—devotee of the creator
Abdul-baasid—(m)—devotee of the expander (allah)
Abdul-baasit—(m)—devotee of the expander
Abdul-baatin—(m)—devotee of allah
Abdul-badee—(m)—slave of the originator, inventor
Abdul-badi—(m)—devotee of the incomparable

Abdul-baith—(m)—devotee of the resurrector
Abdul-baqi—(m)—devotee of the everlasting (allah)
Abdul-bari—(m)—devotee of the creator
Abdul-baseer—(m)—slave of the all-seeing
Abdul-basir—(m)—devotee of the all seeing
Abdul-basith—(m)—devotee of god
Abdul-basit—(m)—devotee of the expander (allah)
Abdul-batin—(m)—devotee of the inward
Abdul-birr—(m)—al-birr is one of name of allah
Abdul-dhahir—(m)—devotee of the manifest
Abdul-elah—(m)—devotee of allah, god
Abdul-fattaah—(m)—slave of the giver of victory
Abdul-ghafaar—(m)—devotee of the forgiver
Abdul-ghaffar—(m)—devotee of the forgiver (allah)
Abdul-ghafoor—(m)—devotee of the forgiver
Abdul-ghafur—(m)—devotee of the all-forgiving
Abdul-ghani—(m)—devotee of the self-sufficient
Abdul-haafiz—(m)—devotee of the guardian (allah)
Abdul-hadi—(m)—devotee of the guide
Abdul-hafeedh—(m)—devotee of the preserver
Abdul-hafeez—(m)—slave of the protector
Abdul-hafee—(m)—devotee of allah
Abdul-hafiz—(m)—devotee of the protector
Abdul-hai—(m)—devotee of the living
Abdul-hakam—(m)—devotee of the arbitrator
Abdul-hakeem—(m)—devotee of the wise (allah)
Abdul-hakim—(m)—devotee of the wise one
Abdul-haleem—(m)—devotee of the forbearing one
Abdul-halim—(m)—devotee of the patient one,
Abdul-hameed—(m)—devotee of the praiseworthy
Abdul-hamid—(m)—devotee of the praised one
Abdul-hannan—(m)—slave of the merciful, forgiving
Abdul-haqq—(m)—devotee of the truth
Abdul-haq—(m)—devotee of the truth (allah)
Abdul-haseeb—(m)—devotee of the reckoner
Abdul-hasib—(m)—esteemed, devotee of the respected
Abdul-hayy—(m)—devotee of the living (allah)
Abdul-jaami—(m)—the devotee of the gatherer

Abdul-jabaar—(m)—devotee of the mighty
Abdul-jabar—(m)—devotee of the mighty (allah)
Abdul-jabbaar—(m)—the devotee of the compeller
Abdul-jabbar—(m)—devotee of the all-compeller
Abdul-jaleel—(m)—devotee of the great, revered
Abdul-jalil—(m)—devotee of the great
Abdul-jameel—(m)—devotee of the beautiful one
Abdul-jame—(m)—devotee of the gatherer
Abdul-jamil—(m)—devotee of the beautiful (allah)
Abdul-jami—(m)—the devotee of the gatherer
Abdul-jawwad—(m)—slave of the most bountiful
Abdul-kabir—(m)—devotee of the great
Abdul-kader—(m)—devotee of the able
Abdul-kareem—(m)—devotee of the most generous
Abdul-karim—(m)—devotee of the generous
Abdul-khaafid—(m)—the devotee of the humbler
Abdul-khaaliq—(m)—devotee of the creator (allah)
Abdul-khabeer—(m)—the devotee of the well acquainted
Abdul-khabir—(m)—slave of the one who is aware
Abdul-khafid—(m)—the devotee of the humbler
Abdul-khafiz—(m)—devotee of the descender
Abdul-khaliq—(m)—devotee of the creator (allah)
Abdul-khallaq—(m)—devotee of allah
Abdul-lateef—(m)—devotee of the kind
Abdul-latif—(m)—devotee of the gentle
Abdul-maajid—(m)—slave of the excellence
Abdul-maalik—(m)—slave of the master, lord
Abdul-maane—(m)—devotee of the withholder
Abdul-maleek—(m)—devotee of allah
Abdul-malik—(m)—devotee of the master
Abdul-manaan—(m)—al-manaan is one of name of allah
Abdul-mani—(m)—slave of one who prevents
Abdul-mateen—(m)—slave of the firm
Abdul-matin—(m)—devotee of the firm
Abdul-mawla—(m)—al-mawla is name of allah
Abdul-moakhir—(m)—devotee of the retarder
Abdul-moez—(m)—devotee of the honourer
Abdul-mohsi—(m)—devotee of the surrounder

Abdul-momit—(m)—devotee of the death-giver
Abdul-moqit—(m)—devotee of the energizer
Abdul-mubdee—(m)—slave of the originator
Abdul-mubdi—(m)—devotee of the originator
Abdul-mubeen—(m)—devotee of allah
Abdul-mueed—(m)—slave of the restorer
Abdul-mueid—(m)—devotee of the restorer
Abdul-mughni—(m)—devotee of the enricher
Abdul-muhaimin—(m)—the guardian, the protector
Abdul-muhaymin—(m)—slave of the protector
Abdul-muheet—(m)—devotee of allah
Abdul-muhsin—(m)—slave of the benefactor
Abdul-muhsi—(m)—devotee of the reckoner
Abdul-muhyi—(m)—devotee of the giver of life
Abdul-muid—(m)—devotee of the restorer
Abdul-muiz—(m)—the exalter
Abdul-mujeeb—(m)—devotee of the responder
Abdul-mujib—(m)—devotee of the responder
Abdul-munim—(m)—slave of the generous
Abdul-muntaqim—(m)—devotee of the revenger
Abdul-muqaddim—(m)—devotee of the promoter
Abdul-muqeet—(m)—slave of the sustainer
Abdul-muqit—(m)—al-muqit is one of name of allah
Abdul-muqsit—(m)—slave of the just
Abdul-muqtadir—(m)—devotee of the powerful
Abdul-musawwir—(m)—devotee of the fashioner (allah)
Abdul-mutaaali—(m)—the devotee of the most high
Abdul-mutaalee—(m)—devotee of the most exalted
Abdul-mutaali—(m)—devotee of the most exalted
Abdul-mutaal—(m)—devotee of the most high
Abdul-mutakabbir—(m)—the devotee of the majestic one
Abdul-mutali—(m)—devotee of the most high (allah)
Abdul-muti—(m)—slave of the giver, donor (allah)
Abdul-muzanni—(m)—a narrator of hadith
Abdul-nafi—(m)—slave of the propitious
Abdul-naseer—(m)—slave of the helper
Abdul-nasir—(m)—protector, devotee of the helper
Abdul-nasser—(m)—devotee of the victorious one

Abdul-noor—(m)—devotee of the light
Abdul-nur—(m)—devotee of the light
Abdul-qaadir—(m)—the devotee of the most capable
Abdul-qabiz—(m)—devotee of the withholder
Abdul-qadeer—(m)—slave of the powerful (allah)
Abdul-qadir—(m)—devotee of the capable
Abdul-qahaar—(m)—devotee of the subduer, almighty
Abdul-qahhaar—(m)—the devotee of the dominant
Abdul-qahhar—(m)—slave of the dominant, subduer
Abdul-qahir—(m)—devotee of the subduer (allah)
Abdul-qaiyoum—(m)—devotee of the self-sustaining
Abdul-qareeb—(m)—devotee of allah
Abdul-qawee—(m)—devotee of the powerful
Abdul-qawi—(m)—devotee of the most strong
Abdul-qayoom—(m)—slave of the self subsistent
Abdul-qayyum—(m)—devotee of the self subsisting
Abdul-quddoos—(m)—devotee of the most holy (allah)
Abdul-quddus—(m)—devotee of the holy (allah)
Abdul-qudoos—(m)—devotee of the most holy
Abdul-raafi—(m)—devotee of the one who raises
Abdul-rabb—(m)—slave of the lord
Abdul-rafi—(m)—devotee of the one who raises
Abdul-rahaman—(m)—devotee of the beneficent
Abdul-raheem—(m)—devotee of the most compassionate
Abdul-rahim—(m)—devotee of the merciful
Abdul-rahman—(m)—slave of god
Abdul-raoof—(m)—the devotee of the merciful one
Abdul-raqib—(m)—slave of the vigilant
Abdul-rasheed—(f)—devotee of the rightly guided
Abdul-rashid—(m)—devotee of the rightly guided one
Abdul-rauf—(m)—devotee of the compassionate
Abdul-razaaq—(m)—devotee of the maintainer (allah)
Abdul-razzaq—(m)—devotee of the maintainer
Abdul-sabur—(m)—devotee of the patient
Abdul-salaam—(m)—devotee of peace
Abdul-salam—(m)—devotee of the peace
Abdul-samad—(m)—devotee of the eternal
Abdul-samee—(m)—devotee of the all-hearing

Abdul-sami—(m)—devotee of the all hearing
Abdul-sattar—(m)—the devotee of the protector
Abdul-shaheed—(m)—devotee of the witness
Abdul-shahid—(m)—devotee of the witness
Abdul-shakur—(m)—devotee of the most thankful
Abdul-tawwaab—(m)—the devotee of the forgiver
Abdul-tawwab—(m)—devotee of the forgiver
Abdul-vajed—(m)—devotee of the finder
Abdul-vakil—(m)—devotee of the implementor
Abdul-waahid—(m)—the devotee of the unique one
Abdul-waajid—(m)—devotee of the finder
Abdul-waali—(m)—devotee of the inheritor
Abdul-waase—(m)—devotee of the vast
Abdul-wadood—(m)—devotee of the all-loving (allah)
Abdul-wadud—(m)—devotee of the loving
Abdul-wahaab—(m)—al-wahaab is one of name of allah
Abdul-wahab—(m)—devotee of the giver
Abdul-wahhab—(m)—devotee of the all-give (allah)
Abdul-wahid—(m)—devotee of god
Abdul-wajid—(m)—devotee of the finder, perceiver
Abdul-wakeel—(m)—devotee of the worthy of trust
Abdul-wakil—(m)—devotee of the trustee
Abdul-waliyy—(m)—the devotee of the protecting
Abdul-waliy—(m)—devotee of the protecting
Abdul-wali—(m)—devotee of the comrade, governor
Abdul-waris—(m)—devotee of the survivor
Abdul-warith—(m)—devotee of the supreme inheritor
Abdul-wasi—(m)—slave of the all embracing
Abdul-zahir—(m)—devotee of the manifest
Abdulaakhir—(m)—devotee of the last
Abdulaalee—(m)—devotee of the most high
Abduladl—(m)—slave of the just
Abdulafuw—(m)—devotee of the forgiver
Abdulahad—(m)—devotee of the only one (allah)
Abdulahi—(m)—one who serves the god
Abdulah—(m)—devotee of allah
Abdulajees—(m)—one with divine wisdom
Abdulaleem—(m)—devotee of the all-knowing

Abdulalim—(m)—devotee of the omniscient
Abdulaliyy—(m)—devotee of the most high
Abdularahman—(m)—devotee of the most gracious
Abdulawwal—(m)—devotee of the first
Abdulazaz—(m)—devotee of uzza
Abdulazeem—(m)—devotee of the mighty
Abdulazeez—(m)—the devotee of the most powerful
Abdulazim—(m)—devotee of the mighty (allah)
Abdulaziz—(m)—devotee of the beloved one
Abdula—(f)—princess, slave of allah
Abdula—(m)—devotee of allah
Abdulbaari—(m)—devotee of the evolver
Abdulbaasit—(m)—creator, devotee of the expander
Abdulbadee—(m)—slave of the originator
Abdulbadi—(m)—devotee of the incomparable
Abdulbais—(m)—devotee of the resurrector
Abdulbaith—(m)—devotee of the resurrector
Abdulbaqi—(m)—devotee of the everlasting (allah)
Abdulbari—(m)—devotee of the creator
Abdulbarr—(m)—devotee of the source of goodness
Abdulbaseer—(m)—devotee of allsagacious (allah)
Abdulbasir—(m)—devotee of the all seein
Abdulbasit—(m)—devotee of the extender, creator
Abdulbatin—(m)—devotee of the inward
Abdulfattah—(m)—devotee of the conqueror (allah)
Abdulgani—(m)—devotee of the self sufficient
Abdulghafaar—(m)—devotee of the forgive
Abdulghafoor—(m)—devotee of the forgiver
Abdulghafur—(m)—devotee of the all-forgiving
Abdulghani—(m)—devotee of the self-sufficient
Abdulhaady—(m)—devotee of the guide
Abdulhaafiz—(m)—devotee of the guardian (allah)
Abdulhadeem—(m)—one who serves a wise man
Abdulhadi—(m)—devotee of the guide (allah)
Abdulhafeez—(m)—devotee of the guardian (allah)
Abdulhafid—(m)—devotee of the protector
Abdulhafiz—(m)—devotee of the protector
Abdulhakam—(m)—devotee of the arbitrator

Abdulhakeem—(m)—devotee of the allwise (allah)
Abdulhakeen—(m)—one who serves a wise man
Abdulhakim—(m)—devotee of the judge (allah)
Abdulhaleem—(m)—devotee of the mild and patience
Abdulhalim—(m)—devotee of the all-element (allah)
Abdulhameed—(m)—devotee of the praiseworthy
Abdulhamid—(m)—devotee of the praiseworthy
Abdulhannan—(m)—slave of the merciful forgiving
Abdulhaqq—(m)—devotee of the truth
Abdulhaq—(m)—devotee of the truth (allah)
Abdulhaseeb—(m)—devotee of the respected, esteemed
Abdulhasib—(m)—devotee of the respected, esteemed
Abdulhayy—(m)—devotee of the living (allah)
Abduljabaar—(m)—devotee of the mighty
Abduljabar—(m)—devotee of the mighty
Abduljabbar—(m)—one who serves the comforter
Abduljabir—(m)—devotee of the comforter
Abduljaleel—(m)—revered
Abduljalil—(m)—devotee of the great, revered
Abduljame—(m)—devotee of the gatherer
Abduljamil—(m)—devotee of the beautiful (allah)
Abduljawwad—(m)—slave of the most bountiful
Abdulkabir—(m)—devotee of the great
Abdulkader—(m)—a name of the al-might allah
Abdulkadir—(m)—one who serves a capable man
Abdulkareem—(m)—generous
Abdulkawi—(m)—one with divine wisdom
Abdulkhaaliq—(m)—devotee of the creator
Abdulkhabir—(m)—devotee of the awar
Abdulkhafiz—(m)—devotee of the descender
Abdulkhalik—(m)—one with divine wisdom
Abdulkhaliq—(m)—devotee of the creator (allah)
Abdullaah—(m)—devotee of allah
Abdullafif—(m)—devotee of the kind one
Abdullahil—(m)—one with divine wisdom
Abdullahi—(m)—father of prophet muhammed
Abdullah—(f)—the devotee of allah
Abdullah—(m)—devotee of allah

Abdullateef—(m)—one who serves a kind man
Abdullatif—(m)—one who serves a kind man
Abdulla—(m)—devotee of allah, devotee of god
Abdullha—(m)—devotee of allah, god
Abdull—(m)—devotee of allah
Abdulmaajid—(m)—slave of the excellence
Abdulmaalik—(m)—devotee of the owner (allah)
Abdulmagid—(m)—devotee of the glorious one
Abdulmajeed—(m)—one who serves a glorious man
Abdulmajid—(m)—devotee of the glorious one
Abdulmalik—(m)—devotee of the master or king
Abdulmanaf—(m)—one with divine wisdom
Abdulmani—(m)—slave of one who prevents
Abdulmannan—(m)—slave of the benefactor
Abdulmateen—(m)—devotee of the firm, strong
Abdulmatin—(m)—devotee of the firm, strong
Abdulmedjid—(m)—devotee of the glorious one
Abdulmejid—(m)—devotee of the glorious one
Abdulmohsen—(m)—one with divine wisdom
Abdulmubdee—(m)—slave of the originator
Abdulmubdi—(m)—devotee of the originator
Abdulmueed—(m)—slave of the restorer
Abdulmueid—(m)—devotee of the restorer
Abdulmughni—(m)—devotee of the enricher
Abdulmuhaimin—(m)—devotee of the supervising
Abdulmuhaymin—(m)—slave of the protector
Abdulmuhsen—(m)—devotee of the charitable one
Abdulmuhsin—(m)—slave of the benefactor
Abdulmuhsi—(m)—devotee of the reckoner
Abdulmuid—(m)—devotee of the restorer
Abdulmujahid—(m)—one with divine wisdom
Abdulmujeeb—(m)—devotee of the responsive
Abdulmujib—(m)—devotee of the responder
Abdulmumin—(m)—devotee of the giver of faith
Abdulmunim—(m)—devotee of the benefactor
Abdulmuntaqim—(m)—devotee of the revenger
Abdulmuqaddim—(m)—devotee of the expediter
Abdulmuqeet—(m)—slave of the sustainer

Abdulmuqsit—(m)—slave of the just
Abdulmuqtadir—(m)—devotee of the powerful
Abdulmusawwir—(m)—devotee of the fashioner
Abdulmutaalee—(m)—devotee of the most exalted
Abdulmutaal—(m)—devotee of the most high
Abdulmuti—(m)—slave of the giver
Abdulmuttalib—(m)—allah's advisor and companion
Abdulmuzanni—(m)—he was a narrator of hadith
Abdulnafi—(m)—devotee of the benefactor
Abdulnaseer—(m)—slave of the helper
Abdulnasir—(m)—devotee of the helper, protector
Abdulnasser—(m)—devotee of the victorious one
Abdulnoor—(m)—slave of the one who is light
Abdulnur—(m)—devotee of the light
Abdulqaadir—(m)—devotee of the capable
Abdulqabiz—(m)—devotee of the withholder
Abdulqadeer—(m)—devotee of the powerful (allah)
Abdulqader—(m)—devotee of the capable
Abdulqadir—(m)—devotee of the capable
Abdulqahhar—(m)—devotee of the subduer
Abdulqawi—(m)—devotee of the most strong
Abdulqayyum—(m)—devotee of the self subsisting
Abdulquddus—(m)—devotee of the most holy
Abdulqudoos—(m)—devotee of the most holy
Abdulqudus—(m)—devotee of the most holy
Abdulraafi—(m)—one who elevates
Abdulrabb—(m)—slave of the lord
Abdulrafi—(m)—devotee of the one who raises
Abdulrahaman—(m)—devotee of a merciful
Abdulraheem—(m)—devotee of the most compassionate
Abdulrahim—(m)—devotee of the merciful
Abdulrahmaan—(m)—devotee of the mercifully gracious
Abdulrahman—(m)—devotee of the mercifully gracious
Abdulraouf—(m)—devotee of the most merciful
Abdulraqib—(m)—slave of the vigilant
Abdulrasheed—(m)—devotee of the rightly guided
Abdulrashid—(m)—devotee of the rightly guided one
Abdulrauf—(m)—devotee of the compassionate

Abdulrazaaq—(m)—devotee of the maintainer
Abdulrazak—(m)—one with divine wisdom
Abdulrazaq—(m)—devotee of the maintainer
Abdulrazzad—(m)—one with divine wisdom
Abdulrazzaq—(m)—devotee of the maintainer
Abdulrehman—(m)—one who serves a merciful man
Abdulsaboor—(m)—devotee of the patient
Abdulsabur—(m)—devotee of the patient
Abdulsalaam—(m)—devotee of the peace
Abdulsalam—(m)—devotee of the peace
Abdulsamad—(m)—devotee of the eternal
Abdulsami—(m)—devotee of the all hearing
Abdulsammad—(m)—one with divine wisdom
Abdulsatar—(m)—one with divine wisdom
Abdulsattar—(m)—devotee of the protector
Abdulshahid—(m)—devotee of the witness
Abdulshakur—(m)—devotee of the most thankful
Abdultawaab—(m)—devotee of the forgiver
Abdultawwab—(m)—devotee of the forgiver
Abdulvajed—(m)—devotee of the finder
Abdulvakil—(m)—devotee of the implementer
Abdulwaahid—(m)—devotee of the one
Abdulwaali—(m)—slave of the governor
Abdulwadood—(m)—devotee of the loving
Abdulwadud—(m)—devotee of the loving
Abdulwahaab—(m)—devotee of the giver
Abdulwahab—(m)—devotee of the giver
Abdulwahhab—(m)—devotee of the giver
Abdulwahid—(m)—devotee of the unique one
Abdulwajid—(m)—devotee of the finder
Abdulwakil—(m)—devotee of the trustee
Abdulwaliy—(m)—devotee of the protecting
Abdulwali—(m)—devotee of the governor
Abdulwarith—(m)—devotee of the supreme inheritor
Abdulwasi—(m)—slave of the all embracing
Abdulyaqzan—(m)—one with divine wisdom
Abdulzahir—(m)—devotee of the manifest
Abdul—(m)—knowledge, devotee of the lord

Abdun-naafe—(m)—devotee of the giver of gains
Abdun-naafi—(m)—the devotee of the propitious
Abdun-nafi—(m)—the devotee of the propitious
Abdun-nasir—(m)—devotee of the helper (allah)
Abdun-noor—(m)—devotee of the light
Abdunnasir—(m)—devotee of the helper (allah)
Abdunnoor—(m)—devotee of the light
Abdun—(m)—king
Abdur-raafi—(m)—the devotee of the elevator
Abdur-rab—(m)—devotee of the lord (allah), se
Abdur-rafi—(m)—devotee of the exalted (allah)
Abdur-raheem—(m)—devotee of the most merciful
Abdur-rahim—(m)—devotee of god, lord
Abdur-raoof—(m)—devotee of the compassionate
Abdur-raqeeb—(m)—devotee of watchful
Abdur-raqib—(m)—devotee of the observer (allah)
Abdur-rasheed—(m)—devotee of the guide to right path
Abdur-rashid—(m)—slave of the guide
Abdur-rauf—(m)—devotee of the most kind (allah)
Abdur-razzaaq—(m)—devotee of the provider (allah)
Abdur-razzaq—(m)—devotee of the provider (allah)
Abdurahman—(m)—one with divine wisdom
Abdurrab—(m)—devotee of the lord (allah)
Abdurrafi—(m)—devotee of the exalted (allah)
Abdurrahman—(m)—one who serves a merciful man
Abdurran—(m)—one with divine wisdom
Abdurraqib—(m)—devotee of the observer (allah)
Abdurrashid—(m)—slave of the guide
Abdurrazzad—(m)—one with divine wisdom
Abdurrehman—(m)—one who serves a merciful man
Abdursalam—(m)—one with divine wisdom
Abdur—(m)—one with divine wisdom
Abdus-saboor—(m)—devotee of the patient (allah)
Abdus-sabour—(m)—devotee of the patient
Abdus-sabur—(m)—slave of the forbearing
Abdus-salaam—(m)—devotee of the source of peace
Abdus-salam—(m)—devotee of the all-peaceable
Abdus-samad—(m)—slave of the eternal

Abdus-sameei—(m)—devotee of the all-hearing
Abdus-samee—(m)—devotee of the all-hearing
Abdus-sami—(m)—slave of the all hearing
Abdus-shafi—(m)—slave of the healer
Abdus-shaheed—(m)—devotee of the witness
Abdus-shahid—(m)—slave of the witness
Abdus-shakur—(m)—devotee of the appreciative
Abdus-smad—(m)—slave of the eternal
Abdus-subbooh—(m)—slave of the extremely pure
Abdus-subhan—(m)—devotee of the glory (allah)
Abdus-subooh—(m)—slave of the extremely pure
Abdush-shafi—(m)—slave of the healer
Abdush-shaheed—(m)—devotee of the witness
Abdush-shahid—(m)—slave of the witness
Abdushshaheed—(m)—devotee of the witness
Abdushshahid—(m)—slave of the witness
Abdussabur—(m)—slave of the forbearing
Abdussalaam—(m)—slave of the giver of peace
Abdussalam—(m)—devotee of peace
Abdussamad—(m)—devotee of the eternal
Abdussami—(m)—slave of the all hearing
Abdusshafi—(m)—slave of the healer
Abdussubbooh—(m)—slave of the extremely pure
Abdussubhan—(m)—devotee of the glory (allah)
Abduz-zaahir—(m)—devotee of the outward
Abduz-zahir—(m)—devotee of the overt, manifest
Abduzzahir—(m)—slave of the manifest
Abdu—(m)—worshipper of god
Abea—(f)—joy of my father
Abeba—(f)—flower
Abeda—(f)—a gift of god
Abedeen—(m)—one with divine wisdom
Abedin—(f)—adorer
Abedin—(m)—worshippers
Abed—(m)—worshipper, adorer
Abeeba—(f)—one who have a knowledge of islam
Abeedah—(f)—adorer, narrator of hadith
Abeeda—(f)—adorer, permanent

Abeedha—(f)—permanent
Abeed—(m)—devotee, worshipper of god, hermit
Abeeha—(f)—her father
Abeel—(m)—healthy
Abeem—(m)—fearless
Abeena—(f)—born on tuesday
Abeerah—(f)—rose
Abeer—(f)—fragrance, perfume
Abeer—(m)—colour, fragrance, strength
Abeesha—(f)—goddess of will
Abeeth—(m)—one with divine wisdom
Abeez—(m)—spark of fire
Abeida—(f)—adorer of god, flower
Abeira—(f)—saffron, perfume
Abena—(f)—born on tuesday, from akan
Abera—(f)—powerful, noble
Abesha—(f)—allah twakl
Abhaar—(m)—seas, oceans, noble and great men
Abhaid—(m)—one who cannot be killed, immortal
Abhaj—(f)—more or most beautiful
Abhaj—(m)—more successful, brilliant
Abhar—(f)—narcissus, arabian jasmine
Abhar—(m)—shining, more brilliant
Abha—(f)—brightness, lustre, shine
Abhidatt—(m)—great
Abhil—(m)—meadow
Abhin—(m)—different, fearless
Abhir—(f)—fragrance, aroma
Abhram—(m)—steady, clear
Abiah—(f)—my father rejoices, yahweh
Abia—(f)—great, my father is the lord
Abia—(m)—god is my father
Abiba—(f)—beloved
Abidaa—(f)—adorers, adorers
Abidah—(f)—adorer, devotee
Abidain—(m)—worshiper, devoted devotee of god
Abidali—(m)—one with divine wisdom
Abidat—(f)—adorers of god

Abida—(f)—adorers, adorers
Abida—(m)—father of knowledge
Abideen—(m)—worshippers
Abidha—(f)—one who worships
Abidh—(m)—worshipper
Abidin—(m)—worshippers, adorers
Abidullah—(m)—worshipper of allah
Abidun—(m)—worshipper of god
Abidu—(m)—worshipper of god, spark of fire
Abid—(f)—adorer of god
Abid—(m)—worshipper of allah
Abigail—(f)—delight, joy to the father
Abigail—(m)—father's joy, wise
Abiha—(f)—the water falls of heaven
Abijah—(f)—god, lord is my father
Abijah—(m)—the lord is my father
Abilah—(f)—beautiful
Abil—(m)—also spelt as abeel, healthy
Abin—(m)—singer, beginning
Abiq—(m)—exhaling, fragrance
Abirah—(f)—noble, powerful, strong
Abira—(f)—strong
Abire—(f)—aroma, fragrance
Abir—(f)—fragrant, strong
Abir—(m)—perfume, colour, thinker
Abisali—(m)—warrior in islam
Abisha—(f)—gift of god
Abish—(m)—sky, gift of god, a ray of light
Abis—(m)—quick, alert, swift
Abiyah—(m)—handsome
Abiyan—(m)—eloquent
Abiya—(f)—brilliant, splendid
Abizer—(m)—father of wealth
Abiz—(m)—spark of fire
Abi—(m)—my father, all given to good
Abkar—(m)—first born, virginal, new, novel
Ablaa—(f)—perfectly formed, a flower
Ablagh—(m)—more or most perfect

Ablah—(f)—perfectly formed, perfectly
Ablaj—(f)—shining, beautiful, fair
Abla—(f)—perfectly formed, a wild rose
Abnat—(m)—strong, strength
Abnaz—(f)—unique, divine aura
Abnus—(m)—ebony
Abod—(m)—father (heb)
Aboobacker—(m)—one with divine wisdom
Abood—(m)—worship
Aboo—(m)—father
Abot—(m)—father
Aboud—(m)—cloudy
Abou—(m)—father
Abqari—(f)—multicoloured, ingenious, genial
Abqar—(m)—wonderland, fairyland
Abqurah—(f)—genius
Abraam—(m)—father of a multitude
Abraar—(m)—loyal
Abrad—(m)—mail, coldest, cool
Abrahah—(m)—father of the people
Abraham—(m)—faultless
Abraha—(m)—one with divine wisdom
Abrahem—(m)—father of a multitude
Abrahim—(m)—form of abraham
Abrahm—(m)—father of a multitude
Abrahum—(m)—one with divine wisdom
Abraiz—(m)—most distinctive
Abraj—(f)—with beautiful eyes
Abraj—(m)—beautiful-eyed
Abrak—(m)—the blessed one
Abrams—(m)—high father, from abraham
Abram—(m)—exalted father
Abran—(m)—exalted father, variant of abram
Abraq—(m)—radiant, brilliant
Abrar—(f)—devoted to god
Abrar—(m)—a truthful person, saint
Abrash—(f)—spotted, dappled
Abrash—(m)—spotted, speckled

Abraz—(m)—most prominent, most distinctive
Abra—(f)—mother of multitude, lesson
Abra—(m)—fire, cloud
Abreena—(f)—queen of arab
Abreeq—(m)—glittering sword
Abree—(f)—female version of abraham
Abreshmina—(f)—made of silk
Abrez—(m)—pure gold
Abrham—(m)—one with divine wisdom
Abrian—(m)—a variation of abraham
Abrik—(m)—precious like gold
Abrina—(f)—queen of arab
Abrin—(f)—unique, divine aura
Abrin—(m)—pure
Abrisha—(f)—full of grace, god's grace
Abrish—(f)—god of grace, full of grace
Abriz—(m)—pure gold
Abri—(f)—female version of abraham
Abroo—(f)—fame, dignity, honour
Abroo—(m)—honour, fame, dignity
Absaar—(f)—vision, insight, keenness
Absaar—(m)—seeing, vision, insight, keenness
Absalom—(m)—god the father of peace
Absana—(f)—fiction
Absara—(f)—moves in the rains in the clouds
Absar—(f)—swift, eye-sight, vision
Absar—(m)—eyes, vision, sight
Absat—(m)—vast, wide, spacious
Absham—(m)—a tree which has scent
Abshar—(m)—one with divine wisdom
Absha—(f)—unique, divine aura
Abshira—(f)—unique, divine aura
Abshir—(m)—one with divine wisdom
Absi—(m)—probably from abasa to frown
Abs—(m)—austere, frowning
Abtab—(m)—grandeur, splendour, brilliancy
Abtahi—(f)—place near makkah
Abtal—(m)—heroes

Abteen—(m)—father of faridoon (a king)
Abthi—(m)—a place near makkah
Abu-al-khayr—(m)—one who does good
Abu-al-qaasim—(m)—the father of qasim
Abu-at-tahir—(m)—the father of tahir
Abu-at-tayyib—(m)—the fater of tayyib
Abu-ayyub—(m)—well-known sahabi
Abu-bakr—(m)—companion of muhammad
Abu-dawud—(m)—author of one of the sahih hadith
Abu-firas—(m)—lion
Abu-huzaifah—(m)—famous sahabi of rasoolullah
Abu-ibrahim—(m)—the fater of ibrahim
Abu-isa—(m)—father of isa
Abu-jayed—(m)—giving, generous
Abu-mirsha—(m)—powerful
Abu-saeed—(m)—father of dignified
Abu-talib—(m)—father of seeker
Abu-turab—(m)—an attributive of caliph ali
Abu-ubaidah—(m)—great sahabi of the prophet
Abu-zar—(m)—great sahabi of the prophet
Abuabdullah—(m)—father of abdullah
Abuahmad—(m)—one with divine wisdom
Abuali—(m)—father of ali
Abualkhayr—(m)—one who does good
Abubacar—(m)—noble
Abubacker—(m)—one with divine wisdom
Abubakar—(m)—noble
Abubaker—(m)—one with divine wisdom
Abubakkar—(m)—one with divine wisdom
Abubakker—(m)—the companion of prophet mohammed
Abubakr—(m)—the companion of prophet mohammed
Abubashir—(m)—one with divine wisdom
Abudah—(f)—adorer, devoted to god
Abudah—(m)—worshipper, devoted to god
Abudain—(m)—worshipper of god
Abudalamah—(m)—father of blackness
Abudarda—(m)—father of a toothless old woman
Abudaud—(m)—father of daud

Abudawud—(m)—author of one of the sahih hadith
Abuda—(m)—worshipper of allah
Abudi—(m)—devoted worshipper of god
Abudujana—(m)—name of sahabi
Abue—(m)—father
Abufiras—(m)—father of a lion
Abufiruz—(m)—one with divine wisdom
Abughalib—(m)—father of ghalib
Abuhabib—(m)—one with divine wisdom
Abuhafs—(m)—father of a lion cub
Abuhamzah—(m)—lion
Abuhanifah—(m)—father of a pious woman
Abuhassan—(m)—one with divine wisdom
Abuhazim—(m)—one with divine wisdom
Abuhisham—(m)—father of hisham
Abuhurairah—(m)—father of a kitten
Abuhurayrah—(m)—one with divine wisdom
Abuidris—(m)—one with divine wisdom
Abuishaq—(m)—one with divine wisdom
Abujafar—(m)—father of ja'far
Abujahl—(m)—father of ignorance
Abujar—(m)—one with divine wisdom
Abujurayj—(m)—one with divine wisdom
Abukathir—(m)—one with divine wisdom
Abul-alaa—(m)—father of glory
Abul-baqa—(m)—immortal
Abul-barakat—(m)—blissful, father of blessings
Abul-bashar—(m)—father of mankind
Abul-farah—(m)—happy, glad, father of joy
Abul-faraj—(m)—comfortable, possessor of comfort
Abul-fath—(m)—victorious, father of victory
Abul-fazl—(m)—father of bounty, grace, grace
Abul-haisam—(m)—sahabi, great scholar of history
Abul-hasan—(m)—father of hasan
Abul-hassan—(m)—the son of ali
Abul-husain—(m)—father of husain, caliph ali
Abul-kalam—(m)—eloquent, father of speech
Abul-khair—(m)—virtuous, father of good work

Abul-khayr—(m)—one who does good
Abul-mahasin—(m)—merits, father of virtues
Abul-qasim—(m)—father of qasim
Abul-yumn—(m)—happy, father of happiness
Abulabbas—(m)—father of abbas
Abulahab—(m)—father of the flame
Abulaina—(m)—father of aina
Abulala—(m)—father of sublimity
Abulasshab—(m)—one with divine wisdom
Abulaswad—(m)—one with divine wisdom
Abulbarakat—(m)—father of blessings, blissful
Abulbashar—(m)—father of mankind
Abulbashr—(m)—father of mankind
Abuldunya—(m)—one with divine wisdom
Abuldurr—(m)—father of the pearl
Abulfadl—(m)—god grace
Abulfaraj—(m)—one with divine wisdom
Abulfath—(m)—one with divine wisdom
Abulfazl—(m)—endowed with bounty, grace
Abulhaija—(m)—father of battle
Abulhaisam—(m)—a sahabi
Abulhasan—(m)—father of hasan
Abulhassan—(m)—the son of ali
Abulhawari—(m)—one with divine wisdom
Abulhusain—(m)—father of husain, caliph ali
Abulhusayn—(m)—one with divine wisdom
Abulkalam—(m)—father of speech, eloquent
Abulkhair—(m)—father of good work, virtuous
Abulkhayr—(m)—one who does good
Abulmahasin—(m)—father of virtues, merits
Abulmahzurat—(m)—father of a scare-crow
Abulmasakin—(m)—father of the poor
Abulmughayyis—(m)—one with divine wisdom
Abulmusawir—(m)—one with divine wisdom
Abulqasim—(m)—father of qasim
Abulsaid—(m)—father of the sa'id
Abultayyib—(m)—one with divine wisdom
Abululu—(m)—father of a pearl

Abulwafa—(m)—father of loyalty
Abulward—(m)—father of flowers
Abulyumn—(m)—father of happiness, happy
Abulzinad—(m)—one with divine wisdom
Abul—(m)—devotee of allah
Abumalik—(m)—father of malik
Abumuhammad—(m)—one with divine wisdom
Abunasr—(m)—one with divine wisdom
Abundrah—(m)—one with divine wisdom
Aburah—(f)—perfume, fragrance
Abusad—(m)—one with divine wisdom
Abusaeed—(m)—father of dignified
Abusahl—(m)—one with divine wisdom
Abushad—(m)—one with divine wisdom
Abushaybah—(m)—one with divine wisdom
Abusuddin—(m)—one with divine wisdom
Abutahir—(m)—father of innocent
Abutalib—(m)—father of seeker
Abutayyib—(m)—one with divine wisdom
Abuthahir—(m)—father of innocent
Abuturab—(m)—one with divine wisdom
Abuyazid—(m)—one with divine wisdom
Abuzair—(m)—one with divine wisdom
Abuzar—(m)—first, top, father
Abuzeid—(m)—one with divine wisdom
Abuzer—(m)—name of sahabi
Abuziar—(m)—one with divine wisdom
Abu—(m)—father (pahlavi), master
Abyaan—(m)—one with divine wisdom
Abyadh—(m)—white
Abyad—(m)—narrator of hadith
Abyan—(m)—very clean, clearer, eloquent
Abyar—(f)—accept
Abyaz—(m)—white, bright, pure
Abya—(f)—joy of my father
Aby—(m)—mazhar, father
Abzal—(m)—one with divine wisdom
Abzari—(m)—seeds, spice, seedsman

Abzar—(m)—powerful, mighty
Abzi—(m)—gift of god, ability
Achernar—(m)—one with divine wisdom
Achmet—(m)—most praiseworthy
Achraf—(m)—most honourable one
Acimah—(f)—praised by god
Ackbar—(m)—greatest, also spelt as akbar
Ackmal—(m)—perfected
Acmal—(m)—perfected
Adaan—(f)—one who happily resides in a place
Adaan—(m)—red earth
Adab—(f)—appropriate breeding, decorum, culture
Adab—(m)—mohamed name, respect
Adad—(m)—power, victory
Adahi—(m)—in the woods
Adah—(f)—from the beautiful scenery
Adail—(m)—just honest
Adain—(f)—resembling the mother, winged
Adaj—(f)—dark, black, with large black eyes
Adala—(f)—justice, noble
Adal—(m)—precious, nobel
Adama—(m)—man
Adam—(m)—red earth, first human being
Adanan—(m)—good fortune, one who is settled
Adana—(f)—feminine of adam, earth
Adaniyaa—(f)—unique, divine aura
Adaniyyah—(f)—one who is from city of aden
Adan—(f)—fire, noble, nobility
Adara—(f)—beauty, fire, noble, virgin
Adar—(m)—ideal, exalted, high, eminent
Adasha—(f)—beauty
Adash—(m)—fire
Adawiyah—(f)—summer plant, a type of plant
Adawi—(m)—a grandson of sayyidina umer
Ada—(f)—graceful and noble, pure, noble
Ada—(m)—fulfilling a duty, paying, beauty
Adbdullah—(m)—allah's person
Adbul-qawi—(m)—devotee of the most powerful

Adbul—(m)—devotee of the most powerful
Addal—(m)—extremely fair, exactly same
Addam—(m)—son of the red earth, man, earth
Addan—(m)—garden of eden, earth
Addeva—(f)—pleasant, gentle
Addin—(m)—delicate, slender
Adeebah—(f)—scholar
Adeeba—(f)—literary woman, authoress
Adeeb—(m)—intellectual, erudite, scholar
Adeefah—(f)—compassionate
Adeelah—(f)—just
Adeela—(f)—equal, upright, justice, virtuous
Adeel—(f)—equal, derived from adeline
Adeel—(m)—judge, honest, the best, justice
Adeema—(f)—rare
Adeem—(m)—rare
Adeenah—(f)—unique, divine aura
Adeena—(f)—goddess, appropriate luck, pious
Adeen—(f)—little fire
Adeen—(m)—obedient, submissive
Adeera—(f)—unique, divine aura
Adeer—(m)—noble, majestic
Adeeva—(f)—pleasant, gentle
Adeiba—(f)—polite, cultured
Adeib—(m)—scholar, literature
Adeis—(m)—hope
Adelina—(f)—graceful, noble kind, adornment
Adeline—(f)—noble, nobility, kind, brightness
Adelky—(m)—one with divine wisdom
Adel—(m)—righteous, upright, sincere
Ademola—(m)—crown is added to my wealth
Adem—(m)—earth, of the earth
Adena—(f)—decoration, tender
Aden—(f)—fire, fiery one
Aden—(m)—attractive, handsome
Adhaan—(f)—call to prayer, announcement
Adhaan—(m)—announcement, call to prayer
Adhaa—(f)—more sensible, intelligent

Adham—(m)—black, son of the red earth
Adhan—(m)—epithet of lord shiva
Adhaviya—(f)—unique, divine aura
Adheel—(m)—justice, honest
Adheem—(m)—great
Adheena—(f)—goddess of art
Adheen—(m)—devotee, follower
Adheeva—(f)—unique, divine aura
Adhif—(m)—generous
Adhnan—(m)—proper name, name of god, bravery
Adhraa—(f)—unique, divine aura
Adhra—(f)—apology, virgin
Adian—(m)—a large bat
Adiat—(f)—rebellious
Adibah—(f)—cultured, refined
Adiba—(f)—etiquette, cultured, polite
Adib—(m)—cultured, well mannered one
Adielah—(f)—adornment of the lord
Adiela—(f)—adornment of the lord
Adiena—(f)—ornament, slender, brightness
Adifaah—(f)—talented, smart
Adifah—(f)—smart
Adifa—(f)—generous, smart
Adif—(m)—generous
Adiha—(f)—god
Adika—(f)—power
Adilah—(f)—justice princess, equal, just
Adila—(f)—equal, just, upright
Adila—(m)—equal, just, honest
Adilia—(f)—honest
Adilla—(f)—just, honest
Adill—(m)—honest
Adilshah—(m)—just king
Adil—(m)—sincere, just, fair, judicious
Adimar—(m)—famous for his kindness
Adim—(m)—entire universe, earth
Adinah—(f)—decoration, slender
Adinan—(m)—bravery, pleasure, name of god

Adina—(f)—decoration, friday, beautiful
Adina—(m)—noble minded, slender, delicate
Adini—(f)—unique, divine aura
Adin—(m)—pleasure given, delicate
Adirah—(f)—unique, divine aura
Adira—(f)—strong, noble, beautiful, powerful
Adir—(m)—noble
Adish—(m)—king of fire, supreme lord, fire
Adit—(m)—from the beginning, first born
Adiva—(f)—pleasant, gentle, agreeable
Adiyaan—(m)—plural of deen
Adiyan—(m)—devotee, devotee, lion, lord shiva
Adiyat—(m)—one with divine wisdom
Adiya—(f)—gods treasure
Adiy—(m)—a companion of the prophet
Adi—(m)—beginning, first born, superior
Adlaa—(f)—just, fairadlai—(f)—just
Adlan—(m)—merciful, fair
Adla—(f)—justice, honest
Adlea—(f)—of justice - fairness
Adleen—(f)—unique, divine aura
Adlie—(m)—yahweh is just, my ornament, just
Adlina—(f)—noble, honourable, of a noble kind
Adli—(m)—juridical, related to fairness
Adly—(m)—just, my ornament, yahweh is just
Adl—(m)—justice, equity
Admaa—(f)—soul
Adman—(m)—a red peony flower
Admin—(m)—a red peony flower
Admira—(f)—admiring
Admir—(m)—strong, famous
Adnaan—(m)—bravery, lion, paradise
Adnaa—(f)—closest
Adnane—(m)—settler
Adnan—(f)—proper name
Adnan—(m)—name of god, proper name
Adna—(f)—paradise, pleasure, delight
Adnen—(m)—settler

Adnin—(m)—settler
Adniyyah—(f)—resident, inhabitant
Adni—(m)—one with divine wisdom
Adnnan—(m)—one with divine wisdom
Adn—(f)—bliss, paradise, heaven
Adolfa—(f)—exalted
Adorer—(m)—worshippers, adorers
Adra—(f)—virgin, beauty, veda, untainted
Adra—(m)—more knowledgeable
Adrian—(m)—dark one, rich, from hadria
Adrina—(f)—dark, the adriatic sea region
Adrish—(m)—lord of mountain, mirror
Adrita—(f)—love, sweetness, kindness
Adriyan—(m)—rich, dark one
Adriz—(m)—one with divine wisdom
Adro—(m)—most righteous
Adsila—(f)—blossom
Adskan—(m)—knight
Adulaziz—(m)—devotee of the beloved one
Adut—(m)—habit
Aduz-zahir—(m)—slave of the manifest
Aduzahir—(m)—slave of the manifest
Aduzzahir—(m)—slave of the manifest
Adviya—(f)—unique, divine aura
Advi—(m)—one who does not need protection
Adwam—(m)—most durable, more lasting
Adwit—(m)—unique, unrivalled
Adwi—(m)—brave, needing no protection
Adyaan—(m)—one with divine wisdom
Adyan—(f)—deen, religion
Adyan—(m)—pious, religious
Adyl—(m)—honest, just
Aeajaz—(m)—one with divine wisdom
Aearif—(m)—knowledgeable, acquainted, devotee
Aeden—(m)—little fire
Aedyn—(m)—little fire
Aeedah—(f)—returning, visiting, reward
Aeena—(f)—mirror

Aeera—(f)—bearer of victory
Aeesha—(f)—woman, alive
Aeeza—(f)—dear one, honored ruler
Aefaz—(m)—helper
Aehaan—(m)—full moon
Aehzaan—(m)—soul of the moon
Aehzan—(m)—soul of the moon, fire
Aeina—(f)—pure, the only one, always
Aeira—(f)—respectful, noble, honourable
Aeisha—(f)—beautiful, obedient
Aeiza—(f)—dear one, mighty one, respected
Aejas—(m)—astonishment, miracle, action
Aejaz—(m)—karma, person who does miracles
Aelaaf—(m)—loving
Aeleena—(f)—unique, divine aura
Aelina—(f)—angel
Aelin—(f)—swift - strong, clever - proud
Aelisha—(f)—god gift
Aelred—(m)—noble counsel
Aema—(f)—plural of imam, leaders
Aema—(m)—leader, variant of imam
Aember—(f)—sky
Aemir—(m)—unbeatable
Aena—(f)—innocent one
Aeni—(f)—original, pure, true
Aerhan—(m)—one with divine wisdom
Aerin—(m)—enlightened
Aesar—(f)—unique, divine aura
Aeshah—(f)—woman, life, alive
Aesha—(f)—love, woman, life, alive, awake
Aesheen—(f)—unique, divine aura
Aesh—(m)—well satisfied
Aetesham—(m)—one with divine wisdom
Aetisham—(m)—preserving himself from sin
Aewaz—(m)—one with divine wisdom
Aeysha—(f)—unique, divine aura
Aezal—(f)—gift of god, the beginning
Aezaz—(m)—honour

Aeza—(f)—obedient, beautiful, noble
Aezza—(f)—respected, noble ones, mighty ones
Afaadh—(m)—one with divine wisdom
Afaaf—(f)—chaste, virtuous, decent, pure
Afaal—(f)—unique, divine aura
Afaan—(m)—forgive
Afaaq—(m)—the place where earth and sky meet
Afaat—(m)—one with divine wisdom
Afaaz-ahad—(m)—slave of the one
Afad—(m)—kind
Afaf—(f)—virtuous, decent, pure, chastity
Afaf—(m)—pure, decent
Afakhim—(m)—greatest
Afak—(f)—please
Afam—(f)—friendly
Afam—(m)—friendly, e
Afanan—(m)—full spreading branches of trees
Afana—(f)—the forgiver, pardoner, chaste
Afandi—(m)—lord, noble, master
Afan—(m)—forgive
Afaq—(f)—world, horizon
Afaq—(m)—deep, depth like sky, the place
Afareen—(f)—worth of praising, to create
Afasana—(f)—storey, romance, fiction
Afasar—(f)—crown
Afashana—(f)—fiction
Afazal—(m)—one with divine wisdom
Afaz—(m)—amazing, helper
Afdaal—(m)—better
Afdal—(m)—better, excellent
Afdhaal—(m)—causing to excel, excellent
Afdhal—(m)—causing to excel, excellent
Afdha—(f)—beautiful
Afea—(f)—strength, shadows, pure
Afeedha—(f)—hearts, consciences
Afeefah—(f)—virtuous, pure, chaste, modest
Afeefa—(f)—maiden, chaste, honest, upright
Afeef—(m)—clean, chaste, modest, pure, pious

Afeeha—(f)—unique, divine aura
Afeek—(m)—one with divine wisdom
Afeela—(f)—unique, divine aura
Afeel—(m)—important
Afeena—(f)—sincerity
Afeen—(f)—one who forgive
Afeen—(m)—one who forgive, pardon others
Afeeq—(m)—honest
Afeerah—(f)—covered with soil or dust, blonde
Afeera—(f)—a type of gazelle
Afeera—(m)—dust, gazelle
Afeesa—(f)—unique, divine aura
Afeesha—(f)—also spelt as afisha
Afees—(m)—one with divine wisdom
Afeetha—(f)—unique, divine aura
Afeeya—(f)—pure, strength, shadows
Afeezah—(f)—a path to paradise
Afeeza—(f)—one who know the recital of quaran
Afeez—(m)—a path to paradise
Afee—(f)—scented river in heaven
Afefa—(f)—pious, chaste, maiden
Afeni—(f)—health
Afera—(f)—young deer, colour of the earth
Affaak—(m)—horizons
Affaan—(m)—name of caliph uthman's father
Affaf—(f)—pure
Affam—(m)—one with divine wisdom
Affana—(f)—virtuous, the forgiver, chaste
Affann—(m)—forgive
Affan—(m)—blessed, forgive
Affeek—(m)—one with divine wisdom
Affera—(f)—colour of the earth, young deer
Affery—(f)—colour of the earth, young deer
Affhida—(f)—unique, divine aura
Affifa—(f)—health, chaste, modest
Affif—(m)—chaste
Affina—(f)—admirer
Affin—(m)—one with divine wisdom

Affiza—(f)—unique, divine aura
Affi—(f)—independent, positive
Affnaa—(f)—unique, divine aura
Affrah—(f)—happiness
Affran—(m)—god, noble
Affra—(f)—colour of earth, young deer
Affrina—(f)—creator
Affrose—(f)—unique, divine aura
Affshad—(m)—one with divine wisdom
Afgan—(m)—one who throws down
Afga—(f)—beautiful
Afhaam—(m)—sense, intelligence
Afham—(m)—intelligent
Afhan—(m)—one with divine wisdom
Afiah—(f)—born on friday
Afiah—(m)—born on friday, fourth born son
Afian—(m)—one with divine wisdom
Afia—(f)—born on friday, from ewe
Afidah—(f)—consciences, hearts
Afida—(f)—consciences, hearts
Afidha—(f)—hearts, consciences
Afid—(m)—consciences
Afif-ud-din—(m)—virtuous of the religion
Afifa-masarrat—(f)—god's angle
Afifah—(f)—chaste, pure
Afifa—(f)—honest, upright, virtuous, pure
Afifi—(m)—one with divine wisdom
Afif—(f)—pure, chaste, honest
Afif—(m)—pure, chaste, modest, virtuous
Afiha—(f)—unique, divine aura
Afija—(f)—unique, divine aura
Afika—(f)—vertex of grace, generosity
Afik—(m)—knowledge, pinnacle of grace
Afila—(f)—intelligent
Afinah—(f)—young doe, cute little deer
Afina—(f)—young
Afin—(m)—one who forgive others
Afiqah—(f)—glorious, honest

Afiq—(m)—generosity, knowledge
Afirah—(f)—a famous, a type of gazelle
Afirat—(f)—heaven
Afira—(f)—pure
Afira—(m)—one with divine wisdom
Afisa—(f)—shining, appropriate luck, transparent
Afishah—(f)—pretty, shining
Afisha—(f)—pretty
Afiyah—(f)—health
Afiyan—(m)—forgiven
Afiyat—(f)—health, freedom from illness
Afiyat—(m)—good health, ease, comfort
Afiya—(f)—health, faithful
Afiya—(m)—good health
Afizan—(m)—honorfied
Afiza—(f)—fresh air
Afizeh—(f)—a pendant
Afiz—(m)—innocent
Afjal—(m)—excellent
Afja—(f)—lucky
Afkar—(f)—intellect thought, plural of fikr
Afkar—(m)—precious, poor, destitute
Afkhar—(m)—finest, bravest, magnificent
Aflaa—(f)—most successful
Aflah—(f)—victory
Aflah—(m)—most successful
Aflak—(f)—heavenly bodies
Aflan—(m)—one with divine wisdom
Aflaq—(f)—light of the morning
Afla—(f)—descending, intelligent
Aflik—(m)—one with divine wisdom
Afnaan—(f)—tree of jannah
Afnaan—(m)—intertwined branches of trees
Afnaaz—(f)—novel, pride, beautiful
Afnaaz—(m)—one with divine wisdom
Afnan—(f)—name of the flower in heaven
Afnan—(m)—branches with leaves
Afnas—(m)—immortal

Afnaz—(f)—fabulous, novel, quickness
Afnaz—(m)—novel, fabulous
Afna—(f)—tree branches of heaven
Afni—(f)—sweet, forever
Afoow—(m)—forgiver
Afraad—(m)—unique, single
Afraah—(f)—white, bright, happiness
Afraan—(m)—happiness
Afraaz—(m)—man who stand like a mountain
Afraa—(f)—white, fair complexioned
Afraa—(m)—happiness
Afrad—(m)—single, unique, matchless
Afrah—(f)—happiness, cheerfulness, teaching
Afrah—(m)—happiness
Afraima—(f)—fertile
Afraj—(m)—one with divine wisdom
Afram—(m)—a river in, africa, river in
Afrana—(f)—unique, divine aura
Afran—(m)—noble, god
Afraq—(m)—love
Afrasiab—(m)—name of a king
Afras—(m)—height
Afraz-iman—(m)—learned in divine law
Afraz—(m)—height
Afra—(f)—white, colour of earth
Afreeda—(f)—produced, created, youth
Afreed—(f)—precious
Afreed—(m)—precious
Afreena—(f)—creator
Afreen—(f)—encouragement, beautiful
Afreen—(m)—beautiful, praise, acclamation
Afreeq—(m)—agreeable
Afreeth—(m)—protection
Afreez—(m)—one with divine wisdom
Afree—(f)—unique, divine aura
Afree—(m)—one with divine wisdom
Afreha—(f)—unique, divine aura
Afrena—(f)—goddess, ruler

Afren—(f)—sweet, name of goddess durga
Africk—(m)—one with divine wisdom
Afrida—(f)—youth, created, produced
Afridha—(f)—produced, youth, created
Afridi—(m)—a cast of afghans, maker
Afrid—(m)—intelligence
Afrihaa—(f)—unique, divine aura
Afriha—(f)—unique, divine aura
Afrina—(f)—creator
Afrin—(f)—happiness, praise, lucky, brave
Afrin—(m)—lucky, to praise
Afriq—(m)—one with divine wisdom
Afrisha—(f)—lovable
Afrish—(m)—lovable
Afrita—(f)—unique, divine aura
Afritha—(f)—created, youth
Afrith—(m)—maker, leadership, enthusiastic
Afriya—(f)—white, born during appropriate times
Afriza—(f)—pure gold, quintessence of fire
Afriz—(m)—pure gold, intelligence
Afri—(f)—dust-coloured, colour of earth
Afroja—(f)—bright
Afroj—(m)—clever
Afrooza—(f)—brightened, quintessence of fire
Afrooz—(m)—one with divine wisdom
Afrose—(f)—enlightening
Afrose—(m)—one with divine wisdom
Afrozaa—(f)—brightened, enlightening
Afroza—(f)—quintessence of fire, brightened
Afroze—(f)—illuminating, enlightening
Afroze—(m)—enlightening
Afroz—(f)—illuminated
Afroz—(m)—king, brighten something
Afro—(m)—from africa
Afrudeen—(m)—one with divine wisdom
Afruja—(f)—clever
Afruza—(f)—unique, divine aura
Afsaana—(f)—storey

Afsaan—(m)—the holy
Afsaar—(m)—crown, explained
Afsahan—(f)—unique, divine aura
Afsahn—(f)—revealed, resolved, gift of god
Afsah—(f)—most eloquent, expressive
Afsah—(m)—most eloquent, expressive
Afsal—(m)—judgement
Afsanah—(f)—storey, fiction
Afsana—(f)—fiction, romance, storey
Afsana—(m)—fiction
Afsaneh—(f)—a fairy tale
Afsaneh—(m)—fairy tale
Afsan—(f)—gift of god, beautiful, best
Afsan—(m)—gift of god, leader, smart, best
Afsar-ara—(f)—adorning the crown
Afsar-ud-din—(m)—adorning the religion
Afsarah—(f)—leader
Afsarara—(f)—adorning the crown
Afsara—(f)—angel
Afsari—(f)—most beautiful, angel
Afsaruddin—(m)—adorning
Afsar—(f)—crown
Afsar—(m)—better, explained, officer, crown
Afsa—(m)—transparent, clear
Afseena—(f)—shine like a star
Afseen—(f)—shine like a star
Afseera—(f)—angel
Afseruddin—(m)—crown of the faith
Afsha-firdus—(f)—happiness of heaven
Afshaan—(f)—glitter, shining, to sprinkle
Afshaan—(m)—to sprinkle, shining, glitter
Afshaar—(m)—one with divine wisdom
Afshaa—(f)—shining
Afshah—(f)—shining, pretty
Afshanah—(f)—fiction, storey, one who scatters
Afshanaz—(f)—fiction, storey
Afshana—(f)—fiction, storey
Afshan—(f)—to sprinkle, glitter

Afshan—(m)—to sprinkle, glitter
Afshara—(f)—an angel
Afshar—(m)—rose, accessorial, fellow
Afsheena—(f)—unique, divine aura
Afsheen—(f)—shine like a star
Afsheen—(m)—shine like star
Afshen—(m)—one with divine wisdom
Afshid—(m)—one with divine wisdom
Afshina—(f)—shine like a star
Afshin—(f)—decorated with sparkles, golden
Afshin—(m)—name of an general
Afshir—(m)—one with divine wisdom
Afshith—(m)—one with divine wisdom
Afshiya—(f)—shining, pretty
Afsia—(f)—gift of god, peace, gift
Afsina—(f)—shine like a star
Afsini—(f)—unique, divine aura
Afsin—(f)—shine like a star
Afsin—(m)—warrior, shining star
Afsiya—(f)—gift, peace, gift of god
Afsna—(f)—imagination
Afsoon—(f)—spell or bewitchment, charm, spell
Aftaab—(m)—the sun
Aftab-azlan—(m)—sun, lion
Aftabuddin—(m)—sun of the religion
Aftab—(f)—the sun
Aftab—(m)—sun, sunlight
Aftan—(f)—more attractive, charming
Aftan—(m)—one with divine wisdom
Aftar—(m)—breakfast the east
Aftash—(m)—one with divine wisdom
Afta—(m)—later born, younger
Afthab—(m)—sun
Afthaf—(m)—sun, god gift
Afusat—(f)—amenable, unique, absolute
Afuww—(m)—the pardoner
Afuw—(m)—one who pardons
Afuza—(f)—unique, divine aura

Afuza—(m)—one with divine wisdom
Afvan—(m)—one with divine wisdom
Afwan—(m)—forgiven, welcome
Afyaan—(m)—forgiven, great king, leader
Afyah—(m)—fragrant, wide, extensive
Afyan—(m)—forgiven, shadow
Afya—(f)—pure, health, strength, shadows
Afzaal—(m)—grace, favours, kindness
Afzaan—(m)—king of king
Afzaa—(f)—augmenting, increasing
Afzad—(m)—one with divine wisdom
Afzaif—(m)—one with divine wisdom
Afzal—(m)—most excellent, grace, kindness
Afzana—(f)—storey, fiction
Afzan—(m)—king of kings
Afza—(f)—augmenting, increasing
Afzhal—(m)—one with divine wisdom
Afzia—(f)—unique, divine aura
Afzida—(f)—unique, divine aura
Afzim—(m)—one with divine wisdom
Afzin—(m)—shining star
Afziya—(f)—unique, divine aura
Afzul—(m)—best, top
Agafia—(f)—appropriate, pure, virginal
Agamis—(m)—one with divine wisdom
Agar—(m)—the beginning
Aghala—(f)—pleasing
Agharid—(f)—tweet
Agharr—(m)—magnanimous, handsome, beautiful
Agha—(f)—master, owner (arabic), fight
Agha—(m)—pre-eminent, master, owner
Aghid—(f)—delicate, young, mistress
Aghigh—(f)—name of a stone
Aghlab—(m)—supreme, superior, conqueror
Aghla—(f)—dearer, most valuable, priceless
Aghnia—(f)—needless, rich ones
Aghniyaa—(f)—needless ones, rich ones
Aghsan—(f)—branch, twig, plural of ghusn

Agim—(m)—morning, early riser, dawn
Agrim—(m)—advance, first, leader
Ahaana—(f)—ray of light, dawn
Ahaan—(m)—dawn, auspicious dawn
Ahab—(m)—prime, uncle, father's brother
Ahada—(f)—unique
Ahadia—(f)—the unique, the one
Ahadiyah—(m)—unity
Ahad—(f)—pledge, commitment, delegation
Ahad—(m)—another name for god
Ahail—(m)—prince
Ahamada—(m)—most praiseworthy
Ahamad—(m)—one who saves
Ahamath—(m)—worthy of praise
Ahamd—(m)—one who saves
Ahamed—(m)—powerful
Ahammod—(m)—one with divine wisdom
Ahanaf—(m)—one with divine wisdom
Ahana—(f)—first ray of sunrise, chaht
Ahana—(m)—gain
Ahanna—(f)—first rays of the sun
Ahan—(m)—morning, dawn
Ahaqq—(m)—deserving, worthier
Ahaq—(m)—deserving, worthier
Aharon—(m)—lofty, exalted, high mountain
Ahasana—(f)—a favour, vigorous
Ahasan—(m)—helpful
Ahaud—(m)—unique, referring to god
Ahaya—(f)—to live
Ahazan—(m)—one with divine wisdom
Ahaz—(m)—one that takes or possesses
Ahbab—(f)—darling, dear, beloved ones
Ahdaa—(f)—better guided
Ahdaf—(f)—aim, goal, plural of hadaf, target
Ahdaf—(m)—goal, aim, target
Ahda—(f)—better guided
Ahda—(m)—best guide, ruler
Ahdia—(f)—unique, the one

Ahdul—(m)—one with divine wisdom
Ahd—(f)—knowledge, smart, science, metal
Ahd—(m)—knowledge, thousand, the only one
Ahed—(m)—best gift
Aheedah—(f)—ally, confederate
Aheed—(m)—he who takes to one side
Aheela—(f)—unique, divine aura
Aheen—(m)—fullness, abundance, whole
Aheera—(f)—unique, divine aura
Ahefaz—(m)—one with divine wisdom
Ahel—(m)—cowboy
Ahemad—(m)—one who saves
Ahemed—(m)—powerful, one who saves
Ahem—(m)—proud, important, necessary
Ahera—(f)—dazzling, brilliant
Ahesan—(m)—a favor
Ahetesham—(m)—one with divine wisdom
Aheya—(f)—to live
Ahezam—(m)—intelligent
Ahfaaz—(m)—brave
Ahfaz—(m)—brave
Ahian—(m)—brother of wine
Ahia—(f)—goat
Ahibbat—(f)—beloved
Ahida—(f)—promiser
Ahidul—(m)—oath-taker, promiser
Ahid—(m)—promiser, oath-taker
Ahill—(m)—ruler, head, prince, commander
Ahilya—(f)—maiden, without any deformation
Ahil—(m)—prince, emperor, ruler, commander
Ahima—(m)—not cold, hot, cloud, water
Ahim—(m)—cloud, water, traveller
Ahina—(f)—poor, ascetic, firm, unshakeable
Ahin—(m)—ascetic
Ahira—(f)—respectful, gift
Ahir—(m)—devotee, fearless
Ahista—(f)—slowly
Ahiyaan—(m)—gift of god

Ahiyan—(m)—gift of god
Ahiya—(f)—unique, divine aura
Ahkaf—(m)—gift from all the gods
Ahkam—(m)—strong, durable
Ahkeel—(m)—thoughtful, wise, king
Ahkeem—(m)—established, wise
Ahlaam—(f)—dreams, utopia
Ahlam—(f)—witty
Ahlam—(m)—witty
Ahlem—(f)—dream
Ahlima—(f)—merciful, kind, gentle, mannered
Ahliyat—(f)—fitness, competence
Ahmaad—(m)—praise worthy
Ahmadullah—(m)—i praise allah
Ahmadzulkifli—(m)—one with divine wisdom
Ahmad—(f)—commendable
Ahmad—(m)—highly praised, commendable
Ahmani—(f)—aspirations, faith, wishes, belief
Ahmaraan—(f)—saffron, gold
Ahmar—(m)—red, ruddy, red coloured
Ahmath—(m)—worthy of praise
Ahmat—(m)—worthy of praise
Ahmaud—(m)—most praiseworthy
Ahmead—(m)—one with divine wisdom
Ahmed-din—(m)—one with divine wisdom
Ahmedullha—(m)—i praise allah
Ahmed—(f)—blessed, gift of allah, fortunate
Ahmed—(m)—leader, one who is praise worthy
Ahmeed—(m)—one with divine wisdom
Ahmer—(m)—gift of allah
Ahmet—(m)—worthy of praise
Ahmida—(f)—unique, divine aura
Ahmmad—(m)—one who is praise worthy, leader
Ahmod—(m)—one who is praise worthy, leader
Ahnaaf—(m)—one of the narrators of hadith
Ahnab—(m)—one with divine wisdom
Ahnaf-huda—(m)—one with divine wisdom
Ahnaf—(m)—straight path, upright

Ahnan—(m)—one with divine wisdom
Ahna—(f)—exist, days, first rays of sun
Ahona—(m)—morning
Ahon—(m)—sunrise, morning
Ahoo—(f)—deer, smart
Ahou—(f)—smart, deer
Ahraaz—(m)—one with divine wisdom
Ahram—(m)—exalted, highness
Ahran—(m)—mountain of strength, enlightened
Ahrar—(m)—winner
Ahraz—(m)—piety, protection, progressive
Ahren—(m)—fighter, enlightened, eagle
Ahriel—(m)—lion of god
Ahrif—(m)—one with divine wisdom
Ahrin—(f)—enlightened
Ahrum—(m)—one with divine wisdom
Ahsaan—(m)—an act of kindness
Ahsab—(m)—nobler, respected
Ahsana—(f)—mercy, an act of kindness
Ahsanullah—(m)—favour of god
Ahsanul—(m)—helpful, helper
Ahsan—(f)—an act of kindness
Ahsan—(m)—an act of kindness, mercy
Ahsa—(m)—strong, valiant men
Ahsham—(m)—one with divine wisdom
Ahsin—(m)—gratitude
Ahsun—(m)—gratitude
Ahtasam—(m)—one with divine wisdom
Ahtesham—(m)—decency, manner
Ahtisham—(m)—manner, decency
Ahtzan—(m)—one with divine wisdom
Ahud—(m)—beautiful
Ahuramazda—(m)—lord, divinity of wisdom
Ahuzam—(m)—possessing vision
Ahuzan—(m)—one with divine wisdom
Ahwas—(m)—having narrow
Ahyaan—(m)—god gift
Ahyad—(m)—noble

Ahyam—(m)—starless night, thirsty
Ahyana—(f)—beautiful flower
Ahyan—(m)—eras, ages, times, god's gift
Ahyum—(m)—one with divine wisdom
Ahzaan—(m)—one with divine wisdom
Ahzab—(m)—troops, parties
Ahzam—(m)—one with divine wisdom
Ahzana—(f)—an act of kindness, mercy
Ahzan—(m)—one with divine wisdom
Ahzik—(m)—one with divine wisdom
Aian—(m)—appear, movement
Aiasha—(f)—prosperous, alive, woman, lively
Aiaz—(m)—great, generous
Aibak—(m)—slave, messenger, ambassador
Aiba—(f)—flower, beautiful
Aibin—(m)—beauty, fair
Aicha—(f)—enthusiasm
Aidah—(f)—noble, kind, returning, visitor
Aidah—(m)—visiting, returning, reward
Aidam—(m)—intelligent, king of own kingdom
Aidana—(f)—tall palm tree, perpetuity
Aidan—(f)—tall palm tree, noble - serene
Aidan—(m)—superior, mystery, intelligent
Aida—(f)—visiting, noble, nobility, reward
Aideen—(m)—born of fire
Aiden—(m)—born of fire
Aidhaan—(m)—one with divine wisdom
Aidhan—(m)—one with divine wisdom
Aidha—(f)—power, splendour, a flame, desire
Aidh—(m)—fame, splendour, ardour, power
Aidil—(m)—honest
Aidin—(m)—clear, enlightened, illuminated
Aid—(m)—little fire
Aieeda—(f)—daily returnees
Aiefa—(f)—beautiful
Aieham—(m)—bravery
Aieman—(f)—righteous, door of the paradise
Aiema—(f)—leader

Aiera—(f)—bearer of victory, gift, lion
Aieshah—(f)—woman, life
Aieza—(f)—dear one, noble
Aiez—(f)—princess
Aiez—(m)—reciter of holy quran
Aifaaz—(m)—helper, successful
Aifan—(m)—forgive
Aifaz—(m)—helper, strong and intelligent
Aifa—(f)—gift, gift of god
Aifa—(m)—smart, gifted, talented
Aifia—(f)—unique, divine aura
Aihaam—(m)—one with divine wisdom
Aihaan—(m)—flower of heaven
Aiham—(m)—brave
Aihan—(m)—a true devotee of allah, kind
Aijaaz—(m)—one with divine wisdom
Aijah—(f)—goat(sanskrit)
Aijan—(m)—soul of the moon, fire
Aijaz—(f)—favour
Aijaz—(m)—blessing, favour
Aijuddin—(m)—one with divine wisdom
Aika—(f)—love song
Aika—(m)—a ngai tahu chief
Aikin—(m)—oaken, made of oak
Aikko—(f)—little loved one
Aiko—(f)—little loved one
Aik—(m)—single, one
Ailaan—(m)—harmony, peace
Ailah—(f)—earthly, almighty, name of a river
Ailan—(m)—announcements
Aila—(f)—name of a river, earthly, noble
Aileena—(f)—messenger of god
Ailin—(f)—rock, transparent, very clear
Ailin—(m)—fair, handsome, rock, comely
Ailiya—(m)—one who is extremely truthful
Ailya—(f)—unique, divine aura
Ailyn—(f)—beauty and shine of moon
Aily—(f)—hazelnut, bird, the juniper tree

Aimaa—(f)—leader
Aimal—(f)—hope
Aimal—(m)—hope, cleaver, young, friend
Aiman—(f)—door of the paradise, righteous
Aiman—(m)—blessed, door of the paradise
Aima—(f)—leader
Aimen—(f)—most congratulated
Aimen—(m)—honest, lucky
Aimer—(m)—fortunate
Aimiah—(m)—one with divine wisdom
Aiminath—(f)—faithful
Aimin—(m)—fortunate
Aimmah—(m)—leader, variant of imam
Aimon—(m)—house, fearless
Aimo—(m)—fair-sized, proper, good
Aimram—(m)—one with divine wisdom
Ain-alsaba—(f)—treasure of the eye
Ainaan—(m)—two eyes, springs, two fountains
Ainah—(f)—pure, virginal
Ainain—(m)—two eyes, springs, plural of ain
Ainalsaba—(f)—treasure of the eye
Ainan—(f)—two eyes, springs, plural of ain
Ainan—(m)—two eyes, springs, two fountains
Ainayn—(m)—two eyes, springs, plural of ain
Ainaz—(f)—beautiful like the moon, gorgeous
Aina—(f)—mirror, lightning
Ainea—(f)—resembling a spring flower
Aineem—(m)—one with divine wisdom
Ainee—(f)—spring flower
Ainey—(f)—resembling a spring flower
Ainin—(f)—unique, divine aura
Aini—(f)—spring, flower, source, the eye
Aini—(m)—genuine, original
Ainuddin—(m)—one with divine wisdom
Ainullah—(m)—eye of god
Ainul—(f)—eye
Ainul—(m)—eyes
Ainy—(f)—resembling a spring flower

Ain—(f)—precious, eye, god was gracious
Ain—(m)—eye, fountain, spring, merciful
Aiqah—(f)—sea shore, beach
Aiqaz—(m)—awake, watchful, vigilant
Aiqunah—(m)—image, picture
Airafat—(m)—one with divine wisdom
Airaf—(f)—unique, divine aura
Airah—(f)—noble, respectful, arabic letters
Airam—(f)—unique, divine aura
Airan—(m)—home of aryans
Airas—(m)—happiness
Aira—(f)—beloved jasmine, of the wind
Airik—(m)—grandfather of king minocheher
Airin—(f)—unique
Airin—(m)—amazing
Aisah—(f)—life, woman, lively
Aisam—(m)—one with divine wisdom
Aisan—(m)—soul of the moon
Aisar—(m)—sacrifice
Aisa—(f)—alive
Aishah—(m)—lively, dear, princes, life
Aishan—(m)—belonging to lord shiva
Aishath—(f)—unique, divine aura
Aishatou—(f)—one who lives, alive
Aishatu—(f)—one who lives, alive
Aisha—(f)—living, prosperous, lively, woman
Aisheen—(f)—unique, divine aura
Aishiah—(f)—one who lives, alive
Aishi—(f)—being fond of poetry, god's gift
Aish—(m)—live, enjoy life, happy
Aisia—(f)—woman, life, livelyaissa—(f)—wonderful, grateful
Aison—(m)—nimble, quick-moving
Aissata—(f)—unique, divine aura
Aissa—(m)—pretty, nice
Aitesham—(m)—one with divine wisdom
Aitzaz—(m)—one with divine wisdom
Aiush—(m)—long life
Aiva—(f)—variant of the feminine name ava

Aiwa—(f)—date from heaven
Aixa—(f)—happiness
Aiyaan—(m)—one with divine wisdom
Aiyaaz—(m)—generous
Aiyad—(f)—small gulf
Aiyan—(m)—gift of god, appear
Aiyat—(f)—miracles, proof
Aiyaz—(m)—generous
Aiya—(f)—bird, beautiful silk
Aiyesha—(f)—alive, she who lives
Aiyla—(f)—moonlight
Aiyman—(m)—lucky, righteous
Aiyna—(f)—endless beauty
Aiyra—(f)—respectable, bearer of victory
Aiysa—(f)—precious
Aiyub—(m)—to repent
Aiyza—(f)—noble, princess
Aizaad—(m)—extension, excess
Aizaam—(m)—one with divine wisdom
Aizaan—(m)—soul of the moon
Aizaa—(f)—dear one, noble
Aizad—(m)—excess
Aizah—(m)—honourable
Aizak—(m)—joyful, cheerful, happy
Aizal—(m)—gift of god
Aizam—(m)—one with divine wisdom
Aizan—(m)—fire, soul of the moon
Aizat—(m)—honourable
Aizaz—(m)—reward, time
Aiza—(f)—noble, dear one, clever
Aizem—(m)—one with divine wisdom
Aizen—(m)—powerful and complete
Aizha—(f)—graceful, powerful, strong
Aizhin—(m)—one with divine wisdom
Aizik—(m)—laughter, one who laughs
Aizin—(m)—decoration
Aizwan—(m)—soul of the moon
Aizza—(f)—noble, life

Aiz—(m)—aizen, mare, new, pretty, loving
Ajaam—(m)—tree, forest
Ajaar—(f)—rewards
Ajaar—(m)—rewards
Ajaaz—(m)—miracle
Ajab—(f)—amazement, wonder
Ajab—(m)—wonder, astonishment, miraculous
Ajad—(m)—independence
Ajah—(f)—god protects
Ajah—(m)—god protects, unborn
Ajal—(m)—period
Ajamil—(m)—a mythological king
Ajam—(f)—date seed, foreign, persian
Ajam—(m)—foreign, persian, date seed
Ajan—(m)—the unborn, love of vishnu
Ajaruddin—(m)—honoured person of the religion
Ajar—(m)—forever, the god
Ajasudheen—(m)—one with divine wisdom
Ajas—(m)—powerful, strong, purity
Ajaweed—(f)—generosity, acts of kindness
Ajaweed—(m)—acts of kindness, generosity
Ajawid—(m)—noble, open-handed, generous
Ajaz—(m)—profitable
Aja—(f)—high priestess of mecca, goat
Ajba—(f)—shine
Ajdal—(m)—lovely, handsome
Ajda—(m)—useful, advantageous
Ajdin—(m)—one with divine wisdom
Ajeebah—(f)—narrator of hadith
Ajeeb—(f)—amazing, wondrous
Ajeeb—(m)—wonder
Ajeel—(m)—fast, quick
Ajeem—(m)—heat, fire
Ajeenah—(f)—unique, divine aura
Ajeer—(m)—he who is rewarded
Ajeesha—(f)—graceful
Ajeez—(m)—proud, respected
Ajee—(f)—unique, divine aura

Ajer—(m)—reward
Ajhan—(m)—descent, birth
Ajhar—(m)—radiant, the most shining, famous
Ajiad—(m)—noble, generous, gracious
Ajia—(f)—quick, fast
Ajiba—(f)—rare, unique
Ajib—(f)—unique, rare
Ajib—(m)—wonderful, strange
Ajida—(f)—unique, divine aura
Ajijul—(m)—one with divine wisdom
Ajij—(m)—fire, flame
Ajilan—(m)—man who commands everything
Ajila—(f)—loyal, love
Ajimal—(m)—smart
Ajima—(f)—daughter of sun
Ajimuddin—(m)—one with divine wisdom
Ajim—(m)—zeal, fire, heat
Ajina—(f)—merciful, unique
Ajinsha—(f)—loving
Ajinsha—(m)—loving
Ajinth—(m)—skilled person
Ajin—(m)—unique, merciful
Ajir—(m)—agile, quick
Ajiza—(f)—strong and proud
Ajiz—(m)—respected, proud
Ajju—(f)—mother
Ajlaan—(m)—lion
Ajlah—(m)—bald, hairless
Ajlan—(m)—the king, lion
Ajla—(f)—brighter, beautiful, smoother
Ajmaal—(m)—one with divine wisdom
Ajmain—(m)—spontaneous
Ajmalkhan—(m)—one with divine wisdom
Ajmal—(f)—pious
Ajmal—(m)—beauty, pious
Ajmani—(m)—beautiful jewel
Ajman—(m)—beautiful jewel
Ajmar—(m)—fastest

Ajmath—(m)—one with divine wisdom
Ajmat—(m)—respected, ambitions
Ajma—(f)—happiness
Ajmeel—(m)—one with divine wisdom
Ajmeena—(f)—unique, divine aura
Ajmeera—(f)—rich woman, princess
Ajmeer—(m)—one with divine wisdom
Ajmel—(m)—beautiful
Ajmia—(f)—moon
Ajmira—(m)—one with divine wisdom
Ajmir—(m)—legend
Ajmi—(f)—moon
Ajmunnisa—(f)—unique, divine aura
Ajnan—(m)—one with divine wisdom
Ajnas—(m)—kind
Ajnat—(m)—cheek
Ajna—(f)—beautiful
Ajrat—(f)—unique, divine aura
Ajra—(f)—it never happens
Ajra—(m)—agile, quick, a field
Ajrin—(f)—unique, divine aura
Ajruddin—(m)—one with divine wisdom
Ajrul—(m)—ruler of world
Ajsal—(m)—best
Ajtaba—(m)—selected, favourite
Ajubah—(m)—wonder, more strange
Ajul—(m)—one with divine wisdom
Ajuma—(f)—priceless
Ajurrum—(m)—religious man, sufi
Ajvan—(m)—one with divine wisdom
Ajveena—(f)—unique, divine aura
Ajwaad—(m)—talented, intelligent
Ajwad—(m)—better, best, more generous
Ajwan—(f)—small gulf
Ajwan—(m)—small gulf
Ajwas—(m)—intelligent, pure hearted
Ajwath—(m)—one with divine wisdom
Ajwa—(f)—name of a date in saudia arabia

Ajwed—(m)—heaven stone
Ajwin—(m)—one with divine wisdom
Ajyaz—(m)—one with divine wisdom
Ajzal—(m)—of great intellect
Akaas—(m)—as vast as the sky
Akabar—(m)—ruler, greatest, powerful
Akalmash—(m)—stainless, pure
Akal—(m)—timeless, chief of a tribe
Akaram—(m)—most generous, excellent
Akarim—(m)—most honourable, most precious
Akbani—(m)—one with divine wisdom
Akbarali—(m)—greatest, powerful
Akbarkhan—(m)—leader, pleader, soldier
Akbarshan—(m)—one with divine wisdom
Akbarsha—(m)—one with divine wisdom
Akbar—(m)—powerful, greatest, bigger
Akber—(m)—big
Akdas—(m)—clean
Akeam—(m)—established, wise
Akeeb—(m)—one with divine wisdom
Akeedah—(f)—trust
Akeef—(m)—one with divine wisdom
Akeel—(m)—world, intelligent, strong
Akeem—(m)—knowledgeable, wise, leader
Akee—(m)—established, wise
Akeil—(m)—wise, thoughtful, intelligent
Akeiyla—(f)—logical, wise, intelligent
Akei—(f)—born in autumn
Akeyla—(m)—honest, responsible
Akfah—(m)—black
Akfash—(m)—one who has weak eyes
Akhangal—(m)—sword
Akhas—(m)—a narrator of hadith, excellent
Akhdan—(m)—best friend
Akheel—(m)—complete
Akhfash—(m)—one with divine wisdom
Akhileshwa—(m)—god
Akhil—(m)—entire, whole, complete, tree

Akhir—(m)—latest
Akhi—(m)—my brother, manly, generous
Akhkaz—(m)—fascinating, thrilling
Akhlak—(m)—character, one
Akhlaqi—(f)—moral
Akhlaq—(m)—more appropriate, behaviour
Akhlas—(m)—sincerity, love, purity
Akhmad—(m)—tranquil, silent, calm
Akhmas—(m)—valiant, brave
Akhram—(m)—active, clever
Akhsam—(m)—broad-sword, lion
Akhtab—(m)—falcon
Akhtaf—(m)—slim, slender
Akhtari—(f)—wife of prophet
Akhtarullah—(m)—belongs to allah
Akhtarzamir—(m)—enlightened mind
Akhtar—(m)—a star, good man, good luck
Akhter—(m)—a star
Akhund—(m)—learned in religious matters
Akhwan—(m)—being, existence
Akhyar—(m)—better, best, virtuous
Akhzam—(m)—male serpent
Akhzari—(f)—greenish
Akhzar—(m)—greenery
Akia—(f)—sister, first born
Akia—(m)—first born
Akib—(m)—last one to arrive, high
Akida—(f)—certain, firm
Akid—(m)—certain, strong, firm
Akief—(m)—attached, focused, devoted
Akielah—(f)—intelligent, logical, wise
Akiel—(m)—steady, wise, intelligent
Akiem—(m)—established, wise
Akifa—(f)—dedicated to, intent, busy
Akif—(m)—focused, attached, intent
Akilah—(m)—wise, intelligent, thoughtful
Akila—(f)—intelligent, complete, total
Akile—(m)—wise, intelligent, thoughtful

Akili—(f)—wisdom, intelligence, cleverness
Akili—(m)—intelligent, from kikuyu
Akill—(m)—lipless, pain, thoughtful
Akil—(f)—wise
Akil—(m)—intelligent, thoughtful
Akimana—(f)—superior
Akim—(m)—god will establish
Akina—(f)—spring flower, relations
Akin—(m)—warrior, hero, brave man
Akira—(f)—gentle flower, a natural
Akira—(m)—intelligent, anchor, bright
Akir—(m)—anchor
Akiva—(m)—protect
Akiya—(f)—first born
Akiyl—(m)—one with divine wisdom
Aki—(f)—autumn, bright, pure milk
Akkim—(m)—one with divine wisdom
Aklaf—(m)—lion
Aklamash—(m)—spotless, pure
Akleema—(f)—beautiful
Aklim—(m)—from karbis
Akl—(m)—food
Akmad—(m)—dark
Akmal—(m)—perfect, whole, complete
Akmar—(f)—brilliant of whiteness
Akmez—(m)—one with divine wisdom
Aknaan—(m)—shelter
Aknan—(f)—shelter
Aknan—(m)—place of retreat, shelter, cover
Akna—(f)—goddess of fertility - childbirth
Akramul—(m)—one with divine wisdom
Akram—(f)—honourable, great, generous
Akram—(m)—excellent, more generous-noble
Akran—(m)—honoured
Akra—(m)—banner, wall, fence, sun, letter
Akrem—(m)—noble
Akrim—(m)—noble
Akroor—(m)—kind, gentle, a yadava chief

Akrum—(m)—noble
Aksad—(m)—one who achieves his aims - goals
Aksam—(m)—lion, broad-sword
Aksan—(m)—undestroyable
Aksar—(m)—imperishable
Aksa—(f)—soul, eye, indestructible
Akshan—(m)—eye
Akshara—(f)—letter, indestructible
Akshara—(m)—unalterable, indestructible lord
Akshithi—(f)—victorious peace
Akshiti—(f)—imperishable, victorious peace
Aksir—(m)—touch stone
Aktabul—(m)—one with divine wisdom
Aktar—(m)—fragrance
Akter—(m)—a star, fragrance
Akthar—(m)—star
Akwan—(m)—existence, creations
Akwas—(f)—prettier, nicer
Akyan—(f)—unique, divine aura
Akyas—(m)—wise, intelligent, ingenious
Akyla—(f)—intelligent, wise, logical
Akyl—(m)—thoughtful, wise, intelligent
Akym—(m)—yahweh will establish, wise
Al-aahab—(m)—the greater, lion
Al-abbas—(m)—description of a lion
Al-adur—(f)—intelligent, righteous, a pious
Al-anood—(f)—eye's of beautiful deer
Al-bara—(m)—wholesome with innocence
Al-burhan—(m)—the proof
Al-faiz—(m)—name of a fatimid caliph
Al-fayan—(m)—shining
Al-hakam—(m)—the arbitrator, the judge
Al-harith—(m)—the ploughman
Al-hasan—(m)—the handsome
Al-husayn—(m)—handsome, the good
Al-kabir—(m)—the great
Al-karimah—(f)—righteous, intelligent, a pious
Al-mahdi—(m)—guided to the right path

Al-mamoon—(m)—seventh abbasid caliph
Al-rafi—(m)—name of god
Al-safi—(m)—clear, fine, pure
Al-siddiq—(m)—the truthful, title of abu bakr
Al-tahir—(m)—nickname of abdullah
Al-tayyib—(m)—nickname of abdullah, the good one
Al-tijani—(m)—crowning
Al-zahar—(m)—one with divine wisdom
Al-zahra—(f)—the illuminated
Ala-al-din—(m)—excellence of faith
Ala-ud-din—(m)—glory of religion (islam)
Alaa-udeen—(m)—excellence of religion
Alaaddin—(m)—paragon of faith
Alaaldin—(m)—excellence of faith
Alaan—(m)—conqueror of the world, leader
Alaaudeen—(m)—excellence of religion
Alaaudin—(m)—excellence of religion
Alaa—(f)—devotee of allah, exaltation
Alaa—(m)—nobility, excellence, greatness
Alabbas—(m)—description of a lion
Alabi—(m)—a rare gem, a genius
Alabras—(m)—one with divine wisdom
Aladdin—(m)—peak, height of faith
Aladean—(m)—one with divine wisdom
Aladeen—(m)—gift of god
Aladino—(m)—paragon of faith
Aladin—(m)—nobility of faith, magic
Aladyn—(m)—paragon of faith
Alaeddin—(m)—peak, height of faith
Alafdal—(m)—one with divine wisdom
Alafdil—(m)—flag holder
Alahuakbar—(m)—god is the greatest
Alahudin—(m)—splendour of the religion
Alah—(f)—noble, honourable, ornament
Alaia—(f)—sublime, virtuous
Alaik—(m)—one who is honoured
Alainah—(f)—princess
Alainna—(f)—unique, divine aura

Alaisha—(f)—unique, divine aura
Alaiyah—(f)—unique, divine aura
Alaiyna—(f)—precious, valuable, fair one
Alaizah—(f)—sweet, love
Alaiza—(f)—love, sweet
Alai—(m)—defender of man
Alal-uddin—(m)—assam
Alala—(f)—war goddess
Alaleem—(m)—he who knows all things
Alaleh—(f)—a flower, buttercup
Alalim—(m)—omniscient
Alam-ara—(f)—adorning the world
Alam-ul-eeman—(m)—the banner of faith
Alam-ul-yaqeen—(m)—the banner of belief
Alamafruz—(f)—en-lightener, light to the world
Alamara—(f)—adorning the world
Alamat—(m)—sign, insignia, symbol, gesture
Alamdar—(m)—flag holder
Alamea—(f)—ripe, precious, whole
Alameda—(f)—grove of cottonwood, promenade
Alameel—(m)—one with divine wisdom
Alameen—(m)—truthfulness
Alame—(m)—world
Alamgeer—(m)—world, world conquering
Alamgir—(m)—conqueror of the world
Alamguir—(m)—world conqueror, catcher
Alamin—(m)—truthfulness
Alamirah—(f)—unique, divine aura
Alamiy—(f)—wise, vivacious
Alamul-hudaa—(m)—banner of guidance
Alamulhuda—(m)—banner of guidance
Alamzeb—(m)—world beauty
Alam—(f)—world, sing, of alameen
Alam—(m)—world, universe, the whole world
Alanah—(f)—attractive, peaceful
Alana—(f)—valuable, precious
Alana—(m)—peace, little rock, precious
Alanin—(m)—sharp mind

Alani—(f)—continues flow, highest
Alannah—(f)—valuable, precious, dear child
Alanna—(f)—fair, beautiful, dear child
Alansari—(m)—one with divine wisdom
Alan—(m)—god of shine, handsome, cheerful
Alaqat—(f)—devotion
Alaqat—(m)—devotion, relationship, attachment
Alaraf—(m)—one with divine wisdom
Alaraph—(m)—sweet
Alasha—(f)—god gifted, nobility
Alashraf—(m)—one with divine wisdom
Alaska—(f)—the great land
Alasqualani—(m)—one with divine wisdom
Alauddeen—(m)—excellence of religion
Alauddin—(m)—glory of religion (islam)
Alaudeen—(m)—one with divine wisdom
Alaudin—(m)—excellence of religion
Alaviaa—(f)—unique, divine aura
Alaviya—(f)—symbol of peace, towards god, life
Alavi—(f)—symbol of peace
Alawiya—(f)—towards god, symbol of peace
Alawi—(m)—smart, beautiful
Alayah—(f)—unique, divine aura
Alayana—(f)—princess, beautiful
Alaya—(f)—lofty, sublime
Alayeha—(f)—unique, divine aura
Alayka—(f)—gift of god, peace
Alaynah—(f)—light, princess, beautiful
Alayna—(f)—beautiful, princess
Alayne—(f)—bright, shining, rock or comely
Alayra—(f)—unique, divine aura
Alaysha—(f)—noble, kind, truthful
Alazae—(m)—one with divine wisdom
Alazet—(f)—unique, divine aura
Ala—(f)—noble, nobility, flag, truthful
Ala—(m)—nobility, excellence, superior
Albaab—(m)—sense, intelligence
Albab—(m)—wise

Albadawi—(m)—one with divine wisdom
Albaghdadi—(m)—one with divine wisdom
Albain—(m)—man from alba
Alban—(m)—from alba, a city on a white hill
Albaqa—(m)—one with divine wisdom
Albara—(m)—wholesome with innocence
Albar—(m)—guard of all
Albash—(f)—ruler
Albawwab—(m)—one with divine wisdom
Alba—(f)—white, blond, fair complexion
Albeena—(f)—fair one, blond, white
Alber—(m)—a quick mind
Albia—(f)—fair one, white, blond
Albinah—(f)—blond, white, fair one
Albina—(f)—white, bright, famous one
Albin—(m)—white, old english for brilliant
Albira—(f)—true to all, truly foreign, truly
Albira—(m)—one with divine wisdom
Albiruni—(m)—one with divine wisdom
Albis—(m)—man from alba
Alborz—(m)—the highest one, mountain
Alburz—(m)—mountain
Albusti—(m)—one with divine wisdom
Albyna—(f)—fair one, white, blond
Aldah—(f)—old, noble, honourable
Aldamiri—(m)—one with divine wisdom
Aldan—(m)—from the old manor, form of alden
Aldaqiq—(m)—one with divine wisdom
Aldar—(m)—from the alder tree
Alda—(f)—old but graceful, rich, old, wise
Aldean—(m)—old friend
Aldeen—(m)—blessed
Alden—(m)—old and wise protector, defender
Aldet—(f)—gift of god
Aldina—(f)—old, prosperous, small winged one
Aldin—(m)—defender, old friend
Aldjahiz—(m)—one with divine wisdom
Aldrei—(m)—one with divine wisdom

Aldric—(m)—old, wise ruler, old leader
Aleaha—(f)—high, exalted
Aleah—(f)—high, sublime
Aleaseya—(f)—saviour
Aleasia—(f)—of a noble kind, honourable
Alea—(f)—exalted, high
Alea—(m)—sublime, lofty, high
Aleeana—(f)—silk of heaven, soft
Aleecia—(f)—nobility, variant of alice
Aleefa—(f)—friendly, kind, compassionate
Aleef—(m)—sociable, amicable, friendly
Aleeha—(f)—exalted, high
Aleei—(m)—high, exalted, sublime
Aleek—(m)—the forehead, heaven
Aleelea—(f)—fair, appropriate looking
Aleem-ul-huda—(m)—banner of guidance
Aleemah—(f)—learned, wise, knowing
Aleema—(f)—wise, knowledgeable, intellectual
Aleemuddin—(m)—learned person
Aleem—(m)—knowledgeable
Aleena—(f)—soft, silk of heaven, beautiful
Aleen—(f)—light, fair, appropriate looking
Aleen—(m)—fair
Aleerah—(f)—unique, divine aura
Aleera—(f)—unique, divine aura
Aleesa—(f)—peace, beautiful, truthful, noble
Aleesha—(f)—noble, nobility, noble sort
Aleesh—(m)—protected by god, truthful
Aleesia—(f)—unique, divine aura
Aleeya—(f)—high born
Aleezah—(f)—joyous, joyful, cheerful
Aleezay—(f)—joyful, cheerful, joyous
Aleeza—(f)—happiness, joy
Aleezeh—(f)—joyful, happiness, cheerful
Aleez—(m)—one who is joyful
Alee—(f)—high, sublime, little rock
Alee—(m)—sublime, high, lofty
Alefiya—(f)—kind, sweet, one in millions

Aleftina—(f)—most beautiful
Aleha—(f)—exalted, ascender
Aleigha—(f)—to ascend
Aleigh—(f)—lofty, high, sublime, nobly famous
Aleigh—(m)—sublime, lofty, high
Alein—(f)—unique, divine aura
Aleisha—(f)—noble, exalted
Alei—(f)—lofty, leaf, nobly, sublime, high
Alemar—(m)—coated in gold
Alem—(m)—wise man, highly qualified
Alena—(f)—torch of light, dear child, torch
Alen—(m)—fair, handsome
Aleqa—(f)—helper - defender of mankind
Alerio—(m)—wise man, eagle
Alesa—(f)—unique, divine aura
Aleser—(m)—lion
Alesha—(f)—of a noble kind, of the noble sort
Alesia—(f)—of a noble kind, help, aid
Alesit—(f)—unique, divine aura
Alessa—(f)—protector of humanity
Alesta—(f)—defender of men
Alex—(m)—form of alexander
Aleyah—(f)—exalted, highest social standing
Aleyana—(f)—precious, awakening
Aleya—(f)—noble, ascender
Aleyna—(f)—bright, shining, rock or comely
Aleysha—(f)—protected by god, nobility
Aley—(f)—of a noble, high, sublime
Aley—(m)—high, lofty, sublime
Aleza—(f)—joy, happiness
Alfaaj—(m)—one with divine wisdom
Alfaan—(m)—unique, the art, attraction
Alfaaz—(m)—words, poetic phrases
Alfadl—(m)—one with divine wisdom
Alfaez—(m)—one with divine wisdom
Alfahd—(m)—one with divine wisdom
Alfah—(f)—guide
Alfah—(m)—first-born, excellent

Alfaiza—(f)—truthful, kind hearted
Alfaiz—(m)—gold, gift by god
Alfaj—(m)—words
Alfana—(f)—the art, unique, attraction
Alfan—(m)—attraction, the art, leader
Alfaqih—(m)—one with divine wisdom
Alfarah—(f)—happiness
Alfaraj—(m)—lovable
Alfaraz—(m)—one with divine wisdom
Alfarid—(m)—aloneness
Alfarin—(m)—son of hlif
Alfar—(m)—beautiful
Alfas—(m)—words (plural of lafz)
Alfathunissa—(f)—unique, divine aura
Alfath—(m)—one with divine wisdom
Alfayan—(m)—shining star, god gift
Alfaz—(m)—word
Alfa—(f)—first born, guide
Alfa—(m)—most important, leader, excellent
Alfeena—(f)—one of the world, respected
Alfeeya—(f)—one in thousand, sweet
Alfee—(m)—old peace, inspired advice
Alfej—(m)—word
Alfera—(f)—unique, divine aura
Alfez—(m)—word
Alfia—(f)—garden of heaven
Alfida—(f)—god's trust
Alfidha—(f)—unique, divine aura
Alfidh—(m)—one with divine wisdom
Alfid—(m)—gift
Alfiesya—(f)—unique, divine aura
Alfie—(m)—counsel from the elves
Alfiha—(f)—one in thousand
Alfija—(f)—unique, divine aura
Alfina—(f)—elf, magical counsel
Alfin—(m)—king, the art, attraction
Alfiono—(m)—one with divine wisdom
Alfisa—(f)—honest, truthful

Alfishahr—(f)—a thousand months
Alfisha—(f)—one in thousand
Alfiyaa—(f)—one in thousand, sweet
Alfiyana—(f)—god gift, shining
Alfiyan—(f)—unique, divine aura
Alfiyan—(m)—shining, god gift
Alfiya—(f)—sweet, one in million
Alfiza—(f)—truthful, honest
Alfi—(f)—elf power
Alfi—(m)—one with divine wisdom
Alfna—(f)—respected, one of the world
Alfran—(m)—one with divine wisdom
Alfred—(m)—wise counsellor, name of a king
Alfteem—(m)—one with divine wisdom
Alfutuh—(m)—one with divine wisdom
Alfya—(f)—one in millions
Alfy—(m)—counsel from the elves
Alghabra—(m)—one with divine wisdom
Alghani—(m)—one with divine wisdom
Alghazali—(m)—one with divine wisdom
Alhaan—(m)—one who shows right path
Alhabhab—(m)—one with divine wisdom
Alhad—(m)—joy, happiness
Alhafiz—(m)—devotee to god
Alhajjaj—(m)—one with divine wisdom
Alhakam—(m)—the arbitrator, the judge
Alhakan—(m)—one with divine wisdom
Alhallaj—(m)—one with divine wisdom
Alhamd—(m)—creative
Alhamid—(m)—one with divine wisdom
Alham—(m)—peace of world, son of allah
Alhana—(f)—beautiful dear child
Alhani—(f)—pale, appropriate voice
Alhann—(m)—pale, good voice
Alhan—(f)—appropriate voice, melody
Alhan—(m)—good voice, pale
Alhaque—(m)—one with divine wisdom
Alhaq—(m)—truth, correct

Alhariri—(m)—one with divine wisdom
Alharith—(m)—the ploughman
Alhasan—(m)—the handsome, the good
Alhazar—(m)—help, sos
Alhena—(f)—a ring
Alhindi—(m)—one with divine wisdom
Alhuda—(f)—unique, divine aura
Alhum—(m)—one with divine wisdom
Alhusain—(m)—the good
Alhusayn—(m)—the good, handsome
Ali-al—(m)—one with divine wisdom
Ali-asgar—(m)—clever, honest
Ali-asghar—(m)—one with divine wisdom
Ali-mohammed—(m)—devotee of god
Aliaa—(f)—most exalted, uppermost, highest
Aliah—(f)—noble, highest social standing
Aliakbar—(m)—one with divine wisdom
Aliana—(f)—noble and gracious
Alian—(m)—high
Alia—(f)—exalted, highest social standing
Alia—(m)—forehead
Alibaba—(f)—great leader
Alibaba—(m)—great leader
Alibux—(m)—one with divine wisdom
Alida—(f)—beautiful dressed
Alidrisi—(m)—one with divine wisdom
Aliea—(f)—unique, divine aura
Alief—(m)—amicable, sociable
Aliena—(f)—bright, of magdala, bird, hazelnut
Alienor—(f)—foreign
Aliesha—(f)—god gifted, a star
Aliezah—(f)—joy
Alieza—(f)—happiness, joyous, delightful
Alie—(m)—high, lofty, sublime
Alifah—(f)—sociable, friendly
Alifa—(f)—friendly, sociable
Aliff—(m)—one with divine wisdom
Alifia—(f)—unique, divine aura

Alifiya—(f)—one in millions, sweet, kind
Alifna—(f)—unique, divine aura
Alifsa—(f)—precious diamond, one in thousand
Alifsha—(f)—one in thousand
Alifta—(f)—unique, divine aura
Alifya—(f)—one in millions
Alif—(f)—one thousand
Alif—(m)—the first character in urdu
Alihamza—(m)—one with divine wisdom
Alihat—(f)—goddess, idol
Aliha—(f)—respectable
Alih—(m)—idol, god, brave
Aliisa—(f)—noble, graceful
Alijaffar—(m)—one with divine wisdom
Alijah—(f)—loving, smart
Alijan—(m)—one with divine wisdom
Alija—(f)—derived from ali
Alika—(f)—noble, kind, truthful
Alikhan—(m)—one with divine wisdom
Alikhshid—(m)—one with divine wisdom
Aliki—(f)—defender of mankind, noble, kind
Alik—(m)—defender of men
Alila—(f)—one who weeps
Alil—(m)—research for the world
Alimah—(f)—skilled in music or dance
Alimaia—(f)—unique, divine aura
Alima—(f)—intelligent, wise, cultured
Alimin—(m)—knowledgeable one
Alimohammed—(m)—devotee of god
Alimuddin—(m)—one with divine wisdom
Alimun—(m)—knowledgeable
Alimuzzaman—(m)—one with divine wisdom
Alim—(m)—learned, scholarly, omniscient
Alinaa—(f)—light, fair, noble, beautiful
Alinah—(f)—shining, bright, little noble one
Alinaz—(f)—unique, divine aura
Alina—(f)—fair, noble, light, beautiful
Alinna—(f)—beautiful

Alinsha—(f)—unique, divine aura
Alin—(m)—fair, handsome
Alirah—(f)—unique, divine aura
Alira—(f)—unique, honest
Alireza—(m)—kind
Alisaa—(f)—of the nobility, god is salvation
Alisah—(f)—noble, kind, great happiness
Alisan—(m)—son of the highborn
Alisa—(f)—kind type, god is salvation, sun
Alisbah—(f)—treasure of the eye
Alisba—(f)—alizba, treasure of the eye
Alishaba—(f)—beautiful sunshine
Alishah—(f)—protected by god, nobility
Alishan—(f)—dignity, dignified, glorious
Alishan—(m)—beautiful, glorious, magnificent
Alishay—(f)—protected by god, of a noble kind
Alisha—(f)—a star, god gifted
Alishbah—(f)—god in my oath
Alishba—(f)—god in my oath, pretty, innocent
Alishbha—(f)—innocent
Alishekh—(m)—one with divine wisdom
Alishfa—(f)—affectionate, simplicity
Alishka—(f)—intelligent, precious jewel
Alishma—(f)—innocent - beautiful
Alish—(f)—impressive, cute
Alish—(m)—power of mind
Alisiya—(f)—noble kind
Alisma—(f)—unique, divine aura
Alissar—(f)—unique, divine aura
Alissa—(f)—noble kind, nobility, rational
Alissya—(f)—of a noble kind, protected by god
Alistair—(m)—variant of alexander
Alista—(f)—feminine of alexander
Alisya—(f)—noble, honourable, of a noble kind
Alis—(m)—brother of cliges
Alith—(f)—short form of alitha
Alitta—(f)—truthful, small winged one
Aliuddin—(m)—one with divine wisdom

Aliul—(m)—one with divine wisdom
Aliva—(f)—beautiful, pretty, sweet
Alivia—(f)—olive branch, symbol of peace
Aliviyah—(f)—symbol of peace, intelligent
Aliviya—(f)—life
Aliyaah—(f)—sublime
Aliyaana—(f)—beautiful, beauty
Aliyaan—(m)—one with divine wisdom
Aliyah—(f)—rising, ascending, high-born
Aliyana—(f)—beauty, beautiful
Aliyan—(m)—name of allah, promise
Aliyas—(m)—one with divine wisdom
Aliyath—(f)—unique, divine aura
Aliya—(f)—highness, exalted, sublime
Aliya—(m)—exalted
Aliyeh—(f)—ornament, noble, honourable
Aliye—(f)—high-born, exalted, noble
Aliyna—(f)—beautiful, beauty
Aliysa—(f)—noble, honourable, ornament
Aliyyah—(f)—exalted, highest social standing
Aliyya—(f)—highest social standing, lofty
Aliyy—(m)—the highest, greatest, excellent
Alizaan—(m)—gift of god
Alizaa—(f)—pious, joyous
Alizah—(f)—god's word, god's promise
Alizan—(m)—son of the highborn
Alizar—(m)—origin, god is my help
Alizay—(f)—beauty of light
Aliza—(f)—joyous, happiness, faithful
Alizba—(f)—treasure of the eye
Alizeha—(f)—happiness
Alizeh—(f)—trade wind
Alizeh—(m)—one with divine wisdom
Alize—(f)—trade wind, joyful
Alizha—(f)—beauty, beautiful
Alizia—(f)—pious, faithful, delightful
Alizra—(f)—unique, divine aura
Aliz—(f)—noble, graceful, kind, happy

Aliz—(m)—graceful, noble, truthful
Ali—(f)—noble and shining
Ali—(m)—elevated, high
Aljahiz—(m)—one with divine wisdom
Aljanah—(m)—the paradise
Aljili—(m)—one with divine wisdom
Aljizi—(m)—king
Aljurjani—(m)—one with divine wisdom
Alkabir—(m)—name of god
Alkaif—(m)—one with divine wisdom
Alkama—(f)—unique, divine aura
Alkamil—(m)—one with divine wisdom
Alkasha—(f)—unique, divine aura
Alkasim—(m)—one with divine wisdom
Alkhadim—(m)—devotee of allah
Alkhattab—(m)—one with divine wisdom
Alkhawas—(m)—one with divine wisdom
Alkhayyami—(m)—one with divine wisdom
Alkhayyat—(m)—one with divine wisdom
Alkhayzuran—(f)—unique, divine aura
Alkhidr—(m)—one with divine wisdom
Alkira—(f)—the sky
Alkumayt—(m)—one with divine wisdom
Allaam—(m)—knowledgeable, extremely wise
Allaana—(f)—unique, divine aura
Allabakash—(m)—one with divine wisdom
Allabakshi—(m)—one with divine wisdom
Allabi—(f)—god gifted
Alladdin—(m)—peak, height of faith
Alladin—(m)—nobility of faith
Allafiya—(f)—peace, one in millions
Allah-bakhsh—(m)—gift of allah
Allahbakhsh—(m)—gift of allah
Allahbukhsh—(m)—gift of allah
Allahdad—(m)—one with divine wisdom
Allahditta—(m)—given by allah
Allahrakha—(m)—run away
Allahuddin—(m)—one with divine wisdom

Allah—(m)—almighty, god
Allaina—(f)—unique, divine aura
Allaiza—(f)—sweet, love
Allal—(m)—comforter
Allamah—(f)—extremely knowledgeable
Allamah—(m)—extremely knowledgeable
Allama—(m)—very learned
Allami—(f)—very wise
Allam—(m)—very knowledgeable, wise, entire
Allana—(f)—dear child, little rock, beautiful
Allannah—(f)—dear child
Allanna—(f)—peace, harmony, little rock
Allan—(m)—harmony, stone, noble, fair
Allarakha—(m)—one with divine wisdom
Allauddeen—(m)—one with divine wisdom
Allauddin—(m)—one with divine wisdom
Allaudeen—(m)—excellence of religion
Allaudin—(m)—excellence of religion
Allavuddin—(m)—one with divine wisdom
Allayna—(f)—light
Alla—(f)—an angel, name of truth, defender
Alla—(m)—defender, the supreme spirit
Alleah—(f)—leader
Allea—(f)—lofty, sublime, nobly, high
Allee—(f)—lofty, nobly famous, sublime, high
Allena—(f)—bright, shining, rock, comely
Allen—(f)—beautiful woman
Allen—(m)—form of alan, noble, comely
Alleyah—(f)—leader
Allfiya—(f)—one in millions, peace
Alliah—(f)—to ascend
Allie—(f)—little rock, noble and shining
Allihmyir—(f)—unique, divine aura
Allina—(f)—bright, shining, rock or comely
Allisha—(f)—protected by god, honourable
Alliyah—(f)—noble, high-born, ascending
Alliya—(f)—unique, divine aura
Alliza—(f)—happiness

Alli—(f)—long-tailed duck, noble, nobility
Alli—(m)—defender of man, noble, high
Allmeera—(f)—aristocratic lady
Allmera—(f)—aristocratic lady
Allmeria—(f)—aristocratic lady
Allmira—(f)—unique, divine aura
Alloula—(f)—unique, divine aura
Alltasha—(f)—unique, divine aura
Allula—(f)—unique, divine aura
Allvera—(f)—speaker of truth, dearly loved
Allyah—(f)—ornament, honourable, noble, joy
Allyiah—(f)—sublime, exalted
Allysa—(f)—great happiness
Allysia—(f)—noble, kind
Allyzza—(f)—joy, happiness
Ally—(f)—noble, graceful, shining
Ally—(m)—harmony, stone, noble, fair
Allzahraa—(f)—unique, divine aura
Almaan—(m)—noble man, willing and wise man
Almaasa—(f)—diamond
Almaas—(f)—diamond, adamant
Almaaz—(m)—diamond
Almahdi—(m)—rightly guided
Almahira—(f)—unique, divine aura
Almaia—(f)—unique, divine aura
Almaida—(f)—unique, divine aura
Almaisha—(f)—grace, desirable as the moon
Almamun—(m)—one with divine wisdom
Almana—(f)—alone
Almanzor—(m)—triumphant
Alman—(m)—kind, willing and wiseman
Almar—(m)—noble man
Almasa—(f)—diamond
Almasha—(f)—desirable as the moon, grace
Almas—(f)—precious stone, a diamond
Almas—(m)—diamond
Almaye—(f)—angel
Almaza—(f)—unique, divine aura

Almaz—(f)—diamond
Almaz—(m)—one with divine wisdom
Alma—(f)—caring, fostering, soul
Alma—(m)—precious man
Almedina—(f)—precious stone
Almeena—(f)—will, helmet
Almeen—(f)—unique, divine aura
Almeerah—(f)—aristocratic lady, clothes basket
Almeera—(f)—aristocratic lady, wealthy female
Almeeria—(f)—aristocratic lady
Almeer—(m)—noble man
Almeira—(f)—aristocratic lady, clothes basket
Almena—(f)—will, helmet
Almen—(m)—a widower, forsaken
Almerah—(f)—aristocratic lady
Almera—(f)—aristocratic lady
Almeria—(f)—aristocratic lady, work ruler
Almer—(m)—infamous, noble man
Almie—(f)—soul, nourishing
Almina—(f)—will, helmet
Almiraa—(f)—princess, truthful
Almirah—(f)—princess, aristocratic lady
Almira—(f)—woman of nobility, princess
Almire—(f)—aristocratic lady, princess
Almir—(m)—prince
Almiya—(f)—cultured
Almyrah—(f)—clothes basket
Almyra—(f)—aristocratic lady
Alnaaz—(f)—most precious, beautiful
Alnaba—(f)—wars passed each other
Alnahdi—(m)—one with divine wisdom
Alna—(f)—conqueror of the world
Aloc—(m)—solider for god
Aloha—(f)—affection, loving, kind-hearted
Aloodra—(f)—virgin
Alouf—(m)—one who is in charge
Aloula—(f)—unique, divine aura
Alparslan—(m)—hero lion

Alphaz—(m)—poetic phrases, words
Alphia—(f)—most important, first-born
Alphiya—(f)—unique, divine aura
Alpona—(f)—design
Alqamah—(m)—one with divine wisdom
Alqa—(f)—a with a lovely hair, beauty
Alquaf—(m)—honest
Alraaz—(f)—mystery
Alrashid—(m)—one with divine wisdom
Alreeza—(f)—unique, divine aura
Alrufian—(m)—one with divine wisdom
Alsaba—(f)—treasure of the eye
Alsaba—(m)—morning
Alsafin—(m)—one with divine wisdom
Alsafi—(m)—pure, clear, fine
Alsaid—(m)—one with divine wisdom
Alsana—(f)—princess
Alsan—(m)—one with divine wisdom
Alsarah—(f)—unique, divine aura
Alseefa—(f)—lovable, trustable, appropriate, homely
Alshaan—(m)—brilliance
Alshada—(f)—unique, divine aura
Alshad—(m)—one with divine wisdom
Alshafa—(f)—the healing
Alshana—(f)—unique, divine aura
Alshara—(f)—unique, divine aura
Alsheefa—(f)—unique, divine aura
Alshefaa—(f)—unique, divine aura
Alshibin—(m)—one with divine wisdom
Alshifaa—(f)—lovable, trustable, appropriate, homely
Alshifah—(f)—appropriate, homely, sweet, lovable
Alshifa—(f)—appropriate, homely, sweet, lovable
Alshifha—(f)—nice
Alshima—(f)—as glorious as moon
Alshina—(f)—god gift, sensitive, creative
Alsifa—(f)—lovable, homely, sweet, trustable
Altaaf—(m)—kindness, graces
Altaam—(m)—correct, right

Altaaz—(m)—one with divine wisdom
Altab—(m)—kindness
Altaf-hussain—(m)—kindness of husain
Altaffeea—(f)—noble
Altafhussain—(m)—kindness of husain
Altaf—(f)—kindness, politeness
Altaf—(m)—kindness, graces, more gracious
Altahir—(m)—nickname of abdullah
Altaira—(f)—bird, high-flying
Altair—(f)—bird, star, flying eagle
Altair—(m)—star, the flyer, flying eagle
Altamash—(m)—front-line army
Altamish—(m)—vanguard, commander, leader
Altar—(m)—one who is old
Altasha—(f)—unique, divine aura
Altayyib—(m)—the good one
Alta—(f)—abbreviation of altagracia
Alteesh—(m)—one with divine wisdom
Althaaf—(m)—more delicate, kindness
Althaff—(m)—more delicate
Althafkhan—(m)—one with divine wisdom
Althaf—(m)—more delicate
Althamees—(m)—one with divine wisdom
Althamish—(m)—commander, vanguard, leader
Althea—(f)—one who heals, sincere, healing
Altijani—(m)—crowning
Altin—(m)—golden
Altisha—(f)—unique, divine aura
Altthea—(f)—sincere
Altufail—(m)—one with divine wisdom
Aludra—(f)—virgin, the maiden
Aluf—(m)—friendly, devoted, faithful
Alula—(f)—singer, first born, winged one
Alvah—(m)—sublime
Alvaka—(f)—unique, divine aura
Alvan—(m)—friend of the elves, sublime
Alva—(m)—noble friend, elf, brilliance
Alveena—(f)—loved one, cared one

Alveen—(f)—elf, noble friend
Alveerah—(f)—truthful
Alveera—(f)—truthful, sweet
Alvee—(f)—treasure, innocent
Alvee—(m)—noble, elf friend
Alvena—(f)—noble, elf friend
Alvera—(f)—speaker of truth
Alvesha—(f)—unique, divine aura
Alvia—(f)—bright, famous
Alvinaz—(f)—unique, divine aura
Alvina—(f)—noble and wise friend
Alvin—(f)—joy of love
Alvin—(m)—noble friend
Alvira—(f)—dearly loved, foreign, true
Alvir—(m)—dearly loved
Alvisa—(f)—feminine of elvis
Alvisha—(f)—unique, divine aura
Alvish—(m)—one with divine wisdom
Alviyah—(f)—unique, divine aura
Alviya—(f)—towards god
Alwaan—(f)—colours, shades
Alwaan—(m)—colours
Alwan—(m)—noble friend
Alwar—(m)—name of a city
Alwaz—(m)—brightness, light
Alwa—(f)—beauty, sweet
Alweena—(f)—unique, divine aura
Alweera—(f)—truthful
Alwera—(f)—beautiful princess
Alwia—(f)—unique, divine aura
Alwina—(f)—elf, noble friend
Alwin—(m)—noble friend, defender
Alwira—(f)—dearly loved
Alyaanah—(f)—great, high in rank and status
Alyaan—(f)—headstrong, bible, ladder
Alyaan—(m)—one with divine wisdom
Alyaa—(f)—heaven, sky, sublimity, lofty
Alyamama—(f)—dove

Alyana—(f)—unique, divine aura
Alyanna—(f)—vibrant, cheerful, prayer to god
Alyan—(f)—tall and healthy
Alyan—(m)—supreme, great, exalted, high
Alyasaa—(m)—a prophet name elisha
Alyas—(m)—brave one
Alya—(f)—from heaven, sky, loftiness
Alya—(m)—pretty
Alyka—(f)—truthful, kind, noble
Alykhan—(m)—spirit from heaven, lovely
Alyma—(f)—sea, skilled in music - dancing
Alyna—(f)—light, of the nobility
Alynna—(f)—brightness, ornament, beautiful
Alyoza—(f)—happiness, joy, daughter of adam
Alysa—(f)—rational, princess
Alysha—(f)—nobility, similar to alice
Alysia—(f)—entrancing, possesive, captivating
Alyssa—(f)—noble, graceful, sweet angel
Alyza—(f)—happiness, joy
Aly—(m)—the high, exalted one
Alzaba—(f)—unique
Alzab—(m)—one with divine wisdom
Alzafa—(f)—genius
Alzahra—(f)—the illuminated
Alzaib—(m)—tiger
Alzaid—(m)—one with divine wisdom
Alzaina—(f)—the woman
Alzaman—(m)—one with divine wisdom
Alzam—(m)—one with divine wisdom
Alzan—(f)—woman
Alzan—(m)—lion
Alzayyir—(m)—intelligent
Alzeena—(f)—woman
Alzena—(f)—the woman
Alzia—(f)—god's light
Alzina—(f)—woman
Alzin—(m)—one with divine wisdom
Alzira—(f)—beauty, ornament

Alzishan—(m)—one with divine wisdom
Alziya—(f)—god's light
Alzubra—(f)—a star in the constellation leo
Amaad—(m)—support, pillar, post
Amaal—(f)—hopes, expectations
Amaal—(m)—amazing, hope, aspiration
Amaanat—(m)—treasure, security, deposit
Amaani—(f)—hope
Amaanullah—(m)—protection treasure
Amaan—(m)—peace, protection, without fear
Amaara—(f)—crown
Amaar—(m)—one who prays five times and fasts
Amaayah—(f)—unique, divine aura
Amaaz—(m)—kind, gracious
Amacei—(f)—plural form for evening
Amac—(f)—plural form for evening
Amadi—(m)—loved by god, rejoicing
Amad—(f)—period of time, time, age
Amad—(m)—serious, much praised
Amahd—(m)—most praiseworthy
Amahira—(f)—only one expertise in every field
Amahl—(m)—hope
Amah—(f)—slave, a woman companion
Amaifa—(f)—unique, divine aura
Amail—(m)—necklace
Amairah—(f)—leader, princess
Amaira—(f)—one who is forever beautiful
Amaisha—(f)—sunshine, most beautiful
Amaiya—(f)—beautiful princess
Amaiyra—(f)—princess
Amai—(f)—sweet
Amala—(f)—the pure one, bird, hope
Amala—(m)—spotless, pure, tree
Amale—(f)—caring, beautiful
Amalia—(f)—industrious, work, striving
Amalillah—(f)—hope with allah
Amalina—(f)—strain
Amalin—(f)—loved, clean, pure

Amaliya—(f)—beloved, rivalling, work
Amali—(f)—specialty, profession, truthful
Amal—(f)—to have hope, bright, clean, pure
Amal—(m)—hope, expectation, bird
Amama—(f)—head cover
Amam—(m)—protective, safety
Amanaat—(f)—guardianship, loyalty
Amanah—(f)—faithful to believe
Amanah—(m)—trust, the gift
Amanatullah—(f)—god's charge, consignment
Amanat—(f)—god's treasure, present or gift
Amanat—(m)—gift of god, security, deposit
Amana—(f)—all, faithful, devotion
Amanda—(m)—active
Amanea—(f)—wishes, belief, faith, aspirations
Amanee—(f)—belief, aspirations, faith, wishes
Amaney—(f)—aspirations, faith, wishes, belief
Amanie—(f)—belief, faith, aspirations, wishes
Amanie—(m)—aspirations, wishes
Amani—(f)—road, one who shows the path
Amani—(m)—peace, wishes, aspiration, belief
Amanuddin—(m)—trust of religion islam
Amanudeen—(m)—one with divine wisdom
Amanullah—(f)—god's peace, protection
Amanullah—(m)—trust
Amanulla—(m)—one with divine wisdom
Amany—(f)—wishes, aspirations
Amany—(m)—aspirations, wishes
Aman—(f)—peace, the one who is peaceful
Aman—(m)—the one who is peaceful
Amapola—(f)—poppy
Amarah—(f)—deathless, full of compassion
Amarah—(m)—deathless
Amara—(f)—elegance, grass, immortal one
Amara—(m)—immortal
Amardad—(f)—immortality
Amare—(m)—one who builds
Amariah—(f)—pledged by god, given by god

Amarina—(f)—rain
Amarissa—(f)—given by god
Amariya—(f)—given by god, pledged by god
Amari—(f)—a miracle from god, special gift
Amari—(m)—protector, strength, builder
Amarvir—(m)—eternally brave, immortal power
Amarya—(f)—unfading flower
Amar—(f)—one who lives forever
Amar—(m)—forever, the immortal one
Amatallah—(f)—unique, divine aura
Amatasalam—(f)—devotee of peace
Amatul-aakhir—(f)—devotee of the last one
Amatul-aala—(f)—devotee of the highest one
Amatul-ahad—(f)—devotee of the one
Amatul-akram—(f)—devotee of allah
Amatul-aleem—(f)—devotee of allah
Amatul-awwal—(f)—devotee of the first one
Amatul-azim—(f)—al-azim is one of name of god
Amatul-aziz—(f)—devotee of allah
Amatul-baatin—(f)—devotee of allah
Amatul-birr—(f)—devotee of the faithful one
Amatul-fattah—(f)—devotee of allah
Amatul-ghafoor—(f)—devotee of allah
Amatul-hadi—(f)—al-hadi is one of name of god
Amatul-hafeez—(f)—devotee of the best protector
Amatul-hai—(f)—devotee of allah
Amatul-hakam—(f)—devotee of the arbitrator
Amatul-haleem—(f)—devotee of allah
Amatul-hameed—(f)—devotee of the praiseworthy one
Amatul-haseeb—(f)—al-haseeb is one of name of god
Amatul-islam—(f)—devotee of islam
Amatul-jabar—(f)—devotee of the mighty one
Amatul-jaleel—(f)—devotee of the almighty one
Amatul-jameel—(f)—devotee of beautiful one
Amatul-kabir—(f)—devotee of the great one
Amatul-khabir—(f)—devotee of the all-aware
Amatul-khaliq—(f)—devotee of the creator
Amatul-maalik—(f)—devotee of allah

Amatul-maleek—(f)—devotee of allah
Amatul-manaan—(f)—devotee of the bestower
Amatul-mateen—(f)—devotee of the firm one
Amatul-mawla—(f)—devotee of the protector
Amatul-mubeen—(f)—devotee of allah
Amatul-mujeeb—(f)—devotee of the responder
Amatul-muqit—(f)—al-muqit is one of name of god
Amatul-mutaali—(f)—devotee of allah
Amatul-mutaal—(f)—devotee of the exalted
Amatul-naseer—(f)—devotee of the supporter
Amatul-qadeer—(f)—devotee of the all-capable
Amatul-qadir—(f)—al-qadir is one of name of god
Amatul-qahir—(f)—al-qahir is one of name of god
Amatul-qareeb—(f)—devotee of the near one
Amatul-qawee—(f)—devotee of the strong one
Amatul-quddus—(f)—devotee of the holy one
Amatul-shaheed—(f)—devotee of the witness
Amatul-wadud—(f)—devotee of the loving one
Amatul-wahaab—(f)—devotee of the bestower
Amatul-waleei—(f)—devotee of the protector
Amatul-waris—(f)—devotee of the inheritor
Amatulislam—(f)—devotee of islam
Amatullah—(f)—female devotee of allah
Amatur-rab—(f)—devotee of the lord, allah
Amatur-raheem—(f)—devotee of allah
Amatur-raqeeb—(f)—devotee of the overseer
Amatur-razzaq—(f)—devotee of the provider
Amatus-samee—(f)—devotee of allah
Amatuz-zaahir—(f)—az-zaahir is one of name of god
Amat—(f)—devotee
Amat—(m)—slave, observation
Amayaa—(f)—unique, divine aura
Amayah—(f)—close to god, night rain
Amayara—(f)—gentle, polite
Amaya—(f)—goddess of nature, night's rain
Amaya—(m)—night's rain, not cunning
Amayera—(f)—princess or leader
Amayira—(f)—princess or leader

Amayraa—(f)—princess
Amayrah—(f)—leader, princess
Amayra—(f)—princess
Amaysja—(f)—pretty
Ama—(f)—lovable, born on a saturday
Ambara—(f)—perfume, ambergris
Ambarin—(f)—perfumed, fragrant
Ambar—(f)—sky
Ambar—(m)—sky
Ambereen—(f)—fragrance, amber, sky
Amberia—(f)—amber
Amberjill—(f)—amber
Amberlee—(f)—a precious jewel
Amberli—(f)—amber
Amberlynn—(f)—a jewel
Amberlyn—(f)—a jewel, amber and lynn
Amberly—(f)—smart, playful, nice, strong
Ambert—(f)—unique, divine aura
Amber—(f)—gemstone, sky, from the stone
Amber—(m)—sky
Ambia—(f)—prophet muhammad's relative
Ambie—(f)—amber
Ambir—(f)—appropriate, beautiful
Ambra—(f)—gemstone, jewel, amber
Ambrea—(f)—amber
Ambreen—(f)—sky fragnance, sky
Ambria—(f)—amber
Ambrim—(f)—ambergris
Ambrin—(f)—scent
Ambyre—(f)—amber
Ambyr—(f)—amber
Amdadul—(m)—one with divine wisdom
Amdad—(m)—growth, increase, gain, expansion
Amdan—(m)—one with divine wisdom
Amean—(m)—trustworthy, faithful, truthful
Ameara—(f)—ruler, commander, emir, prince
Amear—(m)—ruler, prince, emir, commander
Amedha—(f)—beautiful, charming, attractive

Amed—(m)—hopeful, polite person
Ameedah—(f)—chief, prefect
Ameeda—(f)—prefect, chief
Ameed—(m)—leader, chief, prefect
Ameeka—(f)—nectar, sweetness
Ameela—(f)—unique, divine aura
Ameel—(m)—in the sense of being
Ameem—(m)—one with divine wisdom
Ameenah—(f)—trustworthy
Ameenal—(f)—god is with us
Ameena—(f)—trustworthy, faithful
Ameenuddin—(m)—trustworthy in religion (islam)
Ameenulla—(m)—one with divine wisdom
Ameen—(f)—mist, fog, dew drop, appropriate luck
Ameen—(m)—divine grace, honest, faithful
Ameeqa—(f)—unique, divine aura
Ameeraa—(f)—high-born, leader, prosperous
Ameerah—(f)—high-born, princess
Ameera—(f)—leader, princess, rich woman
Ameerhamza—(m)—one with divine wisdom
Ameersha—(m)—one with divine wisdom
Ameeruddin—(m)—one with divine wisdom
Ameerullah—(m)—the order of allah
Ameerul—(m)—one with divine wisdom
Ameerunnisa—(f)—always growing
Ameer—(f)—prince, kind
Ameer—(m)—ruler, prince, superior, chief
Ameesah—(f)—an object of enjoyment, friend
Ameesha—(f)—all coming together, beautiful
Ameeza—(f)—unique, divine aura
Ameez—(m)—one with divine wisdom
Amein—(m)—faithful, truthful, trustworthy
Ameirah—(f)—ruler, commander
Ameira—(f)—commander, emir, prince, ruler
Ameir—(m)—prince
Amelia—(f)—hard-working, courage
Amelina—(f)—imitating, rivalling, work
Ameliya—(f)—trustworthy, courage, pretty

Amel—(f)—aspiration, hope
Amel—(m)—hope, aspiration
Amenah—(f)—god's swear of life
Amena—(f)—beautiful, honest woman
Amenoolahkhan—(m)—one with divine wisdom
Amerah—(f)—high-born girl
Amera—(f)—high-born girl
Ameretat—(f)—goddess of immortality
Ameria—(f)—innocent, gift from jannah
Amerulla—(m)—prince
Amer—(m)—rich, one who builds, great tree
Amesa—(f)—free from guile
Ames—(f)—loves
Amet—(m)—power of an eagle
Ameya—(f)—boundless, devotion, princess
Amgad—(m)—greater glory
Amhara—(f)—beautiful, pleasant, happy
Amhar—(m)—legendary son of arthur
Amiah—(f)—beloved
Amial—(f)—lighthouses
Amial—(m)—lighthouses
Amian—(m)—one who tames or subdues, tamer
Amiara—(f)—high-born, princess, prosperous
Amia—(f)—beloved
Amidah—(f)—chief, prefect
Amida—(f)—chief, prefect
Amidha—(f)—nectar
Amiduddawlah—(m)—support of the state
Amid—(m)—support, leader, chief
Amiee—(f)—nectar
Amiel—(f)—god of my people
Amiena—(f)—faithful, trustworthy
Amien—(m)—truthful, trustworthy, faithful
Amierah—(f)—high-born girl
Amiera—(f)—princess, leader
Amier—(m)—prince, ruler, commander, emir
Amie—(f)—beloved
Amiha—(f)—bright

Amik—(m)—friend, one of melimon
Amilah—(f)—hopeful
Amila—(f)—hopeful, worker, striver
Amilita—(f)—imitating, work, rivalling
Amil—(f)—one in a million
Amil—(m)—invaluable, worker, one who hopes
Amimah—(f)—unique, divine aura
Amima—(f)—full, complete
Amim—(m)—one with divine wisdom
Aminah—(f)—honest, trustworthy, faithful
Aminan—(f)—calm, at peace, not afraid
Aminath—(f)—faithful
Aminatta—(f)—truthful, trustworthy, faithful
Aminat—(f)—trustworthy, loyal
Amina—(f)—trustful, honest, trustworthy
Amindah—(f)—lovable
Aminda—(f)—lovable
Amineh—(f)—faithful, trustworthy, secure
Amine—(f)—trustfully, sincerity
Amine—(m)—fair, trustworthy, honest
Aminin—(m)—safe one, unharmed one
Amini—(f)—reliable, trustworthy, unalterable
Aminollah—(m)—one with divine wisdom
Aminuddin—(m)—trustworthy in religion (islam)
Aminul—(m)—one with divine wisdom
Aminun—(m)—safe one
Aminur—(m)—bright, light
Aminu—(f)—safe, secure, peace
Amin—(m)—divine grace, trustworthy, honest
Amiqa—(f)—unique, divine aura
Amiq—(m)—road, door of heaven
Amiraa—(f)—leader, chief, commander
Amirah—(f)—princess, wealthy, ruler
Amiran—(m)—royal, prince
Amirash—(m)—one with divine wisdom
Amira—(f)—princess, high-born, speech
Amirdeen—(m)—one with divine wisdom
Amire—(m)—ruler, prince, commander, emir

Amirhossein—(m)—one with divine wisdom
Amiri—(m)—leader, officer, prince
Amiroddin—(m)—leader of the faith
Amirr—(m)—rich, leader, from kikuyu
Amiruddin—(m)—leader of the faith
Amirul-hassan—(m)—one with divine wisdom
Amirulhaq—(m)—one with divine wisdom
Amirullah—(m)—god's wish
Amirul—(m)—strong, brave, proud
Amirunnisa—(f)—always growing
Amir—(f)—from the top of the tree or prince
Amir—(m)—rich, leader, wealthy, ruler
Amissa—(f)—friend
Amit—(m)—unlimited, boundless
Amiyah—(f)—delight
Amiya—(f)—nectar, delightful
Amiza—(f)—truth, friend
Amjaad—(m)—honour, glory, plural of majd
Amjadh—(m)—virtuous man
Amjad—(f)—magnificence, splendour
Amjad—(m)—great, noble, gratifying
Amjath—(m)—virtuous man, fit
Amjed—(m)—hard-working, intelligence
Amjitha—(f)—progressive
Amlahan—(f)—dew
Amlah—(f)—kindness, favour
Amlah—(m)—pretty, handsome, beautiful
Ammaarah—(f)—lady of dignity
Ammaar—(m)—long living
Ammal—(m)—hard work, hope, as pure as white
Ammam—(f)—beautiful, pretty, better
Ammam—(m)—a person who is ahead of others
Amman—(m)—peace, comfort
Ammarah—(f)—an inhabitant
Ammarah—(m)—punctual, obedient
Ammara—(f)—a lady with strong imaan
Ammar—(m)—long-living, builder, popularity
Ammatul—(f)—slave of, devotee of

Ammena—(f)—trustworthy, faithful
Ammen—(m)—faithful, trustworthy, truthful
Ammer—(m)—nice
Ammin—(m)—faithful, truthful, trustworthy
Ammuna—(f)—trustworthy, faithful, loyal
Ammuni—(f)—safe, away from harm
Ammura—(f)—beautiful, beloved, captivating
Ammuri—(f)—beautiful, lovable, captivating
Ammu—(m)—mother
Amnah—(f)—faithful to believe
Amnajane—(f)—gift of almighty
Amnan—(f)—safe, secure
Amnan—(m)—safe, secure
Amnas—(m)—young lamb
Amnati—(f)—my hope, wish
Amnaz—(f)—trustworthy
Amna—(f)—peace, soft, desire, safety
Amney—(f)—fantastic, high power
Amnian—(f)—safe, secure
Amniyya—(f)—unique, divine aura
Amona—(f)—precious
Amosa—(m)—encumbered
Amour—(m)—person who loves someone secretly
Amrah—(f)—headgear
Amraj—(m)—i'm the king
Amran—(m)—the people is exalted
Amraz—(m)—prosperity
Amra—(f)—beautiful, princess
Amreena—(f)—sky, beautiful warrior
Amreen—(f)—pray, powerful and complete
Amreen—(m)—pray
Amrinah—(f)—princess, blue sky
Amrina—(f)—princess
Amrinn—(f)—princess, blue sky
Amrin—(f)—blue sky, princess
Amrin—(m)—follow rules of god
Amritta—(f)—immortality, nectar, art
Amri—(m)—power, one who lives a long life

Amroze—(m)—one with divine wisdom
Amrozia—(f)—female of today
Amroz—(m)—one with divine wisdom
Amro—(m)—immortal, love
Amrullah—(m)—the order of allah
Amru—(m)—life and alive
Amr—(m)—order, command, old name
Amsah—(f)—friendly
Amsal—(m)—optimal, exemplary, the best
Amsa—(f)—fairness, fair, dear
Amshaj—(m)—great
Amsha—(f)—to awaken someone
Amtar—(m)—beautiful
Amtullah—(f)—female devotee of allah
Amud—(m)—support, chieftain
Amulya—(m)—precious, priceless, valuable
Amun—(m)—trustworthy, god of mystery
Amur—(m)—wise, sharp sighted
Amyali—(f)—desirous, ambitious for something
Amyali—(m)—desirous, ambitious for something
Amya—(f)—high place
Amyl—(m)—in the sense of being
Amynah—(f)—trustworthy, faithful
Amyn—(m)—trustworthy, faithful, truthful
Amyraa—(f)—princess, high-born
Amyrah—(f)—princess, high-born
Amyra—(f)—high-born, princess
Amyr—(m)—commander, prince, emir, ruler
Amyza—(f)—free from guile
Amzad—(m)—more glorious
Amzan—(m)—beautiful jewel
Amzi—(m)—strong and mighty
Anaaba—(f)—returned to god - became virtuous
Anaam—(f)—all living things on earth
Anaam—(m)—without any name
Anaan—(f)—clouds
Anaas—(m)—pleasant companionship
Anaaya—(f)—exclusive, care, powerful

Anaba—(f)—returning to god, returns from war
Anabia—(f)—paradise door, returning to god
Anabila—(f)—unique, divine aura
Anabiya—(f)—bird of heaven
Anabiya—(m)—birds
Anab—(m)—a grape, a knot
Anadia—(f)—delicate, moist, tender
Anadil—(f)—nightingale, plural of andalib
Anadiya—(f)—without a beginning, immortal
Anaeyza—(f)—beautiful
Anaeza—(f)—unique, divine aura
Anafah—(f)—resembling the heron
Anafa—(f)—resembling the heron
Anahid—(m)—immaculate
Anahita—(f)—goddess of wisdom and fertility
Anahya—(f)—brightness
Anah—(f)—patience, perseverance, answer
Anah—(m)—one who answers, afflicted
Anaiah—(f)—gift of god, god listens to prayer
Anairah—(f)—lovable grade, different
Anaish—(m)—special, answered prayer
Anais—(f)—grace, favour, pure
Anaitha—(f)—unique, divine aura
Anaiza—(f)—respectful, mercy, beauty
Analee—(f)—grace, favour, similar to anna
Anamat—(m)—noun
Anamta—(f)—blessed
Anam—(f)—blessing, noble man with power
Anam—(m)—blessing, grace, reward
Ananda—(f)—happy, joyful, bliss, full of joy
Anandu—(m)—one with a lot of talent
Anangkiti—(f)—unique, divine aura
Anan—(f)—clouds
Anan—(m)—cloud
Anaqat—(f)—beauty, elegance
Anaraka—(f)—unique, divine aura
Anarkkali—(f)—pomegranate blossom
Anar—(f)—pomegranate, priceless, radiant

Anar—(m)—radiant, glowing, pomegranate
Anasat—(f)—lack of fear - worry
Anasat—(m)—a variant of the name anasa
Anasa—(f)—serenity, tranquillity
Anasha—(f)—unique
Anasiya—(f)—friendly, compassionate
Anasi—(f)—friendly, kind
Anasi—(m)—friendly
Anass—(m)—a group of people, affection
Anas—(m)—a group of people, affection
Anat—(f)—response, answer, forbearance
Anat—(m)—response, answer
Anaum—(m)—blessing of allah
Anavia—(f)—trust
Anaviya—(f)—trust, peaceful, lovable
Anayaa—(f)—complete freedom
Anayah—(f)—gift of god
Anayara—(f)—happiness
Anayatullah—(m)—favour, grace
Anayat—(f)—favour, grace
Anaya—(f)—blessing of god, origin
Anaya—(m)—answer of god
Anayeza—(f)—success, beautiful
Anayra—(f)—happiness
Anaysha—(f)—unique, special
Anayt—(f)—grace, favour
Anayza—(f)—respected
Anaz—(m)—friendliness
Ana—(f)—form of anna, gracious
Anbara—(f)—ambergris, perfume
Anbarin—(f)—of ambergris
Anbar—(f)—perfume, ambergris
Anbir—(m)—aspire, aim, strive
Anceena—(f)—unique, divine aura
Ancia—(f)—favoured by god, grace
Anciba—(f)—unique, divine aura
Ancina—(f)—god has blessed
Ancyra—(f)—from ankara

Ancy—(f)—beautiful of all
Andalah—(f)—song of the nightingale
Andalib—(f)—nightingale
Andalib—(m)—nightingale, small bird
Andam—(m)—forever
Andleeb—(f)—nightingale bird
Andleeb—(m)—nightingale
Aneeba—(f)—angel
Aneeb—(m)—one with divine wisdom
Aneeda—(f)—endless
Aneefa—(f)—likes of god
Aneef—(m)—one with divine wisdom
Aneeha—(f)—unwillingness, indifferent
Aneena—(f)—kind, noble
Aneen—(m)—hello, good
Aneeqah—(f)—beautiful
Aneeqa—(f)—beautiful, unique
Aneeq—(m)—valuable
Aneerah—(f)—snow
Aneera—(f)—young woman, girl
Aneer—(f)—girl, young woman
Aneesah—(f)—affectionate, close, intimate
Aneesa—(f)—friendly, of appropriate company
Aneesbegum—(f)—unique, divine aura
Aneesha—(f)—victory, uninterrupted
Aneesh—(m)—brightness, supreme, friendly
Anees—(f)—friendly, of appropriate company, inmate
Anees—(m)—wise man, close friend, companion
Aneetah—(f)—god has shown, god was gracious
Aneethah—(f)—god has shown, god was gracious
Aneezah—(f)—female goat
Aneeza—(f)—happiness and green valleys
Aneez—(m)—one with divine wisdom
Aneif—(m)—brightness, likes of god
Aneira—(f)—man of honour, gold
Anekah—(f)—several, god was gracious
Anen—(m)—sinless, faultless
Anesa—(f)—pure, chaste

Anetra—(f)—god has shown, god was gracious
Anfaal—(m)—one with divine wisdom
Anfal—(m)—one with divine wisdom
Anfani—(f)—dignified
Anfani—(m)—dignified
Anfas—(f)—spirits, souls, breaths
Anfas—(m)—spirits, souls, breaths
Anfaz—(m)—god's gift
Anfa—(f)—self-respect, dignity
Anfa—(m)—self respect, dignity
Anfia—(f)—loyal, honest
Anfina—(f)—unique, divine aura
Anfiya—(f)—unique
Angar—(m)—embers
Angbin—(f)—honey
Angel—(f)—fairy
Angeza—(f)—logic, reason
Angham—(f)—melody, plural of nagham
Angoori—(f)—grape
Angur—(f)—a sweet grape
Anhaar—(f)—river
Anhaar—(m)—river
Anhar—(f)—heaven waves, rivers
Anhar—(m)—river
Anha—(f)—representation of love, beautiful
Aniba—(f)—one who whorship to god
Anida—(f)—obstinate, faithful
Anifa—(f)—bright, dignified
Anif—(m)—noble, lofty
Anika—(f)—grace, favour, god is gracious
Anila—(f)—grace, breeze, air, wind
Animesh—(m)—wakeful, lord buddha, open-eyed
Anin—(m)—having no master, less
Aniqah—(f)—beautiful, stylish
Aniqa—(f)—clever, elegant, beautiful
Aniqha—(f)—unique, divine aura
Aniqua—(f)—bright, unique
Anique—(m)—unique, bright

Aniq—(f)—beautiful, pretty
Aniq—(m)—elegant, blessed, moon
Anira—(f)—intelligent, fearless
Anirha—(f)—powerful
Anisah—(f)—close, intimate, appropriate friend
Anisa—(f)—joy and pleasure, friendly
Anise—(m)—gracious
Anisha—(f)—pure, grace, continuous, day
Anish—(m)—lord krishna, lord vishnu
Anissa—(f)—gracious, merciful, pure
Anisur—(m)—one with divine wisdom
Anis—(f)—pure, chaste, companion
Anis—(m)—close friend, friendly, amiable
Anithah—(f)—god has shown, god was gracious
Anittah—(f)—god was gracious, god has shown
Aniyah—(f)—caring, affectionate
Aniya—(m)—concern, loving
Aniyyah—(f)—unique, divine aura
Anizah—(f)—female goat
Aniza—(f)—mercy, beauty
Ani—(f)—ornament, beautiful
Anjam—(f)—stars, variant of najm (star)
Anjam—(m)—stars
Anjil—(m)—derived from anjan, devdut
Anjoom—(f)—stars
Anjoom—(m)—stars
Anjudiya—(f)—form of anjud
Anjudi—(m)—the attributive form of anjud
Anjud—(f)—plateaus, the plural of word najd
Anjud—(m)—plateaus, the plural of word najd
Anjuman-ara—(f)—adorning the assembly
Anjumanara—(f)—adorning the assembly
Anjuman—(f)—assembly
Anjuman—(m)—a token, a symbol, a garden
Anjumara—(f)—unique, divine aura
Anjum—(f)—star, a token, angel, meeting
Anjum—(m)—name of a star, a token, stars
Anjuna—(f)—beautiful

Anjura—(f)—unique, divine aura
Anjuwara—(f)—unique, divine aura
Anmar—(f)—leopard
Anmol—(f)—priceless, valuable, precious
Anmol—(m)—priceless, precious, valuable
Annaba—(f)—one who returns from war
Annahi—(f)—unique, divine aura
Annaish—(f)—unique, divine aura
Annam—(f)—swan, god's blessing
Annana—(f)—beautiful, appearance
Annan—(m)—from the brook
Annas—(m)—compassion of god
Annaya—(f)—unique
Anna—(f)—present, graceful
Anna—(m)—name of a king, food, grain
Anne-laure—(f)—god has shown, god was gracious
Annella—(f)—god was gracious, god has shown
Annesha—(f)—beautiful, pure, grace
Annettchen—(f)—god was gracious, god has shown
Annida—(f)—god has shown, celtic
Anniki—(f)—god has shown, god was gracious
Annisah—(f)—one, chaste, pure, lamb, intimate
Annissa—(f)—friendly, congenial, form of anna
Annitra—(f)—god has shown, god was gracious
Anniyah—(f)—concern, loving
Annnees—(m)—friendly, of good company, inmate
Annum—(f)—year
Annwar—(m)—light
Anny—(m)—superhero
Ann—(f)—gracious, form of anna
Anoofa—(f)—unique, divine aura
Anoosha—(f)—delighted, happy
Anoosheh—(f)—lucky, happy, fortunate
Anoosh—(f)—delighted
Anorah—(f)—honour
Anosha—(f)—justice, joy, lucky
Anouar—(m)—light, shining
Anoud—(f)—strong-willed, smart, popular

Anoum—(f)—god's blessings
Anoum—(m)—god's blessings
Anousha—(f)—everlasting
Anousheh—(f)—fortunate, happy
Anoushirvan—(m)—name of an ancient king
Anoush—(m)—eternal, everlasting
Anowara—(f)—unique, divine aura
Anowar—(m)—morning air
Anqa—(f)—long necked, most purest one
Ansaar—(m)—helper, kind hearted, supporter
Ansaba—(f)—unique, divine aura
Ansab—(f)—worthier, more appropriate, better
Ansab—(m)—altar stones
Ansad—(m)—one with divine wisdom
Ansaifa—(f)—unique, divine aura
Ansal—(m)—strong, lusty
Ansam—(f)—breath, plural of nasam
Ansam—(m)—plural of nasam
Ansar-ali—(m)—helper
Ansara—(f)—helper
Ansariah—(f)—one who helps
Ansar—(m)—friend, patron, supporter, helper
Ansat—(m)—god is merciful, gracious
Ansa—(f)—beauty queen, goddess of dreams
Ansa—(m)—portion
Anseeda—(f)—unique, divine aura
Anseela—(f)—enlightening
Anseena—(f)—sweet heart
Anseera—(f)—unique, divine aura
Anseer—(m)—helper, friend, supporter
Anser—(m)—one with divine wisdom
Anshab—(m)—one with divine wisdom
Anshad—(m)—strong, brave
Anshahra—(f)—joyful
Anshana—(f)—unique, divine aura
Ansharah—(f)—precious, relief, relaxation
Anshar—(m)—the king of gods
Ansha—(f)—portion, hope

Ansheena—(f)—light
Ansheera—(f)—joyful
Anshiba—(f)—pure, favoured by god
Anshida—(f)—singer
Anshidha—(f)—unique, divine aura
Anshid—(m)—intelligent
Anshifa—(f)—one who can cure
Anshif—(m)—one who can cure
Anshil—(m)—happy, in the old testament
Anshina—(f)—gorgeous, star
Anshirah—(f)—joyful, delight
Anshira—(f)—joyful
Anshi—(f)—gift of god, whole
Anshrah—(f)—relief, precious
Anshra—(f)—unique, divine aura
Anshuka—(m)—one with divine wisdom
Ansiba—(f)—unique, divine aura
Ansifa—(f)—unique, divine aura
Ansila—(f)—enlightening
Ansil—(m)—nobel, god's protection
Ansina—(f)—god has blessed
Ansira—(f)—helper
Ansiya—(f)—gift of god
Ansra—(f)—helper
Ansri—(f)—famous, glorious, beautiful
Anssiya—(f)—gift of god
Ansuma—(f)—unique, divine aura
Ans—(m)—part of whole, portion
Antarah—(m)—fearless bravery
Antar—(m)—rush boldly in to danger, heart
Antasha—(f)—gift, invaluable
Antique—(m)—one with divine wisdom
Antony—(m)—priceless, highly praiseworthy
Antu—(m)—prayer
Anuf—(m)—nose, smell
Anugraha—(f)—divine blessing, favour, kindness
Anul—(m)—wind
Anumullah—(f)—god's blessings, god's bestowals

Anumullah—(m)—god's blessings, god's bestowals
Anum—(f)—gift of allah, god's gift
Anum—(m)—present, blessings of god
Anurita—(f)—glamorous
Anusheh—(f)—fortunate, happy
Anuu—(m)—grape
Anu—(m)—an atom, angel, messenger of god
Anvaar—(m)—prosperity, lighting
Anvara—(f)—lighting, prosperity
Anvar—(m)—prosperity, excellent
Anver—(m)—light
Anvin—(m)—one victory man
Anvir—(m)—excellent, prosperity
Anwaaraddin—(m)—light, brilliance of the faith
Anwaar—(f)—rays of light
Anwaar—(m)—multiple lights, lustre, light
Anwarah—(f)—greatly lighten
Anwara—(f)—ray of light, radiance, glow
Anwari—(m)—radiant, glowing, full of light
Anwarr—(m)—light
Anwarulkarim—(m)—lights of the beneficent allah
Anwarullah—(m)—light of allah
Anwarul—(m)—brightest, lustrous
Anwarus-sadat—(m)—the most brilliant of the sayyids
Anwarussadat—(m)—brilliant
Anwar—(f)—rays of light, blossoms
Anwar—(m)—devotee of god, lustrous, shiny
Anwa—(f)—strong will gathered, temptation
Anwerussadat—(m)—the most brilliant of the sayyids
Anwer—(m)—devotee of god, lustrous
Anya—(f)—inexhaustible, gracious, graceful
Anyra—(f)—golden eyes
Anysa—(f)—lamb, friendly, hunger
Anyta—(f)—god was gracious, god has shown
Anzaar—(m)—god of paradise
Anzala—(f)—unique, divine aura
Anzalna—(f)—unique, divine aura
Anzal—(f)—descendant

Anzal—(m)—one with divine wisdom
Anzana—(f)—dusky, beauty
Anzara—(f)—vision, insight
Anzar—(f)—vision, eyesight, insight
Anzar—(m)—having a good eye sight
Anza—(f)—small
Anzeena—(f)—dusky, beauty
Anzer—(f)—helping
Anziba—(f)—unique, divine aura
Anzik—(m)—sword
Anzil—(m)—devotee of god
Anzina—(f)—beauty, dusky
Anzisha—(f)—angel of heaven
Anzish—(f)—angel of heaven, gift of god
Anziyah—(f)—unique, divine aura
Anziya—(f)—unique, divine aura
Anzla—(f)—bright, enlightening
Anzum—(f)—unique, divine aura
Aoj—(f)—peak, height, apex, climax
Apana—(f)—almond
Aphra—(f)—colour of earth, young deer, dust
Aphsana—(f)—fiction, storey
Apsana—(f)—fiction
Apsara—(f)—angel, beauty, celestial maiden
Apsar—(m)—water-goer, any aquatic animal
Apshana—(f)—fiction
Apsha—(f)—beautiful
Apshu—(f)—beautiful
Apsira—(f)—unique, divine aura
Apsra—(f)—most beautiful
Aqa—(m)—master, owner
Aqball—(m)—destiny, glory
Aqbar—(m)—greatest, honourable, bigger
Aqdas—(f)—pure, sacred
Aqdas—(m)—most holy, more or most sacred
Aqeeb—(m)—follower, behind
Aqeedah—(f)—unique, divine aura
Aqeed—(m)—one who has given a promise

Aqeefah—(f)—dedicated, devoted
Aqeefa—(f)—devoted, dedicated
Aqeef—(m)—dedicated, devoted
Aqeelah—(f)—wise, sensible, reasonable
Aqeela—(f)—the very best, wise, sensible
Aqeel—(m)—wise, intelligent, sensible
Aqeem—(m)—knowledgeable
Aqeeq—(m)—valuable stone
Aqeer—(m)—one with divine wisdom
Aqeil—(m)—knowledgeable
Aqela—(f)—intellectual, wise
Aqheel—(m)—discerning, intelligent, wise
Aqibah—(f)—consequence, aftermath
Aqiba—(f)—result, consequence
Aqib—(m)—one who follows
Aqidah—(f)—creed, belief, faith, tenet
Aqifah—(f)—dedicated, devoted
Aqifa—(f)—dedicated, devoted
Aqif—(m)—devoted, dedicated, focused
Aqilah—(f)—intelligent woman, spouse
Aqila—(f)—clever, bright, intellectual, wise
Aqilla—(f)—gifted with reason, wise
Aqil—(m)—wise, intelligent, leader
Aqisha—(f)—complete, blessing of god
Aqlaam—(m)—pen
Aqlaan—(m)—keen
Aqlam—(m)—pen
Aqlan—(m)—intelligent, keen
Aqleema—(f)—beautiful world
Aqleem—(m)—realm, kingdom, region, zone
Aqlema—(f)—unique, divine aura
Aqlimah—(f)—wise, intelligent
Aqlim—(m)—wise
Aqllan—(m)—keen, intelligent
Aql—(m)—mind, ability to think
Aqmal—(m)—perfect, complete, whole
Aqmar—(f)—light
Aqmar—(m)—bright, brilliant, luminous

Aqqaad—(m)—maker of trimmings
Aqqad—(m)—maker of trimmings, haberdasher
Aqrab—(m)—near, close
Aqram—(m)—variant of akram, generous
Aqra—(f)—to read, educate
Aqsaa—(f)—farthest
Aqsad—(m)—achiever, goal-setter
Aqsam—(m)—hope, lion, broad sword
Aqsara—(f)—unalterable
Aqsat—(m)—most just, fairer
Aqsa—(f)—a mosque, intelligent
Aqsa—(m)—a mosque
Aqshan—(m)—one with divine wisdom
Aqsha—(f)—blessing of god
Aqtaab—(m)—falcon, bird of prey
Aqtaar—(f)—regions
Aqtaar—(m)—region
Aqtab—(m)—one with divine wisdom
Aqtar—(f)—regions
Aqtar—(m)—regions
Aqtasa—(f)—unique, divine aura
Aqteeba—(f)—unique, divine aura
Aquebal—(m)—one with divine wisdom
Aqueeba—(f)—unique, divine aura
Aqueelah—(f)—unique, divine aura
Aquela—(f)—wise, intelligent lady
Aquib—(m)—follower of god
Aquid—(m)—one with divine wisdom
Aquif—(m)—one with divine wisdom
Aquila—(f)—powerful as an eagle
Aquil—(f)—eagle
Aquil—(m)—wise
Aqusa—(f)—name of mosque
Aqwa—(m)—strongest, stronger
Aqyan—(m)—one with divine wisdom
Araaf—(m)—honest, noble
Araam—(f)—comfort, relief
Araan—(m)—nobility

Araaz—(m)—commodities, provisions
Arabia—(f)—evening, desert, ravens
Arabi—(f)—arabian
Arabi—(m)—arabian
Arab—(m)—peaceful
Arad—(m)—name of an angel
Arae—(f)—intelligent, andaji
Arafaa—(f)—a variant of arafah
Arafah—(f)—unique, divine aura
Arafah—(m)—vigil, guard
Arafath—(m)—mountain, mount of recognition
Arafat—(m)—mount of recognition
Arafa—(f)—knowledgeable
Arafa—(m)—knowledgeable
Arafiya—(f)—angel, devotee of god
Araf—(f)—unique, divine aura
Araf—(m)—beautiful
Arahaan—(m)—destroyer of demons
Arahad—(m)—water fall
Araham—(m)—mercy - compassion
Arahan—(m)—one with divine wisdom
Araibah—(f)—wise
Araiba—(f)—wise, skilful, messenger of god
Araiha—(f)—guiding star
Araina—(f)—pure
Araisa—(f)—leader, bright
Araish—(m)—adornment
Araiza—(f)—leader
Araiz—(m)—national leader
Araju—(f)—wish
Araj—(f)—fragrant
Araj—(m)—pray, fragrance
Arakan—(m)—worthy one, hero
Araka—(f)—respected
Araka—(m)—respected
Araman—(m)—desire, wish
Aramazd—(m)—divinity of wisdom
Aram—(f)—righteous woman, high, exalted

Aram—(m)—highness, exalted, quiet
Aran—(m)—righteous
Arar—(m)—powerful
Arash—(m)—bright arrow, a hero
Arastoo—(m)—knowledgeable, wise, best purpose
Arastu—(m)—one with divine wisdom
Arath—(m)—sense, meaning
Arav—(m)—peaceful, smart, beautiful
Arawinda—(m)—one with divine wisdom
Arayana—(f)—utterly pure
Arayna—(f)—vivacious
Araysh—(m)—over-shadower
Araz—(m)—provisions, commodities
Ara—(f)—ornament, brings rain
Arbaaj—(m)—strong, touching sky like eagle
Arbaas—(m)—eagle
Arbaaz—(m)—eagle
Arbab—(f)—people in charge, master, chief
Arbab—(m)—friends, masters, chiefs
Arbad—(m)—masters, lords
Arbaj—(m)—touching sky like eagle
Arban—(m)—fluent, eloquent
Arbas—(m)—eagle
Arbaz—(m)—touching sky like eagle
Arbeena—(f)—queen of arab
Arben—(m)—of the forest
Arbina—(f)—gift
Arbin—(m)—advance
Arbish—(f)—rain of haven, gift of god
Archie—(m)—bold, form of archibald
Ardam—(m)—brave, bold man
Ardan—(m)—a hill, high, aspiration
Ardashir—(m)—one who rules with truth
Ardavan—(m)—protector of righteousness
Arda—(m)—truthful
Ardeen—(m)—great forest
Arden—(m)—high, soaring, eagle valley
Ardhwaan—(m)—one who make justice

Ardia—(f)—burning with enthusiasm
Ardina—(f)—ardent, eager, industrious
Ardin—(m)—burning with enthusiasm, fiery
Ardit—(m)—golden day
Ardi—(m)—valley of the eagle
Arduaan—(m)—one with divine wisdom
Ardvan—(m)—protector of holiness
Areaba—(f)—one who is smart and witty
Areaza—(f)—unique, divine aura
Areba—(f)—wise, sharp
Areebah—(f)—witty - smart, wise, intelligent
Areeba—(f)—brilliant, sharp, beautiful
Areeb—(m)—skillful, adroit, wise
Areefa—(f)—expert, learned, authority
Areef—(m)—learned, expert, authority
Areeha—(f)—fragrance, garden
Areeja—(f)—pleasant smell
Areej—(f)—pleasant smell, flower of heaven
Areej—(m)—fragrant, sweet-smelling
Areeka—(f)—beautiful heart, eyes
Areema—(f)—unique, divine aura
Areem—(m)—one with divine wisdom
Areena—(f)—god gifted, voice of bird
Areen—(f)—sun god, full of joy
Areen—(m)—full of joy, sun god
Areeqa—(f)—unique, divine aura
Areeq—(m)—noble
Areesa—(f)—unique, divine aura
Areesha—(f)—orchard of grapes
Areesh—(m)—built wooden structure
Arees—(m)—peasant, farmer
Areeva—(f)—unique, divine aura
Areeza—(f)—urge
Areez—(m)—friend, respect, leader
Arefeen—(m)—leader
Arefin—(m)—leader, boss
Aref—(m)—knowing, knowledgeable, wise
Areif—(m)—wise, knowledgeable, learned

Arein—(f)—bringer of light
Arella—(f)—angel, golden-haired, messenger
Arel—(m)—sprite, lion of god
Areman—(m)—fighter, leadar
Arena—(f)—holy one creative
Aren—(f)—eagle, ruler, peace
Aren—(m)—eagle, ruler, peace
Aresha—(f)—under an umbrella
Ares—(m)—god of war, quick sighted
Areta—(f)—virtuous, excellent
Aretha—(f)—woman of virtue, morality, best
Arezah—(f)—gold, happiness queen
Arezoo—(f)—longed for, wish
Arezou—(f)—wishful, desire, wish
Arezu—(f)—desire, wish
Arfaad—(m)—brighten
Arfaana—(f)—wisdom, variation of name irfana
Arfaan—(m)—grateful, wisdom
Arfaas—(m)—one with divine wisdom
Arfaat—(m)—mountain
Arfaaz—(m)—respected, most handsome
Arfaa—(f)—very high, uche martaba wali
Arfaa—(m)—very high
Arfad—(m)—delighted
Arfah—(f)—unique, divine aura
Arfain—(f)—unique, divine aura
Arfaj—(m)—respected
Arfana—(f)—wisdom, leader
Arfan—(m)—intelligent, gratitude
Arfas—(m)—respected
Arfath—(m)—king of kings, heavens garden
Arfat—(m)—place of pilgrimage
Arfazz—(m)—one with divine wisdom
Arfaz—(m)—respected
Arfa—(f)—greatness, high, best
Arfa—(m)—high-status, best, sublime
Arfeen—(f)—unique, divine aura
Arfeen—(m)—leader

Arffa—(f)—very high
Arfhan—(m)—gratitude, intelligent
Arfha—(f)—beautiful, best, greatness
Arfia—(f)—devotee of god
Arfina—(f)—leader
Arfin—(m)—leader
Arfitha—(f)—place of pilgrimage
Arfiyaz—(f)—forgiveness, intelligent
Arf—(f)—scent, appropriate scent
Arf—(m)—scent, good scent
Arghavan—(f)—reddish purple
Arhaad—(m)—one with divine wisdom
Arhaam—(m)—merciful, compassion
Arhaana—(f)—giving happiness, worship
Arhaan—(m)—king, winner, angel, ruler
Arhaa—(f)—to become calm, tranquil, serene
Arhab—(m)—scared heart, open-minded
Arhad—(m)—one with divine wisdom
Arhal—(m)—king
Arhama—(f)—mercy, most merciful, kind
Arham—(f)—most merciful, kind
Arham—(m)—most merciful, kind
Arhana—(f)—worship, honour, giving happiness
Arhana—(m)—worship
Arhan—(m)—king of king, ruler, climb
Arhat—(m)—deserving, respectable
Arhm—(m)—heaven, compassion
Arhum—(m)—forgiving
Ariah—(m)—lion, best, excellent
Arianah—(f)—holy one, pure, variant of arianna
Ariana—(f)—the holiest one, pledge
Ariani—(f)—pure, holy one, variant of arianna
Arian—(m)—spares, pledge, oath, golden life
Aria—(f)—gentle music, brings rain, pledge
Aribah—(f)—wise
Ariba—(f)—intelligent, skilful,
Arib—(m)—brilliant, intelligent, clever
Arica—(f)—prediction of the winds

Arid—(m)—king of ruler
Arieba—(f)—one who is smart and witty
Arief—(m)—wise, knowledgeable
Ariege—(f)—fragrance, beautiful scent
Aries—(m)—the ram, pledge, oath
Ariez—(m)—wise
Arie—(f)—nobel
Arifaa—(f)—learned
Arifah—(f)—knowledgeable
Arifan—(m)—one with divine wisdom
Arifa—(f)—knowledgeable, learned
Arifeen—(m)—god
Ariffulla—(m)—one with divine wisdom
Arifin—(m)—brave, saints
Arifuddin—(m)—one with divine wisdom
Arifulaa—(m)—one with divine wisdom
Arifullah—(m)—one with divine wisdom
Arifulla—(m)—one with divine wisdom
Ariful—(m)—global prime minister
Arifunnisa—(f)—unique, divine aura
Arifur—(m)—one with divine wisdom
Arif—(m)—knowing, knowledgeable
Arihan—(m)—one who kills enemies
Ariha—(f)—fragrance, garden
Arij—(f)—fragrance, sweet smell, pleasant
Arikah—(m)—decorated throne
Arika—(f)—water lilly, god of beauty
Arim—(m)—roots, little star, near to god
Arinaa—(f)—peace
Arinah—(f)—precious, winner, beautiful
Arina—(f)—peace
Arine—(m)—sun ray
Arin—(f)—from ireland, enlightened, peace
Arin—(m)—mountain of strength, with spokes
Ariqaat—(f)—noble
Ariq—(m)—deep rooted
Arisaa—(f)—unique, divine aura
Arisah—(f)—bright, happiness queen

Arisa—(f)—bright
Arisha-fatima—(f)—unique, divine aura
Arisha—(f)—peace
Arishfa—(f)—glory of sky, princess
Arishi—(f)—true, real
Arishma—(f)—with beautiful hair
Arish—(m)—righteous, wise, prudent, sky
Arislan—(m)—honest person
Arissa—(f)—bright, best
Aris—(m)—pledge, oath, battle
Arita—(f)—lightness
Arith—(m)—wish, peaceful
Aritoon—(m)—a twinkle, star in the sky
Ariyana—(f)—silver
Ariyanna—(f)—most holy
Ariyan—(m)—first king, warrior
Ariyapala—(m)—one with divine wisdom
Ariya—(f)—noble
Ariyn—(m)—pledge
Ariyya—(f)—lioness of god
Arizaa—(f)—gold, gold coin of islam
Ariza—(f)—sun rises, urge
Arizha—(f)—unique, divine aura
Ariz—(f)—clouds
Ariz—(m)—ruler of nation, leader, firmly
Ari—(f)—brings rain, exalted, on high
Arjaan—(m)—golden life
Arjan—(m)—the archer, a kind of fir, tree
Arjeena—(f)—unique, divine aura
Arjia—(f)—acquiring, earned
Arjina—(f)—beautiful
Arjisha—(f)—acquired, gained
Arjmand—(m)—bountiful
Arjoo—(f)—wish
Arjumand—(f)—beloved, noble, honourable
Arjumand—(m)—respected, noble
Arjuma—(f)—unique, divine aura
Arjumnd-bano—(f)—excellent woman, noble woman

Arjumndbano—(f)—excellent woman, noble woman
Arju—(f)—wish, mountain of strength
Arkaan—(m)—principles
Arkam—(m)—generous
Arkan—(m)—support, pillar, responsible
Arkham—(m)—one with divine wisdom
Arleena—(f)—pledge
Arlin—(f)—promise, variant of arlen, pledge
Armaan—(f)—desire, wish, famous bearer
Armaan—(m)—wish, longing, soldier
Armagan—(m)—gift
Armaghan—(f)—gift
Armaghan—(m)—gift
Armana—(f)—desire
Armand—(m)—french form of herman, army man
Armani—(f)—derivative of imani, faith
Armann—(m)—desire, wish, longing
Arman—(f)—wish, longing, desire
Arman—(m)—longing, wish, hope, desire
Armash—(m)—one with divine wisdom
Armayun—(m)—intelligent
Armeena—(f)—fairy, princess, brave
Armeen—(f)—brings rain
Armeen—(m)—one with divine wisdom
Armen—(m)—high place, castle, palace
Armina—(f)—noble, warrior maiden
Armineh—(f)—desire, goal
Armin—(f)—dweller of the garden of eden
Armin—(m)—protective, soldier, army man
Armish—(f)—quiet
Armish—(m)—quiet
Armiya—(m)—god has appointed, jeremiah
Armun—(m)—earnest, pledge
Arnaaz—(f)—graceful, pretty
Arnab—(m)—sea, ocean
Arnaf—(m)—one with divine wisdom
Arnav—(m)—sea, great ocean, silence of ocean
Arnaz—(f)—graceful

Arna—(f)—ornaments, mountain of strength
Arnob—(m)—sea, ocean
Arof—(m)—respecting, good nature
Arona—(f)—colourful
Aronna—(m)—forest
Arooba—(f)—a woman who love her husband
Aroob—(f)—loving to her husband
Aroofa—(f)—knowledgeable, learned, patient
Aroof—(m)—wise, learned, skilled
Arooj—(f)—height peak, height of something
Arooj—(m)—healthy
Arooma—(f)—unique, divine aura
Aroosa—(f)—bride
Aroosh—(f)—angel of heaven
Aroosh—(m)—angle of heaven
Aroub—(f)—woman loving to her husband
Arouge—(f)—unique, divine aura
Arouna—(f)—dawn
Aroush—(f)—princess of paradise
Arqam—(m)—writer, the best recorder
Arqan—(m)—pillar, responsible, support
Arqa—(f)—refined tastes
Arqum—(m)—one with divine wisdom
Arraf—(m)—heights
Arrant—(m)—one with divine wisdom
Arria—(f)—brings rain
Arriya—(f)—unique, divine aura
Arsad—(m)—pious, honest
Arsalaan—(m)—lion, king of jungle
Arsalah—(f)—the one who was sent
Arsalan—(m)—lion, king of jungle, brave man
Arsalna—(f)—unique, divine aura
Arsal—(m)—the one who was sent
Arsana—(f)—unique, divine aura
Arsan—(m)—prince, king
Arsath—(m)—honest, head of a group
Arsat—(m)—one with divine wisdom
Arsav—(m)—devoting, complete baby

Arseena—(f)—powerful, actress
Arseen—(m)—almighty place
Arsel—(m)—to send, to ship, dispatch
Arshaad—(m)—one with divine wisdom
Arshaan—(m)—brave, righteous
Arshaa—(f)—great, prayer ceremony
Arshad—(m)—pious, honest, obedient
Arshaf—(m)—one with divine wisdom
Arshak—(m)—powerful
Arshala—(f)—one who comes from the sky
Arshal—(m)—the one who was sent
Arsham—(m)—very strong
Arshana—(f)—gift of god
Arshan—(f)—two thrones, name of city in yemen
Arshan—(m)—righteous, brave
Arshaq—(m)—handsome, elegant, graceful
Arshath—(m)—guidance, pious
Arshat—(m)—pious, obedient, head of a group
Arshdullah—(m)—one with divine wisdom
Arshea—(f)—holy, heavenly, divine
Arshed—(m)—one with divine wisdom
Arsheel—(m)—one with divine wisdom
Arsheena—(f)—cultured, gods beauty
Arsheen—(f)—soft, cultured
Arsheen—(m)—soft, cultured
Arsheet—(m)—king
Arsheeya—(f)—heavenly, divine, holy
Arsheq—(m)—elevated, handsome
Arshiah—(f)—heavenly, divine, holy
Arshia—(f)—divine, holy, heavenly
Arshia—(m)—throne
Arshida—(f)—beautiful
Arshidha—(f)—truthful
Arshid—(m)—honest, pious
Arshifa—(f)—glory of sky, princess
Arshik—(m)—saviour
Arshila—(f)—one who comes from the sky
Arshil—(m)—smile, throne of god

Arshiman—(m)—prince of sky
Arshima—(f)—gift of god
Arshina—(f)—blessing
Arshin—(f)—almighty's place
Arshin—(m)—almighty's place
Arshiqa—(f)—unique, divine aura
Arshiq—(m)—one with divine wisdom
Arshith—(m)—part of god, god venkateswara
Arshiyan—(f)—angel, heavens, light
Arshiyan—(m)—light, heaven
Arshiya—(f)—belonging to throne, sky
Arshi—(f)—mirror, heavenly, goddess durga
Arshi—(m)—heavenly, belonging to a throne
Arshlan—(m)—one with divine wisdom
Arshmaan—(m)—king of sky
Arshman—(m)—king of sky, prince of heaven
Arshnoor—(f)—wish, sky light, glow of god
Arshul—(m)—one with divine wisdom
Arshu—(f)—mirror
Arshya—(f)—divine, righteous
Arshy—(f)—righteous, divine
Arsh—(f)—sky, throne, power, dominion
Arsh—(m)—sky, importance, crown, dominion
Arsia—(f)—throne
Arsifa—(f)—glory of sky
Arsika—(f)—one who prays, appointed by god
Arsil—(m)—the one who was sent
Arsima—(f)—unique, divine aura
Arsina—(f)—unique, divine aura
Arsin—(m)—one with divine wisdom
Arsiya—(f)—of sacred descent
Arsi—(m)—mirror
Arslaan—(m)—king of jungle, great hearted
Arslan—(m)—king of lions, brave
Arsleen—(f)—unique, divine aura
Arsman—(m)—one with divine wisdom
Arsu—(m)—water of eyes, unique
Arsylan—(m)—one with divine wisdom

Artah—(m)—narrator of the hadith
Arubah—(f)—faithful woman
Aruba—(f)—loves her husband
Arubiyyah—(f)—fluent, eloquent
Arub—(f)—wife loved by her husband
Arufa—(f)—patient
Aruj—(m)—healthy
Arusah—(f)—bride, doll
Arushi—(f)—first ray of sun, beauty, dawn
Arusi—(f)—calm, bright, the sun, kills
Arus—(f)—bride, spouse
Arva—(m)—fastest motion wind
Arveena—(f)—unique, divine aura
Arveera—(f)—power
Arvil—(m)—fusion of soul
Arvish—(m)—daring, freedom-loving
Arvi—(m)—eagle, noble, talented, warrior
Arwaan—(m)—gift of god
Arwaa—(f)—satisfied, female ibex, softness
Arwah—(f)—breath of air
Arwah—(m)—more delicate, more gracious
Arwan—(m)—brave
Arwarh—(m)—more delicate, more gracious
Arwaz—(m)—one with divine wisdom
Arwa—(f)—pleasant, bright fullness, fresh
Aryaana—(f)—holy, pure
Aryaan—(m)—powerful, the king, innocent
Aryaa—(f)—noble, honoured, goddess paravati
Aryah—(f)—divine light, honoured
Aryam—(f)—god
Aryan—(m)—warrior, honourable, king, noble
Arya—(f)—goddess parvati
Arya—(m)—powerful, noble, great, truthful
Aryika—(f)—unique, divine aura
Aryisha—(f)—under tree or umbrella
Aryka—(f)—unique, divine aura
Aryn—(m)—mountain of strength, enlightened
Aryssa—(f)—best

Arzaan—(m)—angel of paradise, valuable
Arzad—(m)—king of king, prosperous
Arzam—(m)—war, battle
Arzana—(f)—prosperous, worthy
Arzang—(m)—an ancient wrestler
Arzan—(f)—worth, prosperous
Arzan—(m)—worth, worth live
Arza—(f)—cedar panels
Arzeenah—(f)—which can be seen
Arzeena—(f)—which can be seen
Arzeen—(f)—which can be seen, gift of god
Arzen—(m)—which can be seen, gift of god
Arzhan—(m)—worth, a kind of mountain almond
Arzia—(f)—urge
Arzima—(f)—unique, divine aura
Arzina—(f)—precious
Arzisha—(f)—value, price, loveable
Arzish—(m)—price, value
Arziyaan—(m)—request full
Arziyan—(m)—request full
Arzoo—(f)—desire, wish, hope
Arzou—(f)—desire, wish
Arzo—(f)—wish, dream, desire
Arzuan—(m)—one with divine wisdom
Arzuma—(f)—unique, divine aura
Arzun—(m)—amiable qualities
Arzu—(f)—hope, wish, desire
Arzu—(m)—wish, hope, love
Arz—(f)—mountain, breadth, width
Arz—(m)—mountain, breadth, width, length
Asaad—(m)—happier, beautiful, brave
Asaalat—(f)—a variant asala, nobleness
Asaal—(f)—evenings
Asaal—(m)—evening
Asab—(m)—respected
Asadah—(f)—female lion
Asadel—(m)—successful, most prosperous one
Asadollah—(m)—lion of allah

Asadour—(m)—most prosperous one
Asaduddin—(m)—lion of deen
Asadullah—(m)—lion of allah, title of ali
Asadulla—(m)—one with divine wisdom
Asadullha—(m)—one with divine wisdom
Asadul—(m)—tiger of allah
Asadur—(m)—one with divine wisdom
Asad—(m)—virtuous, pious, happier, luckier
Asaf—(m)—gathers
Asah—(f)—plant known for its greenness
Asah—(m)—more correct, proper, healthier
Asaiah—(m)—god made, the lord hath wrought
Asaisha—(f)—unique, divine aura
Asalah—(f)—purity, nobility of descent
Asalina—(f)—little noble one, beautiful
Asali—(f)—made of honey, honey
Asal—(f)—honey, sweet
Asal—(m)—honey, danger, fear
Asama—(f)—sky
Asamuddin—(m)—one with divine wisdom
Asan—(m)—name of lord shiva, lord vishnu
Asaraf—(m)—without grief
Asarat—(f)—lucky
Asara—(f)—remnant, trace
Asardeen—(m)—honoured person of the religion
Asareer—(f)—attractive
Asarfi—(f)—without grief, cultured
Asaruddin—(m)—one with divine wisdom
Asarudeen—(m)—honoured person of the religion
Asarudheen—(m)—honoured person of the religion
Asar—(f)—sign, mark, trace
Asar—(m)—mark, sign
Asawar—(m)—one with divine wisdom
Asaya—(f)—god's creation
Asa—(f)—healer, like, similar to, doctor
Asbaab—(f)—factors, causes
Asbab—(f)—factors, causes
Asbab—(m)—factors, causes

Asbagh—(m)—coloured animal, huge flood
Asbah—(f)—pure as water, beautiful
Asbah—(m)—handsome, beautiful, dawn, morning
Asbat—(m)—more reliable, steadier
Asbeera—(f)—unique, divine aura
Asbira—(f)—unique, divine aura
Asbiya—(f)—unique, divine aura
Asdaq—(m)—trustworthy
Aseeb—(f)—unique, divine aura
Aseed—(m)—narrator of hadith
Aseefa—(f)—unique, divine aura
Aseef—(m)—forgiveness
Aseela—(f)—high-born, of noble origin
Aseel—(m)—son of elite family, evening time
Aseema—(f)—limitless, protector, devotee
Aseem—(m)—longer, boundless, limitless asim
Aseena—(f)—beautiful
Aseen—(m)—pure, beautiful
Aseerah—(f)—unique, divine aura
Aseer—(m)—preferred, noble, exquisite
Aseeya—(f)—unique, divine aura
Aseey—(f)—beautiful, honest
Asefeh—(f)—wise woman, strong storm
Asem—(m)—cast-protector
Asfaan—(m)—merciful
Asfaaq—(m)—lovable, kindness, favours
Asfahan—(m)—beautiful
Asfah—(f)—princess
Asfakulla—(m)—one with divine wisdom
Asfakur—(m)—kind hearten, compassion
Asfak—(m)—one with divine wisdom
Asfal—(m)—one with divine wisdom
Asfana—(f)—princess of heaven
Asfandyar—(m)—created by the holy spirit
Asfand—(m)—month of march
Asfan—(m)—great
Asfaque—(m)—one with divine wisdom
Asfaqulhaq—(m)—one with divine wisdom

Asfaq—(f)—favours, kindness, compassion
Asfaq—(m)—compassion, kind hearten
Asfara—(f)—greatness, morning light
Asfareen—(f)—greatness, morning light
Asfar—(m)—morning light, greatness, lion
Asfa—(f)—beautiful, clearer, purest
Asfa—(m)—pure, clear, tanned sun burned
Asfeeya—(f)—clear, holy, just one, pure
Asfhak—(m)—compassion, kind hearten
Asfia—(f)—pure, enduring, respectable, huge
Asfika—(f)—compassion, kindness
Asfina—(f)—success
Asfin—(f)—unique, divine aura
Asfiqa—(f)—kindness, compassion
Asfiyah—(f)—holy, pure, just one
Asfiya—(f)—pure, holy, clear, just one
Asfiya—(m)—just, holy ones, plural of safee
Asfi—(f)—supporter, helper
Asfoureh—(f)—bird
Asfour—(m)—bird
Asgari—(f)—devotee
Asgar—(m)—devotee, devoted to lord
Asghar-ali—(m)—devoted to lord
Asghari—(f)—little
Asghar—(m)—smaller, younger, shorter, junior
Asghia—(f)—modest people
Ashaab—(m)—friends, companions
Ashaad—(m)—respectful, strong-willed
Ashaar—(m)—fierce, like a lion
Ashaas—(m)—humble, scattered, spread about
Ashaath—(m)—scattered, humble, spread about
Ashaaz—(m)—obedient, one in a million
Ashabanu—(f)—unique, divine aura
Ashab—(m)—reddish, blond, fair
Ashadieeyah—(f)—princess, perfect
Ashadul—(m)—one with divine wisdom
Ashadur—(m)—one who keeps hope
Ashah—(f)—woman, life

Ashaj—(m)—abu addunya almaghrabi
Ashalina—(f)—sweet, always living, shy, loving
Ashal—(m)—most brilliant, bright
Ashana—(f)—daughter of bali, friend
Ashan—(m)—pride
Asharaf—(m)—one with divine wisdom
Asharfi—(f)—cultured, without grief
Asharf—(m)—without grief, more honourable
Ashari—(m)—one with divine wisdom
Ashar—(f)—blessed, prosperous
Ashar—(m)—noble one of god
Ashaz—(m)—one in a million
Asha—(f)—hope, aspiration, wish, desire
Ashbah—(f)—resemblance, image, picture
Ashbala—(f)—unique, divine aura
Ashbir—(m)—prince
Asheeba—(f)—unique, divine aura
Asheeb—(m)—one with divine wisdom
Asheeda—(f)—blessings
Asheef—(m)—one with divine wisdom
Asheeka—(f)—love
Asheel—(m)—god risen from ashes
Asheemah—(f)—unique, divine aura
Asheem—(m)—boundless
Asheena—(f)—beautiful
Asheen—(m)—one with divine wisdom
Asheeqah—(f)—sweet heart, also spelt as aashika
Asheeqa—(f)—lovable, sweet heart, love
Asheerah—(f)—rich
Asheera—(f)—rich, favourable
Asheer—(m)—favourable
Asheeyana—(f)—house, nest
Ashefa—(f)—princess, courageous
Ashel—(f)—god risen from ashes
Asherah—(f)—queen of heaven, grove
Ashera—(f)—unique, divine aura
Asher—(m)—favourable, blessed, fortunate
Ashe—(f)—make you happy

Ashfaaq—(m)—compassionate
Ashfahaan—(m)—one with divine wisdom
Ashfahan—(m)—one with divine wisdom
Ashfah—(f)—princess
Ashfakh—(m)—blessed
Ashfak—(m)—blessed
Ashfana—(f)—success
Ashfan—(m)—successful
Ashfaque—(m)—noble prince
Ashfaqur—(m)—one with divine wisdom
Ashfaq—(m)—noble prince, kindness, compassion
Ashfar—(m)—one with divine wisdom
Ashfa—(f)—princess
Ashfeena—(f)—unique, divine aura
Ashfeen—(m)—success
Ashfeeq—(m)—noble king, prince
Ashfee—(m)—nice
Ashfia—(f)—booster, supporter, storm
Ashfina—(f)—success
Ashfin—(m)—one with divine wisdom
Ashfiqa—(f)—pride, love
Ashfiya—(f)—pure, ruling the sky, helping
Ashhaad—(m)—witness, plural of shahid
Ashhal—(m)—having bluish black eyes
Ashhar—(m)—famous, popular
Ashha—(f)—pour
Ashhub—(m)—shooting stars
Ashiah—(f)—hope, woman, life
Ashiah—(m)—shelter
Ashiana—(f)—shelter, home, house
Ashia—(f)—woman, life, lively
Ashiba—(f)—lucky
Ashida—(f)—blessings
Ashidha—(f)—sky, love, blessings
Ashid—(m)—lord of light, sun
Ashifa—(f)—courageous, princess
Ashiff—(m)—courageous, bold
Ashifur—(m)—independent

Ashif—(m)—bold, courageous, forgiveness
Ashika—(f)—one without sorrow, mercury
Ashikur—(m)—one with divine wisdom
Ashik—(m)—lover, romeo, sweetheart
Ashila—(f)—unique, divine aura
Ashil—(m)—one with divine wisdom
Ashima—(f)—limitless
Ashim—(m)—endless, limitless
Ashina—(f)—she wolf, successful
Ashin—(m)—beautiful, lion, free like a ocean
Ashiqah—(f)—lover, adorer
Ashiqali—(m)—adorer of ali
Ashiqa—(f)—sweet heart, beloved, romantic
Ashiqmuhammad—(m)—adorer of the prophet muhammad
Ashique—(f)—lover, beloved
Ashique—(m)—beloved
Ashiqullah—(m)—lover of allah
Ashiq—(m)—lover, variant of aashiq
Ashiraf—(m)—one with divine wisdom
Ashirah—(f)—female, tenth
Ashira—(f)—wealthy
Ashir—(m)—living
Ashiyaa—(f)—spiritual, spirit of ash tree
Ashiyane—(f)—unique, divine aura
Ashiya—(f)—spirit of ash tree, spiritual
Ashi—(f)—evening, night, reward, smile
Ashja—(m)—more courageous, braver
Ashkaf—(m)—one with divine wisdom
Ashkar—(m)—clear
Ashkeen—(f)—unique, divine aura
Ashlam—(m)—peace, one who salutes
Ashlan—(m)—ash tree
Ashla—(f)—meadow of ash trees
Ashleena—(f)—meadow of ash trees
Ashliah—(f)—essence, ancestor
Ashlina—(f)—dream, petal, meadow of ash trees
Ashlin—(m)—meadow of ash trees
Ashmaan—(f)—heaven

Ashmaan—(m)—heaven
Ashmal—(m)—perfect, complete
Ashman—(m)—son of the sun, sky, stony
Ashmath—(m)—correct path, straight path
Ashma—(f)—rock, mountain of rocks, strong
Ashmeena—(f)—positive thinker
Ashmeen—(f)—positive thinker
Ashmeen—(m)—victory
Ashmeerah—(f)—flower of heaven
Ashmeera—(f)—flower of heaven
Ashmera—(f)—flower of heaven
Ashmida—(f)—unique, divine aura
Ashmila—(f)—derived from ashma
Ashmil—(m)—derived from ashma
Ashmina—(f)—rays of sun light
Ashmin—(f)—unique, divine aura
Ashmin—(m)—rays of sun light
Ashmirah—(f)—heaven's flower
Ashmira—(f)—heaven's flower
Ashmir—(m)—one with divine wisdom
Ashmiya—(f)—jasmine
Ashmiza—(f)—joyful
Ashmy—(f)—admirable
Ashnad—(m)—swimmer
Ashna—(f)—friend, beloved, desire
Ashna—(m)—a friend
Ashnoor—(f)—like a diamond, beautiful
Ashour—(m)—strongest assyrian king
Ashpak—(m)—one with divine wisdom
Ashpiya—(f)—unique, divine aura
Ashqar—(m)—most beautiful
Ashqa—(f)—beloved
Ashqeen—(m)—loved one
Ashraan—(m)—powerful
Ashraf-ali—(m)—most honourable
Ashraf-jahan—(f)—noblest of the world
Ashrafali—(m)—most honourable
Ashrafa—(f)—without grief, cultured

Ashrafdeen—(m)—one with divine wisdom
Ashraff—(m)—without grief, cultured
Ashrafia—(f)—noble
Ashrafiya—(f)—gold coins
Ashrafi—(f)—noble
Ashrafjahan—(f)—noblest of the world
Ashrafulla—(m)—best of the creation
Ashraful—(m)—best of the creation
Ashrafus-sadat—(m)—noble
Ashrafussadat—(m)—most noble of the sayyids
Ashraf—(f)—honourable, nobler or noblest
Ashraf—(m)—cultured, without grief
Ashrah—(f)—happiness, queen of heaven
Ashrat—(m)—mark, sign
Ashra—(f)—happiness
Ashreena—(f)—beautiful, one who is graceful
Ashreen—(f)—powerful, one who is graceful
Ashref—(m)—without grief, honourable
Ashrful—(m)—one with divine wisdom
Ashrifa—(f)—most honourable
Ashriffa—(f)—unique, divine aura
Ashrif—(m)—without grief, cultured
Ashrimah—(f)—rich, beloved one, precious gift
Ashrina—(f)—beautiful, one who is graceful
Ashriya—(f)—modernist, one who gives shelter
Ashrofi—(f)—noble, without grief, honourable
Ashruf—(m)—without grief, cultured
Ashtad—(m)—justice, judge, rectitude
Ashtalfa—(f)—fragrance of a heaven flower
Ashtar—(m)—weapon, sword
Ashvak—(m)—blessed, victorious
Ashwak—(m)—plenty
Ashwan—(m)—prosperity, fame
Ashwaq—(f)—love, affections
Ashwaq—(m)—horse
Ashwa—(f)—horse
Ashwa—(m)—brave, strength like a horse
Ashwida—(f)—unique, divine aura

Ashya—(f)—pious
Asiah—(f)—woman, life, eastern sunrise
Asianne—(f)—the rising sun
Asian—(f)—like a star
Asia—(f)—east, woman, resurrection
Asib—(m)—one with divine wisdom
Asidin—(m)—one with divine wisdom
Asid—(m)—great
Asiefa—(f)—spotless, pure, virtuous
Asief—(m)—one with divine wisdom
Asiem—(m)—limitless, endless
Asifah—(f)—storm, tempest, hurricane
Asifa—(f)—pure, spotless, upright
Asifuddin—(m)—one with divine wisdom
Asiful—(m)—one with divine wisdom
Asifur—(m)—one with divine wisdom
Asif—(f)—tempest, storm, honest
Asif—(m)—forgiveness, pure, clean, gather
Asik—(m)—dagger, sharp
Asilah—(f)—pure, noble origin
Asila—(f)—original
Asil—(f)—pure, true, honest, noble, smooth
Asil—(m)—high-born, pure, pristine
Asimah—(f)—one who protects, chaste woman
Asima—(f)—defender, protector, virtuous
Asim—(m)—limitless, guardian, defender
Asina—(f)—pride, popularity
Asina—(m)—an elamite rebel
Asin—(f)—pure
Asin—(m)—pure
Asique—(m)—sharp, dagger
Asiq—(m)—sharp, dagger
Asira—(f)—honoured, preferred, chosen
Asira—(m)—honoured, chosen, preferred
Asiruddin—(m)—honoured person of the religion
Asir—(m)—selected, chosen, sun
Asiyah—(f)—world of making
Asiyana—(f)—beautiful home

Asiya—(m)—bright, pillar, mediator
Asjad—(f)—gold, jewel
Asjad—(m)—jewel, gold
Asja—(f)—eastern sunrise
Asjeah—(f)—prayer of god
Asjid—(m)—one who prays to god
Askan—(m)—spear of the wood of the ash tree
Askari—(m)—soldier
Askar—(m)—army, warrior
Aska—(f)—pious
Aska—(m)—pious
Askhar—(m)—alphabet
Askina—(f)—unique, divine aura
Aslaan—(m)—one with divine wisdom
Aslaha—(f)—purity, nobility of descent
Aslam—(m)—peace, greeting, safer, freer
Aslan—(m)—the king of lion
Asla—(m)—this name was the name of asfa
Asleena—(f)—dream, symbol of fire
Asleen—(f)—symbol of fire, dream
Asliah—(f)—essence, ancestor, honest
Aslima—(f)—unique, divine aura
Aslin—(f)—beautiful, daughter of god
Asliraf—(m)—honourable
Asli—(f)—sincere, original, pure, genuine
Asmaan—(f)—value, price
Asmaan—(m)—the sky
Asmaa—(f)—sky, shine like the star, names
Asmaa—(m)—sky, higher, precious
Asmabi—(f)—unique, divine aura
Asmah—(f)—brave, bold
Asmaira—(f)—beautiful butterfly
Asman—(f)—sky
Asman—(m)—the sky
Asmara—(f)—beautiful butterfly
Asmara—(m)—love
Asmar—(m)—deep yellow, tawny
Asmath—(f)—friendly, pure, clean

Asmath—(m)—one with divine wisdom
Asmat—(f)—pure, clean
Asmat—(m)—clean, pure
Asmau—(f)—unique, divine aura
Asmaya—(f)—unique, divine aura
Asmayra—(f)—beautiful butterfly
Asma—(f)—sky, excellent, precious, higher
Asma—(m)—sky, he was ibn harithah alaslami
Asmeena—(f)—unique, divine aura
Asmeen—(f)—appropriate heart, sweet-smelling
Asmeera—(f)—heaven's flower
Asmeer—(m)—one with divine wisdom
Asmia—(f)—guardian
Asmihna—(f)—unique, divine aura
Asmila—(f)—powerful
Asmil—(m)—one with divine wisdom
Asmina—(f)—jasmine
Asmin—(f)—god's gift, variant of jasmine
Asmin—(m)—one with divine wisdom
Asmira—(f)—heaven's flower
Asmir—(m)—greater than the sky
Asmiya—(f)—jasmine
Asmi—(f)—i am present, nature
Asnaat—(f)—holy
Asnaf—(m)—one with divine wisdom
Asnam—(f)—idols, statues
Asnan—(m)—one with divine wisdom
Asnat—(f)—god gifted
Asna—(f)—voracious, lamb, light
Asneena—(f)—unique, divine aura
Asneeya—(f)—brightness
Asnia—(f)—brightness
Asnika—(f)—fulfilling desire
Asniyah—(f)—brightness, beautiful
Asniya—(f)—brightness, beautiful
Asni—(f)—a flash of light
Asnu—(f)—precious
Asooda—(m)—prosperous, jolly, happy

Aspak—(m)—king
Asphak—(m)—kind hearten, compassion
Asqan—(m)—one with divine wisdom
Asqara—(f)—small daughter
Asraa—(f)—shelter, pure
Asrafil—(m)—one with divine wisdom
Asrafi—(f)—without grief, shine, diamond
Asraful—(m)—grateful
Asraf—(m)—without grief
Asrah—(f)—pure, sincere
Asran—(m)—lion
Asrar—(f)—secrets, mysteries
Asrar—(m)—mysteries, secret
Asrat—(m)—third
Asra—(f)—generous, nobler
Asra—(m)—travel by night
Asreena—(f)—beautiful angel
Asreen—(f)—appropriate
Asrin—(f)—beautiful angel
Asrin—(m)—one with divine wisdom
Asriyah—(f)—modernist
Asruf—(m)—without grief
Asrul—(m)—lion heart, unbeatable
Assab—(m)—gazelle
Assadulla—(m)—title of ali, lion of allah
Assad—(m)—lion
Assaf—(m)—virtues
Assamad—(m)—one with divine wisdom
Assan—(m)—waterfall
Assar—(m)—to respond, fortunate, blessed
Assa—(f)—fair, beautiful goddess
Assem—(m)—great one
Assia—(f)—protect
Assifa—(f)—unique, divine aura
Assim—(m)—great one
Asslam—(m)—peace, greeting, freer
Assma—(f)—higher, sky
Assyria—(f)—calming

Astaan—(m)—gateway, threshold
Astan—(m)—threshold, gateway
Asta—(f)—ambassador, of the stars
Asub—(f)—queen bee
Asucena—(f)—lily
Asuman—(m)—lord of vital breaths
Aswaada—(f)—unique, divine aura
Aswab—(m)—more correct, sensible, better
Aswad—(m)—islamic name, black stone in moka
Aswah—(f)—gracious, light
Aswana—(f)—unique, divine aura
Aswana—(m)—one with divine wisdom
Aswar—(m)—horse rider, brave
Aswat—(m)—stone of heaven
Aswa—(f)—light, gracious
Aswiya—(f)—unique, divine aura
Ata-al-rahman—(m)—gift of the beneficent
Ata-allah—(m)—gift of allah
Ataallah—(m)—gift of god
Ataalrahman—(m)—gift of the beneficent
Ataa—(f)—gift from god, gift
Ataa—(m)—gift, favour
Atabuk—(m)—protector, guard
Atafah—(f)—affectionate, compassionate
Ataf—(m)—compassionate
Atah—(m)—gift
Atalaya—(f)—guard, watch tower
Atallah—(m)—gift of allah, god gift
Atal—(m)—admiring, immovable, attractive
Atanaz—(f)—father's sweetheart, daddy's girl
Atasee—(f)—common flax, linseed
Atash—(m)—fire
Ataubaq—(m)—handsome, beautiful, helpful
Ataul-mustafa—(m)—a gift of allah
Ataullah—(m)—gift of allah, god gift
Ataulla—(m)—god gift, gift of allah
Ataur-rahman—(m)—gift of the merciful, allah
Ataurrahman—(m)—gift of the merciful allah

Atayat—(f)—gifts, things given freely
Ataya—(f)—bestowal, gift, present
Ataya—(m)—gifts, presents, god helps
Ata—(f)—gift from god, discontinue
Ata—(m)—gift, one of twins, from fante
Ateeba—(f)—unique, divine aura
Ateeb—(m)—very pious, pure, virtuous
Ateefah—(f)—affectionate, compassionate
Ateefa—(f)—affection, sympathy
Ateef—(f)—affectionate, compassionate
Ateef—(m)—kind
Ateeqah—(f)—ancient
Ateeqa—(f)—ancient, noble, feminine of atiq
Ateequa—(f)—ancient, independent
Ateeque—(m)—one with divine wisdom
Ateeq—(f)—most ancient, noble
Ateeq—(m)—freed, liberated, ancient
Ateesha—(f)—supreme, derived from ateesh
Ateet—(m)—past
Ateeyah—(f)—gift, present, gift of god
Atefa—(f)—compassion
Atefeh—(f)—kind-hearted, affection, emotion
Atef—(m)—good, king, kind, honest
Atem—(m)—one with divine wisdom
Atfah—(f)—affection, compassion
Atfat—(f)—affection, compassion
Atfat—(m)—affection, compassion
Athaarah—(f)—trace, remnant
Athari—(f)—unique, divine aura
Atharna—(f)—the things we left behind
Atharunnisa—(f)—most pious among female
Athar—(f)—pure, mark, print, effect
Athar—(m)—mark, print, very pious, pure
Athazaz—(m)—unknown, mystery, maze
Atheefa—(f)—unique, divine aura
Atheef—(m)—compassionate
Atheeka—(f)—liberated, ancient
Atheek—(m)—old name for kahbathullah

Atheel—(f)—noble, deep-rooted, high in status
Atheel—(m)—noble, deep-rooted, high in status
Atheena—(f)—god's friend
Atheeqa—(f)—noble, ancient
Atheeq—(m)—old name for kahbathullah
Atheera—(f)—fragrance
Atheer—(m)—light reflected from a sword
Ather—(m)—the active one
Athfa—(f)—affectionate, sympathetic
Athier—(m)—lion hearted
Athifa—(f)—love, sympathetic, affectionate
Athif—(m)—knowledgeable
Athiha—(f)—kind, pure hearted
Athilah—(f)—firmly established, deep-rooted
Athila—(f)—truth, deep-rooted
Athil—(m)—firmly rooted
Athina—(f)—atina greek goddess
Athique—(m)—one with divine wisdom
Athirah—(f)—flower, glorious
Athir—(f)—favoured, preferred
Athir—(m)—favoured, preferred
Athmah—(f)—narrator of hadith
Athmane—(m)—one with divine wisdom
Athraa—(f)—un pierced pearl
Athyab—(m)—scrupulously clean, refined
Athya—(f)—kind
Atiah—(m)—ready
Atia—(f)—ancient
Atiba—(f)—the most ambitious
Atief—(m)—kind
Atifah—(f)—affectionate, compassionate
Atifat—(f)—kindness, sympathy
Atifa—(f)—empathy, affectionate, sympathetic
Atifeh—(f)—affection
Atifi—(f)—affectionate, loving
Atif—(f)—generous, one with kind heart
Atif—(m)—generous, sympathetic
Atikah—(f)—generous, noble, clear, virgin

Atika—(f)—generous, noble, beautiful
Atikul—(m)—one with divine wisdom
Atikur—(m)—one with divine wisdom
Atik—(m)—world, good, innocent
Atim—(m)—light
Atiqah—(f)—beautiful
Atiqa—(f)—emancipated, a beautiful lady
Atiqua—(f)—independent
Atique—(m)—old valuable thing
Atiqullah—(m)—one with divine wisdom
Atiqur—(m)—one with divine wisdom
Atiq—(f)—most ancient, noble
Atiq—(m)—independent
Atirah—(f)—fragrant
Atira—(f)—pray
Atira—(m)—prayer
Atir—(m)—fragrant, aromatic
Atisa—(f)—unique, divine aura
Atith—(m)—sunday, sunny day
Atiu—(m)—the eldest, famous
Atiyaa—(f)—gift, something given freely
Atiyab—(m)—refined, scrupulously clean
Atiyah—(f)—gift, present
Atiya—(f)—gift from allah, present, gift
Atiyq—(m)—noble
Atiyyaat—(f)—gifts, thing given freely
Atiyyatullah—(f)—gift from god
Atiyya—(f)—gift
Atlantis—(m)—silken
Atman—(m)—the self
Atoofa—(f)—unique, divine aura
Atoof—(m)—compassionate, sympathetic
Atoosa—(f)—daughter of the first king of iran
Atqaa—(f)—conscious of god, appropriate, virtuous
Atqaa—(m)—conscious of god
Atqa—(f)—pious, honest, near to god
Atqa—(m)—most god conscious, fearing
Atqiya—(f)—religious

Atsham—(m)—one with divine wisdom
Attaar—(m)—perfumer, perfume seller
Attaboak—(m)—defender, teacher, guide
Attaf—(m)—affectionate, compassionate
Attar—(m)—perfume, frangrance
Attaullah—(m)—one with divine wisdom
Attawah—(f)—generous
Atthifa—(f)—unique, divine aura
Attiah—(m)—god is helper
Attia—(f)—gift
Attiqa—(f)—a beautiful lady, emancipated
Attiq—(m)—old
Attiullah—(m)—one with divine wisdom
Atufaah—(f)—kind woman
Atufah—(f)—kind woman
Atufa—(f)—kind, merciful
Atuf—(f)—affectionate, kind hearted
Atuf—(m)—affectionate, kind-hearted
Atun—(f)—educator, teacheress
Atushi—(f)—a flower name
Atwaar—(f)—forms, shapes, stages, states
Atwaar—(m)—shape - form, states, phases
Atwar—(f)—shapes, phases, stages, forms
Atwar—(m)—shapes - forms, states, phases
Atyaaf—(f)—thoughts, images in the mind
Atyab—(f)—pure, pious
Atyab—(m)—scrupulously clean, refined
Atyaf—(f)—fantasies
Atyia—(f)—first born daughter
Aubeidulla—(m)—one with divine wisdom
Auday—(m)—one with divine wisdom
Auden—(m)—ancient, old friend, bold one
Audhy—(f)—going up
Aujah—(f)—fair, beautiful, pretty
Auj—(m)—zenith, climax
Auka—(f)—most guarding
Aula—(f)—superior one
Aula—(m)—another name for prophet muhammad

Aunullah—(m)—god's help
Aun—(m)—helping
Aurangzeb—(m)—a person befitting the throne
Aurang—(m)—a throne, wisdom, understanding
Auraq—(f)—dust-coloured, sand-coloured
Auraq—(m)—dust-coloured, sand-coloured
Aura—(f)—air, cloud, rain, wind
Aurelia—(f)—golden, wind, dawn, breeze
Aurin—(f)—bringer of light
Aurin—(m)—one with divine wisdom
Ausaaf—(m)—one with divine wisdom
Ausaf—(m)—qualities, virtues, merits
Ausaq—(f)—loads, the plural of wasq
Aushah—(f)—wife of prophet muhammad
Aushan—(m)—one with divine wisdom
Aus—(m)—to give, gift
Auzma—(f)—blessing of god
Auzmeena—(f)—unique, divine aura
Avaan—(m)—water
Avad—(m)—marvellous
Avaiz—(m)—one with divine wisdom
Avan—(f)—variant of awan, time, moment
Avan—(m)—water, joy, desire, pleasure
Avash—(m)—independent, free
Ava—(f)—a fulfilling sound, voice
Avea—(f)—my god, my father, strength
Aveed—(m)—purity
Aveen—(f)—beauty
Avej—(m)—fire
Aven—(m)—iniquity, force, riches, sorrow
Avez—(m)—fire
Avid—(m)—loving, sweet, cute
Avila—(f)—bird, strength, desired, sun rays
Avin—(m)—affection
Aviram—(m)—father of heights
Avira—(f)—bright, intelligent
Avir—(m)—great
Avita—(m)—life

Aviv—(m)—spring, young
Aviza—(f)—necklace
Avizeh—(f)—pendant
Avlok—(m)—enlightened, heaven
Awaan—(m)—helper, assistant
Awaar—(f)—rays of light, blossoms
Awaatif—(f)—feelings, sympathy, compassion
Awaaz—(m)—voice
Awabin—(m)—one who repent
Awab—(m)—one who always returns to god
Awadil—(m)—one who is fair
Awadini—(m)—eternal, everlasting
Awad—(m)—reward, compensation, kindness
Awaidia—(f)—visitor of the sick
Awaise—(m)—one with divine wisdom
Awaisha—(f)—one who are living well
Awaish—(m)—one who are living well
Awais—(m)—gifted, name of a saint
Awaiz—(m)—decorated, courageous
Awalmir—(m)—prime chief
Awal—(m)—first
Awamila—(f)—active, industrious
Awamil—(m)—active, effective
Awamira—(f)—long-lived
Awamiri—(m)—long-lived
Awamir—(m)—a town full of life - activity
Awanah—(m)—middle-aged, fierce
Awan—(m)—supporter, friend, somebody
Awara—(m)—winner, stroller
Awarif—(f)—intelligent, wise, knowledgeable
Awar—(m)—certain
Awasha—(f)—one who living well
Awatef—(f)—unique, divine aura
Awatif—(f)—emotions, passions, instincts
Awatif—(m)—emotions, passions, instincts
Awayeda—(f)—guide
Awayed—(m)—habit, something accustomed to
Awaz—(m)—sound

Awbia—(f)—one who repents
Awbi—(f)—one who repents
Awbi—(m)—one who repents
Awb—(f)—repentance
Awb—(m)—repentance
Awdaq—(f)—friendly, intimate, genial
Awdaq—(m)—friendly, intimate, genial
Awda—(f)—designation
Awdiya—(f)—valley, plural of waadi, valley
Awd—(m)—to return, to go back somewhere
Aweer—(m)—excellent
Aweeza—(f)—pure
Awej—(m)—fire
Awelijama—(m)—man of somali
Awen—(m)—somebody
Awesta—(f)—the holy book of zarasthura
Awez—(m)—fire
Awfaa—(f)—most faithful, fulfilling
Awfaa—(m)—faithful, more fulfilling
Awfa—(f)—most faithful, more fulfilling
Awfa—(m)—true to higher promise, indeed
Awf—(m)—a plant with a nice smell
Awhad—(m)—unique, peerless
Awish—(m)—pray
Awka—(f)—unique, divine aura
Awlaa—(f)—more deserving
Awlaki—(m)—one with divine wisdom
Awlan—(m)—one who returns often
Awla—(f)—more deserving, worthier
Awla—(m)—more deserving, worthier
Awliyaa—(f)—allies, friends
Awliyaa—(m)—allie, friend
Awliya—(f)—friends, allies
Awliya—(m)—allie, friend
Awlya—(f)—supporter, close friend, allies
Awlya—(m)—close friends
Awmari—(m)—long-lived
Awmar—(m)—long-lived

Awni—(m)—helper, supporter
Awn—(m)—support, to help, assist
Awqa—(f)—most guarding
Awrad—(m)—rose-coloured, rosy
Awsam—(f)—badges of honour
Awsam—(m)—badges of honour
Awsat—(m)—middle one, medium, most moderate
Awsima—(f)—variant of awisma
Aws—(m)—name of a tribe in madinah
Awtaad—(f)—pillars, stakes, poles
Awtaad—(m)—stake, poles, pillar
Awtad—(f)—stakes, pillars, poles
Awtad—(m)—stakes, poles, pillar
Awwaab—(m)—great repenter to god
Awwab—(m)—returning to allah
Awwadi—(m)—dutiful, compassionate
Awwad—(m)—compensation, reward, kind
Awwalan—(f)—those who are ahead, first
Awwalan—(m)—those who are ahead, first
Awwal—(m)—great of the world
Awwazah—(f)—giver of restitution, recompense
Awwaz—(m)—giver of replacement
Awzha—(f)—the moon
Ayaab—(m)—one with divine wisdom
Ayaaf—(m)—honest
Ayaaj—(m)—night breeze
Ayaana—(f)—innocent, pretty flower
Ayaani—(f)—politeness
Ayaan—(m)—first ray of the sun, nature
Ayaash—(m)—gold
Ayaat—(f)—many signs and proofs
Ayaat—(m)—sign, verse of the quran
Ayaaz—(m)—brave, courageous, respected
Ayab—(m)—one with divine wisdom
Ayad—(m)—memory
Ayaf—(m)—perfectionist
Ayah—(f)—sign of god, clear evidence, clue
Ayaiyaz—(m)—one with divine wisdom

Ayaj—(m)—night breeze
Ayamin—(f)—blessed ones, fortunate ones
Ayamin—(m)—blessed ones, fortunate ones
Ayam—(f)—days
Ayam—(m)—does not die
Ayanah—(f)—beautiful blossom, innocent one
Ayanat—(f)—unique, divine aura
Ayana—(f)—goddess saraswati, ethiopian
Ayana—(m)—innocent one, beautiful blossom
Ayani—(f)—politeness
Ayanna—(f)—innocent, beautiful flower, royal
Ayann—(f)—colourful sound, design
Ayann—(m)—speed, bright, gift of god
Ayan—(f)—gift of god, bright, the sun
Ayan—(m)—movement
Ayarin—(f)—unique, divine aura
Ayasha—(f)—little one
Ayasha—(m)—one with divine wisdom
Ayash—(m)—life, long life, gold
Ayasuddin—(m)—honour of the religion
Ayas—(m)—gold
Ayath—(f)—verse, proof, sign
Ayath—(m)—mark, sign
Ayatollah—(m)—sign of god
Ayatullah—(m)—sign of allah
Ayat—(f)—mark, sign, proof
Ayat—(m)—mark, sign
Ayaza—(f)—dear one, daughter of hazrat ali
Ayazuddin—(m)—honour of the religion
Ayaz—(f)—cool breeze
Aybak—(m)—ibn-aybak was a leading historian
Aydaan—(m)—one with divine wisdom
Aydah—(f)—helpful, ornament, visitor
Aydania—(f)—tall - slender
Aydan—(f)—unique, divine aura
Aydan—(m)—fire, mystery, superior
Ayda—(f)—in the moon, benefit, returning
Aydeen—(m)—born of fire

Aydee—(f)—capability, power, strength, hands
Aydee—(m)—hands, power, strength, capability
Ayden—(m)—enlightened, bright, strength
Aydhin—(m)—bright
Aydin—(f)—power, strength, illuminated
Aydin—(m)—educated, illuminated, clear
Aydi—(f)—hands, strength, power
Aydrin—(m)—from the adriatic
Ayd—(f)—strength, power
Ayd—(m)—strength, power
Ayeasha—(f)—successes, woman
Ayeaza—(f)—pretty, beautiful, wonderful
Ayeda—(f)—returning, in the moon
Ayed—(m)—visitor of sick, returner
Ayeena—(f)—mirror, glass
Ayeesah—(f)—woman, life, alive
Ayeesa—(f)—woman, life, alive
Ayeeshah—(f)—woman, life
Ayeesha—(f)—woman, life, alive, living
Ayeeza—(f)—obedient, beautiful, pretty
Ayefa—(f)—life path
Ayeh—(f)—sign, distinct, prophet's daughter
Ayeisah—(f)—woman, life
Ayeisa—(f)—woman, life
Ayeishah—(f)—woman, life
Ayeisha—(f)—woman, life, lively female
Ayema—(f)—unique, divine aura
Ayena—(f)—innocent one
Ayerah—(f)—respectable
Ayera—(f)—respectable
Ayesah—(f)—alive, woman, life
Ayesa—(f)—cute - soft, unique
Ayeshah—(f)—alive, one who lives
Ayesha—(f)—woman, life, small one, simple
Ayesha—(m)—life
Ayessa—(f)—woman, life, successes, small one
Ayessha—(f)—small one, successes, woman, life
Ayet—(f)—bird sparrow, versie of quran

Ayezah—(f)—hazrat ali second wife's daughter
Ayeza—(f)—pretty, obedient, beautiful
Ayfan—(m)—forgive
Ayham—(m)—brave, noble, imaginary
Ayhan—(m)—king of the moon
Ayida—(f)—returning, in the moon
Ayidin—(m)—strength, illuminated, power
Ayiesha—(f)—alive, woman, beautiful
Ayika—(f)—flower petal
Ayina—(f)—mirror, beauty
Ayinde—(m)—we gave praises and he came
Ayiq—(m)—flowering plant known as larkspur
Ayira—(f)—honourable, respectful
Ayisah—(f)—woman, life
Ayisa—(f)—woman, life, journey
Ayisha-nasrin—(f)—flower of heaven
Ayishaa—(f)—unique, divine aura
Ayishah—(f)—woman, life, prosperous
Ayishath—(f)—unique, divine aura
Ayisha—(f)—star, woman, life, lively female
Ayish—(m)—alive, living-well
Ayiza—(f)—dear one, clever, noble
Ayjaz—(m)—favour, karma
Ayka—(f)—flower petal
Ayk—(m)—dawn
Aylah—(f)—entire, little cinders
Aylan—(m)—shield, moon, light (turkish)
Ayleena—(f)—messenger of god
Ayleen—(f)—hazelnut bird, messenger of god
Aylena—(f)—entire, true to, little cinders
Aylia—(f)—angel on paradise
Aylina—(f)—beautiful
Aylin—(f)—moon halo
Aymaan—(m)—lucky
Aymaa—(f)—princess
Ayman—(f)—gift of god, fearless, blessed
Ayman—(m)—lucky, righteous
Ayma—(f)—princess

Aymeen—(m)—fortunate
Aymen—(f)—sacred, brave, old name of arabia
Aymen—(m)—right hand side, blessed
Aymil—(m)—rivalling, imitating
Aymin—(f)—fortunate, blessed one
Aymin—(m)—fortunate, blessed one
Aymi—(f)—beloved
Ayn-ul-ghurr—(m)—the chief of the chosen one
Ayn-un-naeem—(m)—the spring of blessing
Aynah—(f)—beautiful eyes, mirror
Aynan—(m)—two springs, fountains
Aynaz—(f)—beautiful like the moon
Ayna—(f)—mirror, beautiful eyes
Aynoor—(f)—moonlight, beautiful, gorgeous
Aynuddin—(m)—source of the faith (islam)
Aynul-hasan—(m)—hasan like
Aynul-hayat—(f)—fountain of life
Aynul-hayat—(m)—fountain of life
Aynulhasan—(m)—hasan like
Aynulhayat—(f)—fountain of life
Aynulhayat—(m)—fountain of life
Aynun-nahr—(f)—source of the spring
Aynun-naim—(m)—fountain of blessing
Aynunnahar—(f)—lioness, source of the spring
Aynunnahr—(f)—source of the spring
Aynunnaim—(m)—fountain of blessing
Aynun—(f)—unique, divine aura
Ayn—(f)—source of the spring
Ayn—(m)—test, source, pure
Ayon—(m)—god gift, way, speed, path
Ayoob—(m)—messenger, a prophet's name
Ayoon—(f)—eyes, active waterfall
Ayoon—(m)—active waterfall
Ayoosh—(f)—living, content, long-lived
Ayoub—(m)—job, penitent
Ayoun—(m)—eyes, spring water in heaven
Ayrah—(f)—vision filler, respectable, noble
Ayra—(f)—respectable, noble, vision filler

Ayreen—(f)—fiery, made of fire
Ayrene—(f)—holy one
Ayren—(m)—mountain of strength, enlightened
Ayrin—(f)—princess, beautiful, fiery, soft
Ayrin—(m)—one with divine wisdom
Aysaa—(f)—beauty, obedient
Aysan—(m)—an act of kindness
Aysar—(m)—easier, prosperous, living better
Aysa—(f)—obedient
Aysa—(m)—precious
Aysel—(f)—moon stream, moonlight
Ayser—(m)—wealthy, easy in dealing
Ayse—(f)—peace
Ayshaa—(f)—woman, also spelt as aysha, aisha
Ayshabi—(f)—unique, divine aura
Ayshah—(f)—wife of the holy prophet
Aysham—(f)—fragrance, practical
Ayshan—(m)—in gods grace
Aysha—(f)—woman, life
Ayshea—(f)—one who lives, alive
Ayshe—(f)—beauty
Ayshia—(f)—unique, divine aura
Ayshin—(f)—lightning, beautiful
Ayshu—(f)—lively, enjoy life
Aysiah—(f)—unique, divine aura
Aysian—(f)—asia
Aysia—(f)—one who lives, alive
Ayska—(f)—lively
Ayslin—(f)—vision, dream
Aytza—(f)—one who lives, alive
Ayubkhan—(m)—mohammed
Ayub—(m)—king of patience, name of a god
Ayuf—(m)—perfectionist
Ayumi—(f)—pace, walk
Ayunda—(f)—older sister
Ayuni—(f)—eyes
Ayun—(f)—eyes
Ayup—(m)—wealth

Ayusha—(f)—life, life span
Ayush—(m)—life span, long lived, long life
Ayuub—(m)—one with divine wisdom
Ayvah—(f)—lively
Ayva—(f)—variant of ava, lively
Ayyaam—(f)—days
Ayyaam—(m)—days
Ayyad—(m)—powerful person
Ayyah—(f)—a verse in the quran
Ayyam—(f)—days, plural of yawm (day)
Ayyam—(m)—days, plural of yawm (day)
Ayyan—(m)—gift of god
Ayyashi—(m)—one who lives well
Ayyash—(m)—bread-seller
Ayyaz—(m)—courageous, enduring, brave
Ayyoob—(m)—a biblical prophet's name
Ayyubia—(f)—form of ayyub
Ayyubi—(m)—one who is patient, humble
Ayyub—(m)—one who asks for forgiveness
Ayzaad—(m)—one with divine wisdom
Ayzaan—(m)—goodness
Ayzah—(f)—unique, divine aura
Ayzal—(m)—the beginning, gift of god
Ayzam—(m)—one with divine wisdom
Ayzan—(m)—morning
Ayza—(f)—daughter of hazrat ali
Ayzel—(m)—noble
Ayzen—(m)—complete, powerful
Ayzin—(f)—complete
Ayzin—(m)—powerful, strong, complete
Az-zahra—(f)—excellent and smart
Azaad—(f)—care free
Azaad—(m)—liberated, free
Azaaf—(m)—one with divine wisdom
Azaam—(m)—submission, prostration
Azaan—(f)—allah's call for prayer, powerful
Azaan—(m)—powerful, strength
Azaar—(m)—one with divine wisdom

Azaa—(f)—a must have, right, courage
Azab—(m)—sword, pleasant, name of quantum
Azada—(m)—born free, free
Azadeh—(f)—dry earth, detached
Azad—(m)—free, independence, liberated
Azahara—(f)—unique, divine aura
Azahar—(m)—great
Azahin—(m)—one with divine wisdom
Azahra—(f)—excellent and smart
Azah—(f)—loved one, appropriate, successful
Azaiba—(f)—unique, divine aura
Azaien—(m)—decoration
Azaif—(m)—one with divine wisdom
Azaila—(f)—unique, divine aura
Azail—(m)—one with divine wisdom
Azain—(m)—decoration
Azaira—(f)—flowers
Azair—(m)—gift from god
Azajj—(f)—with long lashes
Azaj—(m)—one with divine wisdom
Azaka—(f)—unique, divine aura
Azalea—(f)—a flower, dry, withered flower
Azalfa—(f)—guiding to the right path, angel
Azalia—(f)—spared by jehovah, dry earth
Azaliya—(f)—pre-existence, eternal
Azali—(f)—eternal
Azaln—(m)—lion
Azal—(m)—the beginning
Azamat—(m)—one who is majestic, a proud man
Azama—(f)—blessing of allah
Azam—(f)—the powerful one
Azam—(m)—offspring, variant of a'zam
Azana—(f)—ultimate
Azania—(f)—one who is heard by god
Azaniya—(f)—one who is heard by god
Azan—(f)—call to prayer, announcement
Azan—(m)—muslim call for prayer
Azarah—(f)—fire

Azara—(f)—scarlet
Azara—(m)—one with divine wisdom
Azardeen—(m)—honesty, braveness
Azard—(m)—colour, paint
Azariah—(f)—helped by god
Azariah—(m)—one who hears the lord
Azarias—(m)—yahweh has helped
Azaria—(f)—helper of almighty
Azaria—(m)—god helps
Azarik—(m)—one with divine wisdom
Azariyah—(f)—helped by god
Azarrudin—(m)—honoured person of the religion
Azaruddeen—(m)—honoured person of the religion
Azaruddin—(m)—one with divine wisdom
Azarudeen—(m)—honoured person of the religion
Azarudheen—(m)—honoured person of the religion
Azarul—(m)—unbeatable, lion heart
Azarunnisa—(f)—unique, divine aura
Azar—(f)—flame, shine, fire
Azar—(m)—help, scarlet, fire, king
Azat—(m)—gazelle, -
Azayah—(f)—unique, divine aura
Azayiz—(f)—mighty, powerful, respected
Azazel—(m)—cancerous spirit, the scapegoat
Azaziah—(m)—strength of the lord
Azazzil—(m)—the leader of angels
Azaz—(m)—strong one, giving respect, honest
Aza—(f)—powerful, from kikuyu, comfort
Aza—(m)—comfort
Azbah—(f)—fresh, sweet
Azbak—(m)—independent, autonomous
Azban—(m)—fresh, sweet
Azba—(f)—sweet, bright, beautiful
Azbina—(f)—fresh
Azbin—(m)—one with divine wisdom
Azb—(m)—modern, wonder, astonishment
Azdine—(m)—hope of religion
Azeba—(f)—gift of god, bright, beautiful

Azeebah—(f)—fresh, sweet
Azeeb—(m)—fresh, sweet
Azeed—(m)—god gift
Azeefa—(f)—pure, spotless, heaven
Azeef—(m)—spotless, pure
Azeeka—(f)—unique, divine aura
Azeel—(m)—precious
Azeemah—(f)—great
Azeema—(f)—determination, firm will
Azeemuddin—(m)—one with divine wisdom
Azeemullah—(m)—one with divine wisdom
Azeemunisa—(f)—beautiful
Azeem—(m)—defender, greater, name of god
Azeena—(f)—beauty, beautiful, obedient
Azeen—(f)—beauty, patience
Azeera—(f)—a winner, unperceived pearl
Azeera—(m)—unperceived pearl
Azees—(m)—one with divine wisdom
Azeezah—(f)—esteemed, precious, cherished
Azeezat—(f)—unique, divine aura
Azeeza—(f)—esteemed, precious, cherished
Azeezullah—(m)—one with divine wisdom
Azeez—(f)—dearly, loveable, kind
Azeez—(m)—friend, dear, beloved, respected
Azelfa—(f)—guiding to the right path
Azel—(m)—noble
Azem—(m)—greatest, the powerful one
Azfaar—(m)—fragrances, victories
Azfar—(m)—most victorious
Azfer—(m)—leader
Azfreen—(f)—unique, divine aura
Azgar—(m)—devoted to lord
Azghan—(m)—faithful
Azgharr—(m)—one with divine wisdom
Azgor—(m)—devoted to lord
Azhaam—(m)—one with divine wisdom
Azhaan—(m)—abilities, geniuses, intellects
Azhaar—(f)—flowers, blossoms

Azhaar—(m)—flowers, blossoms
Azhaf—(m)—courageous, elite
Azhagesan—(m)—one with divine wisdom
Azhaire—(m)—bright, shining, light, famous
Azham—(m)—forest, tree, greatest
Azhana—(f)—fire
Azhan—(m)—plural of intelligent
Azharan—(m)—the sun and moon alike, to adopt
Azhara—(f)—flower, bright, shining
Azhare—(m)—luminous
Azharia—(f)—powerful, complete
Azhari—(m)—one with divine wisdom
Azharoddin—(m)—honoured person of the religion
Azharudheen—(m)—honoured person of the religion
Azharudin—(m)—one with divine wisdom
Azhar—(f)—flower, blossoms
Azhar—(m)—famous, luminous, brilliant
Azha—(f)—star
Azheran—(m)—famous
Azher—(m)—famous
Azhia—(f)—unique, divine aura
Azhib—(m)—one with divine wisdom
Azhin—(m)—one with divine wisdom
Azhir—(m)—intelligent, learned
Azhman—(m)—one with divine wisdom
Azhma—(f)—unique, divine aura
Azhmeer—(m)—clever, wise
Azhmyr—(m)—wise, clever
Azhra—(f)—bright, flower, shining
Aziah—(f)—hope
Aziam—(f)—unique, divine aura
Azian—(m)—true
Azia—(f)—the rising sun
Azibur—(m)—one with divine wisdom
Azibu—(f)—friend of allah
Azib—(m)—sweet, friend of allah
Azida—(f)—unique, divine aura
Aziem—(m)—protector

Aziez—(m)—powerful and beloved
Azifah—(f)—spotless, heaven
Azifa—(f)—heaven, spotless, pure
Azif—(m)—the close one
Azijul—(m)—one with divine wisdom
Azila—(f)—protector, guardian
Azil—(m)—protector, guardian
Azimah—(f)—unique, divine aura
Aziman—(f)—sky, heaven
Azima—(f)—defender, resolution, purpose
Azima—(m)—good in all thing
Azimoddin—(m)—defender, great, grand
Azimuddin—(m)—great, defender, grand
Azimullah—(m)—one with divine wisdom
Azimulla—(m)—strong as lion
Azimul—(m)—one with divine wisdom
Azimushan—(m)—one with divine wisdom
Azimushshan—(m)—of mighty concern
Azim—(m)—magnificent, defender, big, great
Azina—(f)—unique, divine aura
Azin—(f)—jewellery, accessories
Azin—(m)—decoration
Azirah—(f)—a rising star
Azira—(f)—a rising star
Azirin—(f)—happy
Azir—(m)—respectful
Azisa—(f)—unique, divine aura
Azita—(f)—name of an iranian princess
Aziyah—(f)—unique, divine aura
Aziyan—(m)—highly rank, famous, friendly
Aziya—(f)—loveable, peace
Azizah—(f)—dear, beloved, esteemed, precious
Aziza—(f)—a friend, precious, gorgeous
Azizi—(f)—precious one
Azizi—(m)—precious one, treasure, valuable
Azizuddin—(m)—one with divine wisdom
Azizul-haque—(m)—true, truth
Azizullah—(m)—dear to allah

Azizulla—(m)—dear to allah
Azizul—(m)—dear to allah
Azizunisa—(f)—unique, divine aura
Azizunnisa—(f)—unique, divine aura
Azizur—(m)—one with divine wisdom
Azizza—(f)—unique, divine aura
Azizz—(m)—powerful and beloved
Aziz—(f)—friendship
Aziz—(m)—powerful, friend, dear one
Azi—(f)—dry, sky blue, azure
Azka—(f)—pious, pure, very ingenious
Azka—(m)—purer, better, pious
Azkhar—(m)—one with divine wisdom
Azlaan—(m)—lion
Azlain—(m)—one with divine wisdom
Azlam—(m)—one with divine wisdom
Azlan—(m)—allah's lion, lion
Azleefa—(f)—unique, divine aura
Azleena—(f)—unique, divine aura
Azlia—(f)—reserved by god, dry earth
Azlida—(f)—unique, divine aura
Azlifa—(f)—knowledge
Azlina—(f)—beautiful
Azlin—(f)—sun, shine
Azliya—(f)—unique, divine aura
Azli—(m)—from the beginning
Azmaan—(m)—beautiful jewel
Azmadul—(m)—one with divine wisdom
Azmah—(f)—blessing of allah
Azmain—(m)—one with divine wisdom
Azmaira—(f)—unique, divine aura
Azmal—(m)—good, strong as lion
Azman—(m)—beautiful jewel, infinite
Azmaray—(m)—lion
Azmara—(f)—blue sea
Azmathulla—(m)—star
Azmath—(f)—unique, divine aura
Azmath—(m)—respect, star

Azmatullah—(m)—star
Azmat—(f)—fixed
Azmat—(m)—firm, fixed, the greatness, might
Azma—(f)—blessing of allah
Azmeel—(m)—one with divine wisdom
Azmeena—(f)—beautiful, shining
Azmeen—(f)—unique, divine aura
Azmeer-ali—(m)—pious, clever
Azmeer—(m)—clever, pious
Azmee—(f)—purposeful, determined
Azmera—(f)—harvest
Azmia—(f)—gold, brave, strong, courageous
Azmik—(f)—princess
Azmik—(m)—beautiful soul
Azmila—(f)—light
Azmil—(m)—light
Azminah—(f)—beautiful, fortunate
Azmina—(f)—beautiful, fortunate
Azmin—(f)—a star
Azmin—(m)—star
Azmira—(f)—unique, divine aura
Azmir—(m)—powerful, a leader
Azmiya—(f)—cute
Azmi—(f)—one who keeps his word
Azmi—(m)—one who keeps his word
Azmol—(m)—strong as lion, good
Azmul—(m)—one with divine wisdom
Azm—(m)—resolution, firmness of will
Aznad—(m)—one with divine wisdom
Aznan—(m)—one with divine wisdom
Azna—(f)—popularity, ultimate
Azneen—(f)—unique, divine aura
Azni—(f)—fire
Azny—(f)—a famed beauty
Azom—(m)—firm of will
Azoom—(m)—determined, firm of will
Azoora—(f)—clear blue sky
Azoor—(m)—one with divine wisdom

Azowa—(f)—unique, divine aura
Azqa—(f)—pure, pious, generous
Azraan—(m)—lion
Azraa—(f)—virgin (used for maryam, mary)
Azraa—(m)—chaste, one who is pure
Azrael—(m)—god's help, god is my help
Azraff—(m)—an elegant man
Azraf—(m)—more elegant, more graceful
Azrah—(f)—beautiful pearl in heaven
Azrah—(m)—chaste, one who is pure
Azranisar—(f)—unique, divine aura
Azran—(m)—one with divine wisdom
Azraq—(m)—blue
Azra—(f)—virgin, young, maiden, pious
Azra—(m)—pure
Azreef—(m)—one with divine wisdom
Azreena—(f)—lovable, happy
Azreen—(f)—lovable
Azrian—(m)—one with divine wisdom
Azriel—(m)—help of god, womanly
Azril—(m)—god is my aid
Azrina—(f)—unique, divine aura
Azrin—(f)—happy
Azrin—(m)—happy
Azriya—(f)—gracious, helper
Azruddin—(m)—honoured person of the religion
Azrudeen—(m)—honoured person of the religion
Azrul—(m)—one with divine wisdom
Azrun—(m)—one with divine wisdom
Azshar—(m)—one with divine wisdom
Azuan—(m)—creativity
Azubah—(f)—assisted, desolate, born on monday
Azuba—(f)—unique
Azucena—(f)—lily, madonna lily
Azududdawlah—(m)—strength of the state
Azududdin—(m)—support of religion islam
Azud—(m)—upper arm, strength, power
Azuleefa—(f)—unique, divine aura

Azulyfa—(f)—unique, divine aura
Azul—(m)—prince
Azuma—(f)—appropriate in all thing
Azumi—(f)—safe residence
Azurah—(f)—azure, sky blue
Azura—(f)—clear blue sky, sky blue
Azuriah—(m)—yahweh has helped, god's help
Azuria—(m)—aided by jehovah, god's help
Azur—(m)—assisted
Azusa—(f)—lily
Azusena—(f)—lily
Azvan—(m)—gold
Azvina—(f)—blessings of allah
Azvin—(m)—one with divine wisdom
Azwad—(m)—one with divine wisdom
Azwah—(f)—limelight, splendour
Azwan—(m)—one with divine wisdom
Azwar—(m)—beautiful face
Azwa—(f)—splendour, limelight
Azweena—(f)—beauty
Azwer—(m)—one with divine wisdom
Azwin—(m)—one with divine wisdom
Azyaan—(f)—plural of zayn, adornments
Azyaan—(m)—decorations
Azyaded—(f)—unique, divine aura
Azyan—(f)—adornments, decorations
Azyan—(m)—decorations, adornments
Azym—(m)—protector, defender
Azzaam—(m)—determined, resolved
Azzaan—(m)—one with divine wisdom
Azzaa—(f)—female gazelle, a variant of azzah
Azzahra—(f)—excellent and smart
Azzah—(f)—young female gazelle, young
Azzain—(m)—decoration
Azzam—(m)—the lord, almighty, determined
Azzann—(m)—prayer
Azzan—(m)—noble, excellent, lofty
Azzar—(m)—scarlet, fire

Azzat—(f)—gazelle, variant of azzah
Azzat—(m)—gazelle, variant of azzah
Azza—(f)—young female gazelle
Azzedine—(m)—one with divine wisdom
Azzedin—(m)—one with divine wisdom
Azzeza—(f)—respected, darling
Azzie—(f)—unique, divine aura
Azziza—(f)—mighty, a friend, precious
Azziz—(m)—liked
Azzi—(m)—one with divine wisdom

TWO

Arabic Baby Names—B

Baabar—(m)—lion, king of jungle

Baadar—(m)—derived from jujube tree

Baadir—(m)—shining

Baadiyah—(m)—name of a sahahiyyah

Baadi—(m)—distinct, evident, plain, clear

Baadshah—(m)—king

Baahir—(m)—dazzling, brilliant

Baahi—(m)—glorious, magnificent

Baakir—(m)—early, eldest

Baaligh—(m)—major

Baani—(m)—founder, originator

Baaqee—(m)—remaining, lasting

Baaqir—(m)—ever lasting

Baaqiyah—(f)—remaining, lasting

Baaqi—(m)—ever lasting, permanent, eternal

Baare—(m)—brilliant, superior, outstanding

Baariq—(m)—shining, lightning, bright

Baarizah—(f)—eminent, prominent

Baariz—(m)—visible, prominent, manifest

Baari—(m)—one of the names of god

Baarr—(m)—just, pious

Baar—(m)—just, pious

Baasha—(m)—he that seeks or lays waste

Baashir—(m)—bringer of good news, tidings

Baasid—(m)—great emperor
Baasil—(m)—brave, courageous
Baasima—(f)—smiling
Baasim—(m)—smiling
Baasiqaat—(f)—high, lofty - towering things
Baasir—(m)—seeing, wise
Baazighah—(f)—shining, radiant, rising
Baazigh—(m)—shining, radiant, rising
Baaz—(m)—falcon
Babajan—(m)—one with divine wisdom
Babak—(m)—name of the father of ardeshir
Babar—(m)—lion, king of jungle, bold
Babbar—(m)—tiger
Babber—(m)—brave, strong
Babeesh—(m)—one with divine wisdom
Baber—(m)—courageous, lion, powerful
Babgha—(m)—parrot
Babik—(m)—law
Babi—(m)—followers of the sufi saint baba
Babrak—(m)—little basilica flower
Babra—(m)—tiger
Babr—(m)—tiger
Babuddin—(m)—one with divine wisdom
Babul—(m)—a tree, gate of god, father
Baburao—(m)—one with divine wisdom
Babur—(m)—joy
Bab—(f)—from the gateway, foreign, gate
Bab—(m)—door, gate entrance, gateway
Bachar—(m)—one who is full of joy
Bachir—(m)—oldest son
Bachra—(m)—joy
Badai—(f)—wonder, marvel, plural of badia
Badariya—(f)—angel of god
Badarul—(m)—one with divine wisdom
Badarunnisa—(f)—full moon of the female
Badar—(m)—full moon, fresh, green
Badawiya—(f)—variant of badawi
Badawi—(m)—nomad

Badaya—(f)—beginnings, initiation, inception
Baddarudin—(m)—full moon of the faith
Baddar—(m)—early and on time, speedy
Badda—(m)—big heart
Baddrun-nisha—(f)—moon of female
Baddur—(f)—little full moon
Badeah—(f)—unique
Badeeah—(f)—astonishing, amazing, marvel
Badeea—(f)—inventor, creator
Badeeda—(f)—example, sample, specimen
Badeeh—(m)—wondrous
Badeel—(m)—replacement
Badeen—(m)—religious, faithful
Badee—(m)—wonderful, marvellous, unique
Badela—(m)—one with divine wisdom
Bader—(m)—full moon
Badhariya—(f)—angel of god
Badhil—(m)—one with divine wisdom
Badhira—(f)—full moon
Badi-al-zaman—(m)—the marvel of time
Badiah—(f)—unprecedented, amazing, admirable
Badialzaman—(m)—the marvel of time
Badia—(f)—unprecedented, amazing, admirable
Badiha—(f)—insight, perceptive faculty
Badilayn—(m)—substitutes, a plural of badeel
Badil—(f)—religious, pious
Badil—(m)—brave, generous
Badira—(f)—full moon
Badir—(m)—shining, full moon
Badiul-alam—(m)—unique in the world
Badiulalam—(m)—unique in the world
Badiullah—(m)—one with divine wisdom
Badiulla—(m)—one with divine wisdom
Badiuz-zaman—(m)—genius of the time
Badiuzzamaan—(m)—wonder of the age
Badiuzzaman—(m)—genius of the time
Badiuz—(m)—genius of the time
Badiyah—(f)—desert

Badiya—(f)—desert, unique
Badiy—(m)—first, new, another name for god
Badi—(m)—inventor, creator, marvellous
Badr-al-din—(m)—full moon of the faith
Badr-aldin—(m)—led by allah
Badr-e-alam—(m)—full moon of the world
Badr-udeen—(m)—full moon of faith
Badraan—(m)—one with divine wisdom
Badrah—(f)—full moon, to be early
Badraldin—(m)—full moon of the faith
Badran—(f)—plural of badr, beautiful
Badran—(m)—the most beautiful
Badrawi—(m)—one who is like the full moon
Badrealam—(m)—full moon of the world
Badria—(f)—like the full moon
Badriyah—(f)—resembling the full moon
Badriya—(f)—resembling full moon, moor-like
Badriyyah—(f)—resembles the full moon
Badri—(f)—full moon
Badri—(m)—old, lord shiva
Badrud-duja—(m)—full moon of the dark
Badruddeen—(m)—one with divine wisdom
Badruddin—(m)—the moon of the faith
Badrudduja—(m)—full moon of the dark
Badrudeen—(m)—full moon of the faith
Badrudin—(m)—full moon of the faith
Badrul—(f)—badrul islam
Badrul—(m)—one with divine wisdom
Badrun-nisa—(f)—full moon of the female
Badrunnisa—(f)—full moon of the female
Badrunnisha—(f)—unique, divine aura
Badru—(m)—born at the full moon, full moon
Badr—(f)—full moon
Badr—(m)—full moon
Badshah—(m)—king, ruler, emperor
Badurudeen—(m)—one with divine wisdom
Badur—(f)—moon
Badusha—(f)—unique, divine aura

Badusha—(m)—king, emperor
Badyah—(f)—clear, knowledgeable person
Badya—(f)—unique
Bady—(m)—a wonderful man
Baegum—(f)—a woman of rank
Baekhyun—(m)—love god
Baghawi—(m)—resident of bagh
Baghel—(m)—ox, royal sovereign
Baghl—(m)—ox
Bagum—(f)—a woman of rank
Baha-al-din—(m)—magnificence of the faith
Baha-udeen—(m)—the magnificent of faith
Bahaadur—(m)—brave, bold
Bahaaldin—(m)—magnificence of the faith
Bahaar—(f)—spring
Bahaddin—(m)—one with divine wisdom
Bahador—(m)—honourable, brave
Bahadur—(m)—fighter, bold
Bahaeddin—(m)—one with divine wisdom
Bahair—(f)—delicate woman
Bahajat—(m)—handsome, lovely
Bahameen—(f)—spring
Bahamin—(f)—spring
Bahar-bano—(f)—blooming princess
Baharak—(f)—spring
Bahara—(f)—brings the spring
Baharbano—(f)—blooming princess
Bahareh—(f)—sprint flower, bringer of spring
Bahare—(f)—bringer of spring, spring flower
Bahar—(f)—spring season, prime of life
Bahar—(m)—spring
Bahati—(f)—luck or be lucky, appropriate fortune
Bahat—(m)—pure, spotless, flawless
Bahauallah—(m)—one with divine wisdom
Bahauddaulah—(m)—ornament of the kingdom
Bahauddawlah—(m)—magnificence of the state
Bahauddin—(m)—glow of the religion islam
Bahaudeen—(m)—the magnificent of the faith

Bahaudin—(m)—the magnificent of the faith
Bahaullah—(m)—god's glory
Baha—(f)—value, price, worth
Baha—(m)—beautiful, magnificent
Baheeja—(f)—happy, beautiful, radiant
Baheej—(f)—beautiful, graceful, charming
Baheej—(m)—beautiful, convivial
Baheen—(m)—exalted, great, noble
Baheerah—(f)—dazzling
Baheera—(f)—dazzling, brilliant
Baheer—(m)—dazzling
Bahera—(m)—superb
Baher—(m)—dazzling, brilliant
Bahgat—(m)—happiness
Bahhas—(m)—scholar, researcher
Bahia—(f)—nice, bahiya - nice
Bahier—(m)—dazzling
Bahiga—(f)—glad, happy, joyful
Bahijah—(f)—magnificent, splendid
Bahija—(f)—glad, happy, joyful, splendid
Bahij—(f)—splendid, happy
Bahij—(m)—splendid, handsome, happy
Bahili—(m)—name of famous people, including
Bahim—(m)—pure, unmixed
Bahirah—(f)—dazzling, brilliant, noble lady
Bahiran—(m)—publicly
Bahirat—(f)—delicate woman
Bahira—(f)—sparkling, dazzling, brilliant
Bahiri—(f)—sparkling, prevailing, luminous
Bahirun—(m)—the plural of bahir, brilliant
Bahir—(m)—luminous, sparkling, dazzling
Bahisa—(f)—seeker, searcher, researcher
Bahisha—(f)—researcher, seeker, searcher
Bahis—(m)—investigator, researcher
Bahiy-udeen—(m)—the magnificent of faith
Bahiyaa—(f)—beautiful, radiant
Bahiyah—(f)—beautiful, from kikuyu, radiant
Bahiyat—(m)—precious

Bahiya—(f)—beautiful, nice, radiant
Bahiyud-din—(m)—radiant
Bahiyuddin—(m)—radiant
Bahiyudeen—(m)—the magnificent of the faith
Bahiyudin—(m)—the magnificent of the faith
Bahiyy-al-din—(m)—magnificence of the faith
Bahiyyah—(f)—beautiful, radiant
Bahiyyaldin—(m)—magnificence of the faith
Bahiyya—(f)—beautiful in arabic
Bahiyy—(m)—magnificence of the faith
Bahiy—(m)—good, magnificent of the faith
Bahi—(f)—beautiful, elegant, graceful
Bahi—(m)—splendid, brilliant, shining
Bahjah—(f)—radiance, joyfulness
Bahjah—(m)—joyfulness, radiance
Bahjat—(f)—bringer of happiness
Bahjat—(m)—happiness, beautiful
Bahja—(f)—happiness
Bahja—(m)—joyfulness, radiance
Bahlawan—(m)—entertainer, acrobat
Bahlol—(m)—leader of a tribe, virtuous king
Bahlul—(m)—one who does good deeds
Bahman—(m)—well-spirited
Bahmat—(m)—kid, child
Bahoos—(m)—researcher, searcher, seeker
Bahraa—(f)—shining, beautiful
Bahram—(f)—winning over resisting people
Bahram—(m)—name of a persian king
Bahrawar—(m)—lion-heart
Bahria—(f)—water, beautiful, grey
Bahriyah—(f)—unique, divine aura
Bahriya—(f)—bright, bold
Bahri—(m)—little, part, vast like the ocean
Bahrul—(m)—one with divine wisdom
Bahr—(f)—ocean, sea
Bahr—(m)—sea, ocean
Baht—(m)—pure, unmixed
Bahualdin—(m)—one with divine wisdom

Bahuj—(m)—handsome, happy - lively
Bahurudeen—(m)—one with divine wisdom
Bahur—(m)—intense heat
Bahu—(m)—a lot, arm
Bahy—(m)—brother
Bahzar—(m)—active, noble
Bahz—(m)—name of bin hakeem
Baidar—(m)—enlightened, attentive
Baid—(m)—another name for god, away
Baigum—(f)—princess, lady
Baihas—(m)—strong, brave
Baijid—(m)—one with divine wisdom
Bailasan—(f)—unique, divine aura
Bainor—(f)—unique, divine aura
Baisha—(f)—daughter of god, beautiful
Baith—(m)—one who raises death
Baiyan—(f)—eloquence
Baizan—(m)—truthful
Baiza—(f)—white, bright, brilliant
Baizid—(m)—devotion of mother
Bajalat—(f)—beautiful woman
Bajala—(m)—venerated, honoured
Bajih—(m)—rejoice
Bajila—(f)—honoured, dignified
Bajul—(m)—respected, honour
Bakarah—(f)—virginity
Bakar—(m)—morning
Bakaullah—(m)—one with divine wisdom
Baka—(f)—crane
Baka—(m)—crane, stork
Bakeet—(m)—lover, paramour
Bakhdan—(f)—delicate girl
Bakhita—(f)—lucky, fortunate
Bakhit—(f)—fortunate, lucky, happy
Bakhit—(m)—lucky, fortunate
Bakhram—(m)—victorious
Bakhshi—(m)—gift, present
Bakhsh—(m)—give, forgive, gift, fortunate

Bakht-rawan—(m)—running luck
Bakhtaawar—(m)—fortunate, lucky
Bakhtari—(m)—a narrator of hadith
Bakhtawara—(f)—lucky
Bakhtawar—(f)—one who brings appropriate luck
Bakhtawar—(m)—one who brings good luck
Bakhtiaar—(m)—lucky, fortunate
Bakhtiar—(m)—lucky, fortunate
Bakhtiyari—(f)—luck, fortunate
Bakhtiyar—(m)—lucky, fortunate
Bakht—(f)—luck, lottery, lot, fate, portion
Bakht—(m)—fortune, luck
Bakhur—(m)—scent, perfume
Bakhyt—(m)—a lucky man
Bakirah—(f)—virgin
Bakira—(f)—virgin, variant of bakir
Bakirin—(f)—one who are early and ready
Bakirin—(m)—one who are early and ready
Bakir—(m)—early in the morning
Baki—(m)—balance, gallant, region
Bakkah—(f)—another name for mecca
Bakkah—(m)—old name of makkah
Bakkar—(m)—a reciter of the quran and author
Bakkur—(m)—early, on time, new
Bakor—(m)—camel
Bakraj—(m)—coffee-pot
Bakri—(m)—one who starts work early
Bakrun—(m)—new, fresh, untouched
Bakr—(m)—camel, first born, new
Bakshu—(m)—blessed
Baktash—(m)—the elder, grandee of a tribe
Baktiyar—(m)—lucky, fortunate
Bakurah—(m)—beginning, dawn
Bakura—(f)—coming early
Bakur—(m)—thunderbolt, horn, glorifies
Balaagh—(m)—proclamation, declaration
Balaghah—(f)—eloquence
Balagh—(m)—delivery of a massage

Balaj—(m)—glitter, shine
Balan—(m)—newly risen, youthful, simple
Balaq—(m)—variety of colours
Balay—(m)—cornice or eaves
Balaz—(m)—one with divine wisdom
Balbala—(f)—nightingale
Balban—(m)—which is holy
Baleegha—(f)—eloquent, lasting
Baleegh—(m)—eloquent, vivid, complete
Baleel—(m)—moisture, one of the prophet
Balhara—(m)—king of kings
Baligha—(f)—eloquent, lasting
Baligh—(m)—eloquent, vivid, learned
Baljat—(m)—brightness, dawn
Balj—(m)—delighted
Balkees—(f)—the queen of sheba
Balkies—(f)—the name of the queen of sheba
Balluri—(f)—crystalline
Balma—(f)—husband, lover, beloved
Balma—(m)—beloved
Balqish—(f)—star
Balqis—(f)—the name of the queen of sheba
Balsam—(f)—balm
Bal—(m)—heart, mind, soul, arm, wing
Bamadhaj—(m)—one with divine wisdom
Bamdad—(m)—name of mazdak's father
Bameen—(m)—one with divine wisdom
Bamshad—(m)—pleasant dawn
Banaan—(f)—fingertips
Banafsaj—(f)—violent flower
Banafsha—(f)—name of flower
Banafsheh—(f)—a flower, violet flower
Banah—(f)—love
Banan—(f)—finger tips, delicate
Banayot—(m)—one with divine wisdom
Banaz—(f)—most beautiful
Bana—(f)—rich
Bandagi—(f)—to pray

Bandagi—(m)—pray
Bandana—(f)—worship
Bandar—(m)—seaport, district capital
Bandenawaz—(m)—one with divine wisdom
Bandgi—(f)—to pray, worship
Baneenzahra—(f)—unique, divine aura
Baneen—(f)—mother of four sons
Bani—(m)—children, speech, an orator
Banna—(m)—builder, architect
Banou—(f)—lady
Bano—(f)—girl, lady, princess
Banujah—(f)—the daughter of al-mahdi
Banu—(f)—princess, lady, flute
Bany—(m)—kind, cute
Ban—(f)—home or village, a kind of tree
Baqais—(m)—one with divine wisdom
Baqai—(m)—immortal
Baqar—(m)—lion, star
Baqat—(m)—bouquet, bunch of flowers
Baqa—(f)—to remain, endure, persist
Baqa—(m)—survival, immortality, eternity
Baqee—(m)—enduring, everlasting
Baqer—(m)—man of knowledge
Baqian—(m)—perpetual, everlasting, firm
Baqilah—(f)—unique, divine aura
Baqir—(m)—deeply learned, genius, scholar
Baqiyyah—(m)—name of a shake
Baqiyya—(m)—remaining
Baqi—(m)—remaining, everlasting, eternal
Baraaa—(f)—excelling
Baraah—(f)—innocence
Baraat—(f)—unique, divine aura
Baraat—(m)—security
Baraa—(f)—purity, excelling, innocent
Baraa—(m)—one who cure, innocent, healed
Barack—(m)—thunder, in vain, soldier
Barahim—(m)—father of the people
Baraim—(f)—blossom, bud, plural of burum

Baraj—(m)—handsome, good-looking
Barakaah—(m)—blessing
Barakaat—(f)—blessings
Barakaat—(m)—blessings, abundance, prosperity
Barakah—(f)—rain, blessing, white one
Barakah—(m)—blessed, blessings
Barakath—(f)—enlargement, growth
Barakath—(m)—prosperity, blessing
Barakatullah—(m)—blessing of allah
Barakat—(f)—blessing
Barakat—(m)—blessings, abundance, prosperity
Baraka—(f)—white one, blessings, increase
Baraka—(m)—a blessing, gift, fortune
Baraki—(f)—unique, divine aura
Barak—(m)—fire bolt, thunder, in vain
Baraq—(m)—electricity
Bararat—(m)—pious, truthful
Barat—(f)—innocence, guiltlessness
Barayek—(f)—blessed
Barayek—(m)—blessed
Baraz—(m)—high, exalted
Bara—(m)—free
Barbat—(m)—lute
Bardia—(m)—name of a prince
Bareck—(m)—one who is noble
Bareea—(f)—innocent, blameless, guiltless
Bareed—(m)—messenger, partner
Bareeha—(f)—the most beautiful
Bareek—(m)—blessed
Bareena—(f)—part of holy
Bareen—(f)—superior
Bareeq—(m)—glitter, flash, lustre
Bareerah—(f)—excellent, kind
Bareera—(f)—kind, appropriate, religious
Baree—(m)—free from the hell, free
Barek—(m)—one who is noble
Baresham—(m)—silk
Barfi—(f)—made of milk and sugar

Bargow—(m)—god
Barhamat—(m)—flower bud
Barhi—(m)—thanks
Bariah—(f)—outspoken, unique, original
Barialy—(m)—one with divine wisdom
Bariat—(f)—beautiful and witty woman
Baria—(f)—excelling, originator
Barida—(f)—unique, divine aura
Barid—(m)—cloud, courier, messenger
Bariha—(f)—unique, divine aura
Barii—(m)—innocent
Barij—(m)—good sailor
Barikaa—(f)—persevering, striving
Barikah—(f)—one who strives
Barika—(f)—bloom, be successful
Barikka—(f)—to bloom, be successful
Barik—(m)—a well watered place
Barina—(f)—the summit, origin is russian
Bariqua—(f)—lighting like stars
Bariq—(m)—bright
Barirah—(f)—faithful and devoted, kind
Barir—(m)—faithful
Bariyya—(f)—the creator, creation
Bariza—(f)—prominent, manifest
Barizia—(f)—visible, prominent
Barizi—(m)—prominent, visible
Bari—(f)—beautiful, brilliant, outstanding
Bari—(m)—creator, deity, sharp, pointed
Barjaa—(f)—of beautiful eyes
Barja—(f)—with beautiful eyes
Barkaat—(m)—blessings
Barkah—(f)—rain, blessing
Barkath—(f)—growth, enlargement
Barkath—(m)—enlargement, growth
Barkatullah—(m)—blessing of allah
Barkat—(f)—blessing, sing, of barakat
Barkat—(m)—growth, enlargement
Barkha—(f)—rain, monsoon

Barlin—(f)—princesses
Barnaly—(f)—unique, divine aura
Barna—(m)—son of comforting, young, youth
Barni—(m)—young, grown up
Baroka—(m)—one with divine wisdom
Barqah—(f)—flash of light
Barqi—(m)—electric light
Barq—(m)—lightening, telegraph
Barraaq—(m)—flashing, bright, brilliant
Barrack—(m)—lightning
Barrah—(f)—narrator of hadith
Barraqa—(f)—bright, brilliant, shining
Barraq—(m)—bright, brilliant, glittering
Barraz—(m)—prominent, clear
Barr—(f)—pious, innocent
Barr—(m)—gateway, form of barretta, a cap
Barsala—(f)—eyelashes
Barsa—(f)—rain, showers, year, queen of rain
Barsha—(f)—rain, monsoon, gift of nature
Barveen—(f)—star
Baryal—(m)—successful
Barzah—(f)—narrator of hadith
Barzakh—(f)—interval, partition, divider
Barzakh—(m)—divider, partition, interval
Barzan—(m)—prominent, visible
Barz—(m)—intelligent
Basaair—(f)—clear sign, proof
Basaair—(m)—clear proof, enlightening proof
Basaam—(m)—smiling
Basaaria—(f)—beautiful, prior
Basafa—(f)—pure
Basah—(m)—beauty
Basair—(f)—enlightening proof, clear proof
Basair—(m)—enlightenment
Basalah—(f)—bravery, courageousness, boldness
Basama—(f)—one who smiles often
Basam—(m)—smiling, one who smiles often
Basan—(f)—beautiful

Basan—(m)—one who uproots fully
Basarat—(m)—one with divine wisdom
Basara—(f)—bringer of appropriate tidings
Basar—(f)—powerful
Basar—(m)—sight, vision, eyesight
Basasiri—(m)—one with divine wisdom
Basaud—(m)—exalted, blessed
Basa—(m)—beauty
Baseeha—(f)—unique, divine aura
Baseel—(m)—brave, lion, courageous
Baseemaa—(f)—one who smiles, happy, cheerful
Baseemah—(f)—one who smiles, cheerful, happy
Baseema—(f)—smiling, spring
Baseem—(m)—smiling
Baseerah—(f)—clear proof
Baseerat—(m)—insight, perception
Baseera—(f)—staying, insight, wisdom
Baseer—(m)—vision, sagacious, all seeing
Baseet—(m)—vast, spacious
Basel—(m)—brave, courageous, lion
Basemah—(f)—smiling
Basem—(m)—smiling, one who smiles, cheerful
Basera—(f)—wisdom, staying
Bashaarat—(m)—good news
Bashaar—(m)—bringer of glad tidings
Bashaer—(f)—appropriate tiding
Bashaira—(f)—roost
Bashair—(f)—appropriate omens
Basharaat—(m)—good omen, prophecy
Basharat—(f)—appropriate news, glad tidings
Basharat—(m)—good omen, prophecy
Bashara—(f)—cause for celebration, appropriate news
Bashari—(m)—human
Bashar—(m)—bringer of glad tidings
Bashasha—(f)—cheerfulness
Bashash—(m)—friendly
Basha—(f)—appropriate tidings, daughter of god
Basha—(m)—stranger, king, emperor, noble

Basheed—(m)—one with divine wisdom
Basheem—(m)—one with divine wisdom
Basheena—(f)—kitty
Basheera—(f)—bringer of appropriate tidings
Basheera—(m)—one with divine wisdom
Basheer—(m)—one who brings good news
Basheir—(m)—well-educated
Bashera—(f)—glad tiding
Bashera—(m)—bringer of good tidings
Basher—(m)—one with divine wisdom
Bashhar—(m)—one with divine wisdom
Bashid—(m)—one with divine wisdom
Bashier—(m)—well-educated
Bashiga—(f)—joyful
Bashiq—(m)—one with divine wisdom
Bashirah—(f)—bringer of appropriate tidings
Bashirat—(m)—prudent, intelligence
Bashira—(f)—joyful, predictor of appropriate news
Bashira—(m)—with perception
Bashiri—(m)—predictor, bringer of good tidings
Bashiruddin—(m)—wise, one who gives good news
Bashirun—(m)—bringers of good news, tidings
Bashir—(m)—one who gives good news
Bashitha—(f)—spoken
Bashith—(m)—one with divine wisdom
Bashiyra—(f)—unique, divine aura
Bashiyr—(m)—one with divine wisdom
Bashnin—(f)—lotus
Bashrah—(f)—appropriate news, appropriate tiding
Bashrat—(m)—glad tidings
Bashshar—(m)—brings good news
Bashsh—(m)—glad, cheerful
Bashurah—(f)—cheerful, glad, optimistic
Bashur—(m)—bringer of good news
Bashush—(m)—friendly
Bashu—(m)—optimistic, joyful, cheerful
Basia—(f)—daughter of god, foreign woman
Basid—(m)—one with divine wisdom

Basilah—(f)—brave, fearless
Basila—(f)—feminine of basil, brave
Basili—(m)—courageous, brave
Basil—(m)—imperial, monarchic, kingly
Basimah—(f)—smiling
Basima—(f)—smiling, feminine of basim
Basimia—(f)—joyful, happy
Basimi—(m)—joyful, happy
Basim—(m)—one who smiles, smiling, happy
Basinah—(f)—kitty, kitten
Basiqat—(f)—high, lofty - towering things
Basiqa—(f)—lofty, outstanding, tall, superior
Basiq—(m)—clear, soaring, lofty, towering
Basiraa—(f)—perceptive, insightful
Basirah—(f)—vision, sight
Basirat—(m)—insight, perception
Basira—(f)—sagacious, endowed with insight
Basira—(m)—pious
Basiruddin—(m)—one with divine wisdom
Basirun—(f)—unique, divine aura
Basita—(f)—generous, giving
Basith—(m)—devotee of the extender, creator
Basit—(m)—expander, spreader
Basi—(m)—that is enough
Basmaan—(m)—smiling a lot
Basmaa—(f)—one who smiles often, cheerful
Basmah—(f)—brilliant, a smile
Basman—(m)—smiling
Basmat—(f)—smile
Basmat—(m)—smile
Basma—(f)—a smile, happy, joyful, cheerful
Basmina—(f)—beautiful
Basmin—(f)—joyful, happy, cheerful
Basmin—(m)—joyful, happy, cheerful
Basm—(f)—smile
Basoomah—(f)—one who smiles often, happy
Basoom—(m)—happy, cheerful
Basrah—(m)—dry land

Basreen—(f)—unique, divine aura
Basr—(m)—eye-sight, wisdom, sight
Bassaam—(m)—frequently smiling
Bassaar—(m)—perceptive, insightful
Bassamat—(f)—unique, divine aura
Bassama—(f)—smiling, feminine of bassam
Bassam—(f)—one who smiles a lot
Bassam—(m)—he who smiles a lot, smiling
Bassel—(m)—courageous, brave
Bassem—(m)—smiling
Bassier—(m)—bringer of glad tidings
Bassil—(m)—brave
Bassima—(f)—smiling
Bassim—(m)—smiling
Bassma—(f)—a smile
Bastaq—(m)—devotee, attendant
Basus—(f)—she-camel
Batal—(m)—brave, hero, champion
Batek—(m)—sharp sword
Bathish—(m)—mighty
Bathshira—(f)—seventh girl-child
Bathsira—(f)—unique, divine aura
Bathul—(f)—unique, divine aura
Batik—(m)—sharp sword
Batinah—(f)—hidden, inner
Batina—(f)—hidden, inner
Batin—(m)—hidden
Batish—(m)—mighty, powerful
Batlaa—(f)—resolved, resolute
Batlah—(f)—independent
Batool—(f)—ascetic virgin, maiden
Batoor—(m)—brave
Batoul—(f)—virgin
Batrisyia—(f)—intelligent
Batshah—(m)—day of judgement
Battaal—(m)—ascetic, virtuous
Battah—(m)—dance
Batula—(f)—ascetic, devoted to god, virgin

Batul—(f)—ascetic virgin, virgin, kind
Bauna—(m)—cool
Bawasim—(f)—one who smiles, cheerful, happy
Bayaan—(f)—elucidation
Bayaan—(m)—elucidation
Bayan—(f)—eloquence, explanation
Bayan—(m)—another name for the holy quran
Bayazid—(m)—name of a saint
Baydah—(f)—adorer, devotee of allah
Baydhaa—(f)—white, feminine of abyaz
Baydhoon—(m)—white
Baydun—(m)—white
Bayd—(m)—worshipper
Bayezid—(m)—name of a saint
Bayhas—(m)—name of the lion
Baysan—(f)—to walk with pride
Bayyinaat—(f)—clear signs - proofs
Bayyinah—(f)—clear sign, proof
Bayyinat—(f)—clear signs, proof
Bayyina—(f)—evidence, proof, clear sign
Bayzaa—(f)—white, pure, moonlit night
Bayza—(f)—white, feminine of abyaz
Bazala—(f)—generous woman
Bazam—(m)—it was the name of the tabiee
Bazan—(m)—a companion of prophet
Bazee—(m)—one who is generous
Bazegha—(f)—bright
Bazela—(f)—generous woman
Bazel—(m)—royal kingly
Bazgar—(m)—peasant
Bazie—(m)—one who is generous
Bazif—(m)—exult, to board
Bazigha—(f)—shining like the sun
Bazigh—(m)—radiating light, radiant, rising
Bazila—(f)—generous, reward
Bazil—(m)—royal, kingly
Bazir—(m)—educated, a great person
Bazish—(m)—aggressive, hard-liner

Bazi—(m)—one who is generous
Bazla—(f)—reward, generous
Bazlur-rahman—(m)—generosity of the all-merciful
Bazlurrahman—(m)—generosity of the all-merciful
Bazl—(m)—prize, reward
Bazm-ara—(f)—beauty of company
Bazmakh—(m)—proud
Bazmara—(f)—beauty of company
Bazriqa—(f)—exalted, great
Bazugh—(m)—sunrise
Bazya—(f)—beautiful
Baz—(m)—royal, kingly, eagle, king
Bebarg—(m)—beautiful tree
Bebeghul—(f)—unique, divine aura
Bebe—(f)—lady of the house, lady
Bechara—(f)—appropriate news
Bechir—(m)—innocence, pure
Bedaruddin—(m)—attentive to the religion
Bedar—(m)—wakeful, attentive, enlightened
Beddis—(m)—one with divine wisdom
Beebee—(f)—lady
Beena—(f)—a musical instrument, seeing
Beenish—(f)—intelligent, genius
Beeran—(m)—lord of warriors
Beesha—(f)—beautiful
Beeta—(f)—unique, singular
Beevi—(f)—angel
Begam—(f)—lady, wife, noble lady
Begum-safrah—(f)—unique, divine aura
Begum—(f)—princess, lady
Begu—(f)—run, escape
Behan—(m)—bee
Behardin—(m)—one with divine wisdom
Behbaha—(f)—best price
Behdad—(m)—excellent gift, of good birth
Behisth—(f)—heaven
Behlol—(m)—leader, a famous saint
Behnam—(m)—man of honour, reputable

Behnaz—(f)—best coquetry
Behraam—(m)—mars, planet
Behram—(m)—mars, planet, victory
Behrang—(m)—good colour
Behrokh—(f)—best face
Behrouz—(m)—having good luck, lucky, fortunate
Behroz—(f)—noble, sacred
Behroz—(m)—sacred, noble
Behruz—(m)—lucky, fortunate, good day
Behr—(m)—sea, wave
Behzaad—(m)—pure, well-mannered
Behzad—(m)—of good birth, of noble family
Bekir—(m)—first born
Belaal—(m)—one with divine wisdom
Belall—(m)—one with divine wisdom
Belal—(m)—white, bright
Bela—(f)—evening time, a flower - jasmine
Belha—(f)—beautiful
Beli—(f)—a flower-jasmine
Belkis—(f)—princess, queen, queen of sheba
Bellal—(m)—one of the solder name
Belma—(f)—husband
Belqis—(m)—one with divine wisdom
Benafsha—(f)—rose, a violet
Benasir—(f)—unique, grace, incomparable
Benazeer—(f)—matchless, unique
Benazer—(f)—unique, incomparable
Benazir—(f)—grace, without like, unique
Benazir—(m)—incomparable, matchless
Benefsha—(f)—rose
Benesa—(m)—one with divine wisdom
Benincasa—(m)—child of qasim
Benjamin—(m)—right hand's son
Benu—(f)—flute
Benyamin—(m)—jacob's youngest son
Benza—(f)—unique, different
Benzeera—(f)—unique, matchless
Benzima—(m)—one with divine wisdom

Beram—(m)—fun, eid, enjoyment
Berkan—(m)—one with divine wisdom
Berka—(f)—increase, growth, breeding
Berngards—(m)—brave as a bear
Besharat—(f)—glad tidings, variant of basharah
Besjana—(f)—oath, pledge
Besmil—(m)—one with divine wisdom
Betelgeuse—(m)—arm of the central one
Bethany—(f)—house of figs, house of poverty
Betoole—(f)—virgin
Betool—(f)—ascetic virgin, maiden
Betulle—(f)—virgin
Betul—(f)—ascetic virgin, maiden
Beulah—(f)—one who is married, bride
Beyza—(f)—extremely white
Bhajat—(f)—splendour, magnificence, pomp
Bhaktiyar—(m)—fortunate, lucky
Bhasheer—(m)—intelligent and discerning
Bhasin—(m)—shining, brilliant
Bhavsar—(m)—ocean
Bhenjir—(f)—most beautiful
Bho—(f)—delights in meditation
Biba—(f)—short form of lover
Bibhakar—(m)—source of light
Bibiana—(f)—alive, lady, full of life, lively
Bibi—(f)—lady, woman, full of life
Bibsbebe—(f)—lady, lady of the house
Bidar—(f)—awake, being early, on time
Bidar—(m)—on time, awake, being early
Bidayah—(f)—beginning, start, inception
Bidayat—(f)—form of bidayah, inception
Bida—(f)—incomparable female
Biddi—(m)—handsome, bidder
Bihaar—(m)—sea
Bihar—(m)—ocean, seas
Bihjan—(m)—one with divine wisdom
Bihzad—(m)—well born
Bijali—(f)—lightening

Bijann—(m)—one with divine wisdom
Bijan—(m)—a character in shahnameh
Bijli—(f)—lightning, bright, electricity
Bijul—(m)—peaceful
Bikhtir—(f)—one who has a graceful gait
Bikr—(m)—first born, eldest
Bilaal—(m)—call to prayer, freshness, river
Bilall—(m)—the chosen one
Bilal—(m)—the chosen one, black man
Bilan—(f)—beauty, gift
Bilawal—(m)—brave
Bilbitri—(f)—unique, divine aura
Bilel—(m)—refreshing
Bilkeesa—(f)—place of queen
Bilkish—(f)—unique, divine aura
Bilkisu—(f)—princess, queen
Billah—(m)—one with divine wisdom
Billal—(m)—satisfies thirst
Billqes—(f)—the queen of sheba
Bilqees—(f)—place of queen, the queen of sheba
Bilqis—(f)—the queen of sheba
Bilquees—(f)—unique, divine aura
Bilquis—(f)—the queen of sheba
Bilqys—(f)—the queen of sheba
Bilsha—(f)—coolness
Bilyaminu—(m)—peace
Bimasha—(f)—unique, divine aura
Bimin—(f)—powerful, strong, brilliant
Binaafsha—(f)—name of a flower
Binad—(m)—hope
Binafsha—(f)—name of a flower
Binat—(m)—humble, modest, variant of vinata
Bina—(m)—wise, seeing, clear-sighted
Binesh—(f)—clever
Binisha—(f)—clever, intelligent, gentle
Binish—(f)—intelligent, clever
Bini—(f)—architect
Binsha—(f)—gift of god

Binte—(f)—with god, urge
Bintiha—(f)—unique, divine aura
Bintulbahr—(f)—daughter of the sea
Bint—(f)—daughter, girl
Binusha—(f)—gift of god, clever
Binyamin—(m)—ploughman, son of the right hand
Bin—(m)—son, form of bingham, crib
Birjees—(f)—a small shining star in the sky
Birjees—(m)—jupiter, planet
Birjis—(f)—authority
Birjis—(m)—planet, planet jupiter
Birrah—(f)—appropriate deed
Birrah—(m)—good deed
Bisaat—(f)—floor covering, spread, expanse
Bisam—(m)—one with divine wisdom
Bisar—(f)—adolescent
Bisat—(f)—floor covering, spread, expanse
Bishaam—(f)—most beautiful
Bisharah—(f)—narrator of hadith, appropriate news
Bisharah—(m)—good news, good tidings
Bisharat—(f)—appropriate news, tidings
Bisharat—(m)—good news
Bishara—(f)—appropriate news, trade
Bisha—(f)—beautiful
Bishma—(f)—beautiful
Bishmi—(f)—starting name of god
Bishrul—(m)—one with divine wisdom
Bishry—(f)—optimistic, cheerful, glad
Bishry—(m)—optimistic, cheerful, glad
Bishr—(m)—joy, solved, based, cheerfulness
Bismah—(f)—freshness, smiling one
Bismal—(f)—fragrance
Bisma—(f)—sliver, freshness and smile
Bismillah—(m)—beginning, commencement
Bismitha—(f)—unique, divine aura
Bismiya-fetheem—(f)—sliver, smiling one
Bismiya—(f)—smiling one, sliver
Bismi—(f)—in god's name, idealistic nature

Bisni—(f)—unique, divine aura
Bisriya—(f)—unique, divine aura
Bisu—(m)—bright star
Bita—(f)—unique, matchless, beautiful
Biva—(f)—sunlight, shine, light
Biyan—(m)—one with divine wisdom
Biya—(f)—refined
Bizziza—(f)—victory
Blessy—(f)—blessing
Bob—(m)—bright, form of robert
Bokhtiar—(m)—fortunate, lucky
Bokil—(m)—one with divine wisdom
Bolour—(f)—crystal
Bony—(m)—pleasant, charming, bones of body
Borak—(m)—the lightning
Borna—(m)—young, youthful
Borzoo—(m)—tall, sohrab's son in shahnameh
Boshry—(f)—gladness, happiness
Boshry—(m)—gladness, happiness
Bostan—(m)—garden
Bost—(m)—pride, blessed, courageous
Botros—(m)—arabic form of peter
Boualem—(m)—one with divine wisdom
Bouid—(m)—one with divine wisdom
Boulos—(m)—small, humble
Boulus—(m)—arabic form of paul
Bouraoui—(m)—one with divine wisdom
Bousseh—(f)—kiss
Boutros—(m)—form of peter, variant of butrus
Bouzid—(m)—thrive
Brada—(m)—one with divine wisdom
Braheem—(m)—father of a multitude
Brahim—(m)—father of multitude
Brahin—(m)—proofs, arguments
Brakat—(m)—prosperity
Breanna—(f)—virtuous, noble, strong
Breeha—(f)—the most beautiful one
Breyaja—(f)—beautiful soul

Bridger—(f)—bridge worker, exalted one
Brishna—(f)—unique, divine aura
Brishna—(m)—light
Brooke—(f)—a small fresh water stream
Bruhier—(m)—name of a sultan
Bubun—(m)—love
Budaid—(m)—example, sample, specimen
Budaili—(m)—replacement, substitute
Budail—(m)—name of a companion of the prophet
Budaira—(f)—little full moon
Budair—(m)—little full moon
Budaiwi—(m)—little bedouin
Budat—(m)—prince
Budayl—(m)—name of a companion of the prophet
Budool—(m)—respected, generous, virtuous
Buduriya—(f)—radiant, beautiful
Budur—(f)—full moon, plural of badr
Budur—(m)—full moon, plural of badr
Buhaan—(m)—proof, evidence
Buhairah—(f)—little sea, lake
Buhairah—(m)—lake
Buhair—(m)—little ocean, little sea, lake
Buhaisah—(f)—walking with pride
Buham—(m)—soldier, brave
Buhaysah—(f)—a narrator of hadith
Buhayyah—(f)—the name of a freed female slave
Buhjah—(f)—joy, delight
Buhmah—(m)—invincible
Buhsum—(m)—firm, hard
Buhthah—(f)—happy
Buhur—(f)—seas, oceans
Buhur—(m)—oceans, seas, river, eye, sight
Bujudat—(m)—one who adheres to his word
Bukair—(m)—new, untouched
Bukrah—(f)—part of the day, early morning
Bukran—(m)—early morning, dawn
Bukrat—(m)—morning, dawn
Bukra—(f)—dawn, early part of the day

Buland—(m)—height, upward
Bulbul—(f)—singing bird, nightingale
Bulbul—(m)—nightingale
Bulhut—(m)—narrator of hadith
Buluj—(m)—glitter, shine
Bulus—(m)—small, humble
Bunaisa—(f)—unique, divine aura
Bunyaan—(m)—structure, formation
Bunyan—(m)—home of pigeons, structures
Buqat—(m)—temple, monastery
Buqayrah—(f)—narrator of hadith
Buqrat—(m)—an ancient physician
Buraid—(m)—chilly, cold
Buraikaat—(f)—blessings
Buraik—(m)—blessed
Burakhdat—(f)—fleshy woman
Buraq—(m)—bright one
Burat—(f)—anklet
Burayd—(m)—mild, cold
Bura—(m)—safe, out of danger
Burhaan—(f)—proof
Burhaan—(m)—proof
Burhan-ud-din—(m)—proof of the religion
Burhanah—(f)—demonstration, clue, proof
Burhanuddin—(m)—proof of the religion islam
Burhan—(m)—proof, evidence
Burhumat—(f)—flower-bud
Burj—(m)—zodiac sign, star, constellation
Bursuq—(m)—badger
Buruj—(m)—signs of the zodiac
Burum—(f)—bud, blossom
Buru—(f)—beauty or wisdom
Busaina—(f)—beautiful woman
Busayna—(f)—unique, divine aura
Busa—(m)—all, universal
Bushair—(m)—enlightenment
Busharat—(m)—good news
Bushara—(f)—happy

Bushirat—(f)—appropriate news
Bushraa—(f)—appropriate news, glad tidings
Bushraa—(m)—giver of good tidings
Bushrah—(f)—appropriate tiding, appropriate news
Bushra—(f)—happy news, glad tiding, glad
Bushra—(m)—good news
Bushr—(m)—joy, happiness
Bushur—(m)—good news
Busrah—(f)—daughter of safwan bin nawfal
Busrat—(m)—rising sun
Busr—(f)—great, wise, humble
Busr—(m)—unripe dates
Bustan—(f)—garden, orchard
Bustan—(m)—orchard, place of perfumes
Busuttil—(m)—one with divine wisdom
Busyna—(f)—unique, divine aura
Buthainah—(f)—of beautiful and tender body
Buthanaya—(f)—having a beautiful body
Buthaynah—(f)—tender body, of a beautiful body
Butros—(m)—rock, form of peter
Butrus—(m)—form of peter, rock, stone
Buurab—(m)—father of earth
Buwayh—(m)—one with divine wisdom
Buyahya—(m)—father of yahya
Buzabiz—(m)—strong, brave
Buzat—(m)—ice-creams

THREE

Arabic Baby Names—C

Cabir—(m)—the great, powerful, leader

Caden—(m)—barrel, fighter

Cadi—(m)—luck

Caeli—(m)—from heaven

Cahmber—(f)—amber

Cailie—(f)—beloved

Cairo—(m)—one who is victorious

Caitlyn—(f)—pure, form of catherine

Cai—(m)—arthur's brother

Calah—(f)—favourable, opportunity

Cala—(f)—fortress, lovely, most beautiful

Caleb—(m)—to be faithful, messenger, bold

Cale—(m)—to be faithful, bold

Calista—(m)—beauty of jannha

Cali—(f)—most beautiful

Cal—(m)—courageous, adorable, well known

Cambar—(f)—amber

Camberia—(f)—amber

Camberise—(f)—amber

Camberlee—(f)—amber

Camberli—(f)—amber

Camberlynn—(f)—amber

Camberlyn—(f)—amber

Camberly—(f)—amber, chief, ruler

Cambra—(f)—amber
Cambur—(f)—amber
Cambyre—(f)—amber
Cambyr—(f)—amber
Camilla—(f)—young ceremonial attendant
Camran—(m)—crooked nose, successful
Cancandanc—(f)—light of allah
Cantarah—(f)—small bridge
Cantara—(f)—small bridge
Cantarrah—(f)—small bridge
Cantarra—(f)—small bridge
Cantar—(f)—small bridge
Canterah—(f)—small bridge
Cantera—(f)—small bridge
Canterrah—(f)—small bridge
Canterra—(f)—small bridge
Captain—(m)—he who is in charge
Careem—(m)—generous
Carim—(m)—generous
Carmen—(f)—garden of god, crimson or red
Carmen—(m)—garden, orchard, son of
Carmin—(m)—covered with hides
Carna—(f)—war horn, goddess of flesh
Cash—(m)—case maker, wealthy man, vain
Casildah—(f)—virgin carrier of the lance
Casilda—(f)—of the home, dwelling place
Casilde—(f)—battler
Casildo—(m)—that carries the lance
Casild—(f)—virgin carrier of the lance
Cassem—(m)—grateful
Cassilda—(f)—virgin carrier of the lance
Cassim—(m)—lord forbid
Cassiopea—(f)—variant of cassiopeia
Cassylda—(f)—virgin carrier of the lance
Casyldah—(f)—virgin carrier of the lance
Casylda—(f)—virgin carrier of the lance
Casylde—(f)—virgin carrier of the lance
Casyld—(f)—virgin carrier of the lance

Casy—(f)—descendant of cathasaigh
Caylie—(f)—beloved, slender
Cayman—(m)—alligator
Celina—(f)—young warrior, rendered to mars
Celmira—(f)—brilliant one
Cemal—(f)—beauty
Cemal—(m)—perfection, beauty, attractive
Centola—(f)—light of knowledge
Cephas—(m)—a rock, stone, war leader
Cesaria—(f)—unique, divine aura
Chaand—(f)—the moon
Chabuk—(m)—agile, clever
Chadia—(f)—gracious
Chadna—(f)—love
Chaesha—(f)—bright, beautiful
Chafia—(f)—look after
Chafika—(f)—to tend
Chafik—(m)—sympathising
Chahat—(f)—desire, love
Chahat—(m)—desire, wish, love, affection
Chahida—(f)—beloved one
Chahid—(m)—witness
Chahrazad—(f)—sensitive
Chahra—(f)—notoriety
Chait—(m)—mind, wisdom
Chaka—(f)—a lark, life, energy centre
Chaker—(m)—thanking
Chakila—(f)—beautiful, appropriate-looking
Chakira—(f)—grateful
Chakir—(m)—chosen one, the chosen one
Chakori—(f)—alert
Chakra—(f)—energy centre of the body
Chalipa—(f)—cross
Challita—(m)—cool
Chaman—(f)—garden
Chamen—(f)—garden of flowers
Chaminda—(m)—shining
Chamini—(f)—love like ocean

Chamis—(f)—sun
Champa—(f)—a flower, essence of sun
Chams—(m)—sun
Cham—(m)—hot, hard worker
Chanan—(m)—god was compassionate, cloud
Chana—(f)—favoured, grave, graceful
Chanchal—(f)—active, spontaneous, lively
Chanchu—(m)—renowned, celebrated, clever, hear
Chandana—(f)—sandalwood, parrot, adorable
Chandani—(f)—moonlight, silver, star, a river
Chanda—(f)—moon
Chanda—(m)—the moon, god's compassion
Chandini—(f)—star, moonlight, moon light
Chandra—(f)—shining moon, the moon, radiant
Chand—(f)—moon
Chand—(m)—moon, shining moon
Changaze—(m)—keen, inventive, reliability
Changeez—(m)—name of king
Changez—(m)—firm, solid
Chan—(m)—nickname for john, light, beloved
Charagh—(m)—light, lamp
Chargul—(m)—jewellery for the nose
Charikar—(f)—unique, divine aura
Chariva—(f)—beautiful
Charugna—(f)—moon
Chasheen—(f)—sweet
Chasmeen—(f)—jasmine
Chawki—(m)—pleasant
Cheekoo—(m)—name of a fruit
Cheherazad—(m)—of noble countenance, funny
Chehra—(f)—face
Cheik—(m)—learned
Chelem—(m)—power, dream
Chema—(f)—god is with us
Chereena—(f)—beautiful, beloved, strong
Chereen—(f)—dear one, darling, beloved
Cheryn—(f)—moon
Chessy—(f)—at peace

Chessy—(m)—peaceful
Chezihan—(m)—beautiful
Chhatrapal—(m)—protector of mankind
Chief—(m)—head, leader
Chikodi—(m)—in the hands of god
Chinar—(m)—name of a beautiful tree
Chiraagh—(m)—lamp, light
Chiragh—(m)—lamp, light
Chirag—(m)—lamp, allaudins lamps, light
Chiraz—(f)—light
Chitnis—(m)—one with divine wisdom
Choti—(f)—little, small
Choyon—(m)—thanks
Chrishan—(m)—awakened, almighty lord
Chunna—(f)—paint
Churagh—(m)—allaudins lamp, light, lamp
Ciara—(f)—black like a raven, dark, black
Cid—(m)—from a large island, lord
Cien—(m)—shadow
Cifran—(m)—one with divine wisdom
Ciji—(f)—cute
Cimrin—(f)—remembrance of god
Clemira—(f)—brilliant princess
Codei—(m)—rockstar
Coman—(m)—noble, bent
Corlissa—(f)—cheerful
Cowie—(m)—hazel, hillside hollow, a twin
Cruinn—(m)—round
Cyd—(m)—lord, a public hill
Cyon—(m)—greenish-blue
Cyra—(f)—beautiful, moon, like the sun
Cyriac—(m)—lord
Cyrille—(f)—of the lord
Cyrine—(f)—sovereign queen

FOUR

Arabic Baby Names—D

Daabir—(m)—secretary

Daaem—(m)—perpetual, constant, continual

Daafi—(m)—one who expels prevents

Daaim—(m)—continual, listing

Daaiyyah—(m)—inviter to truth

Daai—(m)—another name for prophet muhammad

Daajiyah—(f)—living well

Daamin—(m)—surety, guarantor

Daamir—(m)—heart

Daanaa—(m)—wise, intelligent, learned

Daaneesh—(m)—knowledge, wisdom

Daanee—(m)—close, near, hanging low

Daania—(f)—beautiful

Daanish—(m)—clever, knowledge, wisdom

Daaniyah—(f)—close, near

Daani—(m)—near, close

Daan—(m)—the lord is my judge, charity

Daarim—(m)—reader of hadith

Daarina—(f)—love, kindness, beautiful

Daawood—(m)—prophets name

Daa—(m)—the inviter

Dabaran—(m)—those who are behind

Dabbah—(m)—door lock, latch

Dabeer—(m)—teacher, secretary

Daber—(m)—roots, lineage, ancestry
Dabir—(m)—writer, teacher
Daboor—(m)—morning breeze
Dab—(m)—nature, habit, manifestation
Dadapeer—(m)—grand, father of spiritual teacher
Dadbeh—(m)—one with divine wisdom
Dad—(f)—old arabic name
Daeb—(m)—diligent, conscientious
Daee—(m)—caller, evangelist
Dafalla—(m)—one with divine wisdom
Dafeenah—(f)—hidden treasure
Dafinah—(f)—hidden treasure
Dafiq—(m)—jubilant, buoyant, active
Dafiyah—(f)—soft, narrator of hadith
Dafiya—(f)—narrator of hadith
Dafi—(m)—one who keeps away
Dagar—(m)—battle field, open space
Daghfal—(m)—name of first islamic geologist
Daghishat—(m)—darkness
Dagi—(f)—corn, ceremonial grain
Dagwood—(m)—from the bright one's forest
Dahabeah—(f)—the golden child
Dahabea—(f)—the golden child
Dahabe—(f)—the golden child
Dahabiah—(f)—the golden child
Dahabia—(f)—the golden child
Dahab—(f)—gold
Dahah—(f)—beauty
Dahban—(m)—gold-plated
Dahdaah—(m)—short
Dahdah—(m)—short
Dahhaak—(m)—fire mark
Dahhak—(m)—one who laughs much
Dahir—(m)—trustworthy
Dahi—(m)—intelligent, quick-footed, swift
Dahlan—(m)—king, lion
Dahlia—(f)—flower name, valley flower
Dah—(f)—rose

Daiba—(f)—assiduous, persistent, devoted
Daib—(m)—happy fellow
Daidan—(m)—custom, habit
Daieba—(f)—hard worker
Daifallah—(m)—one with divine wisdom
Daifa—(f)—defence
Daif—(m)—weak
Daig—(m)—fire, flame
Daimumat—(m)—duration, endurance
Daim—(m)—permanent, eternal
Dainyat—(f)—to give
Daisha—(f)—pretty and friendly woman
Daiyaan—(m)—protector, good ruler
Daiyan—(m)—a mighty ruler, judge, guard
Daiyat—(m)—one who invites
Daiya—(f)—caller for islam
Daja—(m)—black-eyed
Dajjal—(m)—imposter, big liar
Dakan—(m)—obedient, gentle
Dakheel—(m)—foreigner
Dakhil—(m)—stranger, foreigner
Dakhnas—(m)—strong, muscular
Dalaal—(f)—cuddling, pampering
Dalair—(m)—brave, valiant
Dalaj—(m)—a mufti of baghdad
Dalale—(f)—coquettishness
Dalalle—(f)—coquettishness
Dalall—(f)—coquettishness
Dalal—(m)—agent
Daleela—(f)—guide, proof, leader
Daleel—(m)—conductor, guide
Daleena—(f)—kind, noble
Daleesha—(f)—delight
Daler—(m)—brave, valiant, bold
Dalham—(m)—mad with love
Dalia—(f)—a branch, to draw water
Dalida—(f)—poor, weak, gentle, delight
Dalilah—(f)—guide, leader, clue

Dalila—(f)—gentle, delicate
Dalil—(m)—evidence, proof, guide
Dalim—(m)—pomegranate, one type of fruit
Dalina—(f)—noble, kind
Daliyah—(f)—tree branch
Daliyana—(f)—flower
Daliya—(f)—great, dahlia
Dali—(m)—grape vines, cannot be satisfied
Dalmar—(m)—versatile
Dalma—(m)—dark, very black
Daluh—(m)—another name for the sun
Dalwah—(f)—a bucket, container
Dalw—(m)—bucket, watering-pot
Dalya—(f)—great
Damaa—(f)—river, sea - ocean
Damaleah—(f)—a beautiful vision
Damalea—(f)—a beautiful vision
Damalee—(f)—a beautiful vision
Damaleigh—(f)—a beautiful vision
Damaley—(f)—a beautiful vision
Damalie—(f)—a beautiful vision
Damali—(f)—beautiful vision
Damaly—(f)—a beautiful vision
Dama—(f)—control of the senses
Damdam—(m)—water
Dameer—(m)—conscience, heart
Dameetha—(f)—one of appropriate manners, simple
Damesha—(f)—small noblewoman
Damian—(m)—to tame, subdue, tamer
Damia—(f)—untamed
Damien—(f)—untamed, to tame, subdue
Damil—(m)—respect giver
Damira—(f)—long live the world
Damir—(m)—give peace, heart, love
Damis—(m)—a dark-skinned man
Damsaz—(m)—companion, friend
Damurah—(m)—fire, sparkle of light
Danah—(f)—graceful, intelligent

Danah—(m)—intelligent, knowledgeable
Danal—(m)—god is my judge
Danamir—(f)—looking out for someone
Dananir—(f)—money
Dana—(f)—god is my judge, a dane, judge
Dana—(m)—god is my judge, judge, arbiter
Danean—(f)—dane
Daneen—(f)—princess
Daneer—(m)—radiant, full of light
Danen—(m)—talented
Dania—(f)—judgement day, god is my judge
Daniell—(f)—god is my judge, god has judged
Daniel—(m)—the lord is my judge, joyful
Danin—(m)—liberal, benevolent
Danish-ara—(f)—endowed with wisdom, learning
Danishara—(f)—endowed with wisdom, learning
Danish—(f)—learning, wisdom, clever
Danish—(m)—knowledge, careful, to be clever
Daniyah—(f)—closer, nearer
Daniyal—(m)—intelligent, a prophet name
Daniya—(f)—kind hearted
Dani—(f)—merciful, kindness
Dani—(m)—close, near, god is my judge
Danny—(m)—form of daniel, god is my judge
Danyah—(f)—close, near
Danyal—(m)—prophet
Danya—(f)—god is my judge
Daood—(m)—a prophet's name
Daoud—(m)—beloved, form of david
Daqiq—(m)—fine, thin, delicate
Daqqaq—(m)—seller of flour
Darab—(m)—admiral, big gate
Darakhshaan—(f)—shining, shining of moon
Darakhshan—(f)—shining
Darakhshan—(m)—bright, shining, pearl-like
Darawesh—(m)—wealthy, possesses a lot
Darayavahush—(m)—wealthy
Dara—(f)—mercy, halo of the moon, wisdom

Dara—(m)—lord, wealthy
Dareen—(f)—wise
Darian—(m)—wealthy, upholder of the good
Daria—(f)—owner of appropriateness, wealthy, rich
Daria—(m)—preserver, sea
Darien—(m)—wealthy protector
Darim—(m)—one who takes short steps
Darin—(m)—precious present, great
Daris—(m)—studying, scholar
Dariush—(m)—a good, wealthy protector
Darius—(m)—wealthy protector, prophet
Dariyah—(f)—knowledgeable, aware
Dariya—(f)—learned, wealthy
Darkan—(m)—perceptive, understanding
Darkhshanda—(f)—splendid, glittering
Darmal—(m)—medicine
Darman—(m)—treatment, cure
Darrabah—(m)—clever
Darrah—(f)—wise
Darrak—(m)—intelligent, the wise, perceptive
Darra—(f)—oak tree, small great one, riches
Darsie—(f)—glimpse, vision
Daruj—(m)—fast, swift
Darvesh—(m)—humble, religious, gentleman
Darwesh—(m)—mystic
Darwisa—(f)—glimpse, reflection
Darwish—(m)—mystic, dervish
Daryab—(m)—river
Darya—(f)—sea, river, possesses a lot
Daryush—(m)—good natured
Dasa—(f)—slave
Dastagir—(m)—brave
Dastgeer—(m)—helper, supporter
Dastgir—(m)—helper, supporter, patron
Dastiaar—(f)—helper, assistant
Daudi—(m)—flower, beloved one
Daudy—(m)—beloved
Daud—(m)—david, beloved, darling

Daulah—(f)—wealth, empire, state, power
Daulah—(m)—country, kingdom, empire
Daulat—(f)—power, wealth, variant of daulah
Daulat—(m)—wealth, riches, happiness
Daumaa—(f)—sea, ocean
Davod—(m)—one with divine wisdom
Davood—(m)—beloved one
Davoud—(m)—beloved one
Davud—(m)—beloved, a prophet's name
Davut—(m)—beloved friend
Dawah—(f)—invitation, evangelism
Dawah—(m)—invitation, evangelism
Dawar—(m)—wonderer, another name for god
Dawa—(f)—medicine, born on a monday
Dawa—(m)—born on a monday, moon
Dawha—(f)—lofty tree with many branches
Dawid—(m)—adored, beloved, darling, prince
Dawlah—(f)—wealth, happiness
Dawlah—(m)—riches, happiness
Dawlat-khatoon—(f)—she was from a ruling family
Dawlath—(f)—riches, wealth
Dawlatkhatoon—(f)—she was from a ruling family
Dawmat—(f)—a type of palm tree
Dawoud—(m)—a prophet's name
Dawub—(m)—conscientious, diligent
Dawud—(f)—prophets name
Dawud—(m)—adored, from the david, beloved
Dawwar—(m)—revolving
Dawwas—(m)—strong, brave
Dayaan—(m)—a mighty ruler
Dayanatdar—(m)—honest, pious
Dayanna—(f)—divine, god like
Dayfah—(f)—guest
Dayim—(m)—everlasting, perpetual, for ever
Daylan—(m)—hollow, valley
Dayna—(f)—from denmark, similar to daniel
Daywa—(f)—lord, god, one who is divine, sun
Dayyaan—(m)—good ruler, judge, protector

Dayyan—(m)—one who takes revenge
Dayyar—(m)—resident, inhabitant
Dayyin—(m)—religious, devout
Daza—(m)—joy
Deanna—(f)—divine, variant of diana
Dean—(f)—valley, church official
Dean—(m)—dweller in a valley, hollow
Deebaa—(f)—cloth of silk
Deeba—(f)—silk, goddess laxmi
Deebe—(f)—brocade, gold tissue
Deeb—(m)—wolf, a phonetic variant of zib
Deemah—(f)—honestly
Deema—(f)—rainy cloud
Deem—(f)—beautiful rainbow after the rain
Deenaar—(f)—gold coin
Deenaar—(m)—gold coin
Deenah—(f)—obedience
Deenar—(m)—currency, gold coin
Deena—(f)—divine, god like
Deen—(m)—god will judge, place name
Dee—(f)—mother of perseus by zeus, fear
Dehan—(m)—good
Dekel—(m)—dusty one, devotee, palm tree
Delatam—(m)—calm, peaceful
Delawar—(m)—a person who devote heart
Delbar—(f)—sweetheart, charming
Delilah—(f)—joyous, happy, peaceful
Delila—(f)—hair, lovelorn, delicate, weak
Delishaa—(f)—the one who gives pleasure
Delisha—(f)—gives pleasure, delight
Delkash—(f)—attractive, fascinating, beautiful
Delnaz—(f)—sweetheart, beloved
Delwar—(m)—the loved ones
Del—(f)—devotee of god, noble, nobility
Dema—(f)—the rainy cloud, downpour
Demir—(m)—iron
Deneen—(f)—avenged, vindicated
Deniz—(m)—from the sea, ocean, sea

Denny—(m)—follower of zeus, god of wine
Deore—(m)—dear friend, wine, flower
Derifa—(f)—graceful
Devesh—(m)—kind, name of jesus, god of gods
Deviya—(f)—divine, god gift
Dhaafir—(m)—winner
Dhaahir—(m)—one with divine wisdom
Dhaakiraat—(f)—ones who remember god
Dhaakirah—(f)—one who constantly remembers allah
Dhaakireen—(m)—one who remember god
Dhaakiy—(m)—intelligent, bright
Dhaamin—(m)—responsible, guarantor
Dhahab—(f)—gold
Dhaheer—(m)—supporter
Dhahira—(f)—manifest
Dhahir—(m)—manifest
Dhaigham—(m)—lion, king of jungle
Dhakaa—(m)—deep insight, sharpness of mind
Dhakawaan—(m)—one with divine wisdom
Dhakirah—(f)—one who remembers god frequently
Dhakir—(m)—one who praises allah
Dhakiyah—(f)—bright, intelligent
Dhakiyyah—(f)—intelligent
Dhakiy—(m)—intelligent, bright
Dhaki—(m)—one who has a sharp mind
Dhakwan—(m)—intelligent
Dhameer—(m)—heart, conscience
Dhamin—(m)—responsible, guarantor
Dhamir—(m)—heart, conscience
Dhani—(f)—rich, wealthy
Dhan—(m)—wealth, richness
Dhareef—(m)—one with divine wisdom
Dharr—(m)—darkness
Dharwesh—(m)—mystic
Dhayf—(m)—guest
Dheeshaan—(m)—graceful, distinguished, elegant
Dhheiba—(f)—unique, divine aura
Dhiaa—(m)—light, splendour

Dhikraa—(f)—remembrance, memory
Dhikr—(f)—remembrance of god
Dhikr—(m)—remembrance of god
Dhilaal—(f)—shades
Dhilshana—(f)—joy of heart
Dhiyaa—(f)—radiance, light, lamp
Dhiya—(f)—lamp, give a light, light
Dhiya—(m)—splendour, light
Dhuhaa—(f)—mid morning, forenoon
Dhuha—(f)—forenoon
Dhukaa—(f)—name of the sun
Dhukaa—(m)—dawn, morning, the sun
Dhuka—(f)—name of the sun
Dhul-fiqaar—(m)—name of the prophet's sword
Dhul-fiqar—(m)—name of the prophet's sword
Dhulfaqaar—(m)—name of a celebrated sword
Dhulfiqaar—(m)—name of prophet muhammad's sword
Dhulfiqar—(m)—name of the prophets sword
Dhulipala—(m)—one with divine wisdom
Dhuljalaal—(m)—majestic
Dhulkifl—(m)—name of a prophet
Dhullah—(f)—dark cloud
Dhul—(m)—soil
Dhunnoon—(m)—the man of the whale
Dhunun—(m)—one with divine wisdom
Diar—(m)—an expensive wood
Diaudin—(m)—faith source of light
Dibi—(f)—brocade, gold tissue
Didar—(m)—appearance, sight, view, vision
Didja—(f)—nurse
Dielmith—(m)—one with divine wisdom
Digna—(f)—worthy
Dihana—(f)—light, deity
Dihan—(f)—light, deity
Dihan—(m)—divine
Dihishwar—(m)—beautiful
Dihyah—(m)—commander of troops
Dihyat—(m)—head, general, leader

Dihya—(m)—commander of the troops
Diimuddiin—(m)—one with divine wisdom
Dija—(f)—premature baby
Dijesh—(m)—one with divine wisdom
Dikhlat—(m)—heart, soul
Dil-nawaz—(m)—mind, soothing heart
Dil-shouq—(m)—heart love
Dilaawar—(m)—hearty, daring, courageous, brave
Dilafroze—(f)—attractive, captivating
Dilafroz—(m)—attractive, captivating
Dilalah—(f)—guidance, instruction
Dilan—(m)—loving, son of waves, faithful
Dilara—(f)—lover
Dilara—(m)—adorer of heart
Dilavar—(m)—brave
Dilawar—(m)—brave, hearty, daring, bold
Dilawer—(m)—bold, brave, courageous
Dilbahar—(f)—heart of the spring season
Dilbahar—(m)—heart of the spring season
Dilbar—(f)—close to heart, lover
Dilbar—(m)—lover
Dildaar—(m)—charming, delighting the heart
Dildar—(f)—having a big heart
Dildar—(m)—lover, beloved, friend, charming
Dileesha—(f)—delight
Dilfan—(m)—brave
Dilfa—(f)—brave
Dilhan—(m)—loyal, faithful
Dilhasana—(f)—unique, divine aura
Dilhasu—(f)—joy of heart
Dilisha—(f)—delight
Diljaan—(m)—life, heart, mind
Dilkashan—(m)—attractive, captivating
Dilkasha—(f)—captivating, attractive
Dilkash—(f)—captivating, attractive
Dilkash—(m)—heart happy person
Dilkhas—(m)—one with divine wisdom
Dilksha—(f)—unique, divine aura

Dilkusha—(f)—happy heart
Dillzan—(m)—pride of heart
Dill—(f)—heart, true, sincere, genuine
Dilnaaz—(f)—beautiful heart
Dilnara—(f)—appropriate heart
Dilnar—(f)—appropriate heart
Dilnasheeh—(f)—appropriate heart
Dilnashee—(f)—pleasing
Dilnawaaz—(m)—cherishing
Dilnawaz—(m)—soothing heart, mind
Dilnaz—(f)—sweetheart
Dilna—(f)—heart, appropriate heart
Dilna—(m)—one with good heart
Dilqush—(m)—happy heart
Dilruba—(f)—heart-ravishing, beloved
Dilsaan—(m)—pride of heart
Dilsad—(f)—unique, divine aura
Dilsad—(m)—joyous, happy heart, cheerful
Dilsa—(f)—wrestling goddess
Dilshaad—(f)—happy, sweet, cheerful
Dilshaad—(m)—one with divine wisdom
Dilshaan—(m)—glory of heart
Dilshad-khatoon—(f)—excellent
Dilshada—(f)—beloved, joyful, cheerful
Dilshad—(f)—joyful, happy, initiation
Dilshad—(m)—joyful, joyous, happy heart
Dilshana—(f)—joy of heart
Dilshan—(m)—ruler of hearts, prestigious
Dilshard—(m)—one with divine wisdom
Dilsha—(f)—queen of heart
Dilshida—(f)—wisdom, cheerful
Dilshidha—(f)—cheerful, wisdom, beloved
Dilshiya—(f)—unique, divine aura
Dilwara—(f)—lovely
Dilyan—(m)—one with divine wisdom
Dil—(f)—heart, mind
Dil—(m)—heart, mind
Dimah—(f)—down pour

Dimashq—(m)—one with divine wisdom
Dima—(f)—gentle rain
Dimna—(f)—convenient
Dinaaz—(f)—music, religious song
Dinah—(f)—avenged or judged and vindicated
Dinarah—(f)—gold coin
Dinara—(f)—gold coin
Dinar—(f)—gold coin
Dinar—(m)—gold coin, gold unit of coinage
Dina—(f)—love, god has judged, dinah
Dina—(m)—day, lord of the poor, protector
Din—(m)—great congo, belief, custom
Dipu—(m)—flame, light, shining
Diqrah—(f)—narrator of hadith
Dirar—(m)—cash
Diras—(m)—scholar, one who studies, keen
Dirgham—(m)—lion
Dirrane—(f)—unique, divine aura
Dirran—(f)—very gentle and generous person
Dishad—(m)—perfect
Divina—(f)—like a goddess, divine one
Diwah—(f)—candles, spirit, angel
Diwa—(f)—spirit, angel, candles
Diya-al-din—(m)—brightness of the faith, faithful
Diya-udeen—(m)—brightness of the faith
Diyaa-al-din—(m)—brightness of the faith
Diyaa-udeen—(m)—brightness of the faith
Diyaaldin—(m)—shining religion
Diyaar—(f)—home-land
Diyaar—(m)—homeland
Diyaaudeen—(m)—brightness of the faith
Diyaaudin—(m)—brightness of the faith
Diyaa—(m)—light, brilliance, spender
Diyaeddin—(m)—one with divine wisdom
Diyaelhaqq—(m)—one with divine wisdom
Diyanah—(f)—religion
Diyanat—(f)—creed, religion
Diyana—(f)—divine, light, religion

Diyan—(m)—legend, lamp, leader, bright light
Diyari—(m)—a gift, a present
Diyar—(m)—homeland
Diyauddin—(m)—one with divine wisdom
Diyaudeen—(m)—brightness of the faith
Diyaulhaqq—(m)—one with divine wisdom
Diya—(f)—lamp, light, dazzling personality
Diya—(m)—shining, light, glow, splendour
Dizhwar—(m)—strong
Djamal—(m)—beauty
Djamel—(m)—beauty
Djamila—(f)—gorgeous woman, beautiful
Djamilia—(f)—beautiful
Djamil—(m)—beautiful
Djillali—(m)—considered
Djin—(f)—angel
Dmaurah—(m)—one with divine wisdom
Doaa—(f)—pray, a voice of heart
Doa—(f)—pray, voice of heart
Doha—(f)—god's grace, forenoon
Dolon—(m)—dark-haired
Doniya—(f)—life, world
Donyaa—(f)—world
Donya—(f)—lady of the house, world
Don—(m)—ruler of the world
Doon—(m)—there
Dordaneh—(f)—pearl bead, precious, dear
Doreen—(f)—god's gift, gift, gilded
Dorgham—(m)—one with divine wisdom
Dornaz—(f)—beautiful like pearls
Dorri—(f)—sweet, gift
Dorsa—(f)—pearl-like, pearly, beautiful
Dostmuhammad—(m)—friend of the prophet muhammad
Dost—(m)—friend, sweetheart
Douha—(f)—morning, beautiful
Douha—(m)—forenoon
Dounia—(f)—terrestrial life
Dowana—(m)—one with divine wisdom

Dragomira—(f)—precious - peaceful
Draksha—(f)—shining star, grape
Droon—(m)—respectable
Duaa—(f)—call, prayer
Duah—(f)—a wish, prayer
Dualam—(m)—one with divine wisdom
Dua—(f)—prayer, a wish
Dua—(m)—blessing, prayer
Dubaah—(f)—praying all year
Dubb—(m)—state, condition
Duha—(f)—forenoon, early morning
Duha—(m)—forenoon
Duhmus—(m)—liberal
Duhr—(f)—forenoon
Duhr—(m)—noon
Dujanah—(f)—rain, name of a woman
Dulaamah—(m)—tall, black
Dulaf—(m)—one with divine wisdom
Dulamah—(m)—tall and black
Dulama—(m)—tall, black
Dulari—(f)—dear one, beloved
Dula—(m)—brave and courageous
Duldul—(m)—iman husain's horse
Dulika—(f)—unique, divine aura
Dullah—(m)—devotee of allah
Dulqar—(m)—expressive
Dulqer—(m)—diplomatic, expressive
Dulquar—(m)—diplomatic, expressive
Dulquer—(m)—expressive, diplomatic
Dunaa—(f)—worlds
Dunham—(m)—dark skinned fighter, brown man
Duniah—(m)—the world, dark-featured
Dunia—(f)—the world
Dunia—(m)—the world, dark-featured
Duniya—(f)—world, earth
Dunyana—(f)—world
Dunya—(f)—earth, worldly life
Duoaud—(m)—one with divine wisdom

Duqaq—(f)—kind
Duqaq—(m)—loved
Dur-afshan—(f)—scattered pearls, beads
Dur-e-shahwar—(f)—kings worthy pearl
Durabah—(m)—courage, boldness
Duraid—(m)—one with divine wisdom
Durar—(f)—pearl
Durayd—(m)—wise follower
Durdaana—(f)—single pearl
Durdanah—(f)—pearl
Durdana—(f)—single pearl
Dureshahwar—(f)—kings worthy pear
Duresha—(f)—unique, divine aura
Duriya—(f)—shining, dazzling, brilliant
Durnave—(f)—unique, divine aura
Durrah—(f)—large pearl
Durrah—(m)—companion of prophet muhammad
Durra—(f)—pearl
Durriyah—(f)—shining, bright, brilliant
Durriya—(f)—expensive pearl
Durriyyah—(f)—brilliant, glittering
Durruya—(f)—glittering, twinkling, brilliant
Durr—(f)—pearls
Durr—(m)—pearl, magician
Duryab—(f)—finder, bringer of appropriate things
Duryab—(m)—finder, bringer of good things
Dusya—(f)—hope, tender, delicate, moist
Duva—(f)—pitching wave
Duwar—(m)—idol
Dwivedi—(m)—knower of two vedas
Dyab—(m)—the one who perseveres
Dylan—(m)—from a large sea, winner of mind

FIVE

Arabic Baby Names—E

Eahsan—(m)—an act of kindness, mercy, helpful

Eaiza—(f)—dear one, noble, clever

Eajaz—(m)—astonishment, miracle

Eana—(f)—affection

Eanna—(f)—dark, house of god

Easah—(m)—prophet name

Eashal—(f)—name of flower in the heaven

Eashan—(m)—lord vishnu, shiva

Easin—(m)—one with divine wisdom

Easmatara—(f)—friend

Eazaid—(f)—fifth night, fifteenth

Ebadaah—(m)—prayer to allah

Ebadat—(f)—prayer

Ebadat—(m)—prayer

Ebado—(f)—to worship allah

Ebadullah—(m)—one with divine wisdom

Ebadul—(m)—dynamic, bright

Ebin—(m)—rock

Ebi—(m)—paternal, dark

Eblis—(m)—a devilish man

Ebraheem—(m)—one with divine wisdom

Ebrahem—(m)—from abraham

Ebrahiem—(m)—god's messenger

Ebrahim—(m)—father of many nations

Ebrah—(f)—lesson, wisdom
Ebran—(m)—variant of ibrahim
Ebrar—(m)—one with divine wisdom
Ebrin—(m)—creative
Ebtissam—(f)—smile
Ebzan—(m)—one with divine wisdom
Econ—(m)—strong
Edan—(m)—full of fire, delight, fire
Eden—(m)—place of delight, pleasure
Edina—(f)—ardent, wealthy
Edin—(m)—belief
Edirin—(f)—patience is a virtue
Edmark—(m)—furniture
Ednah—(f)—delight, rejuvenation, pleasure
Ednan—(m)—paradise, delight
Edna—(f)—little seed, kernel
Edrees—(m)—name of prophet
Edrina—(f)—unique, divine aura
Edrish—(m)—invisible, lord of mountain
Eeda—(f)—praise, to deposit, to lodge
Eeda—(m)—to deposit, commit, lodge
Eehaan—(m)—the sun
Eeid—(m)—festival, day of festivity
Eelaaf—(f)—pact, agreement, covenant, safety
Eelaf—(f)—covenant, safety, pact, agreement
Eeman—(f)—faith in god
Eeman—(m)—faith in god
Eema—(f)—universal, all-containing
Eenam—(m)—gift, reward
Eenath—(f)—useful
Eena—(f)—unconquerable, mirror
Eeraj—(f)—air-born, lord hanuman
Eeshah—(f)—life
Eeshah—(m)—life
Eeshal—(m)—cute, name of flower in the heaven
Eetra—(f)—fragrance
Eevi—(f)—life, alive, living, breathing
Eeyan—(m)—one with divine wisdom

Eezal—(m)—one with divine wisdom
Eezan—(f)—permission
Efaaz—(m)—helper
Efath—(f)—virtue, chastity
Efatul—(m)—one with divine wisdom
Efaz—(m)—best amazing neymar, helper
Efa—(f)—prosperity, richness, abundance
Effah—(f)—faithful, pure
Effath—(f)—virtue, chastity
Efrad—(m)—one with divine wisdom
Efrat—(f)—honoured
Efraz—(m)—height
Efshana—(f)—fiction
Eftehan—(m)—one with divine wisdom
Eftekhar—(m)—one with divine wisdom
Eftisham—(f)—unique, divine aura
Efty—(m)—god gift
Ehaad—(m)—love
Ehaam—(m)—one with divine wisdom
Ehaan—(m)—full moon
Ehab—(m)—gift
Ehad—(m)—love, one of a kind
Ehannul—(m)—one with divine wisdom
Ehan—(m)—full moon
Ehfat—(f)—chastity, virtue, honour, purity
Ehfaz—(m)—brave
Ehita—(f)—unique, divine aura
Ehsaan—(m)—favour, good
Ehsana—(f)—appropriateness, compassion
Ehsanullah—(m)—sunrise, wishing
Ehsanul—(m)—helper, favour of god
Ehsan—(f)—charitable, compassion
Ehsan—(m)—charitable, goodness, compassion
Ehtashamul—(m)—modesty, decency
Ehtasham—(m)—glory, honour, greatness
Ehteram—(f)—respect
Ehteram—(m)—respect
Ehtesham—(f)—unique, divine aura

Ehtesham—(m)—magnificent, gift from god
Ehtiram—(m)—respect, high regard, honour
Ehtisham—(m)—decency, modesty
Ehzan—(m)—fire, soul of the moon
Eid—(m)—festival, day of celebration
Eiesha—(f)—light, pleasure, desire
Eifad—(f)—to send someone on a mission
Eifad—(m)—to send someone on a mission
Eifa—(f)—to keep one's promise
Eifa—(m)—to keep one's promise
Eihaa—(f)—to inspire
Eihab—(m)—to bestow, to give freely
Eijaz—(m)—blessings
Eileen—(f)—torch of light, light, beauty
Eiliaz—(m)—one with divine wisdom
Eiliyana—(f)—my god has answered
Eimaan—(f)—faith
Eimam—(m)—leader, chief, a variant of imam
Eiman—(f)—faith
Eiman—(m)—honest loving blessings
Eimen—(m)—miracle
Einas—(f)—to feel at peace
Einas—(m)—to feel at peace
Einat—(f)—eye
Eina—(f)—light, form of eino
Ein—(f)—one who has beautiful large eyes
Eiram—(f)—heaven
Eira—(f)—merciful, snow, gift of allah
Eira—(m)—kindling, to kindle
Eiren—(f)—peace
Eirin—(f)—from ireland
Eisah—(f)—variant of esha, eisha
Eisah—(m)—yahweh is salvation
Eisa—(f)—snow
Eisa—(m)—form of jesus, god is my salvation
Eishaa—(f)—pleasure, desire, pious
Eishal—(f)—flower in heaven
Eisha—(f)—pleasure, desire, pious

Eisra—(f)—happiness, salvation
Eissa—(m)—yahweh is salvation
Eithan—(m)—strong, proud
Eithar—(f)—to love another person
Eithar—(m)—to love another person
Eithen—(m)—long-lived, enduring
Eitzaz—(m)—name of prophet
Eiwa—(f)—to provide refuge, safety
Eiwa—(m)—to provide refuge, provide safety
Ejaaz—(m)—miracle, astonishment
Ejajul—(m)—one with divine wisdom
Ejas—(m)—miracle, astonishment
Ejaz—(f)—miracle, astonishment
Ejaz—(m)—variant of e'jaaz, miracle
Ejhat—(m)—one with divine wisdom
Ejlaal—(m)—honour, to respect, exalt
Ejlal—(f)—to honour
Ekaan—(m)—good
Ekbal—(m)—dignity, lord shiva's daughter
Ekerma—(m)—only one, honour
Ekhlaq—(m)—character
Eknoor—(m)—one light, god's light
Ekrah—(f)—to recite
Ekrama—(m)—only one god rama
Ekramuddin—(m)—one with divine wisdom
Ekramul—(m)—one with divine wisdom
Ekram—(m)—honour
Ekran—(m)—honoured
Ekra—(f)—peaceful
Ekrem—(m)—most generous, noble
Ektiar—(m)—power, authority, control, master
El-amin—(m)—trustworthy
Elaaf—(m)—promise, oath
Eladaria—(f)—park
Eladari—(f)—luxury in paradise
Elaf—(f)—oath, covenant, promise, safety
Elaf—(m)—oath, promise, safety, security
Elaha—(f)—ancient gods

Elaheh—(f)—like a goddess
Elahi—(f)—ony one
Elah—(f)—turpentine, oak tree
Elaina—(f)—shining light, light
Elaiya—(f)—the beautiful one, grow in love
Elakkiya—(f)—literature
Elamin—(m)—trustworthy
Elam—(m)—a young man, a virgin, a secret
Elana—(m)—dolphin
Elani—(f)—light
Elanoor—(f)—light
Elan—(m)—tree, friendly
Elasia—(f)—devoted to god, similar to elissa
Elayna—(f)—shining light, similar to helen
Elayza—(f)—pledged to god
Eleanor—(f)—sympathy, compassion, light
Eleena—(f)—shining light, torch, moon
Eleesha—(f)—god is salvation
Elena—(f)—light, sun ray, shining
Eleonora—(f)—shining light, light, sun
Elessah—(f)—unique, divine aura
Eleyas—(m)—name of prophet
Elfeda—(m)—one with divine wisdom
Elgizouli—(m)—kind, honest
Elhaam—(m)—inspiration
Elhaida—(f)—epic queen of the universe
Elham—(f)—inspiration, revelation
Elham—(m)—inspiration
Elhan—(m)—prince
Eliahu—(m)—a prophet
Eliana—(f)—my god has answered me
Eliash—(m)—name of prophet
Eliass—(m)—one with divine wisdom
Elias—(m)—the god is my lord
Elida—(f)—cute, little, from elide valley
Elif—(m)—slim, tall
Elijah—(f)—sweet, smart, loving, beautiful
Elijah—(m)—yahweh is my god, beautiful

Elija—(f)—beautiful, smart, loving
Elinah—(f)—beautiful, moon elope
Elinaz—(f)—unique, divine aura
Elina—(f)—woman with intelligence, pure
Elinoar—(f)—my god is youth
Elin—(f)—torch, shining, brightness, moon
Elisa—(f)—god is my oath, god's promise
Elisha—(f)—my god is salvation
Elish—(m)—god is salvation
Eliyah—(f)—high-born, rising
Eliyana—(f)—my god has answered
Eliyash—(m)—name of prophet
Eliyas—(m)—name of prophet
Eliyaz—(m)—one with divine wisdom
Eliya—(f)—the beautiful one
Elizah—(f)—precious, unique
Eliza—(f)—god is my oath
Eliza—(m)—oath of god
Elizha—(f)—beautiful, beauty
Elizra—(f)—unique, divine aura
Eljah—(m)—jehovah is god, lord is my god
Elkhan—(m)—one with divine wisdom
Ellaha—(f)—ancient gods
Ellahi—(f)—ony one
Ellaria—(f)—beautiful
Ellena—(f)—light, most beautiful woman
Ellen—(m)—courage
Ellias—(m)—my god is yahweh
Ellina—(f)—bright, all, completely
Ellmeera—(f)—aristocratic lady
Ellmera—(f)—aristocratic lady
Ellmeria—(f)—aristocratic lady
Ellora—(f)—clouds
Ellyana—(f)—unique, divine aura
Elma—(f)—will, desire, helmet
Elmeera—(f)—aristocratic lady
Elmeeria—(f)—aristocratic lady
Elmera—(f)—aristocratic lady

Elmeria—(f)—aristocratic lady
Elmerya—(f)—aristocratic lady
Elmira—(f)—noble, aristocratic lady
Elmiya—(f)—learning of islam
Elmi—(f)—helmet, protection, will
Elmyrah—(f)—aristocratic lady
Elmyra—(f)—noble, aristocratic lady
Elnaaz—(f)—pride of people
Elnaz—(f)—most precious, most beautiful
Elnur—(m)—famous
Elsadig—(m)—one with divine wisdom
Elsamhudi—(m)—love of allah
Elshan—(m)—brilliance
Elsheikhidris—(m)—succeeding
Elsueki—(m)—one with divine wisdom
Elvina—(f)—friend of the elves
Elyana—(f)—my god has answered
Elyasin—(m)—name of a prophet
Elyaz—(m)—one with divine wisdom
Elysha—(f)—consecrated to god
Elzeena—(f)—female
Elzein—(m)—handsome
Elzia—(f)—gods light
Emaad—(m)—pillar, support, confidence
Emaan—(f)—faith
Emaan—(m)—faith
Emaaz—(m)—please
Emadudheen—(m)—the pillar of dheen
Emad—(m)—confidence, pillar, support
Emaifa—(f)—unique, divine aura
Emamul—(m)—spiritual leader
Emam—(m)—leader, chief
Emana—(f)—believer, faith, proud
Emane—(f)—faith, belief
Emanie—(f)—belief, faith
Emani—(f)—faith, believer
Emann—(f)—faith, belief
Eman—(f)—faith

Eman—(m)—god is among us
Emarul—(m)—self-sufficient, strong willed
Emat—(f)—trustworthy
Emaya—(f)—flower
Emaz—(m)—pleasing, kind, affectionate
Emdad—(m)—expressive nature, inspirational
Emefa—(f)—there is peace, ewe of ghana
Emeli—(f)—rival, laborious, eager
Emily—(f)—competitor, industrious
Emil—(m)—challenger, industrious
Emina—(f)—eminent, a noble, lofty maiden
Emine—(f)—faithful, truthful, rival
Emin—(f)—safety, peace
Emin—(m)—trustworthy, confident, honest
Emira—(f)—worthy of merit
Emir—(m)—to command, prince, home ruler
Emmad—(m)—awesome
Emmanuel—(m)—god is with me
Emman—(m)—faith
Emma—(f)—industrious, all-containing
Emna—(f)—believing, believing of love
Emona—(f)—hope, new moon
Emon—(m)—starred, truthful, voice
Emory—(m)—powerfully courageous
Emraan—(m)—one with divine wisdom
Emrah—(m)—older brother, loving friend
Emrana—(f)—achievement, progress
Emran—(f)—progress, achievement
Emran—(m)—progress, achievement
Emrin—(f)—achievement, progress
Emrit—(f)—will be rewarded
Emros—(f)—love respect
Emtehan—(m)—exam
Emthiyas—(m)—one with divine wisdom
Emthiyaz—(m)—one with divine wisdom
Emtiaj—(m)—honest
Emtiaz—(m)—privilege, intelligent
Emtiyaj—(m)—privilege, great king, antique

Emzumana—(f)—unique, divine aura
Enaaya—(f)—beautiful, forgiveness
Enait—(m)—god's gift
Enamullah—(m)—god's gift
Enamul—(m)—prosperity
Enam—(f)—reward
Enara—(f)—brighten
Enas—(m)—one with divine wisdom
Enayah—(f)—light of heaven
Enayath—(f)—kindness, concern attention
Enayath—(m)—kindness, concern attention
Enayat—(f)—goddess
Enayat—(m)—generosity
Enaya—(f)—forgiveness, beautiful
Enayetullah—(f)—healthful
Endadul—(m)—support, helpful
Eness—(f)—kindness
Engy—(f)—glorious, gracious
Enida—(f)—soul, life
Eniyah—(f)—better looking, gift of god
Ennaya—(f)—love
Enny—(f)—the mountain of saudia
Ensar—(m)—great
Ensha—(f)—female, origination
Enshirah—(f)—delight, happiness
Ensimam—(m)—to get together, to unite
Enver—(m)—brightness
Epha—(f)—flying
Eqaan—(m)—believer
Eqbal—(m)—destiny, glory
Eqlima—(m)—one with divine wisdom
Eqra—(f)—to read, educate
Equbal—(m)—one with divine wisdom
Erad—(m)—profit
Eram—(f)—heaven, door of jannat
Eram—(m)—garden in heaven
Eran—(m)—follower, land of aryans, iran
Erbin—(m)—legendary son of custenhin

Erelah—(f)—holy messenger, angel
Ereshva—(f)—righteous, honest, sincere
Erfana—(f)—gratefulness, iron heart
Erfan—(m)—iron heart, gratefulness
Erhan—(m)—king of king, ruler
Erha—(f)—god gifted
Erina—(f)—beautiful lady, from ireland
Eriyadi—(m)—one with divine wisdom
Ermeena—(f)—ermine
Ermina—(f)—noble, friendly
Ermin—(m)—universal, whole
Ernisa—(f)—removes darkness by bringing light
Ersa—(f)—rainbow
Ershad—(m)—god gift forever
Ershath—(m)—one with divine wisdom
Ertaza—(m)—approval
Ertifa—(f)—height
Erum—(f)—heaven, garden of haven
Erza—(f)—protector, strong, kind - safe
Esaaf—(f)—the first to care
Esaan—(m)—one with divine wisdom
Esabah—(f)—pure as water
Esak—(m)—beautiful
Esam—(m)—safeguard
Esa—(m)—god is salvation, desirable
Eshaad—(m)—one with divine wisdom
Eshaal—(f)—flower of paradise, to enliven
Eshaal—(m)—name of a flower in heaven
Eshaan—(m)—desiring and wishing, lord shiva
Eshad—(m)—one with divine wisdom
Eshael—(f)—flower of paradise
Eshak—(m)—never ends
Eshal—(f)—the name of flower in the heaven
Eshal—(m)—music, shell
Esham—(m)—from the iron one's estate
Eshan—(f)—blessed by allah
Eshan—(m)—shining, passion of the sun, lord
Eshaque—(m)—one with divine wisdom

Eshaq—(m)—a prophet's name
Eshat—(f)—love
Eshe—(f)—one who is alive, life
Eshia—(f)—female
Eshina—(f)—blessed by allah to beautify
Eshkashem—(m)—one with divine wisdom
Eshmam—(m)—one with divine wisdom
Eshma—(f)—honey, lucky
Eshrath—(f)—companionship, intimacy
Eshrath—(m)—companionship, intimacy
Eshrat—(f)—enjoyment, wish, affection
Eshra—(f)—companionship
Esita—(f)—desired, one who desires
Eskandar—(m)—defender of mankind
Eslam—(m)—religion
Esmael—(m)—god will hear
Esmaerah—(f)—unique, divine aura
Esmail—(m)—god will hear, name of prophet
Esmam—(m)—kind, helpful, king
Esmat—(f)—sunlight
Esmat—(m)—dignity, pride
Esma—(f)—kind defender, loved, emerald
Esme—(f)—kind defender, esteemed, emerald
Esmin—(m)—a kind man
Esmiya—(f)—jasmine
Esmy—(f)—loved, to love, variant of aime
Esraa—(f)—happiness
Esrafil—(m)—angel who will blow the trumpet
Esrana—(f)—unique, divine aura
Esrat—(f)—shinning, beautiful
Esra—(f)—happiness
Esref—(m)—without grief
Essak—(m)—laughter, joyful
Essam—(f)—safeguard
Essam—(m)—safeguard
Essa—(m)—love, jesus, a prophet's name
Estiak—(m)—one with divine wisdom
Etan—(m)—steady, firmness, steadfastness

Etemaad—(m)—variant of e'temad, faith, trust
Etemad—(f)—reliance, trust
Etemad—(m)—faith, trust, reliance
Etesham—(m)—magnificent
Etham—(f)—strength
Ethibal—(f)—rose peddle
Etimad—(f)—to depend upon, to take refuge in
Etizaaz—(m)—become glorious, become mighty
Ettifaq—(m)—unity, friendship, harmony
Ettra—(f)—heavenly smell
Eusha—(f)—unique, divine aura
Evah—(f)—the juniper tree, alive
Eva—(f)—living and breathing, life
Evey—(f)—life
Evrad—(m)—youthful
Ewaan—(m)—young warrior, born to nobility
Ewazi—(m)—substitute, replacement
Eyaan—(m)—protector of creation - abundance
Eyad—(m)—possesses power
Eyana—(f)—affection, princess
Eyan—(m)—kind, peaceful, well bloomed
Eyasmin—(f)—fragrant flower, sweet smelling
Eyazi—(m)—replacement
Eyaz—(m)—one with divine wisdom
Eyhab—(m)—uncle, father's brother
Eyman—(m)—right side, wright
Eysha—(f)—crowned
Eyza—(f)—noble, honour
Ezaan—(f)—beautiful, obidient
Ezaan—(m)—beautiful, charming, obidient
Ezaj—(m)—believer, flower of heaven
Ezan—(m)—acceptance, obedience
Ezath—(m)—respect
Ezatullah—(m)—one with divine wisdom
Ezaz—(m)—honour, rewarding, popular
Eza—(f)—honour, self-respect, dignity
Ezdan—(m)—one with divine wisdom
Ezdehar—(f)—to love someone by heart

Ezekiel—(m)—strength of god
Ezer—(m)—helper, strong
Ezha—(f)—graceful, star
Ezhilarasi—(f)—queen of beauty
Ezhil—(f)—beautiful, azhagu
Ezhil—(m)—high determination power, beauty
Ezifa—(f)—unique, divine aura
Ezina—(f)—to beautify
Ezlan—(m)—one with divine wisdom
Ezlyn—(f)—freedom
Ezmaray—(m)—one with divine wisdom
Ezmin—(f)—unique, divine aura
Ezrah—(f)—helper
Ezrah—(m)—god is help
Ezra—(f)—humble, salvation, helper
Ezra—(m)—humble, salvation, helper
Ezrin—(f)—generosity, wisdom and tolerance
Ezumi—(f)—self defender
Ezureen—(f)—unique, divine aura
Ezwa—(f)—splendour
Ezzah—(f)—a person who gives the honour
Ezzatollah—(m)—one with divine wisdom
Ezzat—(m)—respect
Ezzi—(m)—help

SIX

Arabic Baby Names—F

Faadhil—(m)—meritorious, abundant

Faadilah—(f)—accomplished, virtuous

Faadil—(f)—generous

Faadil—(m)—outstanding, generous, honourable

Faadin—(m)—king

Faadiyah—(f)—self sacrificing, redeemer

Faadi—(m)—redeemer, sacrificing

Faaeqa—(f)—awake, outstanding

Faaeza—(f)—successful, victorious

Faaghira—(f)—jasmine flower

Faahil—(m)—prince

Faahima—(f)—perceptive, intelligent

Faahim—(m)—perceptive, intelligent

Faahina—(f)—smart

Faahira—(f)—unique, divine aura

Faaid—(m)—gain

Faaiq—(m)—variant of fa'iq, surpassing

Faaizah—(f)—prosperous, successful, victorious

Faaiza—(f)—victorious, successful, triumphant

Faaiz—(m)—victorious, triumphant

Faakeh—(m)—cheerful, amusing

Faakhira—(f)—glorious, magnificent

Faakhir—(m)—proud, excellent

Faakihah—(f)—fruit

Faakih—(m)—funny, humorous
Faakirah—(f)—elegant, splendid, proud
Faalan—(m)—productive
Faalih—(m)—successful, fortunate, lucky
Faarah—(f)—happiness, cheerfulness, glory
Faarees—(m)—horseman, knight
Faareh—(m)—glad, happy
Faariah—(f)—name of sahabiyyah
Faaria—(f)—kind, loving, beautiful, king
Faarihah—(f)—swift female camel
Faariha—(f)—happy, glad, delighted, cheerful
Faarih—(m)—happy, comely, pretty
Faarik—(m)—one with divine wisdom
Faariq—(m)—differentiater
Faarisa—(f)—beautiful, smart, kind
Faaris—(m)—horseman, knight
Faariz—(m)—night
Faari—(m)—tall, towering, lofty
Faasiha—(f)—unique, divine aura
Faasil—(m)—one with divine wisdom
Faateer—(m)—maker, creator
Faateh—(m)—conqueror
Faatihah—(f)—introduction, preface, opener
Faatih—(m)—another name for prophet muhammad
Faatima—(f)—a woman who abstains, captivating
Faatinah—(f)—alluring, enchanting, fascinating
Faatina—(f)—captivating
Faatin—(f)—captivating
Faatin—(m)—captivating
Faatir—(m)—maker, creator
Faazila—(f)—virtuous, honest, excellent
Faazil—(m)—an accomplished person, a scholar
Faazira—(f)—unique, divine aura
Faaz—(m)—victorious, successful, brilliant
Fabah—(f)—grower of beans
Faba—(f)—grower of beans
Fabea—(f)—grower of beans
Fabeeha—(f)—fortunate, appropriate deed

Fabeena—(f)—unique, divine aura
Fabee—(f)—blessing, favour, delight - wealth
Fabeha—(f)—lucky, fortunate
Fabek—(m)—variant of fabian, bean farmer
Fabia—(f)—bean farmer, form of fabian
Fabida—(f)—unique, divine aura
Fabiha—(f)—fortunate, lucky
Fabina—(f)—god
Fabir—(m)—the great leader
Fabiyan—(m)—grower of beans, bean farmer
Fabiya—(f)—appropriate thing
Fabi—(m)—form of fabian, bean farmer
Fabliha—(f)—excellent
Fadahunsi—(m)—royalty has favoured me
Fadah—(f)—silver
Fadal—(m)—generous
Fadeelah—(f)—superiority
Fadee—(m)—saviour
Fadela—(f)—excellent
Fadell—(m)—generous
Fadel—(f)—honourable
Fadel—(m)—excellent
Fadgham—(m)—tall, handsome
Fadheela—(f)—virtuous, outstanding, superior
Fadheeler—(f)—virtue, excellence
Fadhila—(f)—virtuous, outstanding
Fadhiler—(f)—virtue, excellence
Fadhil—(m)—meritorious, abundant
Fadhiya—(f)—gorgeous
Fadhi—(m)—saviour
Fadhl—(m)—gracious
Fadia—(f)—fem, redeemer
Fadie—(m)—saviour
Fadilah—(f)—virtuous, outstanding, superior
Fadila—(f)—attractive, appropriate looking
Fadil—(m)—generous, giving, honourable
Fadin—(m)—freshness
Fadish—(m)—one with divine wisdom

Fadiyah—(f)—redeemer, self sacrificing
Fadiya—(f)—redeemer
Fadi—(m)—redeemer, sacrificer, saviour
Fadl-allah—(m)—favour of allah
Fadl-ullah—(m)—excellence of god
Fadlallah—(m)—favour of allah
Fadli—(m)—my present
Fadlullah—(m)—the excellence of god
Fadlyn—(f)—unique, divine aura
Fadl—(f)—favour, outstanding
Fadl—(m)—outstanding, honourable, gracious
Fadri—(m)—one with divine wisdom
Fadwah—(f)—self-sacrifice, heroism
Fadwa—(f)—name derived from self-sacrifice
Fadwa—(m)—name derived from self sacrifice
Fadyaa—(f)—sacrificing
Fadyla—(f)—gracious
Fady—(m)—sacrificer, saviour
Fad—(m)—saviour
Faeema—(f)—strong female, self sacrifice
Faeem—(m)—famed
Faeeqa—(f)—excellent, awake, superb
Faeezah—(f)—leader
Faeiqa—(f)—superb, excellent
Faeqa—(f)—excellent, awake, outstanding
Faeq—(m)—surpassing, excellent
Faerie—(f)—tall, pretty
Faezah—(f)—unique, divine aura
Faezal—(m)—arbiter, judge
Faezan—(m)—an understanding man
Faezeh—(f)—winner, leader
Fagheara—(f)—resembling the jasmine flower
Fagheera—(f)—resembling the jasmine flower
Fagheira—(f)—resembling the jasmine flower
Faghiera—(f)—resembling the jasmine flower
Faghirah—(f)—resembling the jasmine flower
Faghira—(f)—jasmine flower
Faghir—(m)—flower

Faghyra—(f)—resembling the jasmine flower
Fagirah—(f)—resembling the jasmine flower
Fagira—(f)—resembling the jasmine flower
Fagol—(f)—clever and beautiful
Fahaal—(m)—one with divine wisdom
Fahaan—(m)—life - wind
Fahada—(f)—leopardess
Fahaduddin—(m)—one with divine wisdom
Fahadur—(m)—kind
Fahad—(m)—panther, lynx, lion, leopard
Fahama—(f)—astute, perceptive, discerning
Fahameed—(m)—one with divine wisdom
Fahamida—(f)—unique, divine aura
Fahamitha—(f)—unique, divine aura
Fahammed—(m)—mohammed be praised
Faham—(m)—wise, considerate, intellect
Fahana—(f)—unique, divine aura
Fahan—(m)—life, wind
Faharin—(f)—wanderer, glorified
Fahar—(m)—glory
Fahaz—(m)—victorious minded
Fahdah—(f)—leopardess
Fahdha—(f)—lion
Fahdin—(m)—king
Fahduddin—(m)—leopard of the faith, a brave
Fahdullah—(m)—cheetah of god
Fahd—(m)—panther, lynx, leopard, lion
Faheam—(m)—learned man, scholar
Fahed—(m)—tiger
Faheed—(m)—panther
Faheel—(m)—intelligent, genius
Faheemah—(f)—intelligent
Faheema—(f)—learned, intelligent, perceptive
Faheemudin—(m)—one with divine wisdom
Faheem—(m)—intelligent, judicious
Faheena—(f)—one moment
Faheera—(f)—lucky
Fahee—(m)—from the green field

Faheim—(m)—learned man, scholar
Fahemah—(f)—intelligent, learned
Fahema—(f)—learned, intelligent
Faher—(m)—one with divine wisdom
Fahhaamat—(f)—extremely sympathetic
Fahhaam—(m)—understanding
Fahhama—(f)—very intelligent, learned
Fahham—(m)—very intelligent
Fahia—(f)—fearless, also spelt as fahiya
Fahiba—(f)—bestower, giver
Fahida—(f)—helpful, helpfulness
Fahidha—(f)—helpfulness
Fahid—(m)—panther
Fahiema—(f)—learned, intelligent
Fahiem—(m)—learned man, scholar
Fahika—(f)—unique, divine aura
Fahila—(f)—unique, divine aura
Fahimah—(f)—learned, intelligent
Fahimasulthana—(f)—intelligent queen
Fahimat—(f)—understanding, intelligent
Fahima—(f)—intelligent, learned, understands
Fahimeh—(f)—learned, wise
Fahimudeen—(m)—one with divine wisdom
Fahim—(f)—intelligent, scholar, learned man
Fahim—(m)—wise, learned, prudent, sagacious
Fahina—(f)—unique, divine aura
Fahiqa—(f)—unique, divine aura
Fahiq—(m)—one with divine wisdom
Fahira—(f)—respectful, joyful
Fahirudin—(m)—one with divine wisdom
Fahir—(m)—respectful, glory
Fahisa—(f)—investigator, tester
Fahis—(m)—music
Fahitha—(f)—unique, divine aura
Fahith—(m)—one with divine wisdom
Fahiya—(f)—fearless
Fahiza—(f)—tester, investigator
Fahiz—(m)—brave and successful, music

Fahkir—(m)—proud
Fahlaan—(m)—one with divine wisdom
Fahla—(f)—courageous
Fahm-ara—(f)—intelligent
Fahman—(m)—one with divine wisdom
Fahmara—(f)—adorned with intellect
Fahmat—(f)—understanding, comprehension
Fahmat—(m)—dusk, darkness, understanding
Fahmawi—(m)—understanding, comprehending
Fahma—(f)—intelligence, genius
Fahmeda—(f)—intelligent and wise
Fahmeeb—(f)—variant of fahmi'b, wise
Fahmeedah—(f)—wise, intelligent
Fahmeeda—(f)—intelligent, wise
Fahmeedha—(f)—wise, intelligent
Fahmeena—(f)—precious stone, fish
Fahmee—(m)—perceptive, intelligent
Fahmib—(f)—wise, understanding
Fahmidah—(m)—intelligent, wise
Fahmida—(f)—intelligent and wise, scholarly
Fahmideh—(f)—learned, wise, knowledgeable
Fahmidha—(f)—scholarly, intelligent, wise
Fahmid—(m)—intelligent, wise
Fahmina—(f)—unique, divine aura
Fahmin—(m)—responsible man
Fahmitha—(f)—unique, divine aura
Fahmiya—(f)—learned, understanding
Fahmi—(f)—understanding
Fahmi—(m)—understanding, intelligent
Fahmudeen—(m)—wise, knowledgeable
Fahmun—(m)—understanding, comprehending
Fahm—(f)—intelligence, insight, genius
Fahm—(m)—intellect, understanding
Fahnasin—(f)—unique, divine aura
Fahoom—(m)—intelligent
Fahran—(m)—handsome devotee
Fahra—(f)—gift of god
Fahreen—(f)—blessed, wanderer

Fahreen—(m)—one with divine wisdom
Fahreezan—(f)—unique, divine aura
Fahriah—(f)—unique, divine aura
Fahrin—(f)—glorified, wanderer
Fahriya—(f)—angel, fairy
Fahyaan—(m)—one with divine wisdom
Fahyim—(m)—very clever
Fahzin—(m)—one with divine wisdom
Faiad—(m)—charitable, benevolent, boon
Faian—(m)—trust, belief
Faiaz—(m)—victorious, successful
Faidah—(f)—profit, gain, benefit, advantage
Faida—(f)—plentiful, gain, useful, benefit
Faida—(m)—usefulness
Faidhee—(m)—endowed with super abundance
Faidh—(m)—superabundance, favour
Faid—(m)—benefit, advantage, gain
Faieda—(f)—unique, divine aura
Faieka—(f)—superior, beautiful
Faiez—(m)—victorious, knight, gain, favour
Faihaan—(m)—fragrant
Faihaa—(f)—garden, appropriate smell
Faihami—(m)—understanding, comprehending
Faihan—(m)—fragrant, witness
Faiha—(f)—pleasant smell of paradise
Faih—(f)—perfume, fragrance
Faijaan—(m)—king
Faijal—(m)—lovable
Faijan—(m)—king, lion
Faija—(f)—successful, a beautiful angel
Faijuddin—(m)—one with divine wisdom
Faijul—(m)—victory
Faijunnesha—(f)—unique, divine aura
Faikah—(f)—superior, beautiful, surpassing
Faika—(f)—beautiful, superior
Faik—(m)—superior, excellent
Faila—(f)—arabian jasmine
Fail—(m)—doer, performer

Faima—(f)—peacemaker
Faimeeda—(f)—wise
Faimeena—(f)—lovely
Faimida—(f)—wise, intelligent
Faimina—(f)—lovely
Faimmudin—(m)—one with divine wisdom
Faimudeen—(m)—one with divine wisdom
Fainan—(f)—with beautiful long hair
Fainaz—(f)—greatness, highness
Fainu—(f)—glowing, shining, fairy
Fain—(m)—pleased, joyful
Faiqah—(f)—excellent, surpassing
Faiqa—(f)—genius, extraordinary, superb
Faiq—(m)—superior, excellent, ascendant
Faira—(f)—pleasant, gift of god
Fairiha—(f)—gold
Fairoja—(f)—unique, divine aura
Fairoosa—(f)—unique, divine aura
Fairooza—(f)—a precious gem
Fairooz—(f)—creative, skilful, talented
Fairooz—(m)—a blue stone
Fairosa—(f)—precious stone
Fairose—(m)—precious stone, turquoise
Fairouz—(f)—turquoise stone
Fairoza—(f)—turquoise, precious stone
Fairoze—(m)—turquoise, precious stone
Fairoz—(f)—turquoise
Fairoz—(m)—turquoise
Fairusa—(f)—woman of triumph, turquoise
Fairuzah—(f)—a precious gem
Fairuza—(f)—woman of triumph, gemstone
Fairuz—(f)—turquoise stone
Fairuz—(m)—victorious, triumphant
Faisal—(f)—decisive
Faisal—(m)—decisive, the judge, resolute
Faisan—(m)—generosity, charity, great grace
Faisa—(f)—successful, victorious
Faisel—(m)—bold

Faishad—(m)—one with divine wisdom
Faishal—(m)—resolute, the judge, decisive
Faisha—(f)—a blessing to all
Faisil—(m)—clever
Faisi—(m)—light of the sun
Faisl—(m)—arbiter, judge
Faissal—(f)—decisive
Faisul—(m)—victory
Faisu—(m)—handsome
Fais—(f)—winner
Faitahah—(f)—right guidance
Faitaha—(f)—unique, divine aura
Faitah—(m)—guidance, right direction
Faiva—(f)—attractive
Faiyad—(m)—one with divine wisdom
Faiyaj—(m)—talented, peaceful, artistic
Faiyan—(m)—belief, trust, independent
Faiyaz—(m)—artistic
Faiyed—(m)—one with divine wisdom
Faiyum—(m)—one with divine wisdom
Faiyza—(f)—successful
Faiz-e-rabbani—(m)—possessing divine surplus
Faizaan—(f)—unique, divine aura
Faizaan—(m)—favour, grace, favourite
Faizabad—(m)—one with divine wisdom
Faizad—(m)—one with divine wisdom
Faizah—(f)—victorious, winner, obtaining
Faizah—(m)—achieving, attaining
Faizalkhan—(m)—one with divine wisdom
Faizal—(m)—victory, won
Faizam—(m)—one with divine wisdom
Faizan-anwar—(m)—ruler, favourite, grace
Faizana—(f)—generosity, great grace
Faizanullah—(m)—one with divine wisdom
Faizan—(f)—beneficent, ruler, charity
Faizan—(m)—great grace, beneficence
Faizath—(f)—unique, divine aura
Faizath—(m)—one with divine wisdom

Faiza—(f)—gain, victorious, winner
Faiza—(m)—victorious, winner
Faizeena—(f)—victorious, honest, winner
Faizeen—(f)—winner, honest, victorious
Faizeen—(m)—lion, victorious, winner, grace
Faizee—(f)—bringer, source of abundance
Faizee—(m)—bringer, source of abundance
Faizel—(m)—stubborn, resolute, decisive
Faizerabbani—(m)—possessing divine surplus
Faize—(m)—arbiter, judge
Faizha—(f)—unique, divine aura
Faizia—(f)—successful
Faizin—(m)—champion, creative, great grace
Faiziya—(f)—successful, victorious
Faizi—(f)—liberal
Faizi—(m)—liberal
Faizon—(m)—an understanding man
Faizoon—(m)—winner
Faizuddin—(m)—one with divine wisdom
Faizudeen—(m)—one with divine wisdom
Faizul-anwar—(m)—abundance of light or graces
Faizulanwar—(m)—abundance of light or graces
Faizullah—(m)—abundance from allah
Faizulla—(m)—abundance from allah
Faizul—(m)—victory
Faizum—(f)—unique, divine aura
Faizuna—(f)—unique, divine aura
Faizunisah—(f)—beautiful, the winner
Faizunisa—(f)—the winner, best among female
Faizunissa—(f)—unique, divine aura
Faizunnisa—(f)—the winner, best among female
Faizun—(m)—winner
Faizurrahman—(m)—bounty and plenty from god
Faizur—(m)—successful, victorious
Faizu—(m)—successful, victorious
Faizya—(f)—victorious, successful
Faizy—(f)—victorious, gain, successful
Faizzan—(m)—best, god gift, blessing of god

Faizza—(f)—genius, successful, intelligent
Faiz—(m)—gain, knight, grace, favour
Fajahat—(m)—one with divine wisdom
Fajaruddin—(m)—the first
Fajar—(f)—morning prayer
Fajar—(m)—brave, a great warrior
Fajaz—(m)—powerful
Fajeel—(m)—one with divine wisdom
Fajeena—(f)—rose in desert
Fajer—(f)—daybreak
Fajhan—(m)—nobel, good
Fajila—(f)—cute
Fajisha—(f)—unique, divine aura
Fajitha—(f)—unique, divine aura
Fajiya—(f)—victorious, successful
Fajrah—(f)—dawn
Fajruddin—(m)—dawn of the faith
Fajrullah—(m)—morning of allah
Fajr—(f)—dawn, morning prayer, first light
Fajr—(m)—morning twilight, daybreak, dawn
Fajyaz—(f)—artistic
Fakahat—(m)—good natured
Fakaruddin—(m)—pride of religion
Fakeeaha—(f)—cheerful, happy, humorous, amusing
Fakeehah—(f)—cheerful
Fakeeha—(f)—cheerful
Fakeeh—(m)—cheerful
Fakeer—(m)—a saintly person
Fakharuddawlah—(m)—glory of the kingdom
Fakharuddin—(m)—glory of the religion (islam)
Fakharulislam—(m)—glory of islam
Fakhar—(f)—honour, pride, glory
Fakhar—(m)—pride, fame, jewellery
Fakher—(m)—handsome
Fakhirah—(f)—splendid, elegant
Fakhirah—(m)—precious, honourable
Fakhiraldin—(m)—glorious religion
Fakhira—(f)—glorious, magnificent

Fakhiri—(m)—honorary
Fakhirya—(f)—unique, divine aura
Fakhir—(m)—glory, excellent quality, proud
Fakhitah—(f)—a dove, a ringed turtle dove
Fakhitah—(m)—a dove, a ringed turtle dove
Fakhit—(m)—one with divine wisdom
Fakhr-al-din—(m)—pride of the faith
Fakhr-aldin—(m)—glorious religion
Fakhr-ud-dawlah—(m)—glory of kingdom or state
Fakhr-ud-deen—(m)—pride of the religion
Fakhr-ud-din—(m)—pride of the religion islam
Fakhraldin—(m)—pride of the faith
Fakhrat—(m)—bringing joy
Fakhra—(f)—proud, pride, appropriate, new
Fakhree—(m)—glorious, proud
Fakhria—(f)—unique, divine aura
Fakhridadin—(m)—glorious religion
Fakhriddin—(m)—one with divine wisdom
Fakhriyah—(f)—honorary
Fakhriya—(f)—proud, glory, honorary
Fakhriyya—(f)—glow, pride, glorious, proud
Fakhri—(f)—glory, worthy of being proud of
Fakhri—(m)—glory, honorary, glorious, proud
Fakhrjahan—(m)—pride of the world
Fakhrud-din—(m)—pride of the religion
Fakhruddaulah—(m)—pride of the state
Fakhruddawlah—(m)—glory of kingdom or state
Fakhruddin—(m)—glory of the faith, emperor
Fakhrul—(m)—one with divine wisdom
Fakhrun-nisa—(f)—glory of the female
Fakhrunnisa—(f)—glory, pride of female
Fakhry—(m)—glorious, proud, honorary
Fakhr—(f)—glory, honour, pride
Fakhr—(m)—glory, pride
Fakhtah—(f)—a dove
Fakhta—(f)—dove
Fakihah—(f)—fruit
Fakihat—(f)—fruit of heaven

Fakiha—(f)—fruit
Fakih—(m)—smart, intelligent, humorous
Fakira—(f)—thinker
Fakira—(m)—sage, saint, thinker
Fakirudeen—(m)—pride of religion
Fakir—(m)—a saintly person, saint
Fakiza—(f)—unique, divine aura
Fakra—(f)—proud, pride, glory
Fakra—(m)—pride, glory, proud
Fakruddin—(m)—pride of religion
Fakrudeen—(m)—pride of religion
Fakrudheen—(m)—pride of religion
Fakrudin—(m)—pride of religion
Fakrunnisa—(f)—glory, pride of female
Fakru—(m)—bright
Fakur—(m)—thinker
Falaah—(m)—success, progress, prosperity
Falack—(f)—resembling a star, sky, orbit
Falac—(f)—resembling a star, orbit
Falahah—(f)—great success, deliverance
Falahat—(f)—welfare, benefit
Falah—(f)—happiness, success, long live
Falah—(m)—success, progress, victory
Falakara—(f)—one who decorates the sky
Falake—(m)—an astronomer
Falakh—(f)—the sky, space, orbit
Falaki—(f)—heavenly, celestial
Falaknaz—(f)—sky
Falak—(f)—star, sky, heaven, orbit, space
Falak—(m)—the sky, orbit, space, cosmos
Falaqnoor—(f)—unique, divine aura
Falaq—(f)—break of dawn, daybreak, dawn
Falaq—(m)—top edge, daybreak, dawn
Falasha—(f)—desire, landless ones, jews
Falatun—(m)—mighty powerful
Faleehah—(f)—successful
Faleeh—(m)—successful
Faleena—(f)—descendant

Faleeq—(m)—god of still
Faleesh—(m)—tulip
Faleha—(f)—fortunate, success
Faleh—(m)—victor
Falha—(f)—winner
Falihah—(f)—successful
Faliha—(f)—success, fortunate, lucky
Falihi—(m)—successful, winner
Falih—(f)—successful, prosperous
Falih—(m)—prosperous, successful, victory
Falila—(f)—praise
Falina—(f)—bearing fruit, fruitful, fluffy
Faliq—(m)—creator, one that divides into two
Falisa—(f)—unique, divine aura
Falisha—(f)—happiness, lucky
Faliza—(f)—unique, divine aura
Falkiya—(f)—unique, divine aura
Fallah—(f)—resembling a crow
Fallah—(m)—farmer
Falla—(f)—resembling a crow
Fallgu—(m)—happy, humble
Falooh—(m)—successful, winner
Famai—(f)—bliss, princess, blessed
Famani—(f)—unique, divine aura
Famat—(f)—survived
Fama—(f)—rumour
Fameedah—(f)—wise
Fameeda—(f)—wise, sweet
Fameedha—(f)—wise
Fameeha—(f)—worthy
Fameela—(f)—clever
Fameena—(f)—fish, precious stone
Fameera—(f)—unique, divine aura
Famidah—(f)—sweet
Famida—(f)—scholarly, intelligent, wise
Famidha—(f)—wise
Famila—(f)—unique, divine aura
Famina—(f)—lovely

Famin—(m)—the worshipper of allah, happiness
Famira—(f)—unique, divine aura
Famitha—(f)—gift of god
Famiya—(f)—princess
Famiza—(f)—unique, divine aura
Famiz—(m)—good luck, future, good health
Famnaz—(f)—merciful
Famut—(m)—reading
Famya—(f)—appropriate fame
Famyu—(m)—one with divine wisdom
Fanah—(f)—one who provides light
Fanan—(f)—branch of a tree
Fanan—(m)—branch of a tree
Fanas—(m)—jack fruit
Fanaz—(f)—greatnesh, highness in status
Fanaz—(m)—highness, greatness
Fana—(f)—princess, wealth, honour, light
Faneesha—(f)—heaven flower
Fanha—(f)—passing away
Fania—(f)—free, feminine of francis
Fanila—(f)—able, worthy
Fani—(f)—perishable, changeable, free
Fani—(m)—snake
Fannah—(f)—getting destroyed in love, fun
Fannanah—(m)—female artist
Fannana—(f)—artist
Fannan—(f)—artist
Fannan—(m)—artist
Fanza—(f)—winner
Faouzi—(m)—success
Faoz—(m)—success, victory, advantage, gain
Faqahat—(m)—intelligent, learned
Faqar—(m)—proud, pride
Faqeed—(m)—rare, special
Faqeeha—(f)—knowledgeable, expert, scholar
Faqeeh—(m)—scholar of religious laws, jurist
Faqeer—(m)—poor, sufi mendicant
Faqia—(f)—outstanding, awake

Faqihah—(f)—school mistress
Faqiha—(f)—jurist, expert
Faqih—(m)—jurist, scholar in fight
Faqirah—(f)—wife of murrah al-asadi
Faqir—(m)—poor, sufi mendicant, proud
Faqra—(f)—proud, pride
Faqruddin—(m)—one with divine wisdom
Faqrudin—(m)—pride of religion
Faqrullah—(m)—one with divine wisdom
Faqrunnisa—(f)—glory, pride of female
Faqueeda—(f)—unique, divine aura
Faq—(m)—based
Faraad—(m)—one who has unique opinions
Faraah—(f)—beautiful, joy
Faraaid—(f)—unique, independent-minded
Faraal—(f)—name of lion, height
Faraan—(m)—lonely, happy
Faraasat—(m)—keen eye, discernment
Faraaz—(m)—sword, elevation
Faradis—(m)—paradise
Farad—(m)—unmatched, unique
Farafisa—(f)—companion, bin umayr al-hanafi
Farafisa—(m)—name of a companion
Farag—(m)—cure, improvement, remedy
Farahaat—(m)—variant of farhaat
Farahan—(m)—gladly, cheerfully
Farahath—(f)—liveliness
Farahat—(f)—liveliness
Farahat—(m)—joys, delights
Faraha—(f)—joyful, delight
Farahdokht—(f)—happy, joyous
Farahnaz—(f)—joy, happy and beautiful
Farahna—(f)—cheerful, joyful
Farahnoush—(f)—one who is always happy
Farahrouz—(f)—fortunate, blessed
Farahzad—(f)—bringer of happiness
Farah—(f)—glory, happiness, cheerfulness
Farah—(m)—happiness, paradise's flower, joy

Faraisa—(f)—unique, divine aura
Farajallah—(m)—one with divine wisdom
Farajana—(f)—hospitable and friendly
Farajuddin—(m)—one with divine wisdom
Farajullah—(m)—god's relief, rescue
Faraj—(m)—happiness, ease, relief
Farakh—(m)—secure, wide, spacious
Faranaaz—(f)—leader, loyal
Faranaz—(f)—unique, divine aura
Farana—(f)—glad - joyful
Farani—(f)—sunshine
Faran—(m)—advances
Faraqta—(f)—be with your god
Faraq—(m)—truth
Farasat—(m)—keen eye, discernment, perception
Farashah—(f)—butterfly
Farashah—(m)—moth, butterfly
Farasha—(f)—butterfly, beautiful
Farash—(m)—knight
Faras—(m)—good gift
Farat—(f)—bliss, pleasure, happiness
Farat—(m)—pleasure, bliss
Farazak—(m)—happy, joyful
Farazamed—(m)—bliss
Farazana—(f)—delighted, intelligence
Faraza—(f)—success, height, joyful
Farazuddin—(m)—one with divine wisdom
Farazul—(m)—one with divine wisdom
Faraz—(m)—equitable, above, upon, elevation
Fara—(f)—level measure, beautiful, lovely
Fara—(m)—head, chief of a family, sunset
Farbod—(m)—right, orthodox, keeper
Fardaa—(f)—unique, divine aura
Fardad—(m)—awesome, happy
Fardain—(m)—unique, peerless, plural of fard
Fardanah—(f)—intelligent, wise, unique
Fardan—(f)—unique, peerless
Fardan—(m)—unique, peerless

Farda—(f)—tomorrow
Fardden—(m)—one with divine wisdom
Fardeena—(f)—radiant
Fardeen—(m)—one who has triple strength
Farden—(m)—radiant
Fardifa—(f)—highly illuminated
Fardil—(m)—one with divine wisdom
Fardina—(f)—justified love, love, decorated
Fardin—(f)—unique, divine aura
Fardin—(m)—one who has triple strength
Fardoos—(f)—paradise, garden, heaven
Fardous—(m)—garden, paradise
Fardowsa—(f)—highest garden in paradise, heaven
Fardun—(m)—unique, peerless, singular
Fard—(m)—single, unique
Farea—(f)—towering, tall, lofty, slim
Fareda—(f)—morning
Fareeb—(m)—one with divine wisdom
Fareedah—(f)—unique, matchless
Fareeda—(f)—unique, matchless
Fareedha—(f)—unique, divine aura
Fareed—(m)—unique, incomparable
Fareefta—(f)—devotee, lover
Fareeha—(f)—happiness, happy, joyful
Fareek—(m)—lieutenant general
Fareema—(f)—lovable one
Fareenaa—(f)—unique, divine aura
Fareena—(f)—happiness
Fareen—(f)—wanderer, adventurous, blessed
Fareeq—(m)—distribution, group, band, crew
Fareesa—(f)—light, life
Fareesha—(f)—peaceful, humble, light
Fareess—(f)—life
Farees—(m)—perspicacity
Fareeth—(m)—one with divine wisdom
Fareeya—(f)—unique, divine aura
Fareeza—(f)—light
Fareez—(m)—brave

Faree—(m)—unmatched, unique
Fareha—(f)—happiness, glad, joyful
Fareh—(m)—glad, happy
Fareiba—(f)—beautiful or attractive
Fareshta—(f)—angel
Fares—(m)—knight, down
Farez—(m)—promising, brave
Fare—(m)—tall, lofty, slim, towering
Fargana—(f)—unique, divine aura
Farhaana—(f)—happy, joyful, cheerful, glad
Farhaan—(m)—merry, happy
Farhaat—(m)—happy event, joyous time
Farhaaz—(m)—equitable, above
Farhad—(f)—wise
Farhad—(m)—happiness, digger of mines
Farhah—(f)—happy, lively
Farhaj—(m)—one with divine wisdom
Farhal—(f)—happy
Farhal—(m)—prosperous, bounteous
Farham—(f)—proud
Farhan-ali—(m)—happy, happiness, joyful, glad
Farhanaaz—(f)—loyal, leader
Farhanaa—(f)—beautiful
Farhanah—(f)—happy
Farhanalka—(f)—glad, joyful, happiness
Farhana—(f)—immerse, beautiful, happy, joyful
Farhana—(m)—happiness
Farhang—(m)—good-breeding
Farhani—(f)—unique, divine aura
Farhannah—(f)—joyful, glad
Farhanna—(f)—glad, joyful
Farhanna—(m)—glad, joyful
Farhan—(f)—merry, happy, happiness
Farhan—(m)—happiness, joyful, glad, happy
Farhara—(f)—happiness
Farhas—(m)—knight
Farhatah—(f)—happiness, joy, contentment
Farhath—(f)—happiness

Farhath—(m)—glad, joyous, happy, glorious
Farhatullah—(m)—pleasure, joy of god
Farhat—(f)—happiness, bliss, decent
Farhat—(m)—happiness, joy, mirth, delight
Farhaz—(m)—upon, equitable
Farha—(f)—happiness
Farha—(m)—happiness
Farheem—(f)—unique, divine aura
Farheena—(f)—gift of god
Farheen—(f)—god gifted, great, happy
Farheen—(m)—happy, joyous, jubilant
Farhina—(f)—happiness
Farhin—(f)—jubilant, happiness, sky angel
Farhiya—(f)—happy, pretty, nice
Farhiyyan—(m)—happy, content
Farhi—(f)—glad, happy
Farhi—(m)—happy, joyous, content
Fariah—(f)—name of a companion
Farial—(f)—unique, divine aura
Faria—(f)—a caravan, beautiful
Faribah—(f)—unique, divine aura
Fariba—(f)—mesmerising, enticing, charming
Farib—(m)—intelligent, charming, beautiful
Faridaa—(f)—unique, peerless
Faridah—(f)—unique, matchless
Farida—(f)—turquoise, unique, love, proud
Farida—(m)—unique
Farideh—(f)—delightful, unique, precious
Farideh—(m)—unmatched, unique
Faride—(m)—unmatched, unique
Faridha—(f)—proud, turquoise, unique
Faridoon—(m)—the third child, thrice strong
Fariduddin—(m)—uniqueness of religion
Faridullah—(m)—one with divine wisdom
Faridun—(m)—three times strong, precious gem
Farid—(f)—unique
Farid—(m)—wide, unique, without rival
Farieda—(f)—unique, divine aura

Faried—(m)—unmatched, unique
Farien—(f)—wanderer, wise, glorified
Farihah—(f)—happy, joyful, cheerful, glad
Farihat—(f)—happy, joyful, variant of farihah
Fariha—(f)—happiness, joyful, happy
Fariheen—(f)—joyful, gladly, cheerfully
Farihtah—(f)—angel
Farih—(m)—happy, delight, full of joy
Farija—(f)—beautiful, light
Farik—(m)—lieutenant general
Faril—(m)—heroic, a superior man
Farimah—(f)—happy, joyful, cheerful
Farima—(f)—lovable one
Farima—(m)—one with divine wisdom
Farinah—(f)—unique, divine aura
Farina—(f)—traveller
Farin—(f)—adventurous, wise, wanderer
Farin—(m)—adventurous
Fario—(m)—happiness
Fariqa—(f)—tranquil leader, distinguishing
Farique—(m)—separator
Fariq—(m)—distinguishing, distinctive
Farisaa—(f)—unique, divine aura
Farisa—(f)—smart, beautiful, kind
Farisha—(f)—light, humble, peaceful, life
Farishma—(f)—unique, divine aura
Farishta—(f)—angel, messenger
Farishtha—(f)—unique, divine aura
Farish—(m)—helpful
Farisi—(m)—competent
Fariss—(m)—knight
Farista—(m)—sent by god, angel
Faris—(f)—a forgiving woman
Faris—(m)—horseman, perspicacity, rider
Farita—(f)—brave curious
Faritha—(f)—brave curious
Farith—(m)—guide
Farit—(m)—guide

Fariyaal—(f)—angel
Fariyal—(f)—angel
Fariyaz—(m)—one with divine wisdom
Fariya—(f)—fairy, kind, beautiful
Fariya—(m)—one with divine wisdom
Fariy—(m)—first-born
Farizah—(f)—arch
Fariza—(f)—light, beautiful
Fariz—(m)—determined, promising
Fari—(f)—pretty, beautiful
Fari—(m)—tall, towering, lofty
Farjaana—(f)—beautiful soul, kind
Farjad—(m)—excellent, eminent in learning
Farjam—(m)—perfect
Farjana—(f)—you are kind, home-loving
Farjana—(m)—beautiful soul
Farjat—(m)—freedom from sorrow
Farjia—(f)—comfort, relief
Farjina—(f)—hospitable, friendly
Farjin—(m)—strange
Farjul—(m)—one with divine wisdom
Farjuma—(f)—unique, divine aura
Farj—(m)—duty
Farkhandah—(f)—lucky, happy
Farkhanda—(f)—blessed
Farkhandea—(f)—one who is blessed - happy
Farkhande—(f)—happy, blessed
Farkhandia—(f)—one who is blessed - happy
Farkhand—(f)—one who is blessed and happy
Farkha—(f)—unique, divine aura
Farkhondeh—(f)—joyous, happy
Farkhunda—(f)—prosperous, likeable
Farlin—(f)—beautiful
Farmaan—(m)—decree, verdict, edict
Farmanullah—(m)—order of allah
Farman—(m)—decree, edict, command, order
Farmeena—(f)—unique, divine aura
Farmida—(f)—unique, divine aura

Farnaaz—(f)—unique, divine aura
Farnaz—(f)—glorious coquetry
Farnham—(m)—meadow with ferns
Farod—(m)—unmatched, unique, wicked, unlucky
Farokh—(m)—power of discrimination, happy
Farood—(m)—unique, peerless, singular
Faroogh—(m)—splendour, light, brightness
Farookh—(m)—sprout, shoot, young bird
Farook—(m)—truthful, friendly, good person
Farooque—(f)—fortunate
Farooque—(m)—power of discrimination
Farooqui—(m)—one with divine wisdom
Farooq—(m)—name of prophet's beloved friend
Farooz—(m)—one with divine wisdom
Faroqh—(m)—truth
Faroshan—(f)—unique, divine aura
Farouk—(m)—discerning truth from falsehood
Faroza—(f)—light
Faroz—(m)—success
Farqadin—(m)—two bright stars near the pole
Farqad—(f)—name of a star
Farqad—(m)—bright star
Farq—(m)—beloved man
Farradah—(f)—one who sells jewellery
Farrahah—(f)—happy, jubilant
Farrah—(f)—beautiful, joyful, lovely
Farrajah—(f)—happy, joyous
Farraj—(m)—relief, freedom from grief, happy
Farran—(m)—baker, the land, ardent for peace
Farraz—(m)—above, equitable, upon
Farrel—(m)—brave, hero, man of courage
Farriah—(f)—joyful, pleasant, beautiful
Farrin—(f)—wanderer, adventurous, glorified
Farrin—(m)—blacksmith, the land
Farrisu—(f)—beautiful, intelligent - brave
Farris—(f)—a forgiving woman
Farris—(m)—rock, iron strong
Farriya—(f)—fairy, angel

Farrokhzad—(m)—happily, auspiciously born
Farrokh—(m)—auspicious, happy, fortunate
Farrooh—(m)—happy, joyful
Farrukh—(f)—happy, fortunate
Farrukh—(m)—blessed, auspicious, young bird
Farsad—(m)—wise, learned
Farsana—(f)—intelligent wise
Farsa—(f)—pure
Farseena—(f)—beautiful, intelligent
Farseen—(m)—intelligent, love
Farshad—(m)—soul of the sphere of mercury
Farshana—(f)—unique, divine aura
Farshan—(m)—one with divine wisdom
Farsha—(f)—beautiful, butterfly
Farsheed—(m)—happy
Farshida—(f)—sparkling, illuminated
Farshid—(m)—illuminated, sparkling, happy
Farshiya—(f)—thanks
Farsina—(f)—heaven
Farsin—(f)—unique, divine aura
Farsiris—(f)—princess
Fars—(m)—son of farr
Faruck—(m)—truth, bless full
Farud—(m)—solitary, unique
Farugh—(m)—star
Faruka—(f)—truth, bless, full
Farukh—(m)—power of discrimination, happy
Faruki—(f)—fortunate, happy
Farukk—(m)—power of discrimination
Farukuddin—(m)—one with divine wisdom
Faruk—(m)—bless full, truth, turquoise
Faruqh—(m)—discerning truth from falsehood
Faruq—(m)—divider between vice and virtue
Faruza—(f)—unique, divine aura
Faru—(m)—strongest man
Farveena—(f)—unique, divine aura
Farveen—(f)—unique, divine aura
Farvees—(m)—one with divine wisdom

Farveez—(m)—victorious
Farvins—(m)—one with divine wisdom
Farvin—(f)—star
Farwaan—(m)—wealthy
Farwah—(f)—companion
Farwah—(m)—covering, a crow
Farwan—(m)—wealthy, living in abundance
Farwa—(f)—fur
Farwa—(m)—care, crown, wealth
Farween—(f)—unique, divine aura
Farwin—(f)—blessed
Faryal—(f)—angel
Faryal—(m)—brave
Faryat—(f)—delightful sun-shine
Farya—(f)—friend
Faryda—(f)—unmatched, unique
Faryd—(m)—unmatched, unique
Faryk—(m)—lieutenant general
Farzaad—(m)—splendid
Farzaana—(f)—intelligent, wise
Farzaan—(f)—very beautiful
Farzaan—(m)—wise, intelligent
Farzabeen—(f)—beautiful
Farzad—(m)—splendid birth
Farzak—(m)—powerful gold
Farzam—(m)—worthy, befitting
Farzanah—(f)—intelligent, wise, excellent
Farzana—(f)—intelligence, wise, delighted
Farzana—(m)—intelligent, wise, beautiful soul
Farzand—(m)—child, son
Farzaneh—(f)—wise, beautiful
Farzanna—(f)—intelligent
Farzann—(f)—intelligent
Farzan—(f)—wise
Farzan—(m)—highly knowledgeable, wise, see
Farzeeb—(m)—one with divine wisdom
Farzeena—(f)—unique, divine aura
Farzeen—(f)—learned

Farzeen—(m)—learned, intelligent
Farzhana—(f)—hospitable and friendly
Farzhan—(m)—beautiful soul
Farzia—(f)—happiness, kindness, beauty
Farzib—(m)—one with divine wisdom
Farzim—(m)—worthy
Farzina—(f)—hospitable, friendly
Farzin—(f)—wise, intelligent
Farzin—(m)—learned, man of great speed
Farziyah—(f)—kindness, beauty, happiness
Farziya—(f)—grace, brave, talented
Farzki—(f)—love
Farzu—(f)—religious duty
Farzzana—(f)—delighted, wise
Farz—(m)—religious duty, commandment of god
Fasaahat—(m)—fluency, eloquence
Fasahat—(m)—fluency, eloquence
Fasaludeen—(m)—one with divine wisdom
Fasaludheen—(m)—one with divine wisdom
Fasal—(m)—arbiter, judge
Faseaha—(f)—literary, eloquent
Faseehah—(f)—eloquent
Faseeha—(f)—eloquent
Faseehul-lisaan—(m)—the eloquent of speech
Faseeh—(m)—eloquent, literary, wide, ample
Faseelah—(f)—some distance
Faseela—(f)—distance, shinning star, pretty
Faseel—(m)—one with divine wisdom
Faseem—(m)—variant of waseem
Faseena—(f)—unique, divine aura
Fasel—(m)—justice, justify
Fasha—(f)—beauty
Fashid—(m)—one with divine wisdom
Fashil—(m)—one with divine wisdom
Fashir—(m)—one with divine wisdom
Fashmina—(f)—unique, divine aura
Fasid—(m)—one with divine wisdom
Fasieha—(f)—eloquent

Fasih-ur-rahman—(m)—eloquent
Fasihah—(f)—eloquent
Fasiha—(f)—appropriate for all, literary, eloquent
Fasih—(m)—eloquent, literary, wide, ample
Fasikh—(m)—successful, bounty, bliss
Fasila—(f)—beautiful
Fasilu—(m)—one with divine wisdom
Fasil—(m)—separating, distinguishing
Fasina—(f)—unique, divine aura
Fasir—(m)—one with divine wisdom
Fasitha—(f)—unique, divine aura
Fasith—(m)—one with divine wisdom
Fasiuddin—(m)—bounty of religion islam
Fasiya—(f)—a gentle woman
Faslina—(f)—queen
Fasliya—(f)—unique, divine aura
Fasmiha—(f)—unique, divine aura
Fasmil—(m)—one with divine wisdom
Fasmina—(f)—praised the worship of allah
Fasmir—(m)—one with divine wisdom
Fasmiya—(f)—attraction
Fasnan—(m)—brave
Fasna—(f)—pretty, young
Fastiq—(m)—another name for god
Fasyha—(f)—eloquent
Fas—(m)—wise counsellor
Fatahat—(m)—conquest, victory
Fatah—(f)—young girl, woman bless, happy
Fatah—(m)—the successor, the opener
Fatana—(f)—lovely
Fatan—(m)—intelligent, sagacious, smart
Fatat—(f)—young girl, woman
Fata—(m)—youth, nobility
Fateama—(f)—motherly
Fateam—(f)—chaste, one who abstains, motherly
Fateemah—(f)—daughter of the prophet muhammad
Fateema—(f)—daughter of the prophet muhammad
Fateem—(f)—motherly, chaste, one who abstains

Fateenah—(f)—intelligent
Fateenah—(m)—intelligent
Fateena—(f)—smart, clever
Fateen—(f)—clever, smart
Fateen—(m)—clever, smart
Fateha—(f)—opening, name of surah
Fatehnoor—(f)—beautiful winner
Fateh—(m)—victory, conqueror, triumph
Fateima—(f)—motherly
Fatemah—(f)—one who abstains
Fatema—(f)—daughter of the prophet mohammed
Fatemeh—(f)—a woman who weans her child
Fatemma—(f)—unique, divine aura
Faten—(f)—tempting
Fate—(f)—destiny
Fathan—(m)—guide, conqueror
Fathea—(m)—prosperity
Fatheddin—(m)—conquer for religion
Fatheen—(f)—intelligent
Fathia—(f)—beginning, victory
Fathiha—(f)—unique, divine aura
Fathih—(m)—quran opener
Fathimaa—(f)—unique, divine aura
Fathimah—(f)—daughter of the prophet muhammad
Fathimathul—(f)—unique, divine aura
Fathimath—(f)—unique, divine aura
Fathima—(f)—the prophet mohammad's daughter
Fathin—(f)—enchanting, captivating
Fathiyah—(f)—joy, happiness, new beginning
Fathiya—(f)—triumph
Fathiyyaat—(f)—guide, starter, conqueror
Fathiyyaa—(f)—one who guides others
Fathiyyah—(f)—guide, conqueror, victor
Fathiyya—(f)—conqueror, warrior
Fathi—(m)—victorious, winner, to win
Fathma—(f)—appropriate beginning, pue
Fathmi—(f)—utmost praiseworthy
Fathshah—(m)—triumphant king

Fathuddin—(m)—beginning, guidance
Fathullah—(m)—victory granted by allah
Fathy—(m)—conqueror, prosperity
Fath—(m)—winner, victorious, guidance
Fatia—(f)—abstainer from forbidden things
Fatiema—(f)—chaste - one who abstains
Fatiesha—(f)—happiness, joy, variant of latisha
Fatihah—(f)—opening, start, conqueror
Fatiha—(f)—opening, dawn, introduction
Fatihi—(m)—conqueror, originator
Fatih—(m)—big, opener, conqueror
Fatik—(m)—crystal, deadly, lethal
Fatimah—(f)—accustom
Fatima—(f)—the prophet mohammad's daughter
Fatime—(f)—the weaning, the abstaining
Fatimi—(f)—pertaining to fatimah
Fatimi—(m)—one with divine wisdom
Fatimoh—(f)—god is the worship
Fatim—(f)—divine lady
Fatim—(m)—big
Fatinah—(f)—captivating, alluring, enchanting
Fatina—(f)—captivating
Fatin—(f)—captivating, alluring, enchanting
Fatin—(m)—captivating
Fatiq—(m)—bright, shining, east, dawn
Fatiriyyah—(f)—soft and delicate, relaxed
Fatir—(m)—maker, creator
Fatisha—(f)—joy, happiness, variant of latisha
Fatmah—(f)—motherly
Fatma—(f)—the prophet mohammad's daughter
Fatmir—(m)—lucky
Fatooh—(m)—one who guides others
Fattaah—(m)—victory, conqueror
Fattahah—(f)—conqueror, victor
Fattah—(m)—the one who opens
Fattana—(f)—extremely beautiful, charming
Fattan—(m)—charming, bright
Fattima—(f)—the prophet mohammad's daughter

Fattim—(f)—unique, divine aura
Fattooh—(m)—the little conqueror
Fattuhah—(f)—guidance, conquest
Fatuma—(f)—daughter of the prophet mohammed
Fatunah—(f)—unique, divine aura
Fatun—(m)—intelligent, sharp
Fatyma—(f)—motherly, chaste, one who abstains
Fatyme—(f)—motherly
Faudel—(m)—honest
Faujan—(m)—one with divine wisdom
Fauna—(f)—young deer, fawn, animal life
Fauqiyah—(f)—high grade
Fausat—(f)—triumph
Fausia—(f)—victorious
Fauwaz—(m)—successful, prosperous
Fauzaan—(m)—successful, victorious
Fauzan—(m)—successful, victorious
Fauziah—(f)—successful, victorious
Fauziani—(f)—unique, divine aura
Fauzia—(f)—successful, victorious, triumphant
Fauziyah—(f)—unique, divine aura
Fauziya—(f)—successful
Fauziyya—(f)—success
Fauzy—(m)—gift
Fauz—(f)—triumph, great victory
Fauz—(m)—victory, triumph, indeed
Favas—(m)—successful, winner, prince
Fawaaz—(m)—one with divine wisdom
Fawaduddin—(m)—one with divine wisdom
Fawad—(m)—heart
Fawas—(m)—heart
Fawaz—(m)—always successful, prosperous
Fawez—(m)—one with divine wisdom
Fawha—(f)—breath of fragrance
Fawiza—(f)—successful
Fawiz—(m)—successful, winner, powerful
Fawjida—(f)—unique, divine aura
Fawwaaz—(m)—winner, most successful

Fawwad—(m)—victor
Fawwazaa—(f)—successful, winner
Fawwaz—(m)—successful
Fawzaana—(f)—salvation, successful
Fawzah—(f)—success, win
Fawzan—(m)—victory, successful, salvation
Fawza—(f)—victory, success
Fawzia—(f)—successful, winner, triumph
Fawzie—(m)—victory, success
Fawziyah—(f)—successful
Fawziya—(f)—successful, victorious
Fawziyyaa—(f)—winner, successful
Fawziyyah—(f)—successful, victorious
Fawziyya—(f)—victory, success
Fawziyy—(f)—successful, triumph, victorious
Fawzi—(f)—successful, victorious, triumph
Fawzi—(m)—successful, triumph
Fawzy—(f)—victorious, successful, triumphant
Fawzy—(m)—triumphant, victorious, successful
Fawz—(f)—success, salvation, victory
Fawz—(m)—accomplishes, success, salvation
Faxina—(f)—unique, divine aura
Fayaan—(m)—belief, trust
Fayaaq—(m)—one with divine wisdom
Fayaaz—(m)—kind, generous
Fayab—(m)—one with divine wisdom
Fayadh—(m)—generous
Fayad—(m)—benefit, advantage, welfare
Fayaj—(m)—peaceful, artistic, talented
Fayal—(f)—decisive
Fayana—(f)—fairy, elf
Fayan—(m)—trust, belief, shining
Fayaq—(m)—superior
Fayas—(m)—extremely generous
Fayazdeen—(m)—extremely generous
Fayazuddin—(m)—one with divine wisdom
Fayazudeen—(m)—bounty of religion islam
Fayaz—(m)—extremely generous

Fayda—(f)—plentiful
Fayd—(m)—abundance
Fayed—(m)—one with divine wisdom
Fayeem—(m)—famed
Fayeeza—(f)—successful, victorious
Fayeez—(m)—successful, victorious
Fayeha—(f)—appropriate smell of heaven, fragrant
Fayek—(m)—surpassing, excellent, superior
Fayeq—(m)—superior, surpassing
Fayez—(m)—victorious, successful
Fayhaa—(f)—fragrant
Fayhan—(m)—fragrance
Fayha—(f)—fragrant, appropriate smell of heaven
Fayida—(f)—benefit, gain
Fayid—(m)—winner, benefiter
Fayij—(m)—one with divine wisdom
Fayisa—(f)—victorious, successful
Fayisha—(f)—a blessing to all
Fayis—(m)—the winner
Fayizah—(f)—winner, successful
Fayiza—(f)—successful
Fayiz—(m)—winner, victor
Fayjan—(m)—one with divine wisdom
Fayla—(f)—faith and beauty
Fayma—(f)—leader
Fayona—(f)—beautiful, pretty
Fayqa—(f)—extraordinary, genius, superb
Fayraj—(m)—one with divine wisdom
Fayra—(f)—gift of god, pleasant
Fayrooz—(f)—turquoise
Fayrouz—(f)—turquoise stone
Fayruz—(f)—turquoise, precious stone
Faysal—(f)—decisive
Faysal—(m)—stubborn, resolute, decisive
Faysa—(f)—successful, victorious
Fayum—(m)—famed, strong
Fayyaadh—(m)—generous
Fayyaad—(m)—generous

Fayyadh—(m)—generous, liberal
Fayyad—(m)—overflowing, generous
Fayyah—(f)—repentance
Fayyaza—(f)—a lady who confers great favours
Fayyaz—(m)—charitable, bountiful, merciful
Fayyim—(m)—strong
Fayzaan—(m)—favourite, favour, grace
Fayzal—(m)—romantic
Fayzan—(m)—beneficence
Fayza—(f)—victorious, winner
Fayzel—(m)—arbiter, judge
Fayzi—(m)—blessed with abundance
Fayzuddin—(m)—one with divine wisdom
Fayzul-haq—(m)—grace of the truth (allah)
Fayzulhaq—(m)—grace of the truth (allah)
Fayz—(m)—liberality
Fay—(m)—devil, raven
Fazaan—(m)—ruler, also spelt as fazan
Fazad—(f)—bliss, joyful, happiness
Fazad—(m)—moment, loved
Fazah—(m)—one with divine wisdom
Fazaid—(f)—princess, fifth, earth, love
Fazaid—(m)—happy
Fazaila—(f)—unique, divine aura
Fazail—(m)—superior, scholar
Fazalla—(f)—unique, divine aura
Fazaluudin—(m)—one with divine wisdom
Fazalu—(m)—superiority, grace, excellence
Fazal—(m)—excellence, superiority, reward
Fazamedo—(m)—army
Fazamehrin—(f)—unique, divine aura
Fazanah—(f)—wise
Fazan—(f)—ruler
Fazan—(m)—ruler, profit, ruler of prince
Fazarat—(f)—female leopard
Fazar—(m)—one with divine wisdom
Faza—(f)—bloom, spring
Faza—(m)—victory

Fazeed—(m)—strong, stubborn
Fazeeha—(f)—unique, divine aura
Fazeelah—(f)—superiority, attribute, value
Fazeelath—(f)—virtue, excellence, appropriate traits
Fazeelat—(f)—excellence, merit, virtue
Fazeela—(f)—scholar, intelligent, faithful
Fazeelet—(f)—appropriate traits, merit, excellence
Fazeel—(m)—virtuous, knowledgeable, eminent
Fazeema—(f)—unique, divine aura
Fazeem—(m)—graceful, variant of waseem
Fazeena—(f)—innocent, charming
Fazeen—(f)—increasing, brightness, charming
Fazeen—(m)—increasing
Fazeerah—(f)—unique, divine aura
Fazeera—(f)—gift of angel
Fazeer—(m)—one with divine wisdom
Fazeetha—(f)—moon
Fazela—(m)—one who was praised
Fazel—(m)—learned, decisive
Fazhan—(m)—good, nobel
Faziad—(f)—happy, bliss, powered
Faziad—(m)—one with divine wisdom
Fazia—(f)—successful, victorious
Fazid—(f)—power, love, moments, happiness
Fazid—(m)—admirer, enthusiasm, independent
Fazilah—(f)—scholar
Fazilath—(f)—form of fazilah
Fazilatun-nisa—(f)—excellence of the female
Fazilatunnisa—(f)—excellence of the female
Fazila—(f)—scholar
Fazilla—(f)—unique, divine aura
Fazil—(m)—superior, talented, scholar
Fazima—(f)—unique, divine aura
Fazim—(m)—successful, powerful, love
Fazina—(f)—thanking, gift of allah
Fazin—(f)—queen, god of the feminine
Fazin—(m)—beautiful
Fazirah—(f)—purity, waterfalls

Fazira—(f)—waterfalls
Fazira—(m)—purity
Fazith—(m)—one with divine wisdom
Faziuddin—(m)—bounty of religion islam
Faziya—(f)—successful, victorious
Fazi—(m)—opener, winner
Fazlan—(m)—bright, king of the universe
Fazla—(f)—virtue
Fazle-ilahi—(m)—bounty of allah
Fazle-mawla—(m)—bounty of the lord (allah)
Fazle-rabbi—(m)—bounty of my lord
Fazle-rabb—(m)—bounty of my lord
Fazle-rab—(m)—bounty of lord
Fazleena—(f)—unique, divine aura
Fazleen—(f)—unique, divine aura
Fazlehaq—(m)—bounty of the truth (allah)
Fazleilahi—(m)—bounty of allah
Fazlemawla—(m)—bounty of the lord, allah
Fazlerabbi—(m)—bounty of my lord
Fazlerabi—(m)—bounty of my lord
Fazlerab—(m)—bounty of lord
Fazle—(m)—good and intelligent
Fazlina—(f)—flower, flower in desert
Fazlinn—(f)—unique, divine aura
Fazlin—(f)—flower
Fazliya—(f)—bountiful, graceful, kind
Fazli—(m)—graceful, virtuous, kind
Fazluddin—(m)—excellence
Fazlullah—(m)—grace of god, god's excellence
Fazlul—(m)—a wise leader
Fazlur—(m)—victorious, successful, brilliant
Fazl—(m)—grace, favour, courtesy
Fazmeena—(f)—beautiful
Fazmeer—(m)—one with divine wisdom
Fazmila—(f)—unique, divine aura
Fazmina—(f)—praised the worship of allah
Fazmin—(m)—praised the worship of allah
Fazmir—(m)—precious, energetic

Fazna—(f)—beautiful, winner
Fazon—(m)—an understanding man
Fazool—(m)—one with divine wisdom
Fazra—(f)—queen
Fazrin—(f)—gift of god, queen goddess
Fazrin—(m)—gift of god
Fazrul—(m)—one with divine wisdom
Fazula—(f)—choice
Fazulul-haq—(m)—bounty of the truth (allah)
Fazululhaq—(m)—bounty of the truth, allah
Fazul—(m)—choice, allah's happiness
Fazura—(f)—purity
Fazzah—(m)—victory, powerful
Fazzaid—(f)—happy
Fazzal—(m)—excellent, well-deserving man
Fazzariya—(f)—powerful
Fazza—(f)—joyful
Fazza—(m)—powerful, victory
Fazzilet—(f)—blessing of allah
Fazzina—(f)—power
Fazzin—(m)—loveable, charming, the machine
Fazz—(m)—victorious, a kind of a storm
Feba—(f)—source of light
Febeena—(f)—confidence, independence
Febida—(f)—unique, divine aura
Febinah—(f)—unique, divine aura
Febina—(f)—independence, confidence
Febin—(f)—given by god, moonlight
Febin—(m)—moon light
Feda—(f)—sacrifice, flower
Feebena—(f)—independence
Feeda—(f)—redemption
Feeha—(f)—flower of jannah
Feeidha—(f)—rewarding, generous
Feeiza—(f)—victorious, winner
Feema—(f)—pure
Feerouzeh—(f)—turquoise
Feerozah—(f)—a precious stone

Feeroz—(m)—victorious, happy, fortunate
Feetin—(f)—variant of fit'in, clever, smart
Feeya—(f)—calm, relaxed
Feezan—(m)—one with divine wisdom
Feeza—(f)—nature
Fehaan—(m)—guider, fragrant, clever
Fehan—(m)—guider, clever
Feheema—(f)—intelligent, judicious, learned
Fehim—(m)—slavic, and
Fehleen—(f)—unique, divine aura
Fehmeeda—(f)—unique, divine aura
Fehmeen—(f)—unique, divine aura
Fehmida—(f)—unique, divine aura
Fehmina—(f)—to be wise
Fehmiya—(f)—unique, divine aura
Fehmi—(f)—understanding
Fehrisha—(f)—unique, divine aura
Feida—(f)—plentiful, benefit, gain
Feidha—(f)—gain, plentiful
Feiha—(f)—fragrant, flower of jannah
Feisal—(m)—arbitrator, judge
Feiyaz—(f)—successful
Feiza—(f)—winner, victorious
Feiz—(m)—victorious
Fejura—(f)—beauty
Felana—(f)—loving mankind
Felinah—(f)—lucky, cat-like
Fellah—(f)—arabian jasmine, fields
Felza—(f)—fragrant, beloved one
Femeena—(f)—unique, divine aura
Femena—(f)—cute
Femida—(f)—wise
Femina—(f)—female
Femitha—(f)—unique, divine aura
Fenal—(f)—beautiful, angel of beauty
Fennah—(f)—unique, divine aura
Fenna—(f)—scented flower
Feraaz—(m)—sharpness

Ferah—(f)—beautiful
Feraidoon—(m)—one with divine wisdom
Ferasat—(m)—vision, keenness, acumen
Feras—(m)—perspicacious
Feraz—(m)—sharpness
Fera—(f)—unique, divine aura
Ferbina—(f)—pretty
Ferdin—(m)—one who has triple strength
Ferdnan—(m)—sunshine
Ferdousi—(f)—unique, divine aura
Ferdous—(m)—paradise
Ferdows—(m)—paradise
Ferdoz—(m)—paradise, heaven
Fereshta—(f)—angle of allah
Fereshteh—(f)—angel
Fereydoun—(m)—third
Ferhana—(f)—immerse, joyful, beautiful
Ferhan—(m)—one who rejoices
Ferhas—(m)—joy
Ferhat—(m)—joy
Ferheen—(f)—sky angel, god gifted
Feriba—(f)—unique, divine aura
Ferid—(m)—unique
Feriha—(f)—joyful, happiness
Ferin—(f)—unknown, stranger, gift
Ferin—(m)—glorify, best
Ferjiada—(f)—unique, divine aura
Ferose—(m)—man of triumph
Ferouza—(f)—turquoise
Ferouz—(m)—a classy stone, name of a king
Feroza—(f)—victorious
Feroza—(m)—victorious, name of a stone
Feroze—(m)—man of triumph, successful
Feroziya—(f)—unique, divine aura
Feroz—(f)—shine
Feroz—(m)—name of a king, winner
Ferran—(m)—baker
Feruza—(f)—gem stone, successful, fortunate

Feryale—(f)—possessing the beauty of light
Feryalle—(f)—possessing the beauty of light
Feryall—(f)—possessing the beauty of light
Feryal—(f)—beauty of light
Ferzana—(f)—wise and intelligent
Feshan—(m)—one with divine wisdom
Fethi—(m)—one with divine wisdom
Feyan—(m)—independent
Feyda—(f)—unique, divine aura
Feyha—(f)—fragrant
Feysal—(m)—resolute, judge, stubborn
Fezal—(m)—superiority
Fezan—(m)—a man of the people
Feza—(m)—universe
Fezbin—(m)—one with divine wisdom
Fezin—(m)—love
Fezzah—(f)—pure, silver
Fezza—(f)—nature
Fhahmida—(f)—unique, divine aura
Fhalak—(f)—heaven, sky, space
Fhamed—(m)—powerful
Fhara—(f)—beautiful, pleasant, level measure
Fiah—(f)—fire, flame, a flickering fire
Fiam—(m)—comedy
Fiana—(f)—a warrior huntress
Fian—(m)—one with divine wisdom
Fiaza—(f)—queen
Fiazin—(f)—unique, divine aura
Fiazuddin—(m)—one with divine wisdom
Fiaz—(m)—victory in motion
Fia—(f)—flame, a flickering fire, fire
Fidaan—(m)—person who makes sacrifice
Fidaa—(f)—sacrifice
Fidaa—(m)—sacrifice, ransom, redemption
Fidah—(f)—silver, sacrifice
Fidal—(m)—faithful
Fidan—(f)—sapling
Fidan—(m)—one who makes sacrifice

Fida—(f)—redemption
Fida—(m)—sacrifice, unconditional love
Fiddah—(f)—silver
Fiddah—(m)—silver
Fidda—(f)—silver
Fidel—(m)—loyal, faithful and sincere
Fidhan—(m)—silver
Fidha—(f)—sacrifice
Fidhdhah—(f)—silver, metal
Fidiyan—(m)—person who makes sacrifice
Fidyan—(m)—person who makes sacrifice
Fieroosniza—(f)—pearly
Fieya—(f)—unique, divine aura
Fihaan—(m)—fragrant
Fihan—(m)—courage, happiness, adorable
Fiha—(f)—flower of jannah
Fihr—(m)—stone pestle
Fiiza—(f)—rose from heaven
Fijal—(m)—one with divine wisdom
Fijina—(f)—light
Fikhar—(m)—honour, pride, glory
Fikkir—(f)—very thoughtful
Fikraat—(f)—thoughts, ideas, concepts
Fikrat—(f)—idea, thought, conception
Fikrat—(m)—thought, idea
Fikra—(f)—giver, worry
Fikriyaa—(f)—thoughtful, perceptive
Fikriyah—(f)—intellectual
Fikriyyah—(f)—meditative, thoughtful
Fikriyya—(f)—intellectual
Fikri—(f)—thoughtful, perceptive
Fikri—(m)—intelligent, intellectual
Fikry—(m)—intellectual
Fikr—(f)—thought, concept, conception
Fikr—(m)—thought, concept, conception
Fila—(f)—lover
Filza-fathima—(f)—rose from heaven
Filzah—(f)—light, rose from heaven

Filza—(f)—rose from heaven, light
Filza—(m)—light, rose from heaven
Filziya—(f)—rose from heaven, beloved one
Fima—(f)—blessing, love of god
Fima—(m)—one with divine wisdom
Finaz—(f)—highness in status, winner
Finha—(f)—pale, fair
Finsha—(f)—blond lady
Finza—(f)—winner
Finziya—(f)—pure
Fiona—(f)—white, fair, pale, blond
Fiqra—(f)—unique, divine aura
Fiqri—(m)—one with divine wisdom
Firaas—(m)—knight, perspicacity, sharpness
Firagh—(m)—leisure, happiness, opportunity
Firaq—(m)—separation
Firasah—(f)—acumen, perspicacity
Firasah—(m)—perspicacity, acumen
Firasat—(m)—one with divine wisdom
Firasa—(f)—perspicacity, acumen
Firas—(m)—perspicacious
Firaun—(m)—proud
Fira—(m)—persistent
Firdaush—(m)—enclosure, heaven
Firdausi—(f)—heavenly
Firdausi—(m)—of paradise
Firdaus—(m)—garden of paradise, paradise
Firdaws—(f)—highest garden in paradise, heaven
Firda—(f)—unique, divine aura
Firdevs—(f)—garden in gana
Firdhouse—(m)—entrance of heaven
Firdoos—(f)—highest garden in paradise
Firdoos—(m)—highest garden in paradise
Firdose—(f)—heaven
Firdose—(m)—heaven
Firdosh—(m)—one with divine wisdom
Firdos—(f)—garden, paradise, heaven
Firdos—(m)—heaven, paradise, enclosure

Firdousa—(f)—garden, name of the heaven
Firdouse—(f)—heaven
Firdousi—(f)—unique, divine aura
Firdousi—(m)—belonging to paradise
Firdous—(f)—name of the heaven, garden
Firdous—(m)—paradise
Firdowsa—(f)—highest garden of paradise
Firdows—(m)—paradise
Firdoze—(m)—paradise
Firdusi—(f)—heavenly, of paradise
Firdus—(m)—name of garden in jannat
Firhaan—(m)—one with divine wisdom
Firhad—(m)—smile
Firhun—(m)—one with divine wisdom
Firiha—(f)—unique, divine aura
Firnas—(m)—powerful, brave, thick necked lion
Firnaz—(f)—helper
Firoja—(f)—kind flower, beautiful, stone
Firoj—(m)—stone of sea
Firooza—(f)—beautiful, turquoise
Firoozeh—(f)—woman of triumph, victorious
Firosa—(f)—kind flower, stone of sea
Firose—(m)—gift, winner, precious stone
Firos—(m)—one with divine wisdom
Firouzeh—(f)—turquoise
Firouz—(m)—victorious
Firoz-alam—(m)—blessing, honest, affection
Firoza—(f)—turquoise, beautiful
Firoze—(m)—gift, winner, victorious
Firoz—(f)—victorious
Firoz—(m)—name of a king, overpowering
Firrah—(f)—fair, lovely, beautiful
Firthous—(m)—paradise
Firuwzah—(f)—turquoise
Firuzah—(f)—turquoise
Firuza—(f)—successful, gem stone, turquoise
Firuz—(m)—man of triumph, successful
Firwad—(m)—independent-minded

Firyal—(f)—name, proper name
Firyal—(m)—adornment
Firza—(f)—fortunate, successful, gem stone
Fir—(f)—a sharp weapon
Fisal—(m)—one with divine wisdom
Fishan—(m)—one with divine wisdom
Fishu—(m)—one with divine wisdom
Fitin—(f)—clever, smart
Fitrah—(f)—natural disposition, instinct
Fitrat—(m)—nature, creation
Fiyaan—(m)—independent
Fiyah—(f)—powerful
Fiyam—(f)—intelligent, genius
Fiyana—(f)—independent
Fiyan—(m)—independent
Fiyas—(m)—king, artistic
Fiyaza—(f)—woman of god
Fiyaz—(m)—artistic
Fiya—(f)—powerful
Fizaana—(f)—part of breeze, grace
Fizaan—(f)—grace, breeze
Fizaan—(m)—breeze
Fizaa—(f)—breeze, also spelt as fiza
Fizah—(f)—silver
Fizain—(f)—lovely princess
Fizain—(m)—lion
Fizana—(f)—part of breeze
Fizan—(m)—king, popularity
Fiza—(f)—breeze, air, nature
Fiza—(m)—breeze
Fizee—(f)—bringer, source of abundance
Fizul—(m)—one with divine wisdom
Fizva—(f)—valuable with intelligent
Fizzah—(f)—silver, pure
Fizzaq—(f)—unique, divine aura
Fizza—(f)—nature, silver, precious, pure
Fizza—(m)—silver, ibn abu mawdood
Fizziyah—(f)—silvery, made of silver

Fizzi—(f)—silvery, made of silver
Fizzi—(m)—silvery, made of silver
Flavia—(f)—golden, yellow haired, blond
Flieder—(f)—a flowering shrub
Flora—(f)—flower, the goddess of flower
Flower—(f)—blooming, flower, form of florence
Foizah—(f)—winner, obtaining
Fojan—(f)—loud voice or sound
Folat—(m)—one with divine wisdom
Folla—(f)—arabian jasmine flower
Foram—(f)—fragrance, pleasant smell
Forhad—(m)—happiness
Forhana—(f)—happy, joyful, cheerful
Forida—(f)—unique, proud, turquoise
Forogh—(f)—brilliance or dawn
Foroohar—(m)—essence
Forough—(f)—brightness
Forouzandeh—(f)—shining
Forouzan—(f)—shining
Forozaan—(f)—vivid, gleaming
Fouad—(m)—heart
Foujina—(f)—beautiful, intelligent
Foumida—(f)—wise, intelligent
Fouseena—(f)—unique, divine aura
Fousia—(f)—triumphant, victory
Fousiya—(f)—winner
Fouzaan—(m)—victorious, successful
Fouzan—(m)—victorious, successful
Fouziah—(f)—victorious, successful
Fouzia—(f)—victory, triumphant
Fouziya—(f)—victorious, triumphant, successful
Fouzya—(f)—triumphant, victorious, successful
Fowjia—(f)—victorious, triumphant, successful
Fowmitha—(f)—researcher, mysterious, skill
Fowzia—(f)—victorious
Fowziya—(f)—victorious
Fozan—(m)—one with divine wisdom
Fozhan—(f)—loud voice or sound

Foziah—(f)—successful
Fozia—(f)—successful, conquer
Foziya—(f)—beautiful, like a moon, successful
Fraaz—(m)—elevation, sword
Frasha—(f)—beautiful, butterfly
Fravardin—(m)—guardian spirit
Fravash—(m)—guardian angel
Fraya—(f)—princess of god, highborn lady
Frdeen—(m)—one who has triple strength
Fredj—(m)—one with divine wisdom
Freeda—(f)—elf, power
Freidoon—(m)—one with divine wisdom
Frelashia—(f)—propspure and clever
Freya—(f)—goddess of love
Frhaan—(m)—happiness
Frhan—(m)—happiness
Fridah—(f)—precious pearl or gem, matchless
Fridaws—(f)—unique, divine aura
Frida—(f)—woman of peace, joy, safety
Frogh—(m)—luminosity
Frozaan—(f)—luminous, radiant, gleaming
Fshd—(m)—lynx
Fuaad—(m)—heart
Fuadah—(f)—heart, spirit, conscience
Fuada—(f)—heart, feminine of fuad
Fuad—(m)—conscience, heart, soul, king
Fudael—(m)—of high moral character
Fudaili—(m)—one with divine wisdom
Fudail—(m)—excellent in character
Fudale—(m)—of high moral character
Fudayl—(f)—scholar, learned
Fudayl—(m)—of high moral character
Fudhail—(m)—excellent in character
Fuhaad—(m)—one with divine wisdom
Fuhad—(m)—one with divine wisdom
Fuhaim—(m)—understanding, comprehending
Fujita—(f)—field
Fukaena—(f)—knowledgeable

Fukaiha—(f)—unique, divine aura
Fukaina—(f)—knowledgeable
Fukairaa—(f)—thoughtful, intelligent
Fukana—(f)—knowledgeable
Fukayna—(f)—intelligent
Fulaihan—(m)—successful
Fulaih—(m)—successful
Fula—(f)—light, beams of light or soar
Fullah—(f)—unique, divine aura
Fullan—(f)—blooming
Full—(f)—arabian jasmine
Funoon—(f)—variety, art
Fuqqah—(m)—flower, bud
Furaat—(f)—cold - refreshing water
Furaat—(m)—cold - refreshing water
Furada—(m)—unique, single
Furaiah—(f)—name of a sahabiyah
Furaihaat—(f)—happy, joyous
Furaihah—(f)—happy, joyous
Furaihat—(f)—happy, joyous
Furaniq—(m)—leader of an army
Furat—(f)—sweet water
Furat—(m)—fresh, sweet water
Furayah—(f)—well-built, attractive
Furhan—(m)—cheerful
Furhat—(f)—joy, cheerfulness
Furjah—(f)—relief, rescue, comfort
Furkaan—(m)—one with divine wisdom
Furkan—(m)—intelligent, beautiful
Furkhan—(m)—beautiful, intelligent
Furoogh—(m)—splendour, light, brightness
Furookh—(m)—sprout, shoot, young bird
Furoozan—(f)—luminous, radiant
Furozh—(m)—light
Furqaan—(m)—evidence, proof
Furqana—(f)—proof
Furqana—(m)—proof, evidence
Furqan—(m)—evidence

Furqhan—(m)—proof, evidence
Furquana—(f)—evidence
Furquan—(m)—proof, evidence, doer
Fursat—(m)—leisure, freedom, relief
Furud—(m)—unique, single, alone
Furughuddin—(m)—light of religion
Fusaila—(f)—narrator of hadith
Fusaylah—(f)—some distance
Fuseelah—(f)—narrator of hadith
Fusilat—(f)—detailed, well explained
Fusilat—(m)—detailed, elaborate
Fussilat—(f)—detailed, well explained
Fussilat—(m)—detailed, well explained
Futaihah—(f)—guidance, conquest, beginning
Futaih—(m)—prince, guidance, beginning
Futooh—(m)—conquests, victories
Futtehkhan—(m)—winner, beginner
Futuhat—(m)—victories
Futuh—(m)—victories, conquests
Futun—(f)—fascinations
Fuwaad—(m)—heart
Fuwad—(m)—heart, mind, soul
Fuwaiz—(m)—successful, winner
Fuyum—(m)—strong men
Fuyuzat—(m)—generosity
Fuzaid—(m)—talented
Fuzailah—(f)—excellence, virtue, generosity
Fuzailan—(m)—excellent, praiseworthy, generous
Fuzail—(f)—a form of faazil
Fuzail—(m)—excellence, reward, grace, favour
Fuzaina—(f)—unique, divine aura
Fuzain—(m)—bright lights stars
Fuzzal—(m)—excellent, praiseworthy
Fyan—(m)—runner
Fyaz—(m)—the warrior
Fyha—(f)—fragrant, appropriate smell of heaven
Fyneen—(f)—a beautiful daughter
Fyruz—(f)—fill with wealth

Fysal—(m)—decisive, resolute
Fysha—(f)—victorious, successful
Fyzah—(f)—success
Fyzullah—(m)—abundance from allah

SEVEN

Arabic Baby Names—G

Gabba—(m)—the capital of queensland

Gabber—(m)—a proud and strong man

Gabir—(m)—comforter, consoler

Gabriella—(f)—god gives strength

Gabriel—(m)—christian, god is my strength

Gabr—(m)—compulsion name of a companion

Gaby—(m)—god is my strength, hero of god

Gaddy—(m)—my fortune

Gadee—(m)—my fortune

Gadiel—(m)—god is my fortune

Gadie—(m)—my fortune

Gadil—(m)—forest, god is my wealth

Gadi—(m)—god is my fortune, my wealth

Gady—(m)—my fortune

Gaeti—(f)—angel

Gafar—(m)—little stream, rivulet, a river

Gaffar—(m)—most forgiving

Gaffoor—(m)—forgiver, merciful

Gafoor—(m)—merciful, forgiver

Gafur—(m)—invincible

Gahez—(m)—morning

Gaitha—(f)—beautiful, lucky

Gaith—(m)—rain

Gajal—(f)—song, love

Gakeemah—(f)—unique, divine aura
Galaad—(m)—one with divine wisdom
Galai—(f)—hail, a gift form allah
Galal—(m)—a roll or wheel, round, wave
Galeeb—(m)—one with divine wisdom
Galel—(m)—wave of god
Galib—(m)—name of a great poet
Galilah—(f)—god shall redeem
Galila—(f)—god shall redeem, greatness
Galisha—(f)—beautiful, fortunate woman
Gamaal—(m)—camel
Gamaleddin—(m)—tiger
Gamali—(m)—camel
Gamall—(m)—mountain, beautiful
Gamal—(f)—beauty
Gamal—(m)—camel, handsome
Gambo—(m)—child born before twins
Gameala—(f)—beautiful
Gameelah—(f)—beautiful
Gameela—(f)—beautiful
Gamelia—(f)—beautiful
Gamilah—(f)—beautiful
Gamila—(f)—gorgeous, beautiful, elegant
Gamilia—(f)—beautiful
Gamilla—(f)—beautiful
Gamille—(f)—beautiful
Gamil—(m)—tiger man, handsome, beautiful
Gami—(f)—beautiful
Ganief—(m)—one with divine wisdom
Gani—(m)—gold
Garan—(f)—guards, guardian
Garda—(f)—guarded, shelter, protected
Gardez—(m)—one with divine wisdom
Garima—(f)—warmth, proud, dignity, prowess
Garrath—(m)—gentle
Gassan—(m)—one with divine wisdom
Gasser—(m)—a courageous man
Gathbiyya—(f)—attractiveness

Gathibiyyah—(f)—unique, divine aura
Gauhar—(f)—a pearl
Gauhar—(m)—cow like, white, the pearl
Gausia—(f)—bright as moon
Gawahir—(f)—precious stones, jewels
Gawa—(f)—joy
Gawdat—(m)—goodness, excellence
Gawhar—(f)—a pearl
Gayas—(m)—one with divine wisdom
Gayazuddin—(m)—one with divine wisdom
Gayaz—(m)—one with divine wisdom
Gazalaa—(f)—unique, divine aura
Gazala—(f)—a deer
Gazali—(m)—famous, mystic
Gazbiyyah—(f)—sweet, beautiful
Gazbiyya—(f)—attractive, charming
Gazish—(m)—one with divine wisdom
Gaziyan—(m)—conqueror, fighter
Gazi—(m)—leader
Gazza—(m)—spear, brave with the spear
Gehad—(m)—married man
Gelareh—(f)—eyes
Gemail—(m)—white sparrow
Gemeala—(f)—beautiful
Gemeela—(f)—beautiful
Gemila—(f)—beautiful
Gemilla—(f)—beautiful
Gemyla—(f)—beautiful
George—(m)—earth worker, farmer
Gereshk—(f)—unique, divine aura
Gervasius—(m)—spear
Ghaada—(f)—beautiful, a small song
Ghaafirin—(m)—forgiver
Ghaafir—(m)—forgiver
Ghaaib—(m)—hidden, absent, away
Ghaaliba—(f)—victor
Ghaaliboon—(m)—winner, overcomers, dominant one
Ghaalib—(m)—victor, conqueror, dominant

Ghaaliya—(f)—fragrant, which can be sung
Ghaali—(m)—precious, valuable, dear, beloved
Ghaamid—(m)—strong
Ghaanim—(m)—winner, successful
Ghaaniyah—(f)—ghaniyah 'beautiful
Ghaazee—(m)—war champion, hero, conqueror
Ghaaziya—(f)—warrior, conqueror
Ghaazi—(m)—conqueror, war champion, hero
Ghabashir—(m)—twilight of the morning
Ghabra—(f)—earth, land
Ghadaat—(f)—to leave between dawn and sunrise
Ghadah—(f)—beautiful
Ghadat—(f)—young girl, young lady
Ghada—(f)—charming, graceful woman
Ghaddah—(f)—graceful lady
Ghadda—(f)—graceful lady
Ghadeer—(f)—brook, rivulet, small stream
Ghadeer—(m)—small stream
Ghadef—(m)—one who drives a boat
Ghadhanfar—(m)—lion, king of jungle
Ghadia—(f)—morning, cloud
Ghadir—(m)—a sword, pond, pool
Ghadiya—(f)—early morning rain clouds
Ghadi—(m)—early riser
Ghadra—(m)—dark
Ghaena—(f)—ornament
Ghafar—(m)—forgiving
Ghaffaar—(m)—forgiving
Ghaffara—(f)—forgiving
Ghaffari—(m)—forgiver, forgiving
Ghaffar—(m)—most forgiving, merciful, forgiver
Ghafira—(f)—one who hides other's sins
Ghafirin—(m)—forgiver
Ghafiri—(m)—forgiving, one who pardons
Ghafir—(m)—forgiving, merciful
Ghafoor—(m)—forgiver, merciful
Ghafr—(m)—mercy, forgiveness
Ghafuri—(m)—forgiving, pardoning

Ghafur—(m)—forgiving, merciful
Ghaib—(m)—hidden, absent, away
Ghaidaa—(f)—unique, divine aura
Ghaidan—(m)—delicate, slender
Ghaida—(f)—sun
Ghaida—(m)—young
Ghailam—(m)—good-looking
Ghailan—(m)—demon
Ghailum—(m)—good-looking, handsome
Ghairat—(m)—zeal, self respect, vigilant care
Ghaisan—(m)—one who brings, does much good
Ghaisat—(f)—rain
Ghaisullah—(m)—god's bounty, blessings
Ghais—(f)—beautiful, rain
Ghais—(m)—street light
Ghaith—(m)—rain
Ghaiyyas—(m)—helper, reliever, winner
Ghaiz—(m)—desert, forest, jungle
Ghakhtalay—(m)—strong
Ghalbah—(m)—superiority, conquest
Ghalb—(m)—victory, superior power
Ghaleayah—(f)—high-priced
Ghaleaya—(f)—high-priced
Ghaleb—(m)—be loved
Ghaleeyah—(f)—high-priced
Ghaleeya—(f)—high-priced
Ghaleyah—(f)—high-priced
Ghaleya—(f)—high-priced
Ghaliaa—(f)—precious, valuable
Ghalia—(f)—valuable, dear, beloved, precious
Ghalibah—(f)—dominant
Ghaliba—(f)—conqueror, victor, winner
Ghalibi—(m)—winner, victor
Ghalibun—(m)—winner, dominant one
Ghalib—(m)—excellent, winner, conqueror
Ghalinus—(m)—physician
Ghaliyah—(f)—fragrant, beloved, valuable
Ghaliya—(f)—sweet-smelling, precious

Ghali—(m)—expensive, scare, costly
Ghallaab—(m)—ever victorious, triumphant
Ghallab—(m)—ever victorious, triumphant
Ghamay—(m)—precious stone
Ghamir—(m)—giving a lot of charity
Ghamzah—(m)—signal, hint
Ghamza—(f)—gestures
Ghamzeh—(f)—coquetry
Ghana—(m)—dark, war chief, wealth, profit
Ghandoor—(m)—dandy
Ghandur—(m)—dandy
Ghaneei—(m)—rich, needless
Ghaneemah—(f)—spoils
Ghaneem—(m)—winner
Ghanem—(m)—successful
Ghania—(f)—fair, beautiful
Ghanimat—(m)—reward
Ghanimi—(m)—winner, one who always wins
Ghanim—(m)—good man, successful
Ghaniyah—(f)—pretty girl, beautiful woman
Ghaniyah—(m)—independent, prosperous
Ghaniya—(f)—pretty, beautiful
Ghani—(m)—independent, prosperous
Ghannam—(m)—shepherd
Ghannan—(m)—two friends of prophet muhammad
Ghanum—(m)—winner, acquirer of riches
Ghanyan—(m)—wealthy, needless
Gharab—(m)—gold, silver
Gharam—(f)—hot, infatuation, love, devotion
Gharam—(m)—infatuation, love, devotion
Gharan—(f)—beauty
Ghareebah—(f)—foreign, strange
Ghareeb—(m)—humble, poor, needy, stranger
Ghareer—(m)—young, good manners
Gharib—(m)—stranger, visitor, traveller
Gharisullah—(m)—a young tree planted by god
Ghariy—(f)—beautiful
Gharizah—(m)—nature, character

Gharra—(f)—noble
Gharra—(m)—brilliant, shining
Ghasaan—(m)—old arabic name
Ghasan—(m)—old arabic name
Ghashiah—(m)—devotee, attendant
Ghashia—(f)—guidance, overwhelming happiness
Ghasiq—(m)—moon, pearls
Ghasna—(f)—bud, blossom
Ghassaan—(m)—ardour, vigour (of youth)
Ghassan—(m)—father of a tribe
Ghassedak—(f)—a flower, dandelion
Ghassen—(m)—youthful
Ghathe—(m)—rain
Ghatiya—(f)—dynamic, moving
Ghatola—(f)—tulip
Ghatool—(m)—tulip
Ghatrif—(m)—leader, brave, noble
Ghaur—(m)—consideration, depth, attention
Ghausiazam—(m)—great helper
Ghaus—(m)—cry for help, defender, succour
Ghauth—(m)—succour, helper, defender
Ghawalib—(m)—victorious, triumphant
Ghawani—(f)—beautiful, needless
Ghawani—(m)—modest, singer, chaste
Ghawsaddin—(m)—rescuer of the faith
Ghawth—(m)—help, succour
Ghayab—(m)—disappear
Ghayad—(f)—delicacy, slender
Ghayat—(f)—aim, form of ghayah
Ghayat—(m)—aim, goal, destination
Ghayaz—(m)—one with divine wisdom
Ghayb—(m)—hidden, absent, away
Ghaydaa—(f)—young and delicate
Ghaydah—(f)—graceful lady
Ghayda—(f)—young and delicate
Ghayid—(m)—gentle, soft, delicate
Ghaylan—(m)—great
Ghayoor—(m)—self-respecting

Ghaysaa—(f)—a land where rain has fallen
Ghaysah—(f)—rain, rescues a dry land
Ghays—(m)—shower of mercy
Ghaythah—(f)—unique, divine aura
Ghayth—(m)—rain
Ghayur—(m)—zealous, eager, high minded
Ghayyas—(m)—winner, helper, reliever
Ghayyath—(m)—the one rushing to help
Ghayyoor—(m)—self- respecting
Ghazaalah—(f)—singer of beautiful songs
Ghazaala—(f)—gazelle, deer
Ghazaali—(m)—deer-like
Ghazaal—(f)—deer, gazelle
Ghazaal—(m)—gazelle, young deer, fawn
Ghazalaat—(f)—gazelles, the plural of ghazalah
Ghazalah—(f)—fawn, deer, gazelle
Ghazalan—(m)—spinner
Ghazala—(f)—gazelle, deer
Ghazaleah—(f)—gazelle
Ghazalea—(f)—gazelle
Ghazaleh—(f)—gazelle
Ghazale—(m)—resembling a deer
Ghazaliah—(f)—gazelle
Ghazalia—(f)—gazelle
Ghazallah—(f)—gazelle
Ghazalla—(f)—gazelle
Ghazal—(f)—poem, lyric poem, love poetry
Ghazal—(m)—resembling a deer
Ghazanfar—(m)—lion, title of caliph ali
Ghazan—(m)—holy war fighter
Ghazarat—(m)—abundance, plenty
Ghazari—(m)—pigeon
Ghazawan—(m)—warrior
Ghazee—(m)—war champion, conqueror
Ghazian—(m)—warrior
Ghazia—(f)—conqueror
Ghazia—(m)—child of god
Ghazir—(m)—comfortable, abundant, ample

Ghaziuddin—(m)—warrior of religion
Ghaziyah—(f)—warrior
Ghaziya—(f)—female warrior
Ghaziz—(f)—fresh and tender bud of a tree
Ghazi—(m)—war champion, hero, conqueror
Ghazlaan—(f)—so beautiful
Ghazulah—(f)—spindle
Ghazwaan—(m)—one on expedition, to conquer
Ghazwan—(m)—to conquer, one on expedition
Ghazwi—(m)—militant, warlike, heroic
Ghazy—(m)—conqueror
Ghazzal—(m)—vendor of cotton thread
Ghezaal—(f)—deer
Ghiath—(m)—sun
Ghifari—(m)—of the ghifar tribe
Ghilibba—(m)—victory
Ghiman—(m)—clouds
Ghina—(f)—melody, song
Ghirnauq—(m)—fair, handsome
Ghitamm—(m)—ocean, huge, vast
Ghitbah—(f)—narrator of hadith
Ghitreef—(m)—noble, great, famous man
Ghitref—(m)—noble, great, famous man
Ghiyaas—(m)—full of succour
Ghiyaath—(m)—succourer, help
Ghiyam—(m)—mist, fog
Ghiyas-ud-din—(m)—helper of the religion (islam)
Ghiyasud-din—(m)—helper of the religion
Ghiyasuddin—(m)—helper of the religion islam
Ghiyas—(m)—another name for god
Ghiyath—(m)—aid, succoured
Ghizala—(f)—gazelle, young deer
Ghizlan—(f)—from gazzalle, gazelles
Ghiz—(f)—bud, flower
Ghofran—(m)—pardon, forgiveness
Gholaam—(m)—lad, youth
Gholamhossein—(m)—variant of gulam
Gholam—(m)—lad, youth

Ghoncheh—(f)—bud of the flower
Ghoroob—(f)—sunset
Ghoroob—(m)—sunset
Ghorzang—(m)—long strides, panther strides
Ghotai—(f)—bud
Ghouseuddin—(m)—leadership, individuality
Ghousia—(f)—princess, light for life
Ghudaf—(m)—black raven
Ghudan—(f)—early morning
Ghudwah—(f)—early morning
Ghufair—(m)—forgiving, merciful
Ghufraan—(f)—forgiveness
Ghufraan—(m)—forgiveness
Ghufrah—(f)—female baby mountain goat
Ghufrana—(f)—remission of sins, forgiveness
Ghufran—(f)—forgiveness, pardon
Ghufran—(m)—leave, mercy, forgiveness
Ghulaam—(m)—slave, devotee, youth
Ghulam-ahmad—(m)—variant of gulam
Ghulam-hassan—(m)—variant of gulam
Ghulam-mohammed—(m)—variant of gulam
Ghulamahmad—(m)—variant of gulam
Ghulamhassan—(m)—variant of gulam
Ghulamkhan—(m)—keeps smile
Ghulamrasool—(m)—red flower
Ghulam—(m)—slave, devotee
Ghuljaan—(f)—unique, divine aura
Ghulubba—(m)—victory
Ghulumat—(m)—youthfulness
Ghumair—(m)—saffron
Ghumaysa—(f)—her kuniyah was umm sulaym
Ghumr—(m)—saffron
Ghunaim—(m)—a person who takes booty
Ghunayn—(m)—one who collects booty
Ghuncha-gul—(m)—bunch of flowers
Ghuncha—(f)—bunch of flowers
Ghunwah—(f)—indispensable, song
Ghunyah—(f)—indispensable

Ghurabat—(m)—beginning, edge of a sword
Ghuraibah—(f)—gold, silver
Ghuraib—(m)—gold, silver
Ghurar—(m)—ornaments, stars
Ghurian—(f)—unique, divine aura
Ghurnuq—(m)—tender, comely, delicate
Ghurrah—(f)—chief, leader
Ghurrah—(m)—chief, leader
Ghurran—(m)—grace, bright, brilliant
Ghurra—(f)—princess
Ghurub—(f)—sunset
Ghurub—(m)—sunset
Ghur—(m)—honoured chief, fair-skinned
Ghusayn—(m)—branch of a tree
Ghusn—(f)—branch, twig
Ghusoone—(f)—branches of a tree
Ghusoon—(f)—branches of a tree
Ghusoun—(f)—branches
Ghusune—(f)—branches of a tree
Ghusun—(f)—branches of tree
Ghusun—(m)—branches of tree
Ghutaif—(m)—a well of a person, well to do
Ghutayf—(m)—affluent
Ghuthayfah—(m)—companion of the prophet
Ghuwishat—(f)—bangle
Ghuzaila—(f)—unique, divine aura
Ghuzayyah—(f)—narrator of hadith
Giaa—(f)—sweet heart, life
Gian—(m)—god is merciful
Giasuddin—(m)—one with divine wisdom
Gias—(m)—helping
Gibran—(m)—tree shadow
Gibril—(m)—angel gabriel
Gidaan—(m)—one with divine wisdom
Giladi—(m)—moon
Gilad—(m)—hump of a camel, name of mountain
Gilam—(m)—joy of a country
Gildun—(m)—star

Gilead—(m)—hill of witness, hump of a camel
Gileem—(m)—blanket, warmth, protection
Gilsha—(f)—god of flowers
Ginni—(f)—precious gold coin
Ginton—(m)—a garden
Giraami—(m)—precious, respectable, dear
Girnauq—(m)—delicate, slender youth
Gishnu—(m)—synonymous of lord, singer
Giti—(f)—grape presser, world, song
Givon—(m)—hill, high place, heights
Gizala—(f)—deer
Glory—(f)—glory, form of gloria
Godalupe—(f)—wolf, reference to the virgin mary
Gogal—(m)—vocal cords
Gohar-tab—(m)—shining like bead, stone
Gohar—(f)—precious stone
Gohar—(m)—diamond, precious stone
Golan—(m)—a place of refuge
Golbahar—(f)—winter aconite, spring flower
Gold—(f)—treasure
Goli—(f)—round shaped, tablet
Golnar—(f)—flower of the pomegranate tree
Golnaz—(f)—cute like a flower, a flower
Golnisa—(f)—the most beautiful woman
Golshan—(f)—a flower garden
Gomal—(f)—unique, divine aura
Goolam—(m)—devotee
Gool—(f)—a flower
Gorbat—(m)—eagle
Gormal—(f)—unique, divine aura
Gouhar—(f)—jewellery, a pearl
Gousepak—(m)—friend of god
Gowsya—(f)—pearl
Gow—(m)—a smith
Grace—(f)—mercy, god's favour, grace
Grana—(f)—dear
Gran—(m)—dear, beloved
Greeshma—(f)—warmth, summer season, hot season

Gresilda—(f)—unique, divine aura
Grishma—(f)—warmth, summer season
Grismaa—(f)—summer season, warmth
Guadaloupa—(f)—wolf river
Guadaloupe—(f)—wolf river
Guadaloupe—(m)—wolf river
Guadalupana—(f)—wolf river
Guadalupe—(f)—from wolf's river
Guadalupe—(m)—plenty, river of the wolf
Guadalupi—(f)—wolf river
Guada—(f)—wolf river
Guadlupe—(f)—wolf river
Guadulupe—(f)—wolf river
Gudalupe—(f)—wolf river
Guda—(m)—supreme, he who is praised
Guddan—(f)—wisdom, faith
Gudia—(f)—doll, excellence
Gudiya—(f)—doll
Gufrana—(f)—forgiveness, remission of sins
Gufran—(m)—forgiver, forgiveness
Gufrina—(f)—innocent
Guftar—(m)—one with divine wisdom
Guhika—(f)—voice of birds
Guita—(f)—a kind of song
Guiti—(f)—world, universe
Gul-azra—(f)—unique, divine aura
Gul-badan—(f)—beautiful body resembling rose
Gul-bahar—(f)—rose spring
Gul-bano—(f)—princess of flowers
Gul-barg—(f)—rose petal
Gul-baz—(m)—playing with flowers
Gul-chehra—(f)—beautiful as flower
Gul-e-ranaa—(m)—a beautiful flower
Gul-e-rana—(f)—sweet-smelling rose
Gul-e-rana—(m)—a beautiful flower
Gul-hasham—(m)—flower name
Gul-izar—(f)—rosy-cheeked
Gul-jan—(m)—gul - flowers, jan - life

Gul-mast—(m)—gul - flowers, mast - excitement
Gul-mehtab—(f)—moon like flower
Gul-mina—(f)—lovely flower
Gul-nasreen—(f)—forest flower
Gul-panrha—(f)—flower petal
Gul-rang—(f)—rose-coloured
Gul-rang—(m)—colour of flowers
Gul-rukh—(f)—rose-face
Gul-ru—(f)—rosy-faced
Gul-warin—(f)—one who sprinkles flower
Gul-yar—(m)—loving flowers
Gul-zaman—(m)—zaman means times
Gul-zar—(m)—flower, garden
Gulaab—(f)—rose, flower
Gulaalaim—(f)—unique, divine aura
Gulabhsha—(f)—beautiful fragrant flower
Gulabsah—(f)—blooms like flower
Gulabsha—(f)—beautiful, fragrant flower
Gulab—(f)—rose, beloved's tears
Gulab—(m)—rose, flower
Gulafsan—(f)—rose, beautiful
Gulafsa—(f)—beautiful
Gulafshan—(f)—flower
Gulafshan—(m)—one with divine wisdom
Gulafsha—(f)—blossom flower, flavour rain
Gulalai—(f)—gorgeous, beautiful
Gulala—(f)—gorgeous
Gulali—(f)—gorgeous
Gulamali—(m)—strong
Gulamnabi—(m)—poet, devotee
Gulamrasool—(m)—one with divine wisdom
Gulam—(m)—slave, devotee
Gulaphsa—(f)—flower
Gulapsa—(f)—blooms like flower
Gulapsha—(f)—beautiful
Gulbadan—(f)—beautiful body resembling rose
Gulbadeen—(m)—one with divine wisdom
Gulbahar—(f)—like a rose in spring

Gulbano—(f)—lady like a beautiful flower
Gulbarg—(f)—rose petal
Gulbar—(m)—shredder of flowers, generous
Gulchin—(f)—name of flower
Guldin—(f)—out of flowers
Gule-ranaa—(m)—a beautiful flower
Guleen—(f)—one with beautiful smile
Gulerana—(f)—sweet smelling rose
Gulerana—(m)—a beautiful flower
Gulerina—(f)—smelling rose
Gulesha—(f)—god of flowers
Gulfam—(f)—rosy, beloved
Gulfam—(m)—flower's colour, rose faced
Gulfana—(f)—unique, divine aura
Gulfana—(m)—one with divine wisdom
Gulfan—(m)—one with divine wisdom
Gulfishah—(f)—unique, divine aura
Gulfisha—(f)—sweet smiling, rose
Gulfsa—(f)—beautiful
Gulfsha—(f)—blossom flower
Gulhamid—(m)—one with divine wisdom
Gulhashi—(f)—unique, divine aura
Gulika—(f)—ball, anything round, a pearl
Gulinara—(f)—resembling the pomegranate
Gulinarea—(f)—resembling the pomegranate
Gulinare—(f)—resembling the pomegranate
Gulinaria—(f)—resembling the pomegranate
Gulinar—(f)—pomegranate flower
Gulinear—(f)—pomegranate flower
Gulineir—(f)—resembling the pomegranate
Gulishta—(f)—garden of flowers
Gulistan—(f)—garden, rose garden
Gulista—(f)—flower garden
Gulizar—(f)—rosy-cheeked
Guljaan—(f)—beautiful flower
Guljar—(m)—one with divine wisdom
Gullisha—(f)—unique, divine aura
Gull—(f)—god

Gull—(m)—glutton
Gulmehak—(f)—appropriate fragrance
Gulmir—(m)—one with divine wisdom
Gulmohar—(f)—name of a flower
Gulnaaj—(f)—cute like a flower
Gulnaar—(f)—flowery
Gulnaax—(f)—unique, divine aura
Gulnaaz—(f)—cute like a flower
Gulnahar—(f)—unique, divine aura
Gulnaj—(f)—cute like a flower
Gulnara—(f)—flower of the pomegranate tree
Gulnar—(f)—flower of the pomegranate tree
Gulnasheen—(f)—unique, divine aura
Gulnas—(f)—a flower, cute like a flower
Gulnaz—(f)—cute like a flower, a flower
Gulnoor—(f)—beautiful flower
Gulnur—(f)—beautiful flower
Gulpari—(f)—flower angel
Gulraiz—(f)—rose-sprinkle
Gulraiz—(m)—rose-sprinkle, always happy
Gulrang—(f)—rose-coloured
Gulrej—(m)—red rose
Gulrez—(f)—rose-sprinkle
Gulrukh—(f)—rose-face
Gulru—(f)—rosy-faced
Gulsahar—(f)—unique, divine aura
Gulsah—(f)—unique, divine aura
Gulsanara—(f)—unique, divine aura
Gulsana—(f)—unbelievable flower
Gulsan—(f)—garden of flowers
Gulsan—(m)—a flower garden
Gulsar—(f)—garden, from the garden of roses
Gulshad—(m)—garden of flowers
Gulshama—(f)—unique, divine aura
Gulshana—(f)—from the gardens
Gulshanea—(f)—from the gardens
Gulshania—(f)—from the gardens
Gulshan—(f)—garden of roses, garden

Gulshan—(m)—garden of flowers, rose garden
Gulsheen—(f)—garden of roses, flower garden
Gulsher—(m)—king of flowers
Gulshiya—(f)—god of flowers
Gulussa—(m)—helper
Gulvez—(m)—one with divine wisdom
Gulvish—(m)—one with divine wisdom
Gulwan—(m)—early youth
Gulwareena—(f)—flower shower
Gulyani—(m)—one with divine wisdom
Gulyar—(m)—one with divine wisdom
Gulzaar—(f)—garden
Gulzaar—(m)—bed of roses, a garden
Gulzan—(f)—unique, divine aura
Gulzara—(f)—from the gardens
Gulzarea—(f)—from the gardens
Gulzare—(f)—from the gardens
Gulzaria—(f)—from the gardens
Gulzar—(f)—from the garden of roses, garden
Gulzar—(m)—gardener
Gul—(f)—flower, rose, bouquet
Gul—(m)—the rose flower, flower
Gunjbuksh—(m)—one with divine wisdom
Gunjoor—(m)—one with divine wisdom
Gurdanakhan—(m)—mangoes
Gutaif—(m)—a well of a person, well to do
Guzar—(m)—one with divine wisdom
Guzeeda—(f)—the chosen one
Guzeena—(f)—adopting, selecting
Guzeen—(m)—selecting, adopting
Guzeer—(m)—help, remedy
Gwadalupe—(f)—wolf river

EIGHT

ARABIC BABY NAMES—H

Haadhir—(m)—present, attending

Haadin—(m)—guide

Haadiya—(f)—guide to righteousness

Haadi—(m)—director, leader

Haady—(m)—guiding to the right

Haad—(m)—the leader

Haafidhaat—(f)—protectors

Haafidheen—(m)—protector, guardian

Haafidhoon—(m)—protector

Haafidh—(m)—protector

Haafil—(m)—one with divine wisdom

Haafira—(f)—unique, divine aura

Haafiya—(f)—kind

Haafizah—(f)—having a appropriate memory

Haafiza—(f)—protector

Haafiz—(m)—keeper, guardian, preserve

Haaiz—(m)—acquirer, getter

Haajarah—(f)—unique, divine aura

Haajara—(f)—prophet ismail's mother

Haajar—(f)—hard as a rock

Haajar—(m)—he abandoned

Haajeeth—(m)—beautiful

Haajib—(m)—eyebrow, chamberlain, doorkeeper

Haajid—(m)—one with divine wisdom

Haajira—(f)—terrific
Haajrah—(f)—unique, divine aura
Haakima—(f)—the wise
Haakim—(m)—wise, healer, physician, ruler
Haalah—(f)—a crescent shaped ear-ring
Haala—(f)—aureole, lunar halo, glory
Haalik—(m)—purity
Haalimah—(f)—dreaming
Haalim—(m)—grown up
Haameda—(f)—one who praises allah
Haamed—(m)—one who offers approval
Haamidah—(f)—one who praises
Haamida—(f)—god loving
Haamid—(m)—praising (god), grateful
Haamim—(m)—another name for prophet muhammad
Haamish—(m)—one with divine wisdom
Haamiz—(m)—intelligent
Haami—(f)—protector
Haami—(m)—protector, patron, helper
Haana—(f)—happiness
Haanee—(m)—happy, delighted, content, joyful
Haanish—(m)—delighted
Haaniya—(f)—happy, delighted
Haani—(f)—pleasant
Haani—(m)—happy, delighted, content
Haarib—(m)—one with divine wisdom
Haarisah—(m)—protector, guard
Haarish—(m)—lord siva, vishnu, krishna
Haaris—(m)—vigilant, watchman, guardian
Haaritha—(f)—unique, divine aura
Haaritheh—(f)—a heavenly messenger
Haarithe—(f)—a heavenly messenger
Haarith—(m)—old arabic name, ploughman, tiller
Haaroon—(m)—a prophet's name
Haarun—(m)—name of the prophet
Haasan—(m)—handsome, laughter
Haashid—(m)—one who rallies people
Haashim—(m)—generosity

Haashira—(f)—unique, divine aura
Haashir—(m)—collector
Haasim—(m)—decisive, dwefinite
Haathib—(m)—one with divine wisdom
Haatib—(m)—a person who collects wood
Haatim—(m)—judge, unavoidable
Haayi—(m)—modest, bashful
Haazima—(f)—generosity, prophet's grandfather
Haazim—(m)—precautions, generosity
Haaziq—(m)—skilful, intelligent
Haazira—(f)—intelligent, wise
Habaab—(m)—aim, goal
Hababah—(f)—a daughter of ajlan
Hababa—(f)—two lovers
Habab—(m)—fine dust, aim, goal
Habash—(m)—guinea fowl, turkey
Haba—(m)—favourite
Habbab—(m)—affable, lovable
Habbae—(f)—one who is much loved
Habbah—(m)—berry, grain, seed
Habbai—(f)—one who is much loved
Habban—(m)—loving, affectionate
Habbaye—(f)—one who is much loved
Habbay—(f)—one who is much loved
Habbiba—(f)—beloved one, gift from god
Habbib—(m)—dear, beloved
Habeba—(f)—sweetheart, beloved
Habeebah—(f)—dear one
Habeeballah—(m)—one with divine wisdom
Habeeba—(f)—beloved, sweetheart, darling
Habeebullah—(m)—beloved of allah
Habeeb—(f)—friend, to be loved
Habeeb—(m)—to be loved, friend, sweet heart
Habeekah—(f)—wave, wave of the sea
Habeesa—(f)—appropriate character, of the highlands
Habib-ullah—(m)—beloved of allah
Habibah—(f)—beloved, sweetheart, darling
Habiballah—(m)—friendship

Habiba—(f)—form of habib, beloved one
Habiba—(m)—beloved one, form of habib
Habibeh—(f)—beloved
Habibiyyah—(f)—beloved, loving
Habibi—(f)—loved one, beloved
Habibollah—(m)—beloved of allah
Habibullah—(m)—beloved of allah, dear to god
Habibulla—(m)—beloved of allah
Habibur-rahman—(m)—beloved friend of allah
Habibur—(m)—one with divine wisdom
Habibu—(f)—beloved
Habib—(f)—loveliness, loved one
Habib—(m)—beloved one, darling, dear
Habid—(m)—habib, beloved
Habijul—(m)—one with divine wisdom
Habikah—(f)—the road
Habika—(f)—sweetheart
Habinullah—(m)—one with divine wisdom
Habiri—(m)—colourful clouds
Habisha—(f)—of the highlands
Habita—(f)—curious
Habiyyah—(f)—little
Habiza—(f)—companion
Habiz—(m)—companion
Habi—(f)—picture
Hablah—(f)—a woman who earns a lot
Habon—(f)—helpful, hopeful, kindness
Habriyah—(f)—blessed, knowledgeable, virtuous
Habrur—(m)—blessed, living in luxury
Habr—(m)—virtuous, scholar, blessings
Habsa—(f)—daughter of prophet umme hani
Habsha—(f)—born to hanif
Habushun—(m)—one with divine wisdom
Habwat—(m)—gift, present
Hachem—(m)—name of prophet mohammed
Hachim—(m)—one with divine wisdom
Hackim—(m)—wise
Hadaaiq—(f)—garden

Hadabbas—(m)—tiger
Hadad—(m)—joy, noise, clamour, mighty
Hadaf—(m)—respected, target, aim
Hadah—(f)—she who radiates joy, ornament
Hadaiq—(f)—garden
Hadal—(f)—peaceful
Hadan—(m)—heathen
Hadara—(f)—bedecked in beauty, glory
Hadar—(m)—glorious, splendour, ornamented
Hadassah—(f)—myrtle tree, like a star
Hadas—(m)—new, happening for the first time
Hadaya—(f)—gift, present
Hadaya—(m)—gift, present
Hada—(f)—salty place, she who radiates joy
Hada—(m)—myrtle tree
Hadbaa—(f)—one with long eye lashes
Hadbar—(m)—beautiful
Haddad—(m)—smith, blacksmith
Haddaq—(m)—wise
Hadda—(f)—noble, one who radiates
Haddin—(m)—child of the heather-filled valley
Haddiqa—(f)—unique, divine aura
Haddiyah—(f)—unique, divine aura
Haddi—(m)—guide, leader, calm, quiet
Hadeal—(f)—cooing of pigeons, cooing
Hadeed—(f)—iron, mineral, sharp, perceptive
Hadeed—(m)—iron, sharp
Hadeefah—(f)—unique, divine aura
Hadeefa—(f)—unique, divine aura
Hadeel—(f)—bird
Hadeem—(m)—one with divine wisdom
Hadeeqah—(f)—garden
Hadeeqa—(f)—gorgeous
Hadeer—(m)—beautiful
Hadeesa—(f)—unique, divine aura
Hadees—(f)—speech, dialogue, new, modern
Hadees—(m)—speech, dialogue, new, modern
Hadeeth—(f)—speech, storey, narrations, news

Hadeeth—(m)—speech, news, storey, narrations
Hadeeya—(f)—gift
Hadee—(m)—guiding to the right, director
Hadeil—(f)—cooing, cooing of pigeons
Hadfah—(f)—aim, target
Hadhdh—(f)—fortune, luck
Hadhdh—(m)—fortune, luck
Hadheer—(m)—present, attending
Hadhik—(m)—one with divine wisdom
Hadhil—(m)—one with divine wisdom
Hadhiqah—(f)—intelligent, active
Hadhirah—(f)—unique, divine aura
Hadhir—(m)—present, attending
Hadhish—(m)—khashayar's palace in persepolis
Hadhiya—(f)—gift of god
Hadhi—(m)—present
Hadi-aman—(m)—peaceful leader
Hadiah—(f)—guide to righteousness
Hadia—(f)—guide to righteousness
Hadib—(m)—devoted, kind, compassionate
Hadidah—(m)—sword, weapon
Hadida—(f)—unique, divine aura
Hadid—(f)—iron, the mineral, sharp
Hadid—(m)—the th surah of the quran, iron
Hadiel—(f)—cooing, cooing of pigeons
Hadie—(m)—quiet, leader, calm, guide
Hadifah—(f)—unique, divine aura
Hadifa—(f)—unique, divine aura
Hadif—(m)—target, respected
Hadil—(f)—cooing like a pigeon
Hadinah—(f)—unique, divine aura
Hadina—(f)—guide to righteousness
Hadin—(m)—guide, leader
Hadiqah—(f)—garden
Hadiqa—(f)—walled garden, secure
Hadir—(m)—sound of thunder, glorified man
Hadisa—(f)—unique, divine aura
Hadisha—(f)—unique, divine aura

Hadish—(m)—heaven
Hadis—(m)—history, tradition
Hadith—(m)—narrations, storey, speech
Hadiyah—(f)—guide to righteousness
Hadiya—(f)—gift, guide to righteousness
Hadiyyah—(f)—gift
Hadiyya—(f)—gift
Hadiza—(f)—one with no desire
Hadi—(f)—no limit, guide
Hadi—(m)—guide, leader
Hadjara—(f)—forsaken, variant of hajar
Hadji—(m)—one with divine wisdom
Hadrami—(m)—a quran reciter of basrah
Hadrian—(m)—someone adria, hadria
Hadriel—(m)—majesty of god
Hadus—(m)—new, fresh, young
Hadyah—(f)—calm, guide, leader, quiet
Hadya—(f)—well-behaved, gift
Hadya—(m)—gift
Hadyl—(f)—cooing, cooing of pigeons
Hady—(f)—one who guides
Hady—(m)—calm, leader, quiet, guide
Haedar—(m)—lion
Haeda—(f)—a woman who repents a lot
Haefah—(f)—delicate
Haefa—(f)—delicate
Haemah—(f)—crazy in love
Haetham—(m)—young eagle
Haezal—(f)—leader, the colour of rising sun
Hafawat—(m)—friendly, welcoming
Hafa—(f)—gentle rain
Hafeeda—(f)—protect
Hafeedha—(f)—protect, preserver
Hafeedh—(m)—preserver
Hafeefa—(f)—all of appropriate
Hafeei—(f)—gracious, gentle
Hafeei—(m)—gracious, gentle
Hafeela—(f)—unique, divine aura

Hafeel—(m)—one with divine wisdom
Hafeem—(m)—one with divine wisdom
Hafeena—(f)—unique, divine aura
Hafeera—(f)—beautiful
Hafees—(m)—guardian, protector
Hafeey—(m)—very merciful
Hafeezah—(f)—keeper of the sacred book, exalt
Hafeeza—(f)—guardian, protector
Hafeez—(m)—protector, guardian
Hafez—(m)—protector, preserver
Haffafa—(f)—glittering, shining, thin
Haffaz—(m)—protector, protective
Haffeza—(m)—one with divine wisdom
Haffez—(m)—one with divine wisdom
Haffifa—(f)—unique, divine aura
Haffizur—(m)—one with divine wisdom
Hafia—(f)—loveable
Hafida—(f)—protect
Hafidh—(m)—preserver
Hafid—(m)—offspring, descendant, helpful
Hafiez—(m)—a guardian
Hafifah—(f)—rustle, swish
Hafifa—(f)—unique, divine aura
Hafija—(f)—one who taking of care
Hafijul—(m)—one with divine wisdom
Hafijur—(m)—one with divine wisdom
Hafij—(m)—guardian, protected
Hafila—(f)—keeper of the quran, gift of god
Hafil—(m)—diligent, industrious
Hafina—(f)—lots of things in hand
Hafira—(f)—unique, divine aura
Hafisah—(f)—honour
Hafisa—(f)—honour
Hafisha—(f)—honour
Hafis—(m)—the one who knows quran by heart
Hafiya—(f)—kind
Hafiy—(m)—one with divine wisdom
Hafizah—(f)—guardian, protector, successful

Hafizah—(m)—guardian, administrator, manager
Hafizat—(f)—protector
Hafiza—(f)—protected
Hafizha—(f)—one who taking care of
Hafizin—(m)—protector, guardian
Hafizullah—(m)—remembrance of allah
Hafizulla—(m)—remembrance of allah
Hafizul—(m)—one with divine wisdom
Hafizun—(m)—protector
Hafizur—(m)—one with divine wisdom
Hafiz—(m)—protected, guardian, keeper
Hafi—(m)—affectionate, compassionate
Haflat—(m)—all, everything
Hafnah—(f)—lots of things in hand
Hafna—(f)—lots of things in hand
Hafran—(m)—forgiver, virtuous, forgiveness
Hafsahh—(f)—young lioness
Hafsah—(f)—to collect, to rest
Hafsana—(f)—beauty
Hafsara—(f)—paradise woman
Hafsa—(f)—paradise woman, sound judgement
Hafseena—(f)—unique, divine aura
Hafseen—(f)—beautiful
Hafshah—(f)—young lioness
Hafshan—(m)—young lioness
Hafsha—(f)—young lioness
Hafsheen—(f)—unique, divine aura
Hafsina—(f)—beautiful
Hafsin—(f)—beautiful
Hafsiya—(f)—intelligent
Hafs—(f)—to collect, to rest
Hafs—(m)—young lion, collecting, gathering
Hafthah—(f)—preserved, protected
Haftha—(f)—one who is protected by god
Hafzaan—(m)—one with divine wisdom
Hafzah—(f)—appropriate judgement
Hafzal—(m)—one with divine wisdom
Hafzana—(f)—unique, divine aura

Hafzan—(m)—one who memorise the holy quran
Hafza—(f)—sound judgement, cub
Hafza—(m)—sound judgement
Hafzid—(m)—one with divine wisdom
Hagara—(f)—forsaken, flight
Hagar—(f)—a stranger, one that fears
Hager—(f)—travel
Hagir—(f)—forsaken
Hagi—(f)—one who has been abandoned
Hahnis—(m)—gift of god
Haian—(m)—very beautiful, life
Haia—(f)—heart, happy, shy
Haibaa—(f)—giant and strong
Haibah—(f)—charm
Haiba—(f)—charm
Haidan—(m)—a variant of hayden
Haidarali—(m)—lion, strong
Haidar—(m)—lion, derived from hadara
Haida—(f)—heart
Haideh—(f)—repentant
Haiderali—(m)—one with divine wisdom
Haiderbux—(m)—one with divine wisdom
Haider—(m)—lion, king of jungle, intelligent
Haidha—(f)—heart
Haidine—(m)—self confident, strong in decision
Haidin—(m)—heathen
Haidor—(m)—lion
Haidun—(m)—heathen
Haifaa—(f)—beautiful body, slender
Haifah—(f)—delicate
Haifa—(f)—slender, of beautiful body, slim
Haijuman—(f)—large pearl
Haikal—(m)—tale
Haika—(f)—beauty
Haiman—(m)—leader, warrior
Haima—(f)—snow, winter, gold, singer
Haima—(m)—snow, frost, dew, golden
Haimi—(f)—golden, goddess parvati, snow

Haimi—(m)—golden
Haim—(m)—life
Hainah—(f)—unique, divine aura
Haina—(f)—beautiful flower
Haiqa—(f)—truly, obedient of god
Hairah—(f)—a narrator of hadith
Haira—(f)—stone like diamond
Hairia—(f)—stone like diamond
Hairin—(f)—god gifted, most beautiful
Hairum—(m)—pious
Hairuneesa—(f)—unique, divine aura
Hairunnisa—(f)—unique, divine aura
Hairun—(m)—one of name of prophet
Haisam—(m)—strong man, brave
Haisa—(f)—gold
Haisha—(f)—unique, divine aura
Haisiyat—(m)—capacity, ability
Haitam—(m)—lion
Haitat—(m)—caution, care
Haitham—(m)—lion, eagle
Haithem—(m)—young eagle
Haithum—(m)—one with divine wisdom
Haiyam—(m)—part of heart
Haiyan—(m)—one with divine wisdom
Haiya—(f)—heart
Haiyoom—(m)—quite
Haizaan—(m)—smart
Haizal—(m)—soldier
Haizam—(m)—bold, young eagle
Haizan—(m)—one with divine wisdom
Haiza—(f)—royalty
Haizin—(m)—one with divine wisdom
Haizoom—(m)—one with divine wisdom
Haizyn—(f)—unique, divine aura
Haiz—(m)—from the hedged enclosure
Hajarah—(f)—very hot afternoon
Hajarah—(m)—calm
Hajaratali—(m)—going from one place to another

Hajarat—(m)—one with divine wisdom
Hajara—(f)—helpful
Hajara—(m)—equal to one thousand
Hajarul—(m)—one with divine wisdom
Hajar—(f)—stone, forsaken
Hajar—(m)—forsaken
Haja—(m)—one with divine wisdom
Hajeera—(f)—joy love beauty
Hajee—(m)—born during the hajj
Hajera—(f)—abraham's wife
Hajera—(m)—one with divine wisdom
Hajer—(f)—traveller, one who migrates
Hajib—(m)—doorman, janitor, bailiff
Hajid—(m)—one who sleeps
Hajij—(m)—pilgrim
Hajima—(f)—courage
Hajim—(m)—one with divine wisdom
Hajirafazal—(f)—unique, divine aura
Hajirah—(f)—midday heat
Hajira—(f)—wife of prophet ibrahim
Hajiriy—(m)—handsome, beautiful
Hajir—(m)—migratory, emigrant, noble
Hajisha—(m)—desire
Hajith—(m)—one with divine wisdom
Hajiyah—(m)—pilgrim
Hajiz—(m)—partition, curtain
Haji—(f)—purify
Haji—(m)—pilgrimage to mecca
Hajjaaj—(m)—one who prevails in the argument
Hajjah—(f)—narrator of hadith
Hajjaj—(m)—one who argues a lot
Hajji—(m)—pilgrim
Hajjra—(f)—graceful, peaceful
Hajna—(f)—the daughter of nusayb
Hajraa—(f)—needless, independent
Hajraha—(f)—unique, divine aura
Hajrah—(f)—the wife of prophet ibrahim
Hajratsab—(m)—one with divine wisdom

Hajra—(f)—wife of hazrat ibrahim
Hajreen—(f)—luck
Hajrifa—(f)—unique, divine aura
Hajveri—(m)—of hajver, a saint's name
Hakamat—(m)—scholarship, wisdom
Hakam—(m)—judge, commander
Hakeeb—(m)—will power, aspiration, ambition
Hakeemah—(f)—sage, philosopher, physician
Hakeema—(f)—wise, sage, judicious, prudent
Hakeem—(m)—wise, all-knowing
Hakem—(m)—ruler, governor
Hakib—(m)—will power, ambition, aspiration
Hakiem—(m)—doctor
Hakimah—(f)—judicious, wise
Hakima—(f)—sensible
Hakimi—(m)—dominion, power, rule
Hakimuddin—(m)—one with divine wisdom
Hakim—(m)—almighty, judge, wise
Hakkeem—(m)—all-knowing
Hakkim—(m)—one with divine wisdom
Halaat—(f)—sword gems
Halab—(m)—fish, milk
Halah—(f)—nimble, aureole
Halah—(m)—glory
Halan—(m)—hollow, devotee in the hall
Halawa—(f)—charm
Hala—(f)—halo around the moon, plough
Hala—(m)—halo around the moon, plough
Haleamah—(f)—mild-mannered, gentle
Haleefa—(f)—friend, companion
Haleef—(m)—ally, confederate
Haleel—(m)—intimate friend
Haleemah—(f)—gentle, forgiving
Haleemath—(f)—calm, patient
Haleema—(f)—gentle, patient, sympathetic
Haleem—(m)—lord of sound, patience
Haleena—(f)—like one
Haleh—(f)—halo

Haleima—(f)—mild-mannered, gentle
Halfrida—(f)—peaceful heroine
Halia—(f)—knowing, aware
Halideen—(m)—one with divine wisdom
Halidh—(m)—one with divine wisdom
Halid—(m)—strong
Halifa—(f)—unique, divine aura
Halif—(m)—ally, confederate
Halik—(m)—one with divine wisdom
Halila—(f)—rightful wife
Halil—(m)—close, intimate friend, flute
Halimah—(f)—gentle, soft-spoken, patient
Halimat—(f)—generous, gentle, mild-mannered
Halima—(f)—patient, merciful, poisonous
Halima—(m)—merciful, patient
Halime—(f)—mild, gentle
Halim—(m)—gentle, generous, compassionate
Halinah—(f)—shining one, woman of serenity
Halina—(f)—woman of serenity, light
Halis—(m)—beautiful
Halitha—(f)—unique, divine aura
Halith—(m)—continuous
Haliyah—(f)—adorned with jewellery
Haliya—(f)—adorned with jewellery
Haliza—(f)—unique, divine aura
Haliz—(f)—unique, divine aura
Hali—(f)—unique, the beautiful ocean
Hali—(m)—unique, graceful, kind, sweet
Hallaj—(m)—cotton refiner
Hallamah—(f)—dreamer, forbearing, enduring
Hallam—(m)—lives at the hall's slopes
Hallas—(m)—seller of coarse carpets
Halla—(f)—peace, princess, sweet and kind
Hallim—(m)—dweller in the remote valley
Hallumah—(f)—forbearing, enduring, patient
Halwani—(m)—confectioner, student of hadith
Halyah—(f)—moon's halo
Halyan—(m)—adorned, adorned with good manners

Halyat—(f)—jewel, ornament
Halyma—(f)—gentle, mild-mannered
Halym—(m)—mild, patient, gentle
Halyna—(f)—shining one, bright one
Hamaad—(m)—one who praises god a lot, praised
Hamaama—(f)—unique, divine aura
Hamaas—(m)—enthusiasm
Hamadan—(m)—the praised one
Hamada—(m)—praising (god)
Hamadi—(m)—one who is praised
Hamadullah—(m)—the thanks of allah
Hamad—(m)—to praise, all, whole, beautiful
Hamaid—(m)—one with divine wisdom
Hamail—(m)—things suspended
Hamalah—(m)—lamb
Hamal—(m)—lamb
Hamama—(f)—dove, pigeon
Hamam—(m)—pigeon, dove
Haman—(m)—abraham's brother, noise, tumult
Hamaroon—(m)—one with divine wisdom
Hamasat—(m)—enthusiasm, zeal
Hamasa—(f)—courage
Hamasi—(f)—enthusiastic, zealous, thrilling
Hamas—(f)—low and soft sound, heartbeat
Hamas—(m)—enthusiasm
Hamath—(f)—from the mighty fortress, anger
Hamaya—(f)—greatness
Hamayun—(m)—fortunate, blessed, sacred
Hamazat—(m)—strength
Hama—(f)—shore
Hama—(m)—verily, truly, shower, rain
Hamdaan—(m)—praises to be allah
Hamdah—(f)—praising allah, praiseworthy
Hamdanah—(f)—praise, one who praises god
Hamdan—(f)—much praise, a tribe in arabia
Hamdan—(m)—praiseworthy, the praised one
Hamdast—(m)—friend, one who remains close
Hamdat—(f)—praise, the form of word hamdah

Hamdat—(m)—praise, form of word hamdah
Hamda—(f)—peaceful, blessed by god, praised
Hamdeen—(m)—praised
Hamdee—(m)—of praise
Hamden—(m)—praised
Hamdhan—(m)—praises to be god
Hamdha—(f)—blessed off allah
Hamdhy—(m)—sympathy, blessing
Hamdiyah—(f)—one who praises a lot
Hamdiya—(f)—praiseworthy, admirable, noble
Hamdi—(f)—brave, praise
Hamdi—(m)—of praise, commendable
Hamdoona—(f)—unique, divine aura
Hamdoon—(m)—one who praise
Hamdrem—(m)—commendable, praised
Hamdunah—(f)—harun al rashid's daughter
Hamdun—(m)—praiseworthy, praised
Hamd—(m)—praise, commendation, lauding
Hameadah—(f)—praised, commendable
Hameada—(f)—commendable, praised
Hamead—(m)—commendable, praised
Hameda—(f)—thankful
Hamedha—(f)—gracious
Hamed—(m)—one who praises, thankful
Hameedah—(f)—praise worthy
Hameeda—(f)—praiseworthy, commendable
Hameedha—(f)—commendable, praiseworthy
Hameedh—(m)—praiseworthy, commendable
Hameedullah—(m)—devotee of the all-laudable
Hameed—(m)—praiseworthy, friend
Hameef—(m)—virtuous
Hameema—(f)—close friend, allah's friend
Hameem—(f)—close, intimate friend
Hameem—(m)—allah's friend, friend
Hameera—(f)—unique, divine aura
Hameer—(m)—very rich king
Hameesh—(m)—one with divine wisdom
Hameesi—(m)—patron, supporter, protector

Hameeza—(f)—wise
Hameez—(m)—intelligent, strong, brave
Hameidah—(f)—commendable, praised
Hameida—(f)—praised, commendable
Hamet—(m)—brave
Hamidaa—(f)—gracious, praiseworthy
Hamidah—(f)—praiseworthy, praising allah
Hamidat—(f)—variant of hamidah
Hamidat—(m)—form of hamidah
Hamida—(f)—gracious
Hamida—(m)—praiseworthy
Hamideh—(f)—praiseworthy
Hamidha—(f)—gracious
Hamidi—(m)—to be commended, praise
Hamidullah—(m)—the appreciation of allah (swt)
Hamidul—(m)—fast
Hamidur—(m)—one with divine wisdom
Hamid—(m)—friend, praiseworthy
Hamiedah—(f)—commendable, praised
Hamieda—(f)—commendable, praised
Hamied—(m)—commendable, praised
Hamil—(m)—carrier, bearer
Hamimah—(f)—devoted, loyal
Hamima—(f)—close friend
Hamim—(f)—close, devoted, intimate friend
Hamina—(f)—golden, moon's rays
Hamin—(m)—a great leader
Hamira—(f)—unique, divine aura
Hamirudeen—(m)—one with divine wisdom
Hamir—(m)—good, vest, a raga
Hamisa—(f)—unique, divine aura
Hamisa—(m)—joyful, happy
Hamisha—(f)—happiness, joyful
Hamish—(m)—edge, corner, supplanter
Hamisi—(m)—born on thursday
Hamis—(m)—happy, active, joyful
Hamit—(m)—praised, commendable
Hamiya—(f)—greatness

Hamiz—(m)—firm, vigorous, summer
Hami—(f)—golden
Hami—(m)—protector, defender, patron
Hamlin—(m)—little home-lover
Hammaad—(m)—a person who praises
Hammadah—(f)—one who praise often
Hammadah—(m)—one who praises often
Hammada—(f)—praising god
Hammadiyyah—(f)—praiseworthy, one who praises god
Hammadi—(m)—pertaining to hammad
Hammad—(m)—praised
Hammam—(m)—chief, hero, great man
Hammar—(m)—hammer
Hammed—(m)—one who praises
Hammood—(m)—thankful, grateful
Hammou—(m)—one with divine wisdom
Hammsa—(m)—swan
Hammudah—(f)—praiseworthy
Hammud—(m)—thankful, grateful, praiseworthy
Hammza—(m)—lion, steadfast, strong
Hamnaa—(f)—blessed sparrow of heaven
Hamnah—(f)—bird of paradise
Hamna—(f)—appropriate grapes
Hamood—(m)—one who praises allah
Hamool—(m)—patient, enduring
Hamraaz—(m)—one who has the secret
Hamraa—(f)—red coloured female
Hamran—(m)—one who is remembered by god
Hamraz—(m)—confidant
Hamra—(f)—fair woman, red
Hamsa—(f)—bird, swan hamsavahini
Hamsa—(m)—swan
Hamshad—(m)—always victorious
Hamsha—(f)—jewellery, love, cute
Hamshid—(m)—one with divine wisdom
Hamsini—(f)—one who rides a swan
Hamsiya—(f)—unique, divine aura
Hamuda—(m)—one with divine wisdom

Hamud—(m)—praiseworthy
Hamu—(m)—alert
Hamyaa—(f)—protector, defender
Hamydah—(f)—commendable, praised
Hamyda—(f)—praised, commendable
Hamyd—(m)—commendable, praised
Hamzaa—(m)—strong, lion, steadfast
Hamzad—(m)—comrade, companion
Hamzah—(f)—brave, steadfast, strong
Hamzah—(m)—lion, good man, strong, steadfast
Hamzan—(m)—one with divine wisdom
Hamza—(f)—name of the companion
Hamza—(m)—lion, strong, sour leaves, smart
Hamzeh—(m)—steadfast, brave
Hamze—(m)—strong, steadfast, lion
Hanaaf—(m)—one with divine wisdom
Hanaan—(m)—affection, love
Hanaa—(f)—joy, peace, happiness
Hanadhi—(f)—with radiant face
Hanad—(m)—with radiant face
Hanafi—(m)—true believer, monotheist
Hanah—(m)—happiness
Hanaimah—(f)—unique, divine aura
Hanai—(m)—of happiness
Hanaliya—(f)—happy
Hananan—(m)—another name for god, generous
Hanana—(f)—gracious
Hanane—(f)—love, friendliness, affection
Hananiah—(f)—favoured by god
Hanani—(f)—favoured by god
Hanani—(m)—one who is merciful, my grace
Hananna—(f)—tenderness
Hanan—(f)—compassion, gracious, sympathy
Hanan—(m)—mercy, grace, compassionate
Hanayah—(f)—shine, bright, beautiful, fairy
Hanaya—(f)—every time new, florist, eyes
Hana—(f)—happiness, flower, blossom
Hana—(m)—brahma, happiness, form of john

Hanbal—(m)—pristine, purity
Hanbel—(m)—pure
Haneafah—(f)—pure muslim
Haneafa—(f)—pure muslim
Haneefah—(f)—pure muslim
Haneefa—(f)—true believer
Haneefa—(m)—true believer
Haneef—(f)—true believer, upright, true
Haneef—(m)—one who believes in one god
Haneek—(m)—one with divine wisdom
Haneena—(f)—jewellery, bright
Haneen—(f)—appropriate girl, pretty, bright
Haneen—(m)—yearning, desire
Haneesa—(f)—god of weather
Hanees—(m)—god of weather
Haneeya—(f)—pleasant, pleased
Haneez—(m)—the lord is gracious, merciful
Hanee—(m)—happy, delighted, joyful
Haneifah—(f)—pure muslim
Haneifa—(f)—pure muslim
Hanein—(f)—yearning, emotion
Hanes—(m)—god is gracious
Haney—(m)—happy
Hanfi—(m)—school follower
Hani-ah—(f)—of happiness, bliss
Haniah—(f)—bliss, happiness, pleasant
Haniah—(m)—a spirit warrior
Hania—(f)—grace, favour, apricot from nara
Haniefah—(f)—pure muslim
Haniefa—(f)—true believer, pure muslim
Hanief—(m)—pious, follower of prophet abraham
Hanie—(m)—happy
Hanifaa—(f)—variant of hanifah
Hanifah—(f)—true believer, upright
Hanifah—(m)—upright
Hanifa—(f)—true believer, pure
Hanifa—(m)—true, upright, a believer of islam
Hanife—(m)—true believer

Haniff—(m)—upright, true, a believer of islam
Hanifiyyah—(f)—pure religion
Hanifud-din—(m)—true of religion (islam)
Hanifuddin—(m)—true of religion islam
Hanif—(m)—orthodox, pious
Haniif—(m)—one with divine wisdom
Hanik—(m)—graceful like a swan
Hanim—(m)—one with divine wisdom
Hanina—(f)—devotee girl, maid
Hanin—(f)—emotion, longing, yearning
Hanin—(m)—yearning, desire, affectionate
Hanisah—(f)—unique, divine aura
Hanisa—(f)—beautiful night
Hanisha—(f)—beautiful night, sweetest
Hanishma—(f)—unique, divine aura
Hanish—(m)—ambition, god, god of weather
Haniska—(f)—grace, beautiful
Hanis—(f)—god is gracious
Hanis—(m)—god is gracious, lord shiva
Haniyah—(f)—pleasant, bliss
Haniyah—(m)—a spirit warrior
Haniya—(f)—pleased, happy, encampment
Haniya—(m)—a spirit warrior
Haniyyah—(f)—pleased, happy
Haniyya—(f)—pleasant, encampment
Hani—(f)—droplet, pleasant, delighted
Hani—(m)—happy, content, delighted
Hanlala—(m)—one with divine wisdom
Hannaan—(m)—beautiful, compassionate
Hannad—(m)—one with divine wisdom
Hannah—(f)—gracious, grace, grace of god
Hannah—(m)—grace, wife, favour
Hannanah—(f)—affectionate, sympathetic, caring
Hannan—(f)—warm feelings
Hannan—(m)—merciful, compassionate
Hannath—(f)—lucky life
Hanna—(f)—garden, happiness, joy, grace
Hanna—(m)—name of mother of maryam (mary)

Hannen—(m)—having warm feelings
Hannia—(f)—resting place, pleasant
Hannin—(m)—having warm feelings
Hanni—(f)—god is gracious, grace
Hannon—(m)—having warm feelings
Hannufah—(f)—monotheist
Hannufa—(f)—unique, divine aura
Hanoofa—(f)—unique, divine aura
Hanoona—(f)—compassionate, feminine of hanun
Hanoon—(f)—compassionate, merciful
Hanoon—(m)—compassionate, merciful
Hansal—(m)—smiling
Hansika—(f)—swan, love, baby of swan
Hantama—(f)—pitcher, vessel
Hanuj—(m)—one with divine wisdom
Hanunah—(f)—affectionate, tender
Hanuna—(f)—affectionate
Hanun—(m)—merciful, gracious
Hanyah—(f)—happy
Hanya—(f)—happy
Hanyfah—(f)—pure muslim
Hanyfa—(f)—pure muslim
Hanym—(f)—lady, woman
Hany—(m)—rules an estate
Hanzalah—(m)—pond, water ditch
Hanzala—(m)—water, adjust everywhere, pond
Hanzal—(f)—the beauty of eyes
Hanzal—(m)—pond
Hanzar—(m)—one with divine wisdom
Hanzhalah—(m)—name of a tree
Hanzul—(f)—artistic
Hanz—(m)—gift from god, god is gracious
Haola—(f)—name of a sahabiah
Hapsa—(f)—unique, divine aura
Haqaiq—(m)—truths, facts
Haqam—(m)—quranic name
Haqeeq—(m)—befitting, suitable, obligated
Haqikah—(f)—honest

Haqika—(f)—truthful
Haqiqat—(m)—reality, sincerity
Haqiq—(m)—worthy, deserving, befitting
Haqqaat—(f)—rights, privileges, truths
Haqqani—(m)—correct, right, proper
Haqqi—(m)—a person who upholds the truth
Haqqullah—(m)—right of god, prayer
Haqq—(m)—just, right, true
Haque—(m)—truth
Haquikah—(f)—truthful
Haquika—(f)—truthful
Haqyka—(f)—truthful
Haq—(m)—right, justice, truth
Haraam—(m)—sacred
Haraan—(m)—one with divine wisdom
Harabat—(m)—friday
Harafa—(f)—unique, divine aura
Harana—(f)—a great mountaineer
Haran—(m)—terah's son, brother of abraham
Harar—(m)—free, of noble birth
Harayir—(f)—free, pure, generous
Haraz—(m)—make fun, comedy
Harbi—(m)—son of owen
Harby—(m)—king
Harb—(m)—war, warrior
Hareeb—(m)—one with divine wisdom
Hareef—(m)—pungent, hot
Hareem—(f)—house, walls of house of kabba
Hareem—(m)—respectable
Hareena—(f)—most beautiful
Hareen—(f)—most beautiful
Hareer—(f)—silk
Harees—(m)—eager, keen, desirous
Hareeza—(f)—unique, divine aura
Hareez—(m)—almighty, desirous
Haresa—(f)—daughter of the sun
Hares—(m)—lord shiva, krishna, almighty
Hareth—(m)—good provider

Harib—(m)—highly alienated, name of allah
Harif—(m)—pungent, hot
Harim—(m)—companion, friend, destroyed
Harin—(m)—success, deer
Hariqat—(m)—burning, glowing
Harir—(f)—silk
Harir—(m)—silk
Harisah—(f)—farmer, companion
Harisah—(m)—farmer
Harisa—(f)—cultivator, lioness
Harishah—(m)—guard, protector
Harissa—(f)—cultivator, lioness
Haris—(m)—protector, farmer, watchman
Harithah—(f)—a heavenly messenger
Harithah—(m)—good provider
Haritha—(f)—green, lovely, beautiful princess
Haritha—(m)—green, cultivator, farmer
Harithe—(f)—a heavenly messenger
Harithe—(m)—good provider
Harith—(m)—lion, green colour, surya's horse
Harit—(m)—green, lion
Harizz—(m)—one with divine wisdom
Hariz—(m)—strong, secure, guarded
Hari—(m)—almighty
Harmalah—(f)—a plant
Harmalah—(m)—a plant
Harman—(m)—variant of herman, soldier
Harmayn—(m)—one with divine wisdom
Harmeen—(f)—beauty, fish of god
Harmen—(m)—high ranking soldier
Haron—(m)—loving full person, loving fuel
Haroof—(m)—one with divine wisdom
Haroona—(f)—hope, protector of chief
Haroon—(m)—hope, achievement, heroic warrior
Haroun-al-rachid—(m)—aaron the upright
Haroun—(m)—superior, exalted, on high
Harrah—(f)—seizer, sound, voice
Harrar—(m)—very noisy

Harron—(m)—powerful
Harsahib—(f)—highest of all
Harsallah—(m)—happiness of lord
Harsam—(m)—lion
Harshad—(m)—happiness, one who gives pleasure
Harshat—(m)—happiness
Harsheena—(f)—beautiful
Harshin-begam—(f)—happiness, beautiful, pretty
Harshin—(m)—one who delights
Harshi—(f)—happy, joyous
Harul—(m)—god's mountain
Harun-al-rachid—(m)—aaron the upright
Harunalrachid—(m)—aaron the upright
Harunalrashid—(m)—celebrated abbasid caliph
Haruna—(m)—springtime vegetables
Harundas—(m)—devotee of god
Haruni—(f)—messenger-ship
Harun—(m)—mountain of strength, messenger
Harzin—(m)—protector
Hasaan—(m)—form of hassan, handsome
Hasab—(m)—good deed, generosity, pedigree
Hasad—(m)—harvest
Hasain—(m)—handsome
Hasam—(m)—sword
Hasanaat—(f)—appropriate deeds
Hasanaa—(f)—beautiful
Hasanah—(f)—appropriate deed
Hasanain—(m)—two hasans (hasan and husain)
Hasanali—(m)—one with divine wisdom
Hasanat—(f)—beautiful, fair, elegant
Hasanat—(m)—good deeds, kind acts, favours
Hasana—(f)—first born of twins, appropriate deed
Hasani—(m)—handsome, excellence
Hasanna—(f)—beautiful, beautifier, appropriate
Hasanul—(m)—one with divine wisdom
Hasanur—(m)—one with divine wisdom
Hasanuz—(m)—one with divine wisdom
Hasan—(f)—handsome, chaste woman

Hasan—(m)—laughter, good, beautiful
Hasba—(f)—respected
Hasbeena—(f)—unique, divine aura
Hasbina—(f)—unique, divine aura
Hasbiya—(f)—unique, divine aura
Hasbi—(m)—gift of god
Haseeba—(f)—respected, noble
Haseebulla—(m)—one with divine wisdom
Haseeb—(m)—accounter, omnipotent
Haseefa—(f)—wise, judicious
Haseef—(m)—judicious, wise, prudent
Haseela—(f)—unique, divine aura
Haseemah—(f)—diligent, assiduous, persevering
Haseema—(f)—diligent, assiduous, persevering
Haseem—(m)—diligent, assiduous, persevering
Haseenah—(f)—pretty
Haseena—(f)—smile, beautiful, pretty
Haseen—(f)—beautiful
Haseen—(m)—beautiful, smart, good-looking
Haseer—(m)—one with divine wisdom
Hasees—(m)—sensitive, perceptive
Hasefa—(f)—judicious, wise, prudent
Haseim—(m)—decisive one
Hasem—(m)—decisive
Hasena—(f)—appropriate, pretty, beautiful, smile
Hasen—(m)—good-looking, laughing
Hashaam—(m)—form of hashim
Hashaan—(m)—love
Hashami—(m)—an ancestor of prophet muhammad
Hasham—(m)—form of hashim
Hashan—(m)—love
Hashash—(m)—mirthful, happy, tidy, pleased
Hasha—(f)—piousness, cheerfulness, to laugh
Hashbin—(m)—romantic
Hasheem—(m)—crusher of evil
Hasheena—(f)—most beautiful
Hasheer—(m)—one with divine wisdom
Hasher—(m)—collector

Hashib—(m)—one with divine wisdom
Hashida—(f)—unique, divine aura
Hashid—(m)—one who rallies people, crowded
Hashifa—(f)—unique, divine aura
Hashif—(m)—one with divine wisdom
Hashil—(m)—joyful
Hashimel—(m)—one with divine wisdom
Hashimi—(m)—an ancestor of prophet muhammad
Hashim—(m)—magnificent, destroys evil
Hashina—(f)—most beautiful
Hashique—(m)—one with divine wisdom
Hashiq—(m)—one with divine wisdom
Hashira—(f)—another name for prophet muhammad
Hashir—(m)—collector
Hashi—(m)—companion (avestan)
Hashmat—(f)—modesty, bashfulness, decency
Hashmat—(m)—glory, joyful, decency, dignity
Hashmeen—(f)—beautiful
Hashmil—(m)—one with divine wisdom
Hashmina—(f)—unique, divine aura
Hashmir—(m)—one with divine wisdom
Hashmi—(m)—generous
Hashmullah—(m)—one with divine wisdom
Hashna—(f)—happiness, saviour
Hashrat—(f)—wish
Hashr—(m)—raising, collecting
Hasibah—(f)—reckoner, esteemed
Hasiba—(f)—high-born, respected, noble
Hasibul—(m)—one with divine wisdom
Hasibur—(m)—one with divine wisdom
Hasib—(m)—respected, accountant, avenger
Hasid—(m)—one with divine wisdom
Hasiem—(m)—decisive one
Hasiena—(f)—appropriate
Hasifah—(f)—wise
Hasifa—(f)—judicious, wise, prudent
Hasif—(m)—firm, judicious, steady, joyful
Hasika—(f)—smiling

Hasik—(m)—skillful
Hasil—(m)—acquirer, producer, farmer
Hasima—(f)—beautiful, prettiest
Hasim—(m)—definite, decisive
Hasinaa—(f)—unique, divine aura
Hasinah—(f)—beautiful, pretty, appropriate-looking
Hasina—(f)—appropriate, cheerful, beautiful, pretty
Hasini—(f)—happy, joyful, an atom, pretty
Hasinna—(f)—attractive, pretty, beautiful
Hasin—(f)—beautiful, elegant
Hasin—(m)—beautiful, strong
Hasirah—(f)—clean
Hasisah—(f)—swift, rapid, inspired, spurred
Hasiya—(f)—unique, divine aura
Hask—(m)—acme of mountain
Haslina—(f)—beautiful angel
Haslin—(f)—love
Hasmat—(m)—one with divine wisdom
Hasma—(f)—elegant, prettiest
Hasmina—(f)—clever, unique, strong mind
Hasmira—(f)—unique, divine aura
Hasmiya—(f)—unique, divine aura
Hasmi—(m)—one with divine wisdom
Hasmuddin—(m)—one with divine wisdom
Hasnaat—(f)—beautiful, plural of hasnaa
Hasnaa—(f)—beauty, from swahili, pretty
Hasnah—(f)—pretty, beautiful
Hasnain—(m)—smart, handsome
Hasnat—(f)—beautiful, fair, elegant, wise
Hasnaw—(f)—beautiful, pet form of hasnaat
Hasna—(f)—beautiful, laughing, pretty
Hasniyah—(f)—beautiful
Hasniya—(f)—beautiful
Hasni—(f)—always happy
Hasni—(m)—happy
Hason—(m)—strong
Hasoun—(m)—virtuous, chaste
Hasrah—(m)—wanting

Hasrat—(m)—wish, desire, grief, distress
Hasrin—(f)—smiling face
Hassaan—(m)—beautiful
Hassain—(m)—brave, protector of people
Hassam—(m)—sword
Hassanah—(f)—most pious, beautiful
Hassanain—(m)—beauty, handsome
Hassanaskaree—(m)—early imam (leader) of islam
Hassanaskari—(m)—early imam (leader) of islam
Hassana—(f)—twin girl
Hassan—(m)—good, handsome, beautiful
Hassen—(m)—one with divine wisdom
Hasshir—(m)—an assembler
Hassian—(m)—one with divine wisdom
Hassiba—(m)—one with divine wisdom
Hassib—(m)—the reckoner a name for allah
Hassina—(f)—very beautiful
Hassin—(m)—strong, beautiful
Hassive—(f)—unique, divine aura
Hassnain—(m)—handsome, beauty
Hassna—(f)—beautiful, appropriate, beautifier
Hassona—(f)—beautifier, beautiful, appropriate
Hasson—(m)—one with divine wisdom
Hassoun—(m)—one with divine wisdom
Hassunah—(f)—beautiful
Hassun—(m)—stone, handsome, good-looking
Hastee—(f)—existence
Hasti—(f)—laughing, happy, existence
Hasunah—(f)—one who is well-behaved, appropriate
Hasuna—(f)—appropriate, one who is well-behaved
Hasun—(m)—brave, strong
Hasurah—(f)—unique, divine aura
Hasu—(m)—smile
Haswar—(m)—lion
Haswin—(m)—horse rider, strong men
Hataf—(m)—mars
Hatam—(m)—generous, helper
Hateef—(m)—a sound from heaven

Hateem—(m)—king, steadfast, ruler, judge
Hatem—(m)—judge, decider, justice
Hatham—(m)—young eagle
Hatheem—(m)—ruler, steadfast, king
Hathifa—(f)—sensitive
Hathim—(m)—one with divine wisdom
Hathirullah—(m)—one with divine wisdom
Hathir—(m)—one with divine wisdom
Hathun—(f)—beautiful
Hatibah—(m)—one with divine wisdom
Hatib—(m)—a wood collector, judge
Hatifa—(f)—unique, divine aura
Hatifi—(f)—pertaining to an angel
Hatif—(m)—one who summons
Hatima—(f)—generous, ender of doubts
Hatim—(m)—judge, inevitable, ruler, king
Hattabah—(f)—wood gatherer, seller
Hattan—(m)—a sophisticated, from manhattan
Hattem—(m)—one with divine wisdom
Hauba—(f)—person, individual, soul
Haujamat—(f)—red rose
Hauled—(f)—crown
Haumat—(m)—great battle, battlefield
Haura—(f)—extremely fair
Haurvatat—(f)—perfection, health
Haushab—(m)—name of son of imam muslim (ra)
Haussam—(m)—the sward
Hautat—(m)—prudence, caution
Havin—(m)—sanctuary, safe harbour
Haviva—(f)—precious
Hawaa—(f)—eve
Hawadah—(f)—pleasant
Hawada—(f)—a pleasant woman
Hawah—(f)—desire, air, wind
Hawari—(f)—friend, companion, helper
Hawari—(m)—apostle, supporter, follower
Hawazin—(f)—name of an arabic tribe
Hawazzudin—(m)—one with divine wisdom

Hawa—(f)—air, longing, desire, eve, female
Hawa—(m)—loving, desiring
Hawis—(m)—thought, idea, concept
Hawit—(m)—clever, smart
Hawiya—(f)—dominant
Hawiz—(m)—able, active
Hawla—(f)—active, intelligent
Hawraa—(f)—white, fair, perfectly healthy
Hawra—(f)—white, fair-skinned
Hawshab—(m)—a son of imam
Hawwaa—(f)—one who follows the truth
Hawwah—(f)—a lively woman, air
Hawwa—(f)—eve
Hawwa—(m)—life, life-giving
Hayaam—(f)—deliriously in love
Hayaan—(m)—life, happy
Hayaat—(f)—life, existence
Hayaat—(m)—life, existence
Hayaa—(f)—modesty, chastity, virtue
Hayah—(f)—life, gift of god
Hayam—(f)—deliriously in love
Hayana—(f)—eyes
Hayana—(m)—one with divine wisdom
Hayan—(f)—alive, life, shine, lord shiva
Hayan—(m)—lord shiva, alive, life, shine
Hayath—(m)—soft, skill
Hayati—(f)—presence
Hayat—(f)—life
Hayat—(m)—life, existence
Haya—(f)—modesty, decency, shyness, shame
Hayba—(f)—charm, variant of haiba
Haybek—(m)—one with divine wisdom
Haybin—(m)—one with divine wisdom
Haydan—(m)—independent
Haydara—(f)—lioness
Haydar—(m)—peaceful, lion
Hayda—(f)—heart
Hayden—(m)—from the hedged in valley

Hayder—(m)—lion, another name of ali
Haydin—(m)—strong, independent, loving
Hayed—(f)—movement, motion
Hayee—(m)—ever alive
Hayet—(f)—life
Hayfah—(f)—delicate
Hayfa—(f)—slender, well-shaped
Hayiyyah—(f)—modest, bashful
Hayi—(f)—alive, living, existence, wish
Hayla—(f)—merlin bird
Haylin—(f)—unique, divine aura
Hayooda—(f)—from the mountain
Hayood—(f)—from the mountain
Hayrin—(f)—most beautiful, god gifted
Haysam—(m)—lion
Haysha—(f)—unique, divine aura
Haytham—(f)—unique, divine aura
Haytham—(m)—young hawk, eagle, lion, strong
Haythem—(m)—young eagle
Hayub—(m)—to be feared, venerable
Hayudah—(f)—from the mountain
Hayuda—(f)—from the mountain
Hayud—(f)—beautiful, soft
Hayyaan—(m)—alive
Hayyan—(m)—lively, energetic
Hayyee—(m)—modest, bashful
Hayyin—(f)—easy, facilitated
Hayyin—(m)—easy, facilitated
Hayyi—(m)—good-looking, handsome
Hayy—(m)—alive, having life, living
Hayzam—(m)—one with divine wisdom
Hayzan—(m)—beneficence
Hazaan—(m)—one with divine wisdom
Hazafa—(f)—the too much affection
Hazah—(m)—gift of god
Hazal—(f)—dream, tree name
Hazam—(m)—companien of prophet muhammad
Hazana—(f)—born during autumn

Hazan—(f)—fall
Hazan—(m)—clever
Hazaq—(m)—learning the quran by heart
Hazarah—(f)—civilization, culture
Hazarat—(m)—dignity, power, prophet
Hazara—(f)—from the town of fountains
Hazare—(f)—resembling a nightingale
Hazarra—(f)—resembling a nightingale
Hazarre—(f)—resembling a nightingale
Hazarr—(f)—resembling a nightingale
Hazar—(f)—hard working
Hazar—(m)—ready, attention, vigilant
Hazeeb—(m)—one with divine wisdom
Hazeela—(f)—unique, divine aura
Hazeel—(m)—one with divine wisdom
Hazeema—(f)—unique, divine aura
Hazeem—(f)—thunder, the sound of hooves
Hazeem—(m)—thunder, the sound of hooves
Hazeena—(f)—autumn, treasure, forever
Hazeen—(m)—one with divine wisdom
Hazeerah—(f)—wise
Hazeera—(f)—intelligent, wise
Hazel—(f)—hazelnut, a nut-bearing tree
Hazem—(m)—strict, resolute
Hazera—(f)—beautiful, wise, clean
Hazera—(m)—clean, wise
Hazibaba—(m)—one with divine wisdom
Hazib—(m)—on a masculine people
Hazifa—(f)—beautiful
Hazif—(m)—joyful
Hazika—(f)—intelligent
Hazik—(m)—intelligent, skillful
Hazima—(f)—firm, energetic, judicious
Hazim—(m)—strict regulator, thunder, keen
Hazina—(f)—exchequer, treasury
Hazin—(m)—treasure
Haziqah—(f)—clever, intelligent, beautiful
Haziqa—(f)—clever, shrewd, intelligent

Haziq—(m)—skilful, intelligent
Hazirah—(f)—clean
Hazira—(f)—wise, intelligent, beautiful
Hazir—(m)—another name for god, present
Hazlan—(m)—lion
Hazlaqat—(m)—skilfulness, dexterity
Hazlina—(f)—unique, divine aura
Hazmina—(f)—unique, divine aura
Hazmiya—(f)—unique, divine aura
Hazm—(m)—digestion
Hazoora—(f)—ultimate, wise
Hazrah—(f)—presence
Hazrah—(m)—presence
Hazrath—(m)—dignity, prophet, power, presence
Hazrat—(m)—prophet, jesus, presence, dignity
Hazra—(f)—presence
Hazra—(m)—ultimate
Hazrik—(m)—creativity, wisdom, generosity
Hazriya—(f)—unique, divine aura
Hazur—(m)—eloquent
Hazwani—(f)—unique, divine aura
Hazwa—(f)—gift of god
Hazza—(f)—beautiful
Hazza—(m)—delight, pleasure
Hazz—(m)—pleasure, delight, luck
Haz—(f)—fortune, luck
Haz—(m)—fortune, luck
Healing—(f)—merciful, patience
Heam—(m)—loveable
Hebah—(f)—young, generous gift
Heba—(f)—the gift, blessing of god
Hedayat—(m)—guidance
Hedaya—(f)—give
Hedeyah—(f)—gift
Hediyeh—(f)—gift
Hedi—(m)—director, leader
Heeba—(f)—gift of god
Heelai—(f)—beautiful

Heela—(f)—hope
Heena—(f)—henna, myrtle, fragrance
Heerad—(m)—appearing fresh and healthy
Heer—(f)—diamond
Heeza—(f)—lucky
Hefaizt—(m)—one with divine wisdom
Hefza—(f)—protective angel, brave
Heifa—(f)—slender, well-shaped
Heira—(f)—stone like diamond
Heisal—(f)—the colour of rising sun
Heitham—(m)—lion
Heizan—(m)—one with divine wisdom
Heiza—(f)—royalty
Heizen—(m)—heat
Hejira—(f)—lady
Hekmat—(m)—intuition
Helai—(f)—swan bird
Helal—(m)—new moon
Helan—(f)—torch, sun ray, shining light
Helay—(f)—unique, divine aura
Hela—(f)—moonlight
Heleamah—(f)—gentle, mild-mannered
Heleama—(f)—gentle, mild-mannered
Heleemah—(f)—mild-mannered, gentle
Heleema—(f)—gentle, mild-mannered
Helena—(f)—light, torch, sun ray, corposant
Helen—(f)—torch, sun ray, shining light
Helimah—(f)—mild-mannered, gentle
Helima—(f)—very soft, gentle
Helma—(f)—protective, will-helmet
Helna—(f)—shining light, lights
Helyma—(f)—gentle, mild-mannered
Hemda—(f)—charming
Hemeda—(m)—one with divine wisdom
Hemesh—(m)—clever, cute
Hemil—(m)—smart, handsome, cute, loving kid
Hemin—(m)—calm
Hemma—(f)—golden

Hemraz—(m)—one with divine wisdom
Hemu—(f)—gold
Hena—(f)—on who is polite, a flower
Hena—(m)—flower, rose
Hengameh—(f)—wonder, marvel causing admiration
Henith—(m)—tiger, leader, protector
Hennah—(f)—favour, blessed
Henna—(f)—golden creeper, home ruler
Henna—(m)—blessed
Henza—(f)—gift of god
Herat—(m)—soul
Hera—(f)—queen of gods, protector, heroine
Heria—(f)—diamond
Hermez—(m)—heap of stones, cairn
Heru—(m)—sun god
Hesamuddin—(m)—one with divine wisdom
Hesam—(m)—a sharp sword
Hesa—(f)—piece of pearl
Hesham—(f)—pounding, generous
Hesham—(m)—generous, noble, handsome
Heshan—(m)—brilliant
Heskel—(m)—god strengthens, wisdom
Hessami—(f)—unique, divine aura
Hessa—(f)—piece of pearl, destiny
Hessa—(m)—destiny
Hethin—(m)—one with divine wisdom
Hevin—(f)—delightful, heaven, otherworldly
Hewad—(m)—homeland
Heyam—(f)—cute, infinite love
Heyan—(m)—heart, light of god
Heydar—(m)—like a lion
Heysan—(m)—beneficence
Heyza—(f)—beautiful angel
Heza—(f)—beautiful, precious, charming
Hezba—(f)—unique, divine aura
Hezreen—(f)—a flower
Hezzah—(f)—precious, beautiful, love
Hezzah—(m)—precious

Hezza—(f)—precious
Hiam—(m)—life
Hibah—(f)—a gift from god, gift, grant
Hibah—(m)—gift, grant, donation
Hibaq—(f)—beautiful flowers
Hibat-allah—(f)—gift of god
Hibatallah—(f)—gift of god
Hibathulla—(m)—gift of allah
Hibatullah—(f)—gift of god, gift of allah
Hibatullah—(m)—gift of allah
Hiba—(f)—gift, present, gift from god
Hiba—(m)—gift of god
Hibbaan—(m)—fleshy
Hibbah—(f)—gift of god, beloved
Hibban—(m)—lovers, beloved one
Hibba—(f)—gift from allah
Hibb—(m)—darling, dear
Hibr—(m)—ink, virtuous man, scholar
Hibza—(f)—obedience, gift
Hicham—(m)—energetic, generous
Hichem—(m)—generous
Hidaayat—(m)—guidance, instruction
Hidash—(m)—independent
Hidayah—(f)—guidance
Hidayat-ul-haq—(m)—guidance of the truth (allah)
Hidayathulla—(m)—instruction, guidance of allah
Hidayath—(f)—guidance, instruction
Hidayath—(m)—guidance
Hidayati—(f)—light
Hidayatulhaq—(m)—guidance of the truth (allah)
Hidayatullah—(m)—guidance of allah
Hidayatul—(m)—one with divine wisdom
Hidayat—(m)—guidance, instruction
Hidaya—(f)—precious gift
Hida—(f)—present, gift, warrior, friendly
Hiddah—(f)—strength, activity, swiftness
Hidda—(m)—one with divine wisdom
Hidhayath—(m)—instruction, guidance

Hidha—(f)—gifts of god, gift
Hidir—(m)—expressive
Hidiyah—(f)—as one
Hifaaz—(m)—protective, hope, guardian
Hifazat—(m)—security, safety
Hifaza—(f)—protective angel, queen
Hifaz—(m)—one with divine wisdom
Hifa—(f)—gold, extreme rich, fortunate
Hifjaan—(m)—one with divine wisdom
Hifsa—(f)—angel protector
Hifsha—(f)—unique, divine aura
Hifzaan—(m)—praise
Hifza—(f)—queen, protective angel
Hifzur-rahman—(m)—remembrance of the beneficent
Hifzurrahman—(m)—remembrance of the beneficent
Hifz—(m)—one who is memorable
Hijab—(f)—veil
Hijas—(f)—believer of god
Hijas—(m)—believer of god
Hijazi—(m)—believer of god
Hija—(f)—daughter
Hijrat—(m)—going from one place to another
Hijra—(f)—to leave, avoid
Hijriyyah—(f)—related to the hijrah
Hikmah—(f)—wisdom
Hikmah—(m)—wisdom
Hikmati—(m)—clever, wise
Hikmat—(f)—wisdom, knowledge, justice
Hikmat—(m)—wisdom
Hikma—(f)—wisdom
Hilaal—(m)—crescent
Hilah—(f)—moon's halo, halo
Hilali—(m)—crescent-like
Hilal—(f)—arabian tribe
Hilal—(m)—moon, crescent, happiness
Hilani—(f)—carried in the arms of heaven
Hilar—(m)—cheerful
Hila—(f)—praise or appreciation

Hilda—(f)—battle maid, war
Hilel—(m)—cheerful, the new moon, crescent
Hilf—(f)—treaty, alliance, confederacy
Hilf—(m)—treaty, alliance, confederacy
Hillda—(f)—comrade in arms
Hilli—(m)—belonging to hillah
Hilmiyat—(m)—gentleness, mildness
Hilmiyya—(f)—snow, winter
Hilmi—(m)—gentle, calm
Hilm—(m)—calmness, patience, intelligence
Hilyah—(f)—adornment, jewellery
Hilya—(f)—adornment, jewellery
Himaayat—(m)—help, support, protection
Himaa—(f)—snow, gold, golden, haven
Himaira—(f)—purity like snow
Himaja—(f)—ice, born from gold, snow
Himam—(m)—destiny
Himansha—(f)—cool, mountain covered with snow
Himar—(m)—ice
Himayah—(f)—care, safekeeping, guardianship
Himayat—(f)—guarding, defence
Himayat—(m)—help, protection, guardianship
Himaya—(f)—protection, snow
Himayun—(m)—sacred, fortunate, blessed
Himaz—(m)—one with divine wisdom
Himel—(m)—cold
Himmat—(m)—courage, desire, strength
Himmi—(m)—one with divine wisdom
Himsha—(f)—unique, divine aura
Hims—(m)—whisper
Hinaa—(f)—henna, myrtle
Hinadi—(f)—leader
Hinaya—(f)—shine, bright, beautiful, fairy
Hina—(f)—henna, a shrub, fragrance
Hindah—(f)—wife of abu sufyan
Hindal—(m)—taker of india
Hinda—(f)—female deer, doe
Hinde—(f)—over camels

Hind—(m)—india, hundred camels
Hinnah—(f)—sword of the finest steel
Hinna—(f)—henna, myrtle
Hinza—(f)—lovable, gift of god
Hiqa—(f)—truth speaker
Hirad—(m)—appearing fresh and healthy
Hirah—(f)—name of a mountain
Hiral—(f)—bright, queen, lustrous, wealthy
Hiras—(m)—beautiful, talented
Hira—(f)—diamond, sacred cave
Hirkil—(f)—noble, beautiful
Hirun—(m)—one of name of prophet
Hirza—(f)—unique, divine aura
Hirz—(m)—another name for god
Hisaan—(f)—beautiful one, appropriate looking
Hisaan—(m)—beautiful one, good-looking
Hisabuddin—(m)—one with divine wisdom
Hisad—(m)—lions
Hisamuddin—(m)—one with divine wisdom
Hisam—(m)—sword
Hisana—(f)—beauty, appropriate, beautiful
Hisan—(f)—beautiful, appropriate-looking
Hisan—(m)—good-looking beautiful, handsome
Hisa—(f)—long lasting
Hisba—(f)—accountability
Hisein—(m)—good, variant of husayn, nice
Hishaam—(m)—generous, name of a companion
Hisham—(m)—generous, noble, handsome
Hishana—(f)—beautiful and attractive lady
Hishan—(m)—one with divine wisdom
Hisha—(f)—beautiful
Hishem—(m)—one who crushes, smashes
Hishmat—(m)—state, dignity
Hishma—(f)—generous
Hisra—(f)—joyful
Hissana—(f)—beautiful, appropriate, beauty
Hissa—(f)—star, proud
Hissa—(m)—home ruler

Hitaishi—(f)—well wisher
Hitbah—(f)—unique, divine aura
Hiwaaya—(f)—unique, divine aura
Hiyam—(f)—love
Hiyam—(m)—love
Hizaan—(m)—one with divine wisdom
Hizamezrin—(f)—unique, divine aura
Hizam—(m)—bold, sword, strong man
Hizana—(f)—the most beautiful
Hizan—(m)—warrior
Hizaqat—(m)—intelligence
Hizaq—(m)—sharpness, quickness
Hizazi—(m)—belonging of hijaz
Hiza—(f)—lucky, fortunate
Hizba—(f)—unique, divine aura
Hizbullah—(m)—army of allah
Hizha—(f)—gold
Hizqil—(m)—god strengthens
Hizrat—(m)—freshness
Hizra—(f)—presence
Hizzah—(f)—fortunate
Hmidou—(m)—one with divine wisdom
Hobb—(m)—love, affection
Hobibur—(m)—one with divine wisdom
Hocine—(m)—joyful
Hodah—(f)—thankful
Hoda—(f)—thankful
Hokhmah—(f)—unique, divine aura
Homaira—(f)—unique, divine aura
Homair—(m)—reddish
Homayoon—(m)—royal, fortunate
Homayoun—(m)—royal, fortunate
Homayra—(f)—beautiful, reddish
Homayun—(m)—royal, fortunate
Homa—(f)—a mythical bird
Homeira—(f)—reddish
Homera—(f)—woman who cannot see
Hooda—(f)—right guidance

Hooman—(m)—good nature, having a good soul
Hoorain—(f)—lovely-eyed
Hoorein—(f)—angel of heaven
Hooriah—(f)—unique, divine aura
Hooria—(f)—angel of heaven
Hooria—(m)—angel
Hooriyah—(f)—splendid companion of paradise
Hooriya—(f)—angel of heaven
Hoori—(f)—splendid companion of paradise
Hoor—(f)—a celestical, virgin of paradise
Hoosen—(m)—good, handsome
Hooshmand—(m)—wise
Hooshyar—(m)—wise
Hootan—(m)—one with divine wisdom
Hoque—(m)—real
Hora—(f)—keeper of the hours
Horeezah—(f)—princess
Horia—(f)—angel, the truth
Horiyah—(f)—woman of the gardens
Horiya—(f)—woman of the gardens
Hormat—(f)—honour
Hormazd—(m)—divinity of wisdom
Hormizd—(m)—divinity of wisdom
Hormuzd—(m)—divinity of wisdom
Hosaam—(m)—sword
Hosain—(m)—good or handsome
Hosai—(f)—unique, divine aura
Hosam—(m)—sword of justice
Hosban—(f)—calculation, computation
Hosban—(m)—calculation, computation
Hosein—(m)—good, handsome
Hosen—(m)—one with divine wisdom
Hoshana—(f)—unique, divine aura
Hoshedar—(m)—pure love
Hosneara—(f)—beautiful, beauty of world
Hosni—(m)—goodness, excellence, handsome
Hosn—(f)—beauty, appropriateness
Hosn—(m)—beauty, goodness

Hossain—(m)—good or handsome
Hossai—(m)—one with divine wisdom
Hossan—(m)—one with divine wisdom
Hossein—(m)—handsome, beautiful, good
Hossen—(m)—good, handsome one
Hossina—(f)—beautiful
Hossin—(m)—one with divine wisdom
Hotha—(m)—one with divine wisdom
Houdah—(f)—correct counsel
Houda—(f)—right guidance, variant of huda
Houd—(m)—a prophet's name
Houria—(f)—fairy, angel
Houriya—(f)—maiden of paradise
Houri—(f)—fairy
Housni—(m)—one with divine wisdom
Houssam—(m)—sword edge, variant of husam
Houssein—(m)—handsome one
Hoyam—(f)—passionate love
Hozaifah—(m)—a companion of the prophet
Hozaifa—(m)—a companion of the prophet
Hozai—(m)—prophet
Hrehaan—(m)—god's chosen
Hridan—(m)—voice from heart, gift of heart
Hrida—(f)—pure
Hrihan—(m)—lord vishnu
Hubaab—(m)—aim, friendship, bubble of water
Hubabah—(f)—beloved
Hubab—(f)—aim, goal, beloved
Hubab—(m)—aim, friendship, friendly
Hubaibah—(f)—love, loving, beloved
Hubaibi—(m)—loving, beloved
Hubairah—(f)—unique, divine aura
Hubair—(m)—little scholar, ink
Hubaish—(m)—well known bird, name of a tabi
Hubayl—(m)—one with divine wisdom
Hubayshah—(f)—poetess
Huba—(f)—love, friendship, favour
Hubbah—(f)—love, affectionate

Hubbat—(m)—beloved, love
Hubbee—(m)—loving, affectionate
Hubb—(m)—love, wish, desire
Hubed—(m)—one with divine wisdom
Hubnuqat—(m)—flute
Huboor—(f)—happiness
Hubur—(m)—happiness, joy
Hub—(m)—love
Hudaafrin—(f)—unique, divine aura
Hudaa—(f)—guidance
Hudaa—(m)—guide
Hudad—(m)—name of a pre-islamic arabic king
Hudah—(f)—correct counsel
Hudaiba—(f)—devoted
Hudaif—(m)—immortal, unbreakable spirit
Hudayfa—(m)—boss man
Huda—(f)—right guidance
Huda—(m)—right guidance
Hudhafah—(m)—one with divine wisdom
Hudhaifah—(m)—companion of prophet muhammad
Hudhaifa—(m)—companion of prophet
Hudhayfah—(m)—short-statured, name of companion
Hudhayfa—(m)—boss
Hudie—(f)—one who chooses the right path
Hudi—(f)—one who chooses the right path
Hudn—(m)—peace, calm, quiet
Hudun—(f)—to become quiet
Hud—(m)—hooded, those who ask forgiveness
Hufaizah—(f)—protector
Hufaiz—(f)—unique, divine aura
Hufaiz—(m)—protector
Hufsa—(f)—young lioness
Huful—(m)—plenty, abundance
Hugheen—(m)—heart
Huhjat—(m)—argument, proof
Hujaf—(m)—one with divine wisdom
Hujaifa—(m)—gift of god
Hujaimah—(f)—name of a sahabiah ra

Hujaina—(f)—unique, divine aura
Hujaira—(f)—unique, divine aura
Hujaymah—(f)—attack
Hujayrah—(f)—she was a narrator of hadith
Hujayyah—(m)—father of ajlah bin abdullah
Hujefa—(m)—one with divine wisdom
Hujjatulislam—(m)—proof of islam
Hujjatullah—(m)—proof of god
Hujjat—(f)—reasoning, proof, argument
Hujjat—(m)—argument, proof, reasoning
Hujja—(f)—argument, reasoning, proof
Hukmi—(f)—dutiful, obedient
Hukm—(m)—order, command, lord of hearts
Hulaa—(f)—jewellery
Hulah—(f)—enchanting woman
Hulayl—(m)—old arabic name
Huljat—(m)—argument, proof
Hullah—(f)—costume, dress, garment
Hulm—(m)—forbearance, patient, leniency
Hulou—(f)—sweet, opposite of bitter
Hulum—(m)—dream, vision
Hulwah—(f)—beautiful, sweet
Hulyah—(f)—jewellery, ornament, finery
Humaam—(m)—brave, noble, courageous, generous
Humaayoon—(m)—blessed, auspicious
Humaa—(f)—lucky bird, phoenix
Humaera—(f)—a generous woman
Humahirah—(f)—unique, divine aura
Humaidaan—(m)—one with divine wisdom
Humaidan—(m)—praiseworthy
Humaida—(f)—praised, feminine of humaid
Humaid—(m)—great, one who glorifies god
Humaila—(f)—golden necklace
Humail—(m)—one with divine wisdom
Humaima—(f)—unique, divine aura
Humaina—(f)—able to determine
Humairaa—(f)—red coloured girl
Humairah—(f)—of reddish complexion

Humaira—(f)—reddish
Humairra—(f)—reddish
Humair—(m)—red
Humaisa—(f)—unique, divine aura
Humaisha—(f)—unique, divine aura
Humaiza—(f)—minted, gods gift
Humaiz—(m)—minted
Humai—(f)—of appropriate essence
Humama—(f)—honoured, courageous, pigeon
Humamuddin—(m)—brave
Humam—(f)—brave and noble, magnanimous
Humam—(m)—generous, courageous, honoured
Human—(m)—a character in shahnameh
Humaria—(f)—auspicious
Humasa—(f)—victory
Humasha—(f)—gift of god
Humat—(m)—protector, good thought
Humayan—(m)—one with divine wisdom
Humaya—(f)—unique, divine aura
Humaydah—(f)—narrator of hadith
Humayd—(m)—praised
Humayl—(m)—companion of prophet muhammad
Humayon—(m)—fortunate
Humayoon—(m)—fortunate
Humayraa—(f)—a generous woman
Humayrah—(f)—red, beautiful
Humayra—(f)—beautiful
Humaysha—(f)—unique, divine aura
Humayun—(m)—fortunate
Humayu—(m)—fortunate
Huma—(f)—bird of paradise
Humdan—(m)—the praised one
Humd—(m)—praise of allah
Humeaira—(f)—unique, divine aura
Humeira—(f)—a beautiful raaga
Humerah—(f)—unique, divine aura
Humera—(m)—imaginary bird
Humerya—(m)—one with divine wisdom

Humira—(f)—reddish
Humiyza—(f)—unique, divine aura
Hummad—(m)—one with divine wisdom
Hummaira—(f)—unique, divine aura
Humma—(f)—bird
Humna—(f)—princess of heaven
Humraan—(m)—happiness
Humraz—(m)—one who knows the secret
Humra—(f)—beautiful, rose
Humumera—(f)—unique, divine aura
Humur—(m)—red
Humzah—(m)—brave
Humza—(m)—precious, brave
Humzia—(f)—unique, divine aura
Hunafaa—(f)—one who devoted to god
Hunafaa—(m)—one who are devoted to god
Hunafa—(f)—one who devoted to god
Hunafa—(m)—one who believe in god's oneness
Hunaidah—(f)—diminutive of hind
Hunaid—(m)—happiness
Hunaifah—(f)—devoted believer, virtuous
Hunaifiya—(f)—unique, divine aura
Hunaif—(m)—one with divine wisdom
Hunaina—(f)—unique, divine aura
Hunain—(f)—the literal
Hunaira—(f)—happiness
Hunaisa—(f)—gift of god
Hunais—(m)—one with divine wisdom
Hunaizah—(f)—gift of god
Hunaiza—(f)—gift of god
Hunaiz—(m)—gift of god
Hunaydah—(f)—she was a narrator of hadith
Huna—(f)—golden necklace
Huna—(m)—listening
Hunduj—(m)—name of the arab poet imrul qais
Huneina—(f)—unique, divine aura
Hunera—(f)—happiness
Huneza—(f)—gift of god

Hunoon—(f)—another name for jamaad al-ula
Hunus—(f)—pious, chaste
Huraima—(f)—queen of angel
Hurain—(f)—angel of heaven
Hurairah—(f)—a red-haired woman
Huraira—(f)—red start, reddish
Hurais—(m)—one with divine wisdom
Huraiva—(f)—kitten
Huraiz—(m)—protector
Huram—(f)—unique, divine aura
Hurasim—(m)—lion
Hurayra—(f)—a red-haired woman
Hurays—(m)—a small cultivator
Hurayth—(m)—small cultivator
Hura—(f)—free woman
Hurbuj—(m)—big
Hureaira—(f)—red start, reddish
Hureen—(f)—most beautiful, heavenly female
Hureyn—(f)—lovely-eyed, splendid
Huriaa—(f)—variant of the huriyyah
Huriyah—(f)—angel
Huriya—(f)—fairy, nymph
Huriyyah—(f)—angel
Hurlin—(f)—eyes beauty
Hurman—(m)—mind and intellect
Hurmat—(f)—respect
Hurmat—(m)—sacred, chastity
Hurmuz—(m)—lord of existence, ahura mazda
Hurraah—(m)—free
Hurrah—(m)—free, liberal
Hurrein—(m)—one with divine wisdom
Hurriyat—(m)—freedom, liberty, independence
Hurriya—(f)—freedom, liberty
Hurriyyah—(f)—angel
Hurr—(m)—independent, liberal, noble
Huru—(f)—free
Hurya—(f)—fairy, virgin of paradise
Hur—(f)—fair, black-haired female, sun

Husaam-al-din—(m)—sword of the faith
Husaama—(f)—sword
Husaamudeen—(m)—one with divine wisdom
Husaamudin—(m)—the sword of the faith
Husaam—(m)—sword
Husaiba—(f)—unique, divine aura
Husaifah—(f)—name of sahabi
Husaifa—(f)—name of sahabi
Husaifa—(m)—short-statured, name of sahabi
Husaif—(m)—one with divine wisdom
Husaimah—(f)—diligent, assiduous, persevering
Husaim—(m)—diligent, assiduous, industrious
Husainah—(f)—beautiful
Husaina—(f)—diminutive of beauty
Husaini—(f)—pertaining to husain
Husain—(m)—small beauty, good
Husam-al-din—(m)—sword of the faith
Husamah—(f)—sword blade, sharp, cutting sword
Husamaldin—(m)—sword of the faith
Husamuddaulah—(m)—sword of the kingdom
Husamuddawlah—(m)—sword of the state
Husamuddin—(m)—sword of religion islam
Husamudeen—(m)—the sword of the faith
Husam—(m)—sword edge
Husanah—(f)—very beautiful
Husani—(m)—handsome
Husan—(f)—very beautiful
Husarat—(m)—lion
Husayni—(m)—of husayn
Husayn—(m)—good, beautiful
Husay—(f)—deer, gazelle
Husbaan—(f)—calculation, computation
Husbaan—(m)—computation, calculation
Husbana—(f)—the one who calculates
Husein—(m)—handsome, diminutive of hasan
Husena—(f)—one who arrived first
Husen—(m)—saint
Huseyn—(m)—islamic thinker, saint

Hushaima—(f)—modesty
Husham—(m)—sword
Husian—(m)—one with divine wisdom
Husn-ara—(f)—adorned with beauty
Husnaa—(f)—most beautiful, precious, pious
Husnabanu—(f)—possessive, beauty
Husnain—(m)—pure in the eyes
Husnan—(m)—handsome
Husnara—(f)—adorned with beauty
Husna—(f)—beautiful, a belle, kindness
Husnbano—(f)—beauty, possessive
Husneara—(f)—unique, divine aura
Husnia—(f)—beauty
Husniyah—(f)—beautiful
Husniya—(f)—beautiful
Husniyyah—(f)—beautiful
Husniyya—(f)—test
Husni—(f)—possessing beauty
Husni—(m)—goodness, handsome, excellence
Husn—(f)—beauty, appropriateness
Hussaina—(f)—twin girl
Hussaini—(f)—unique, divine aura
Hussain—(m)—saint, good
Hussana—(f)—beautifier, appropriate, beautiful
Hussan—(m)—one with divine wisdom
Hussayn—(m)—good
Hussa—(m)—one with divine wisdom
Hussein—(m)—beautiful, handsome one, good
Hussena—(f)—beautiful
Hussen—(m)—handsome one
Hussien—(m)—grandson of beloved prophet
Hussin—(m)—saint, legend of islam
Huss—(m)—saffron
Husul—(m)—happening, event
Hutaf—(f)—cheering
Hutaiba—(f)—unique, divine aura
Hutaim—(m)—pure, judge, ruler
Huthama—(m)—one with divine wisdom

Huthayfa—(m)—old arabic name
Hutud—(m)—remain, stay
Hutun—(f)—clouds with rain
Huuwaija—(m)—want, desire
Huwaidah—(f)—gentle
Huwaida—(f)—to express
Huwainaa—(f)—serenity, composure, leniency
Huwairis—(m)—one with divine wisdom
Huwaydah—(f)—gentle
Huwa—(m)—another name for god
Huyai—(m)—alive, vibrant
Huzaaf—(m)—one with divine wisdom
Huzabir—(m)—lion
Huzafa—(m)—one with divine wisdom
Huzaib—(m)—gift of god
Huzaiel—(m)—bin shurah bil had this name
Huzaien—(m)—one with divine wisdom
Huzaifah—(f)—unique, divine aura
Huzaifah—(m)—companion of prophet muhammad
Huzaifa—(f)—the secret keeper
Huzaifa—(m)—name of sahabi, an old name
Huzaiffa—(m)—name of a sahaaba
Huzaif—(m)—son of haroon, brave
Huzaila—(f)—unique, divine aura
Huzaima—(f)—unique, divine aura
Huzaina—(f)—diminutive of beauty
Huzain—(m)—gift of god
Huzairah—(f)—narrator of hadith
Huzaira—(f)—narrator of hadith
Huzair—(m)—armed solider
Huzayfah—(m)—curtailed, short
Huzayfa—(m)—companion of prophet muhammad
Huzayl—(m)—bin shurah bil had this name
Huzayma—(f)—firm believer
Huzeeb—(m)—disciplined
Huzefa—(f)—pure heart
Huzefa—(m)—pure heart
Huzeila—(f)—unique, divine aura

Huzeir—(m)—armed solider
Huzer—(m)—successful
Huzfur—(m)—noble, illustrious
Huziafa—(m)—one with divine wisdom
Huzia—(f)—priceless
Huzifa—(f)—name of sahabi
Huzrah—(f)—presence
Huzumat—(m)—prudence, resolution
Huzur—(m)—title of respect, presence
Huzuz—(f)—fortune, appropriate luck, plural of hazz
Huzya—(m)—gift, present
Huzzaq—(m)—ingenious, clever
Hwas—(m)—having narrow or contracted eye
Hyannis—(f)—search
Hyatt—(f)—from the high gate
Hyat—(f)—from the high gate
Hyat—(m)—long life
Hydan—(m)—independent
Hydar—(m)—lion, kind heart
Hyda—(f)—heart
Hydee—(f)—honourable, of a noble kind
Hyden—(m)—one with divine wisdom
Hyderali—(m)—kind heart
Hyder—(m)—lion, derived from hadara
Hydhar—(m)—kind heart, lion, variant of hydar
Hydin—(m)—independent, strong
Hyfa—(f)—slender
Hymad—(m)—whole, to praise
Hymah—(f)—beautiful, rose
Hyna—(f)—beauty
Hynes—(m)—ivy, descendant of eidhin
Hyrah—(f)—beauty of perfection
Hyra—(f)—beauty of perfection
Hyrine—(f)—most beautiful
Hyrin—(f)—most beautiful
Hyrin—(m)—horse, lion
Hyrunnisa—(f)—unique, divine aura
Hyrunnissa—(f)—unique, divine aura

Hysham—(m)—one who crushes, smashes
Hyuheen—(m)—heart
Hyzaan—(m)—beneficence
Hyzam—(m)—bold
Hyzan—(m)—beneficence
Hyza—(f)—beautiful angel
Hyzen—(m)—beneficence
Hyzin—(m)—treasure

NINE

Arabic Baby Names—I

Iamar—(f)—moon

Ianat—(f)—assistance, help, aid

Iara—(f)—watchful, vigilant

Iayan—(m)—prince

Iaza—(f)—fairy

Ibaadah—(f)—worship

Ibaadah—(m)—worship

Ibaadat—(f)—worship, prayer, devotion

Ibaad—(f)—devotee of god, plural of abd

Ibaad—(m)—prayer, devotees of god

Ibadaat—(f)—acts of worship, appropriate deeds

Ibadah—(f)—worship, obedience of god

Ibadah—(m)—worship, obedience of god

Ibadat—(f)—prayer, worship

Ibadat—(m)—prayer, worship, devotion

Ibada—(f)—adored

Ibada—(m)—adoration, adored

Ibadullah—(m)—worshippers of god

Ibad—(f)—plural of abd, devotee of god

Ibad—(m)—devotees, slaves

Iban—(m)—god is gracious

Iba—(f)—pride, disdain

Ibdar—(m)—light of the full moon

Ibda—(f)—innovation

Ibhar—(f)—stigma of flower, breadth

Ibhraim—(m)—prophet's name

Ibkar—(m)—early morning
Ibnabbas—(m)—son of abbas
Ibnah—(f)—daughter
Ibna—(f)—gift
Ibn—(m)—son
Ibraan—(m)—one with divine wisdom
Ibraham—(m)—father of a multitude
Ibraheem—(m)—a prophet's name
Ibrahima—(m)—form of ibrahim
Ibrahim—(m)—my father is exalted
Ibrah—(f)—wisdom, advice
Ibran—(m)—variant of ibrahim
Ibrar—(m)—peaceful, helpful
Ibrees—(m)—a titan, pure gold
Ibreez—(f)—pure gold
Ibreez—(m)—pure gold
Ibrisami—(f)—silk
Ibrisam—(f)—silk
Ibriz—(f)—pure gold
Ibr—(m)—ibrahim, prophet abraham
Ibsan—(m)—beauty, beautiful
Ibtasam—(f)—smile
Ibtehaj—(f)—joy, delight
Ibtesam—(f)—smile
Ibtesam—(m)—smile
Ibthaj—(f)—joy
Ibthesam—(f)—smiling
Ibthisham—(m)—one with divine wisdom
Ibtida—(f)—invention, discovery
Ibtighaa—(f)—to seek
Ibtigha—(f)—to seek
Ibtihaaj—(f)—joy
Ibtihaj—(f)—joy, delight, happiness
Ibtihaj—(m)—joy, gladness, delight
Ibtihal—(f)—supplication, prayer
Ibtihal—(m)—supplication, humble prayer
Ibtihl—(f)—prayer, supplication
Ibtikar—(m)—innovation

Ibtisaama—(f)—smile
Ibtisama—(f)—smile
Ibtisam—(f)—smile
Ibtisam—(m)—smiling
Ibtissam—(f)—smile
Ibtissem—(f)—smile
Ibukun—(f)—blessings, appropriate wishes
Ibu—(m)—one who is creative
Ibzan—(m)—father of a target
Icah—(f)—light
Idaan—(m)—king
Idah—(f)—pure, kind, noble
Idalat—(m)—victory
Idalika—(f)—queen
Idam—(m)—one with divine wisdom
Idane—(f)—unique, divine aura
Idan—(m)—a historic period, age
Idara—(m)—joy
Iddi—(m)—moonlighting
Idd—(m)—power, victory
Iden—(m)—wealthy, prosperous
Idhan—(m)—king, a historic period, age
Idhar—(f)—fluff
Idil—(f)—battle
Idin—(m)—unity
Idir—(m)—noble
Idraak—(m)—intellect, perception, achievement
Idrak—(f)—intellect, perception
Idrak—(m)—accomplishment, achievement
Idrees—(f)—prophet name
Idrees—(m)—a prophet's name, lord of fiery
Idress—(m)—fiery leader
Idrish—(m)—not visible, invisible
Idris—(f)—powerful, wealthy, ardent lord
Idris—(m)—studious person, one who instruct
Idriz—(m)—one with divine wisdom
Idul—(m)—one with divine wisdom
Ieashah—(f)—woman, life

Ieasha—(f)—woman, life, alive
Ieashiah—(f)—woman, life
Ieashia—(f)—woman, life
Ieeshah—(f)—woman, life
Ieesha—(f)—woman, life
Ieeshiah—(f)—woman, life
Ieeshia—(f)—woman, life
Ieethaar—(m)—sacrifice, selflessness
Iefan—(m)—yahweh is merciful, gracious
Ieisha—(f)—alive, she who lives
Ieishia—(f)—unique, divine aura
Iena—(f)—illuminate, mirror, reflection
Iesa—(m)—a prophet's name
Ieshah—(f)—woman, life
Iesha—(f)—alive, she who lives, life, living
Ieshia—(f)—alive and well, alive
Ieta—(f)—the earth, wish
Ifaan—(m)—knowledge
Ifaasha—(f)—shining, pretty
Ifaaz—(m)—helper
Ifadat—(f)—modesty
Ifada—(f)—chaste
Ifadha—(f)—useful, chaste
Ifad—(m)—to be high and above something
Ifah—(f)—modesty, purity
Ifana—(f)—joyness
Ifan—(m)—season, time, yahweh is merciful
Ifasha—(f)—pretty, shining
Ifath—(f)—pure, chaste, intelligent
Ifatul—(m)—one with divine wisdom
Ifat—(f)—pure
Ifaya—(f)—forgiveness
Ifaza—(f)—light
Ifaz—(m)—helper
Ifa—(f)—keeping faith, satisfying
Iffadath—(f)—modesty
Iffah—(f)—purity, modesty
Iffan—(m)—time, season

Iffat-ara—(f)—decorator of chastity
Iffatara—(f)—decorator of chastit
Iffath—(f)—chastity, virtue
Iffath—(m)—virtue
Iffat—(f)—respect, honour, virtue, chastity
Iffat—(m)—virtue, chastity
Iffa—(f)—invulnerability against attraction
Iffra—(f)—unique, divine aura
Ifham—(f)—friendly, favourable speech
Ifham—(m)—favourable speech
Ifiyan—(m)—forgiven
Iflah—(f)—happy, success
Ifni—(m)—one with divine wisdom
Ifraan—(m)—identity
Ifraaz—(m)—altitude
Ifraa—(f)—happiness
Ifrah—(f)—to make happy
Ifran-rahaman—(m)—one with divine wisdom
Ifran—(m)—identity
Ifraq—(m)—love
Ifrat—(f)—honoured
Ifraz—(m)—height, altitude, elevation
Ifra—(f)—height, giving happiness
Ifreen—(f)—intelligent, brave, attentive
Ifrith—(f)—fairy, angel
Ifrith—(m)—one with divine wisdom
Ifrit—(f)—fairy, angel, jinn
Ifroz—(m)—one with divine wisdom
Ifsah—(f)—break forth, clear, distinct
Ifser—(m)—useful
Ifshana—(f)—fiction
Ifsha—(f)—shining, pretty
Iftah—(f)—unique, divine aura
Iftajul—(m)—one with divine wisdom
Iftar—(m)—one with divine wisdom
Iftasham—(f)—magnificent
Iftekar—(m)—gift of allah
Iftekharalamkhan—(m)—proud

Iftekhar—(m)—honour, glory
Iften—(m)—light
Ifteqar—(m)—one with divine wisdom
Iftequar—(m)—royal parson
Iftesam—(f)—smile
Iftesham—(f)—magnificent
Ifthekar—(m)—one with divine wisdom
Ifthika—(f)—pride
Ifthin—(f)—light
Iftiaha—(f)—unique, divine aura
Iftia—(f)—gift of god
Iftikar—(f)—pride
Iftikar—(m)—self respect
Iftikhaar—(m)—honour, glory
Iftikhar-ud-din—(m)—pride of the religion (islam)
Iftikharllah—(m)—glory, pride of allah
Iftikharuddin—(m)—pride of the religion islam
Iftikharussadat—(m)—pride of the chiefs
Iftikhar—(f)—pride, glory
Iftikhar—(m)—glory, honour
Iftinan—(f)—enchantment, captivation
Iftisa—(f)—gift of god
Iftisham—(f)—unique, divine aura
Iftisha—(f)—unique, divine aura
Iftitan—(f)—unique, divine aura
Ifty—(m)—one with divine wisdom
Ifzal—(m)—eminence, superiority
Ifzan—(m)—gift of god
Ifza—(f)—protective angel
Igal—(m)—redeemed, defiled
Ighlaf—(m)—one with divine wisdom
Ighla—(f)—praise, admiration
Igider—(m)—one with divine wisdom
Igmi—(m)—joyful
Ihaab—(m)—gift, leather
Ihaan—(m)—leader, pioneer, morning, dawn
Ihaa—(f)—inspiration
Ihab—(f)—granting, giving, gift, leather

Ihab—(m)—gift, leather
Iham—(m)—expected
Ihana—(m)—delight
Ihan—(m)—full moon
Iha—(f)—the earth, wish
Iher—(m)—one with divine wisdom
Ihisha—(f)—one who lives, alive
Ihkam—(f)—decisiveness, excellence, mastery
Ihram—(f)—special, white cloth
Ihram—(m)—white cloth, special
Ihsaan—(m)—beneficence, charity, give
Ihsanah—(f)—unique, divine aura
Ihsana—(f)—favour, the best of the appropriate
Ihsane—(f)—charity
Ihsanul-haq—(m)—kindness of the truth (allah)
Ihsanulhaq—(m)—kindness of the truth (allah)
Ihsan—(f)—appropriate deeds, kindness, favour
Ihsan—(m)—beneficence, charity, compassion
Ihsen—(m)—charity
Ihshana—(f)—unique, divine aura
Ihtesham—(m)—magnificent
Ihtiraam—(m)—honour, hold in honour
Ihtiram—(f)—consideration, esteem, regard
Ihtiram—(m)—honour, respect, consideration
Ihtishaam—(m)—pomp, magnificence, chastity
Ihtisham—(f)—chastity, modesty, decency
Ihtisham—(m)—pomp, magnificence, chastity
Ihtsham—(m)—strength
Ihzaan—(m)—kindness, beneficence
Iihan—(m)—considered
Iima—(f)—air
Iizhar—(m)—submission, clearness, expression
Ijaaz—(m)—miracle
Ijada—(f)—knowledge, excellence
Ijajul—(m)—one with divine wisdom
Ijaj—(m)—kind-hearted, soft
Ijan—(m)—soul of the moon, fire
Ijar—(m)—one with divine wisdom

Ijas—(m)—knowledge, glow, shine
Ijazul-haq—(m)—inimitability of the truth
Ijazulhaq—(m)—inevitability of the truth (allah)
Ijaz—(f)—inevitability of the quran
Ijaz—(m)—miracle, astonishment
Ijlaal—(m)—glorification, exaltation
Ijlal—(f)—respect, honour, grand, splendid
Ijlal—(m)—glorification, exaltation
Ijliyah—(f)—population
Ijnanya—(f)—love
Ijtiba—(m)—chosen
Ikan—(m)—fish, star
Ikara—(f)—fragrance of rose
Ika—(f)—gentle, feminine of ike
Ikbal—(m)—glory, destiny
Iken—(m)—well-ordered
Ikha—(f)—brotherhood, sisterhood
Ikhlaaq—(m)—morals, virtues
Ikhlaas—(m)—frankness, sincerity, purity
Ikhlaq—(m)—morals, virtues
Ikhlas—(f)—sincerity, purity, devotion
Ikhlas—(m)—frankness, sincerity, purity
Ikhtiyar—(m)—choice, preference, selection
Ikhwaan—(m)—brother
Ikhwan—(m)—brothers
Ikleel—(f)—crown, garland
Ikleel—(m)—chief of prophets, crown, garland
Iklil—(f)—crown, garland, wreath
Iklil—(m)—crown, garland
Ikraam—(f)—honour, hospitality, generosity
Ikraam—(m)—tribute, to honour someone
Ikrah—(f)—to recite
Ikram-ul-haq—(m)—glory of the truth (allah)
Ikramah—(m)—female pigeon
Ikramuddin—(m)—honour respect
Ikramulhaq—(m)—glory of the truth (allah)
Ikramullah—(m)—glory of allah
Ikramul—(m)—one with divine wisdom

Ikram—(f)—honour, hospitality, generosity
Ikram—(m)—honour respect, esteem, veneration
Ikran—(m)—honoured
Ikrash—(m)—attractive
Ikra—(f)—recite read, start
Ikremah—(m)—female pigeon, a sahabi
Ikrimah—(m)—female version of a pigeon
Ikrima—(m)—a female pigeon
Iksaar—(m)—one with divine wisdom
Ikseer—(m)—elixir
Iksir—(m)—elixir
Iktiyar—(m)—preference, choice, selection
Ilaaha—(m)—one with divine wisdom
Ilaan—(m)—god gift, intelligent
Ilaf—(f)—agreement, safety, covenant
Ilaha—(f)—goddess
Ilahi-bakhsh—(m)—gift of allah
Ilahibakhsh—(m)—gift of allah
Ilahi—(m)—my lord (for allah), divine
Ilaina—(f)—tree
Ilam—(m)—my enemies are many
Ilana—(f)—sunshine, tree, to soften
Ilani—(f)—beautiful soul
Ilann—(m)—intelligent
Ilan—(m)—tree, good person
Ilash—(m)—another name for god
Ilayda—(f)—angela tears
Ilderimkhan—(m)—one with divine wisdom
Ileana—(f)—light, trojan, shining, brilliant
Ileen—(f)—light
Ilfan—(m)—unique, the art, attraction
Ilfa—(f)—origin, soft heart
Ilhaam—(f)—intuition
Ilhaam—(m)—lord of the earth, inspiration
Ilhaan—(m)—precious, respectfull
Ilham—(f)—inspiration
Ilham—(m)—revelation, inspiration
Ilhana—(f)—happiness, excellent

Ilhan—(f)—respectfull, nice, precious
Ilhan—(m)—ruler, emperor, prince
Ilhem—(f)—inspiration
Ilhem—(m)—inspiration
Iliana—(f)—bright, shine, shining, trojan
Ilias—(m)—the lord is my god
Ilifat—(m)—kindness, obligation, friendship
Ilina—(f)—queen
Ilisha—(f)—queen of the earth, ruthful
Iliyaas—(m)—one with divine wisdom
Iliyana—(f)—my god has answered
Iliyash—(m)—name of prophet
Iliyas—(m)—singer of natures
Iliyaz—(m)—beautiful viewer
Iliza—(f)—god is my oath
Ilka—(f)—torch of light, light of hymns
Illani—(f)—tree
Illan—(m)—youth
Illias—(m)—jehovah is god, lord is my god
Illima—(f)—flower
Illiyas—(m)—god is god
Illiyeen—(f)—highest of the high
Illyas—(m)—god is god
Ilmaa—(f)—resolute protector
Ilman—(m)—knowledgeable person
Ilma—(f)—resolute protector, strong helmet
Ilmiya—(f)—cultured, learning of islam
Ilm—(f)—slave belonging to zubaydah
Ilm—(m)—knowledge, science
Ilqis—(f)—queen of sheeba
Ilsa—(f)—pledged to god, god's promise
Iltaf—(m)—poetry
Iltifaat—(m)—regard, attention
Iltifat—(m)—friendship, kindness, obligation
Iltika—(f)—god's gift
Iltimas—(f)—urge, appeal, entreaty
Iltimas—(m)—request, entreaty, appeal
Ilyaasin—(m)—name of a prophet

Ilyana—(f)—sun ray, softness, leniency
Ilyasin—(m)—name of prophet
Ilyas—(f)—name of a prophet of allah
Ilyas—(m)—name of a prophet
Ilyaz—(m)—one with divine wisdom
Ilya—(f)—noble, high class
Ilya—(m)—the lord is my god
Ilzana—(f)—unique, divine aura
Ilzan—(m)—muhammed, strong
Ilza—(f)—god's promise, god is my oath
Imaad-al-din—(m)—pillar of the faith
Imaad-udeen—(m)—pillar of the faith
Imaadudeen—(m)—pillar of the faith, deen
Imaadudin—(m)—the pillar of the faith
Imaad—(m)—proud, support, pillar, confidence
Imaam—(m)—leader, chief
Imaana—(f)—believer
Imaani—(f)—faithful, blessing
Imaan—(f)—faith, belief
Imaan—(m)—faith, belief, faithfu
Imaarah—(f)—to visit, tend
Imaaz—(m)—kind, pleasing, affectionate
Imad-ad-din—(m)—pillars of the religion
Imad-al-din—(m)—pillar of the faith
Imadaldin—(m)—pillar of the faith
Imadallah—(m)—one with divine wisdom
Imaduddin—(m)—pillar of the faith
Imadudeen—(m)—the pillar of the faith
Imadudin—(m)—the pillar of the faith
Imadullah—(m)—supporter of allah
Imad—(f)—brave
Imad—(m)—support, pillar, confidence
Imah—(f)—now, work, imitating, rivalling
Imala—(f)—disciplinarian, disciplines
Imama—(f)—leadership, command
Imamuddin—(m)—leader of the faith
Imamul—(m)—spiritual leader
Imamu—(m)—leader, minister, preacher

Imam—(f)—leader of faith
Imam—(m)—leader, chief
Imana—(f)—believer, supreme god
Imana—(m)—supreme god
Imanee—(f)—faith, belief
Imane—(f)—belief
Imania—(f)—faith, belief
Imanie—(f)—faith, belief
Imani—(f)—faithful person, trustworthy
Imani—(m)—trustworthy
Imany—(f)—belief, faith
Iman—(f)—faith, belief, faithful
Iman—(m)—name of a raga, faithful, respect
Imarah—(f)—strong
Imaran—(m)—strong
Imara—(f)—strong, firm, stubbornness
Imara—(m)—powerful, strength, persistent
Imar—(m)—bow warrior, archer
Imasha—(f)—unique, divine aura
Imaya—(f)—unique, divine aura
Imayne—(f)—faith, belief
Imayn—(f)—faith, belief
Imaz—(m)—kind, pleasing, affectionate
Imdaad—(m)—help, support
Imdad—(m)—charity, help, support, assistance
Imed—(m)—column, pillar
Imeldah—(f)—universal battle
Imene—(f)—powerful
Imen—(f)—faith, belief
Imen—(m)—faith, belief, variant of iman
Imhal—(f)—forbearance, to be patient
Imhal—(m)—forbearance, to be patient
Imian—(m)—one with divine wisdom
Immad—(m)—helper
Immama—(f)—leadership, command
Immeghar—(m)—one with divine wisdom
Immel—(m)—flowers
Immi—(f)—one who pour water from a jug

Immu—(m)—god with us
Imonee—(f)—faith, belief
Imoni—(f)—believer
Imon—(m)—truthful, starred
Impra—(f)—queen
Imraan—(m)—a prophet's name, prosperity
Imraaz—(m)—one with divine wisdom
Imrah—(f)—long life, prosperity, a rebel
Imraj—(m)—one with divine wisdom
Imram—(m)—form of amram
Imrana—(f)—population, socialism, powerful
Imrana—(m)—prosperous, socialism
Imrankhan—(m)—powerful, prosperity, prosperous
Imranullah—(m)—prosperous, powerful
Imranul—(m)—prosperity
Imran—(m)—prosperity, powerful, prosperous
Imrat—(f)—cute, love
Imrat—(m)—one with divine wisdom
Imraz—(m)—prosperity
Imra—(f)—prosperity, firm
Imroja—(f)—unique, divine aura
Imrose—(m)—today
Imroz—(m)—today
Imrul—(m)—strong willed, self-sufficient
Imseera—(f)—wise
Imshaz—(m)—loving
Imsha—(f)—intelligent
Imtaiz—(m)—one with divine wisdom
Imtayaz—(m)—mark of honour, distinction
Imtaz—(m)—the chosen one
Imteyaj—(m)—antique, great king, privilege
Imteyaz—(m)—distinction, mark of honour
Imthias—(m)—the chosen one
Imthiaz—(m)—the chosen one
Imthithal—(f)—polite obedience
Imthiyas—(m)—the chosen one, gift of god
Imthiyaz—(m)—innocent, decent
Imtiaaz—(m)—privilege, distinction

Imtiaj—(m)—honest, great
Imtias—(m)—distinction, privilege
Imtiazuddin—(m)—prominence
Imtiaz—(m)—intelligent
Imtihal—(f)—obedience, polite
Imtinaan—(f)—gratitude, gratefulness, thankful
Imtinan—(f)—gratitude, thankfulness
Imtisal—(f)—obedience, conforming to
Imtisal—(m)—to follow, idolise, imitate
Imtithaal—(f)—polite obedience
Imtithal—(f)—polite, polite obedience
Imtiyaaz—(m)—one with divine wisdom
Imtiyaj—(m)—one with divine wisdom
Imtiyas—(m)—the chosen one, unique
Imtiyaz—(f)—distinction, mark of honour
Imtiyaz—(m)—antique, distinct, great king
Imtyaj—(m)—privilege, antique, great king
Imtyaz—(m)—the chosen one
Imza—(f)—signature
Imziya—(f)—beautiful, caring
Imzumana—(f)—unique, divine aura
Inaad—(m)—one with divine wisdom
Inaamulhaq—(m)—one with divine wisdom
Inaam—(f)—act of kindness, benefaction
Inaam—(m)—king of the earth, reward, favour
Inaarah—(f)—eternal light, heaven's light
Inaara—(f)—eternal light, heavenly daughter
Inaayah—(f)—concern
Inaayat—(m)—gift, favour, kindness
Inaaya—(f)—gift of god, angel, gift of allah
Inab—(f)—grape
Inab—(m)—grape
Inam-ul-haq—(m)—gift, blessing from god
Inama—(f)—beginner
Inamul-haq—(m)—gift of truth (allah)
Inamul-hasan—(m)—beautiful gift of allah
Inamulhaq—(m)—gift of truth allah
Inamullah—(m)—god's gift

Inamul—(m)—prosperity
Inamurrahman—(m)—gift from al-rahman
Inam—(f)—gift, blessings from god
Inan—(f)—flower
Inan—(m)—sun, lord, master, king
Inarah—(f)—eternal light, ray of light
Inara—(f)—ray of light, shining, light
Inasa—(f)—sociability
Inass—(f)—sociability
Inas—(f)—capable, sociability, sweet voice
Inas—(m)—capable, sociability, able
Inayaah—(f)—gift
Inayaat—(f)—care, consideration, protection
Inayah—(f)—concern
Inayath—(f)—favour, concern attention
Inayath—(m)—kindness, favour
Inayatuddin—(m)—care of religion islam
Inayatullah—(f)—god's care and protection
Inayatullah—(m)—care of allah
Inayatur-rahman—(m)—care of the most gracious (allah)
Inayaturrahman—(m)—care of the most gracious allah
Inayat—(f)—blessing of god, kindness
Inayat—(m)—concern attention, kindness
Inayazohra—(f)—gracious blossom
Inaya—(f)—beautiful, concern, solicitude
Inayra—(f)—ray of light
Inay—(f)—gift from god
Inbar—(f)—gemstone
Inbihaj—(f)—cheerfulness, delight, joy, mirth
Inbihaj—(m)—cheerfulness, delight, joy, mirth
Inbisat—(f)—cheerfulness, joyfulness, comfort
Inbisat—(m)—cheerfulness, joyfulness, comfort
Indadullah—(m)—helpful, support
Indamira—(f)—guest of the princess
Indela—(f)—like nightingale
Indyra—(f)—beauty, splendour
Inesa—(m)—a strong king, lord vishnu
Ines—(f)—sacred, chaste, partner, virgin

Inez—(f)—pure, chaste, gentle, virginal
Infari—(m)—sweet
Infisal—(f)—divergence, separation, distance
Infisal—(m)—divergence, separation, distance
Inhaan—(m)—one with divine wisdom
Inham—(m)—shining, favour, reward
Inia—(f)—body of water
Inisha—(f)—sun light, strong, superior
Iniyat—(f)—concern attention
Injah—(f)—success, to cause something
Injah—(m)—success, to cause something
Injamamul—(m)—one with divine wisdom
Injamam—(m)—one with divine wisdom
Injeela—(f)—the gospels, the word
Injila—(f)—shine, brilliant, glittering
Innaira—(f)—ray of light, shining
Innama—(f)—beginner
Innara—(f)—shining, ray of light
Innayath—(f)—kindness, favour
Innayat—(f)—generosity, kindness
Innaya—(f)—gift for god
Inna—(f)—coming from water of strength
Insaaf—(m)—justice, impartiality
Insaf—(f)—justice, fairness, equity
Insaf—(m)—justice, impartiality, fairness
Insar—(m)—helper, supporter
Insa—(f)—chaste
Inseya—(f)—mysterious, challenging
Inshaf—(m)—equity, justice
Inshah—(f)—creation, origination
Insham—(m)—one with divine wisdom
Inshan—(m)—god's grace, gift
Insharah—(f)—spreading happiness
Insha—(f)—origin, origination, creation
Inshera—(f)—relief, joyful, delight
Inshia—(f)—female, origination
Inshifa—(f)—one who can cure
Inshiraah—(m)—delight, happiness

Inshirah—(f)—joy, delight, happiness
Inshrah—(f)—delight, cheerfulness, joy
Inshra—(f)—precious, relief
Inshu—(f)—delight, happiness, pure
Insiah—(f)—woman, also spelt as insia
Insia—(f)—female, mystical, birth of love
Insimamm—(m)—to get together, to unite
Insirah—(f)—cheerfulness, relief, joyful
Insith—(m)—a leader's heart
Insiyah—(f)—woman
Insiya—(f)—someone who remembers
Intaj—(m)—king, magnificent
Intakhab—(m)—election, last dream
Intekhab—(m)—chosen
Intesar—(m)—waiting
Intessar—(f)—victory
Intezar—(m)—to wait
Inthiyaz—(m)—one with divine wisdom
Intiha—(f)—completion, conclusion, finish
Intiha—(m)—completion, conclusion, finish
Intikhab—(m)—selection, choice
Intisaar—(f)—triumph
Intisaar—(m)—triumph, victory
Intisam—(m)—one with divine wisdom
Intisarat—(f)—victory, triumph
Intisara—(f)—triumphant
Intisar—(f)—successful, famous, beautiful
Intisar—(m)—victory, triumph
Intiyas—(m)—one with divine wisdom
Intizara—(f)—triumphant
Intizar—(f)—anticipation, period of waiting
Intizar—(m)—wait, anticipation
Inunna—(f)—unique, divine aura
Inyra—(f)—ray of light
Inzamamul—(m)—one with divine wisdom
Inzamam—(m)—to unite, to get together
Inza—(f)—chaste, small
Inzemam—(m)—one with divine wisdom

Inzimam—(m)—one with divine wisdom
Inziya—(f)—someone who remembers, female
Inzmam—(m)—to get together, to unite
Iqamat—(f)—calm, peace, staying
Iqbaal—(m)—prosperity, wealth, advance
Iqbal—(f)—wealth
Iqbal—(m)—prosperity, wealth, glory destiny
Iqdam—(m)—boldness, courageousness
Iqfiya—(f)—unique, divine aura
Iqlas—(f)—trustful
Iqlas—(m)—well mannered
Iqleem—(m)—land, zone, continent, region
Iqlima—(f)—unique, divine aura
Iqmal—(m)—white soul
Iqraah—(f)—heaven
Iqraam—(m)—to be of assistance, respect
Iqraan—(m)—honoured
Iqraa—(f)—to recite, first word of quran
Iqrah—(f)—heaven, recite
Iqrama—(f)—beautiful
Iqramuddin—(m)—one with divine wisdom
Iqramullah—(m)—one with divine wisdom
Iqrana—(f)—unique, divine aura
Iqran—(m)—honoured
Iqrash—(m)—attractive
Iqra—(f)—educate, read, garden in heaven
Iqra—(m)—garden in heaven
Iqreema—(f)—princess
Iqrit—(m)—amusing, man of early islam
Iqtidaar—(m)—capability, power
Iqtidar—(m)—capability, power, office
Iqubal—(m)—wealth, prosperity
Iquebal—(m)—one with divine wisdom
Iqurah—(f)—sweet voice
Iqyan—(m)—gold
Iqzaana—(f)—unique, divine aura
Iraaz—(m)—arsh se farsh tak line
Iradat—(f)—wish, desire, intention

Irad—(m)—heap of empire, dragon
Iraf—(m)—name of the father of arda
Iraida—(f)—descendant of hera
Iraides—(f)—seeker
Iraj—(f)—flower
Iram-faiza—(f)—unique, divine aura
Iram—(f)—garden in paradise
Iram—(m)—the effusion of them, a high heap
Irana—(f)—unique, divine aura
Iranna—(f)—happy, lovely
Iranshi—(f)—part of earth
Iran—(f)—iran, the land of aryans
Iran—(m)—the land of aryans, lord of braves
Iraq—(m)—shore, river bank
Irasha—(f)—bond of peace, peaceful
Iraten—(m)—one with divine wisdom
Irat—(f)—unique, divine aura
Iravat—(m)—rain clouds, ocean, son of arjuna
Ira—(f)—earth, goddess saraswati
Ira—(m)—watchful, wind, descendants
Irdina—(f)—pride
Ireena—(f)—like the goddess of peace
Ireen—(f)—peace
Irem—(f)—garden in heaven
Irene—(m)—peace
Irfaan—(m)—thankfulness, knowledge, wisdom
Irfadh—(m)—one with divine wisdom
Irfad—(m)—helpful
Irfana—(f)—thankfulness, brilliant
Irfanullah—(m)—word of wisdom, brilliant
Irfan—(m)—wisdom, gratefulness
Irfaque—(f)—self
Irfath—(f)—place of pilgrimage
Irfat—(f)—place of pilgrimage
Irfa—(f)—knowledge, wisdom, recognition
Irfhan—(m)—knowledgeable, wisdom
Irhaan—(m)—ruler, winner
Irhaa—(f)—to make calm, to make serene

Irham—(m)—loveable, merciful
Irhan—(m)—ruler, winner
Irim—(m)—bright
Irine—(f)—peace
Irin—(f)—peaceful
Irman—(m)—wish
Irmas—(m)—strong, tough
Irma—(f)—universal, constant movement
Irphan—(m)—knowledgeable, wisdom
Irrfan—(m)—wisdom, knowledgeable
Irsadah—(f)—unique, divine aura
Irsad—(m)—honest, pious
Irsana—(f)—unique, divine aura
Irsan—(m)—king
Irsa—(f)—rainbow, iris
Irshaad—(m)—signal, guidance, direction
Irshaan—(m)—righteous
Irshad—(m)—sweet wards, guidance, direction
Irshal—(f)—unique, divine aura
Irshana—(f)—rainbow
Irshan—(m)—righteous, lion
Irshath—(f)—guidance
Irshath—(m)—direction, guidance
Irshat—(m)—guidance
Irshefan—(m)—one with divine wisdom
Irshith—(m)—guidance
Irsia—(f)—colours of wonders, rainbow
Irtaba—(f)—street of heaven, a tree name
Irtaza—(m)—one with divine wisdom
Irteeza—(f)—contentment, approval
Irtezaah—(f)—unique, divine aura
Irteza—(f)—contentment, woman of virtue
Irteza—(m)—one with divine wisdom
Irtifa—(f)—height
Irtija—(f)—unique, divine aura
Irtika—(f)—end
Irtiqa—(f)—going higher, ascension
Irtiqa—(m)—ascended, evolved, going higher

Irtisa—(f)—noble, contentment
Irtiza-husain—(m)—approval of husayn
Irtizahusain—(m)—approval of husayn
Irtiza—(f)—contentment, approval
Irtiza—(m)—contentment, approval
Irtza—(f)—approval, contentment
Irufan—(m)—gratefulness, wisdom, iron heart
Irufa—(f)—wisdom, patient
Irum—(f)—paradise, heaven
Irum—(m)—bright
Irvaan—(m)—prophets name
Irvan—(m)—prophets name
Irwin—(f)—jesus of drum, always happy
Irzam—(m)—one with divine wisdom
Irzan—(m)—prosperous, worth live
Irza—(f)—cool
Is-haaq—(m)—a prophet's name
Isaac—(m)—one who brings laughter
Isaad—(f)—blessing, favouring
Isaad—(m)—making happy
Isaamm—(m)—safeguard
Isaam—(m)—safeguard, guard
Isaan—(m)—bestower of riches, supreme ruler
Isaaq—(m)—honest, trustworthy
Isaar—(m)—selflessness
Isabhani—(m)—one with divine wisdom
Isad—(f)—to bring happiness
Isad—(m)—making happy or prosperous
Isaf—(f)—relief, help
Isah—(f)—night prayer
Isaiah—(m)—the lord helps me, god's helper
Isak—(m)—laughter, he will laugh
Isamail—(m)—god will hear
Isamm—(m)—safeguard
Isam—(m)—self-made, security, pledge
Isana—(f)—strong willed, charitable, giving
Isan—(m)—bestower of riches, supreme ruler
Isaq—(m)—trustworthy, honest

Isar—(f)—fascinating
Isar—(m)—eminent, lord shiva
Isas—(f)—plenty, splendour, increase
Isa—(m)—prophet, love, jesus
Isbaah—(f)—daybreak
Isbaah—(m)—daybreak
Isbahani—(m)—from isbahan, abu bakr ibn ashtah
Isbah—(f)—daybreak
Isbah—(m)—daybreak
Isbana—(f)—unique, divine aura
Isbell—(f)—unique, divine aura
Isbha—(f)—morning
Isfaar—(m)—intelligent
Isfahan—(m)—town in iran
Isfand-yar—(m)—one with divine wisdom
Isfandiyar—(m)—one with divine wisdom
Isfaque—(m)—compassion, favours, kind hearten
Isfa—(f)—treasure, lovely
Ishaak—(m)—happiness
Ishaal—(f)—beauty queen, heaven's flower
Ishaal—(m)—one with divine wisdom
Ishaam—(m)—one with divine wisdom
Ishaana—(f)—goddess durga
Ishaan—(m)—the sun, one who bestows wealth
Ishaaq—(m)—isaac, a prophet's name
Ishack—(m)—laughter, one who laughs
Ishac—(m)—laughter, love
Ishaheen—(f)—unique, divine aura
Ishah—(f)—protector
Ishakh—(m)—isaac
Ishak—(f)—never ends, love
Ishak—(m)—never ends
Ishal—(f)—prosperity, flower of heaven
Ishal—(m)—flower, prosperity
Ishama—(f)—queen of india, candle light
Ishaml—(f)—flower
Isham—(m)—from the iron one's estate
Ishan-ansari—(m)—responsible

Ishana—(f)—prosperous, rich, goddess durga
Ishanda—(f)—unique, divine aura
Ishandiyar—(m)—one with divine wisdom
Ishan—(m)—sun, supreme ruler
Ishaque—(m)—powerful
Ishaq—(m)—laughs, a prophet's name
Isharat—(f)—unique, divine aura
Ishara—(f)—a sign, phenomenon
Isharullah—(m)—one with divine wisdom
Ishar—(m)—god, godly
Ishat—(m)—superior, happiness
Ishayu—(m)—full of strength, sun
Isha—(f)—one who protects
Isha—(m)—supreme ruler, one who protects
Ishfaaq—(m)—compassion, kindness, sympathy
Ishfak—(m)—kindness, compassion, sympathy
Ishfaq—(f)—affection, compassion
Ishfaq—(m)—compassion, kindness, sympathy
Ishfar—(m)—one with divine wisdom
Ishfa—(f)—unique, divine aura
Ishia—(f)—woman, life, form of aisha
Ishika—(f)—sacred, sacred paint brush
Ishiqa—(f)—sacred, the queen of the water
Ishir—(m)—another name for agni
Ishmael—(m)—son of abraham, god hears
Ishmail—(m)—god will hear
Ishmam—(m)—a star seen by everyone
Ishmatah—(f)—safeguarding, infallibility
Ishma—(f)—purity, modesty, infallibility
Ishma—(m)—superior
Ishmel—(m)—god will hear, love
Ishna—(f)—lord krishna
Ishqa—(f)—love, sacred
Ishq—(m)—love
Ishraaq—(f)—radiance
Ishraaq—(m)—to radiate, shine
Ishraa—(f)—companionship, fellowship
Ishrah—(f)—companionship, fellowship

Ishraque—(m)—one with divine wisdom
Ishraq—(f)—radiance, daybreak, illumination
Ishraq—(m)—to radiate, shine, sunrise
Ishrat-jahan—(f)—delightful world
Ishrath—(f)—sunrise, happiness, companionship
Ishrath—(m)—intimacy, companionship, society
Ishrat—(f)—wish, affection, enjoyment
Ishrat—(m)—affection
Ishra—(f)—related to god
Ishreena—(f)—unique, divine aura
Ishrin—(f)—perfect formed
Ishtaq—(m)—one with divine wisdom
Ishtar—(f)—the babylonian goddess of love
Ishtayaq—(m)—desire, eagerness, wish
Ishteiq—(m)—one with divine wisdom
Ishteyaq—(m)—one with divine wisdom
Ishtiak—(m)—one with divine wisdom
Ishtiaq—(m)—longing, craving
Ishtiyak—(m)—peace
Ishtiyaque—(m)—desire, wish
Ishtiyaq—(m)—wish, desire, yearning, eagerness
Ishtyak—(m)—one with divine wisdom
Ishtyaq—(m)—one with divine wisdom
Ishya—(f)—spring season
Isir—(f)—inspirational, strong
Isis—(f)—supreme goddess
Iskafi—(m)—iskaf is a shoe-maker
Iskandar—(m)—defender of mankind, alexander
Islaah—(f)—to fix - improve
Islaah—(m)—reform, improvement
Islaam—(m)—peaceful, very safe
Islah—(f)—making right, making appropriate
Islah—(m)—reform, improvement, betterment
Islamuddin—(m)—one with divine wisdom
Islam—(m)—from kikuyu, peaceful, very safe
Isli—(m)—one with divine wisdom
Ismaael—(m)—a prophet's name
Ismaa—(f)—safeguarding

Ismad—(m)—bodyguard
Ismaeel—(m)—name of a prophet
Ismael—(m)—a prophet's name
Ismah—(f)—purity, modesty, infallibility
Ismah—(m)—preservation, infallibility
Ismaila—(m)—lord, prophet
Ismaile—(m)—god will listen, lord, he hears
Ismailkhan—(m)—prophet
Ismail—(m)—farsi for ishmael
Ismal—(m)—god will hear
Ismat-ara—(f)—decorator of modesty
Ismatah—(f)—infallibility, preserving
Ismatara—(f)—decorator of modest
Ismata—(f)—preserving, safeguarding
Ismate—(f)—infallibility, preserving
Ismathullah—(m)—one with divine wisdom
Ismath—(f)—greatness, modesty
Ismath—(m)—one with divine wisdom
Ismatta—(f)—infallibility, preserving
Ismatte—(f)—safeguarding, preserving
Ismat—(f)—purity, modesty, infallibility
Ismat—(m)—chastity, purity, safeguarding
Ismaw—(m)—protection
Ismayil—(m)—prophet's name
Ismayl—(m)—god will hear
Isma—(f)—safeguarding
Ismeal—(m)—god will hear
Ismeil—(m)—god will hear
Isme—(f)—esteemed, kind defender
Ismial—(m)—a prophet's name
Ismita—(f)—individuality
Ismit—(m)—honour
Ismiya—(f)—jasmine
Ismi—(f)—knowledgeable
Ismotara—(f)—thanks
Ism—(m)—god's favourite
Isnah—(f)—beautiful
Isood—(f)—a woman of delicate body

Isoud—(f)—lover of tristan
Israah—(m)—one with divine wisdom
Israail—(m)—the chosen one
Israar—(m)—secrecy, privacy, mystery
Israa—(f)—night journey, variant of isra
Israeli—(m)—one who struggles with god
Israel—(m)—contender with god
Israfeel—(m)—gods dearest angel
Israfil—(m)—angel who will blow the trumpet
Israh—(f)—night travel
Israh—(m)—one who is free
Israil—(m)—wrestled with god
Israq—(m)—one with divine wisdom
Israr—(m)—secrecy, privacy, mystery
Israth—(f)—unique, divine aura
Israti—(f)—unique, divine aura
Israt—(f)—happiness, healthy, delightful
Isra—(f)—freedom, nocturnal, night journey
Isra—(m)—night travel, free
Isrea—(f)—night travel
Isria—(f)—night travel
Isrra—(f)—free, night journey
Issah—(f)—prophet name
Issak—(m)—joyful, laughter
Issam—(f)—safeguard
Issam—(m)—safeguard, self-made
Issaq—(m)—joyful, laughter, love
Issar—(m)—sacrifice
Issa—(f)—the messiah
Issa—(m)—the messiah, from kikuyu
Istabaraq—(f)—a cloth that cover jannah
Istabraq—(f)—brocade
Istack—(m)—one with divine wisdom
Istakhri—(m)—shafaee jurist
Isteyak—(m)—hope, sturdy
Isthiyaq—(m)—hope, sturdy
Istiaq—(m)—one with divine wisdom
Istibshar—(f)—to become happy, hopeful

Istibshar—(m)—to become happy, to have hope
Istifa—(m)—to choose, to prefer
Istighfaar—(m)—ask for forgiveness from god
Istighfar—(f)—ask for forgiveness from god
Istighfar—(m)—to ask for forgiveness from god
Istikar—(m)—one with divine wisdom
Istilah—(f)—agreement
Istiqlal—(f)—independence, sovereignty
Istiqlal—(m)—independence, sovereignty
Istiyak—(m)—hope
Istiyaq—(m)—sturdy
Istkar—(m)—one with divine wisdom
Isuf—(m)—brilliant
Iswa—(f)—role model, appropriate example
Isyana—(f)—unique, divine aura
Itab—(f)—censure
Itaf—(f)—star, clock
Itakh—(m)—the name of abu mansur, the turk
Itban—(m)—censured, blamed
Itbir—(m)—one with divine wisdom
Itedaal—(f)—balance, temperance, moderation
Itemaad—(f)—trust
Ithaar—(m)—selflessness
Ithan—(m)—proud, strong
Ithar—(f)—preference
Ithris—(m)—one with divine wisdom
Itia—(f)—god is with me
Itidale—(f)—moderation
Itidalle—(f)—moderation
Itidall—(f)—moderation
Itidal—(f)—symmetry, balance, temperance
Itidal—(m)—moderateness, clemency
Itimaad—(m)—reliance, dependence
Itimad—(f)—reliance, dependence
Itimad—(m)—dependence, confidence, reliance
Itqan—(f)—proficiency, excellence, mastery
Itrat—(f)—lineage
Itri—(m)—one with divine wisdom

Itsaf—(m)—the one who praise
Itsam—(f)—happy, joy, cleverness
Ittesum-sultana—(f)—drawing
Ittifaq—(m)—unity, friendship, harmony
Ivaan—(m)—god is gracious, undefeatable
Ivan—(m)—god is merciful, gift of god
Iwaana—(f)—god is gracious
Iwad—(m)—one with divine wisdom
Iwana—(f)—god is gracious
Iwan—(m)—welsh form of john, gift of god
Iwazullah—(m)—god's restitution
Iwin—(m)—invisible masquerade, silent
Ixzi—(m)—one with divine wisdom
Iyaad—(m)—generous
Iyaan—(f)—time
Iyaan—(m)—lord shiva, gift of god
Iyaas—(m)—compensation
Iyaaz—(m)—generous
Iyad—(m)—a big mountain
Iyali—(m)—name of abu jafar
Iyamina—(f)—unique, divine aura
Iyanah—(f)—innocent one, beautiful blossom
Iyana—(f)—god is gracious, mirror, princess
Iyanna—(f)—god is gracious, life, woman
Iyanya—(f)—woman, god is gracious
Iyan—(f)—time, era, epoch
Iyan—(m)—gift from god, time, era, epoch
Iyas—(m)—consoling
Iyazuddin—(m)—one with divine wisdom
Iyaz—(m)—refuge, shelter, generous
Iydin—(m)—one with divine wisdom
Iyesha—(f)—form of iesha
Iyka—(f)—beautiful, love
Iyman—(f)—lucky, brave honest
Iymina—(f)—unique, divine aura
Iyra—(f)—earth, respectable
Iyrin—(f)—peaceful
Iysha—(f)—living, prosperous, lively, woman

Iyyad—(m)—one with divine wisdom
Iyyas—(m)—one with divine wisdom
Iyzah—(f)—beautiful
Izaad—(m)—advocacy, loyalty, support
Izaam—(m)—one with divine wisdom
Izaana—(f)—powerful woman
Izaan—(f)—submission, obedience, acceptance
Izaan—(m)—respect, obedience
Izaaz—(m)—one with divine wisdom
Izaa—(f)—a variant of izzah, might
Izad—(m)—god, angel, yazata
Izaf—(m)—leaf
Izahet—(f)—completing the work
Izah—(f)—dearest, beautiful
Izah—(m)—god is my oath
Izaiah—(m)—god is salvation
Izain—(m)—one with divine wisdom
Izaj—(m)—one with divine wisdom
Izam—(m)—the powerful one
Izana—(f)—powerful woman
Izan—(m)—obedience
Izaq—(m)—one with divine wisdom
Izara—(f)—scarlet
Izar—(f)—star
Izar—(m)—star
Izas—(m)—one with divine wisdom
Izath—(m)—respect
Izat—(m)—respect
Izazuddawlah—(m)—honour of the state
Izaz—(f)—honour, esteem, regard, affection
Izaz—(m)—honour, esteem, regard, affection
Iza—(f)—god is my oath
Izbah—(f)—unique, divine aura
Izba—(f)—house
Izdihaar—(f)—flourishing, blossoming
Izdihara—(f)—flourishing, blossoming
Izdiharea—(f)—blossoming, flourishing
Izdihare—(f)—blossoming, flourishing

Izdiharia—(f)—blossoming, flourishing
Izdiharra—(f)—flourishing, blossoming
Izdiharre—(f)—flourishing, blossoming
Izdihar—(f)—flourishing, blooming
Izelah—(f)—a princess, a devoted woman
Izellah—(f)—a devoted woman, a princess
Izen—(m)—one with divine wisdom
Izereena—(f)—unique, divine aura
Izfaar—(m)—help someone attain victory
Izfa—(f)—treasure
Izhaan—(m)—one who follows god's rules
Izhaar—(m)—express, declaration
Izhan—(m)—beautiful, precious
Izhar—(m)—submission, clearness, expression
Izhin—(m)—one with divine wisdom
Izhna—(f)—angel
Izik—(m)—laughter
Izin—(f)—permission
Izin—(m)—gift of god, permission
Izlia—(f)—unique, divine aura
Izmaa—(m)—higher place
Izmam—(m)—one with divine wisdom
Izmat—(f)—might, importance, greatness
Izma—(f)—higher position
Izmet—(f)—shining, beautiful, great fullness
Izna—(f)—energetic, light
Izraf—(m)—one with divine wisdom
Izran—(m)—star, knowledge
Izrath—(f)—unique, divine aura
Izra—(f)—night journey
Izreen—(f)—lovable
Izrin—(f)—beautiful
Izrin—(m)—beautiful
Izum—(m)—obedient, sincere
Izwan—(m)—one with divine wisdom
Izwa—(f)—splendour
Izyaan—(m)—intelligent
Izyan—(f)—intelligent

Izyan—(m)—one who possess wisdom
Izz-al-din—(m)—mighty of the faith
Izz-an-nisa—(f)—narrator of hadith
Izz-udeen—(m)—might of the faith
Izza-an-nisa—(f)—a narrator of hadith
Izzaah—(f)—honoured
Izzaan—(m)—acceptance, submission, obedience
Izzaa—(f)—might, power, strength
Izzaddin—(m)—honour of the faith
Izzah—(f)—honoured
Izzaldin—(m)—might of the faith
Izzana—(f)—powerful woman
Izzannisa—(f)—she was a narrator of hadith
Izzan—(m)—intelligent
Izzath—(f)—honour, respect, noble, fame
Izzati—(f)—noble
Izzatuddeen—(m)—honour of the religion (islam)
Izzatudden—(m)—honour of the religion (islam)
Izzatulislam—(m)—honour of the religion (islam)
Izzat—(f)—respect, might, glory, honour
Izzat—(m)—power, honour, fame, high rank
Izza—(f)—honour, power, fame, wealthy
Izzi—(f)—mighty
Izzuddin—(m)—honour of the religion
Izzudeen—(m)—might of the faith
Izzudin—(m)—might of the faith
Izzul-arab—(m)—the honour of arabs
Izz—(m)—fire, power, might, honour, glory
Continued in Part 2...

Printed by Libri Plureos GmbH in Hamburg,
Germany